KU-639-812

Introduction to

The Gambia

The Gambia is West Africa at its most accessible. Stable, peaceful, affordable and within comfortable flying distance of northern Europe, this former British colony has been a popular winter holiday destination for over three decades, and its appealing tropical climate, lively beach resorts and friendly atmosphere are enough to keep sunseekers returning time and time again. You can fully immerse yourself in the real West Africa here, by travelling up-country, where you'll discover picturesque mud-built villages, rice fields and palm groves, vibrant markets where you can haggle over batiks and balafons, and local festivals – invariably exuberant displays of colour, energy and noise.

The country also has a great deal to offer nature enthusiasts: it's well established as a top birdwatching destination, and its greatest natural feature, the River Gambia, is becoming a major draw for ecotourists. There's a rich seam of history to explore too in the Gambia valley, with heritage sites dating from prehistoric times to the slave trading era and the later colonial period. And, while ancient customs and traditions are still widely practised, younger Gambians are blending the old with the new and adding their own effervescent spin to traditional music and dance.

iii

■

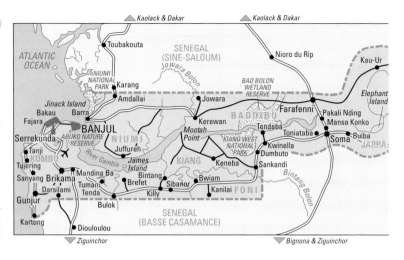

The Gambia's unique charm lies in its **smallness**: even the largest settlements, where crowds jostle along narrow streets brimming with heat, colour and noise, have an overgrown-village atmosphere. Elitism is hard to maintain in this close-knit environment – there's a rapidly acquired feeling of knowing everyone, and you can find yourself in conversation with the likes of senior government officials at the hotel bar without even realizing it. Gambians are generally multilingual, speaking English and a variety of West African languages, and they have a well-earned reputation for being unpretentious, accepting and approachable, and for making strangers feel completely at home.

Wherever you go, you're never far from the **River Gambia**, which gives the country its name and determines its bizarre, elongated shape. The river rises in the Fouta Djalon hills in Guinea, winds erratically through southern Senegal, crosses into The Gambia at its eastern limit, then cuts a five-hundred-kilometre swathe down the middle of the country to the Atlantic. Up-country in eastern Gambia, the river is freshwater and bordered by lush green tropical forest, while the lower reaches are mangrove-fringed. Long-distance boat trips allow you to enjoy the river environment at its peaceful best, watching the changing scenery unfold and listening to the different sounds at dawn, daytime and dusk. The fertile river valley, watered and drained by the daily cycle of tides and the annual swing of flood and drought, is a magnet for native and migrant wildlife species, including a remarkable profusion of birds.

The Gambia is a developing country in the poorest corner of the poorest continent, and **tourism** here has always been inhibited by a lack of resources – even the busiest resort areas have a down-to-earth, rough-

The Gambia

written and researched by

Emma Gregg and Richard Trillo

ROUGH
GUIDES

NEW YORK • LONDON • DELHI

www.roughguides.com

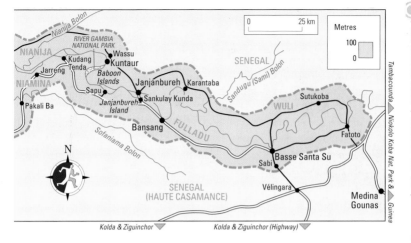

Kolda & Ziguinchor ▽   Kolda & Ziguinchor (Highway) ▽

edged charm that appeals to those who don't like their travel experiences too packaged. With more than sixty kilometres of Atlantic coastline, the winter holiday brochures portray the country as a beach paradise. In reality, however, while the best beaches come close to the broad, empty, palm-fringed ideal, most can't compare with those found in the Caribbean or on the Indian Ocean. Nor does The Gambia have the scenic drama and conspicuously abundant game animals of Africa's great safari destinations. What it can boast, however, is an unusually wide variety of natural habitats, including not only beaches but also river, mangrove, tropical woodland and savanna, all crammed into a small area that's easy to travel around by a combination of driving, boating, cycling and walking.

With The Gambia's wilderness so accessible, far-sighted tour operators are beginning to appreciate the country's potential as an **ecotourism destination**. Low-impact holidays are growing in popularity, allowing visitors both to appreciate the natural environment and also learn about traditional Gambian society, by combining boat-trips or bush-drives with visits to rural villages or music and dance lessons. There's a move, too, to attract high-spending tourists, and new top-range hotels and lodges are opening on the coast and up-country. Improvements to the basic infrastructure are also well under way, and, with a youthful and dynamic government in power, there's an optimistic, energetic buzz to the country, despite spiralling inflation and erratic water, fuel and electricity supplies.

You don't need to be a rugged adventurer to enjoy The Gambia to the full – in fact, if you've never been to Africa, it's one of the best places to start. Independent travel is reasonably cheap and straightforward, and there are plenty of day-trips and longer expeditions which open up the interior

Fact file

- At 11,300 square kilometres (about the size of Yorkshire or Connecticut), The Gambia is one of Africa's smallest and most densely populated countries. The **population** is more than 1.5 million, and growing rapidly, with a birth rate of more than five infants per child-bearing woman. Ethnic groups include Mandinka (42%), Fula (18%), Wolof (16%), Jola (10%), Serahule (9%), other Africans including Serer and Aku (4%), Europeans and Lebanese (1%).

- The Gambia is one of the world's **poorest countries**, with a national debt of £375 million ($600 million), nearly twice the value of its annual exports of goods and services. The average annual income is less than £200 ($320). Most Gambians are subsistence farmers or fishermen, and are self-sufficient for most of the year. The main export crop is groundnuts (peanuts), although tourism is also becoming an important source of revenue.

- Since independence from Britain in 1965, The Gambia has been a multiparty democracy. The president, His Excellency Al-Haji Yahya AJJ Jammeh, is only the country's second; his predecessor, Dawda Jawara, was ousted by Jammeh's military coup in 1994.

to those who prefer guided tours. The Gambia also makes an ideal starting point for anyone wishing to explore West Africa in greater depth. Apart from its Atlantic coast, the country is completely surrounded by Senegal, and it's within easy reach of Mali, Guinea-Bissau and Guinea. The Gambia has much in common with its neighbours, and its hotels, guesthouses and restaurants, many of them right on the beach, allow you to acclimatize in comfort while getting to grips with the West African way of life.

Where to go

The Gambia's biggest attraction for most visitors is the string of **Atlantic beach resorts** in the northern Kombos, the districts closest to the capital, **Banjul**. Few visitors spend more than a day or so in the city itself; far more rewarding targets in the coastal region include the **southern Kombos**, the southwestern districts bordered by

the Atlantic and the Casamance region of Senegal, between the fishing settlements of Ghana Town and Kartong. Here, the beaches, backed by lush countryside, are emptier and wilder than those in the resort areas.

If you have time to explore the **interior** of the country, you'll quickly find yourself deep in classic West African landscapes scattered with traditional villages and crisscrossed by red-earth roads. Here, women with their babies bound to their backs tend vegetable plots or stir spicy stews outside shaggy-thatched, mud-brick houses, and men clear fields with machetes or discuss village politics under shade trees. The up-country animal and birdlife is diverse and exotic, and ornithologists will recognize many wintering migrants from Europe; there are also coconut groves and rice fields, and mangrove swamps and creeks plied by dugout canoes – and, of course, the mighty **River Gambia** itself to explore.

Throughout the country, the north bank of the river is much less visited than the south bank, with the exception of **Juffureh** and **James Island**: once colonial slave-trading stations, they're now essential stops on The Gambia's heritage trail. The south bank market town of **Brikama** – home to many of The Gambia's most celebrated musicians – and the main centres further east offer an insight into up-country urban life, while the more far-flung **villages** can be fascinating places to learn about rural tradition. Both **Soma** and **Farafenni** are junction towns on the Trans-Gambia route between

Kora music

The gentle acoustic *kora* music of the *jalis*, the traditional musicians of the Mandinka tribe, is Gambian music at its most melodic and contemplative. This distinctive harp-lute is usually played solo, to accompany lilting songs which praise the *jalis'* benefactors or relate folk histories. You'll often come across *kora* players busking in the resort area hotels and restaurants, and it's easy enough to track down a tutor who will introduce you to the basics of playing, or even make a *kora* to your own specifications. In recent years, some contemporary *kora* masters like Jaliba Kuyateh (below) and Tata Dindin have given the ancient instrument a new twist by amplifying the sound and playing against explosive backing groups of drummers and *balafon* players, with acrobatic dancers completing the high-energy line up. Live performances, often continuing late into the night, are an unmissable introduction to Gambian social life at its most exuberant.

northern and southern Senegal, and each has a distinctive atmosphere: Soma is a bustling transport stop that benefits from the south bank's superior infrastructure, while Farafenni, on the less developed north bank, is a characterful rural town with a lively and colourful weekly market. Mid-river, **Janjanbureh Island**, location of the old colonial outpost of Georgetown, is an emerging ecotourism centre, well placed for birdwatching and river-trips, as well as for visits to the **Wassu stone circles**, the country's most famous prehistoric site. **Basse**, a cosmopolitan trading town, is a good stopover on up-river explorations.

When to go

The Gambia's peak tourist season roughly coincides with the coastal **dry season**, which lasts around eight months from mid-October to mid-June, when the **rainy season** starts. Up-country, where temperatures are more extreme, the dry season lasts a few weeks longer.

The **best month to visit** is November, when the rains are over, humidity has dropped, the dirt roads are passable, and the bush is still green and busy with birdlife. December and January see the highest concentration of visitors. It's not unusual to have weeks of unbroken sunshine at this time, but there can sometimes be grey days and chilly nights. By March, the up-country landscape is a near-uniform golden brown and hazy with airborne dust; the last three months of the dry season are normally totally rainless.

While daytime **temperatures** in the resort areas vary little all year, **humidity** levels fluctuate considerably, rocketing at the end of the dry season and remaining high until October – nights can be very sticky from June to September. Some of the tourist hotels are closed from May to October, when there's a much reduced choice of charter flights. The country gets around 1300 millimetres (51 inches) of rain from mid-June to mid-October – nearly double London's yearly average – most of it falling at night, with August by far the rainiest month. The malaria risk is higher than usual during the rains, and some roads are waterlogged; however, birds, flowers and fresh vegetation are all abundant at this time, mangoes are in season, the resorts are pleasantly uncrowded, the sea is at its warmest, and, between the spectacular thunderstorms, the days are bright and clear.

Average temperatures and rainfall

	Jan	Feb	Mar	Apr	May	Jun	Jul	Aug	Sep	Oct	Nov	Dec
Banjul												
Daytime temp (°C)	31	32	34	33	32	32	30	29	31	32	32	31
Night-time temp (°C)	15	16	17	18	19	23	23	23	23	22	18	16
Days with rainfall	0.1	0.3	0	0	0.9	5	16	19	19	8	0.8	0.2
Rainfall (mm)	3	3	0	0	10	58	282	500	310	109	18	3

things not to miss

To help you get the most out of your stay in The Gambia, we have put together a personal selection of the country's highlights: special cultural events, historical sites and unspoilt stretches of wilderness. Arranged in five colour-coded categories indicating the best things to see, do and experience, each has a page reference to take you straight into the guide, where you can find out more.

01 Sanyang beach Page **143** • Sanyang has soft sand, sparkling sea and laid-back beach bars – it's a great place to chill out and watch the fishermen rolling brightly painted pirogues up the beach to unload the day's catch.

02 Katchikali crocodile pool Pages **111–112** • You might never get closer to a crocodile than this – Charlie is The Gambia's most approachable reptile, and resides at a sacred pool in Bakau.

03 Eating alfresco Pages **39–44** • Gambian favourites like chicken yassa or grilled barracuda are best enjoyed outdoors, on shady restaurant terraces or at one of the cool beach bars scattered all the way down the coast from Cape Point to Kartong.

04 Long-distance river trips Page **56** • Spend an adventurous few days cruising the River Gambia, enjoying the sights and sounds of the riverine wilderness, passing through the River Gambia National Park, and maybe spotting chimpanzees or hippos.

05 Tumani Tenda ecotourism camp Pages **158–159** • This rural camp, surrounded by beautiful woods, farmland and mangrove creeks, will appeal to anyone wanting to learn about local wildlife and traditional Jola lifestyles.

06 Jinack Island Pages **176–180** • A remote strip of land cut off from the mainland by a creek, Jinack Island is a haven for wildlife and an unspoilt beach retreat.

07 **Sindola Safari Lodge, Kanilai** Pages **189–191** • This comfortable and relaxing up-country bush lodge makes the perfect base for visiting Foni district, the heartland of traditional Jola culture.

09 **Roots pilgrimage to Juffureh** Pages **50–51** • The one-day pilgrimage to the up-country village of Juffureh, immortalized in Alex Haley's novel *Roots*, is one of the highlights of The Gambia's biennial International Roots Festival; the village itself has a small but thought-provoking museum of slavery.

08 **Microlight flights** Page **97** • Get a bird's-eye view of snaking mangrove creeks and long-shadowed palm trees – an exhilarating experience, but not for the faint-hearted.

10 **Mandina Lodge** Pages **157–158** • Overlooking a beautiful creek, on the edge of Makasutu Culture Forest, this luxury bush lodge is a superb place to relax, with one of the loveliest pools in the country.

11 **Wassu stone circles** Pages **210–212** • A tangible remnant of a mysterious prehistoric culture, Wassu is one of the most impressive megalithic sites in the Senegambia region.

12 Southern Kombos beaches Pages **142–145** • Along the palm-fringed bays between Brufut and Kartong, you can walk for miles and barely see another soul – though you may encounter cows, sea birds or even turtles.

13 Albert Market, Banjul Page **93–94** • The capital's main market is a bright, bustling place to browse, with a huge array of vividly patterned fabric, household goods, musical instruments, natural remedies, home-made beauty products and local fruit and vegetables.

14 Creek trips by dugout pirogue Page **56–58** • The Gambia's complex network of mangrove creeks is a haven for birds and a breeding ground for fish. To enjoy the tranquil environment to the full, take a trip through the narrowest waterways by dugout pirogue.

15 Bao Bolon Wetland Reserve Pages **201–202** • The largest protected area in The Gambia is also the least explored, and a rewarding destination for the adventurous, with salt flats, marshland and well-preserved wetland areas that are excellent for birdwatching.

17 **Janjang Bureh Camp**
Page **219** • This quirky and charming riverside lodge is a friendly place to unwind after a long journey up-country; it also makes a perfect base for local birdwatching and river-trips.

16 **Country markets** Pages **199–200** • The *lumos* (country markets) held once a week on the outskirts of rural towns like Farafenni are lively events, with fabric stalls, *juju*-makers, kola-nut sellers and great heaps of seasonal produce.

18 **James Island** Pages **175–176** • With its atmospheric ruined fort and skeletal baobab trees, this bleak mid-river island is an essential stop for anyone tracing the history of the West African slave trade.

20 **Kankurang dancers**
Page **255** • Colourful *kankurang* dancers and other masquerades have a crucial role in traditional rites, and they also entertain the crowds at major festivals.

19 **Abuko Nature Reserve**
Pages **132–135** • Only a short drive from the coastal resorts, Abuko's gallery forest and woodland savanna is easy to explore on foot, making it one of the best places in The Gambia to get really close to wild birds, reptiles and monkeys.

Birds of The Gambia

The Gambia's remarkable diversity of accessible habitats makes it an ideal birdwatching destination. Over 560 bird species have been recorded in the country, including Palearctic migrants which arrive in the late rainy season, and for which The Gambia is the first vital belt of green after the long flight south along the arid coast of northwest Africa.

This field guide provides a quick reference to help you identify some of the most common varieties. It includes a representative selection of native species and a few migrants, presented in conventional taxonomic order. The notes for each bird give you pointers about its usual habitat; how widespread and common it is; typical songs and calls; and general tips about seasonal variations in plumage, feeding habits and other characteristics.

HABITAT   DISTRIBUTION   SONG   ✓ SIGHTING TIPS

Pink-backed pelican
Pelicanus rufescens

Ocean, river and creeks.

Common on the coast; breeds up-country in baobab trees, eg a t Kwinella, near Tendaba.

Claps its bill, hisses and croaks noisily when nesting, otherwise silent.

Large, stately bird, with pinkish back feathers visible in flight; perches on wrecks of ships in the Banjul area.

Hammerkop
Scopus umbretta

Ponds, rice fields and creeks.

Common throughout The Gambia.

Harsh guttural or cackling call; rowdy.

All brown with an unmistakably shaggy, anvil-like crest, which it raises when alarmed; its famously large nests are used year after year, eg at Abuko.

Western reef heron
Egretta gularis

Saltwater creeks, swamps and beaches.

Common throughout The Gambia.

Harsh crow-like *kaw*.

Blue-black with a white throat; follows other water birds and darts at fish that they miss.

Striated heron
Butorides striatus

Mangrove creeks and swamps.

Common, especially in the rainy season.

Forceful *tchack-tchack*.

Brown when immature, blackish green and grey in adulthood; short tail; climbs through tangled vegetation.

  HABITAT DISTRIBUTION SONG SIGHTING TIPS

Intermediate egret
Egretta intermedia

🌴 Open coastal waters, flooded fields and creeks.

🐦 Common throughout The Gambia.

🎵 Hissing call when breeding, otherwise silent.

✓ White plumage and yellow bill, which in both sexes turns bright red when breeding; often solitary.

Marabou stork
Leptoptilos crumeniferus

🌴 Widespread, but prefers semi-arid areas.

🐦 Common in central Gambia.

🎵 Claps its bill when breeding, otherwise silent.

✓ Massive bill and pink gular sac, bald head; gregarious; shares carrion with vultures.

Hooded vulture
Necrosyrtes monachus

🌴 Urban tips, abattoirs, fishing beaches and bush.

🐦 Common, especially near human settlements.

🎵 Mostly silent, but can emit a high-pitched squeak.

✓ Dark brown and scruffy-looking; omnivorous: food includes winged termites, oil palm fruit, insects and carrion.

Palm-nut vulture
Gypohierax angolensis

🌴 Coastal woodland and mangrove creeks.

🐦 Common in western Gambia.

🎵 Mostly silent, but can growl and squeak.

✓ Brown when immature, black and white in adulthood; eagle-like; feeds on oil-palm fruit and dead fish.

African jacana
Actophilornis africanus

🐦 Freshwater ponds and rice fields.

🦅 Common throughout The Gambia.

🎵 Single screeches or loud rapidly repeated *kreep-kreep-kreep*.

✓ Carries its chicks under its glossy chestnut wings before they can fly; often eaten by crocodiles.

Whimbrel
Numenius phaeopus

🐦 Beaches and mangroves.

🦅 Common Palearctic migrant, abundant in western Gambia Aug–April.

🎵 Seven-note tittering call as it takes flight.

✓ Largish brown wader, with distinctively striped crown; picks over mudbanks for insects and crabs.

Egyptian plover
Pluvianus aegyptius

🐦 Riverbanks, jetties and lakesides.

🦅 Migrant, common in eastern Gambia Sept–Dec, eg in Basse area.

🎵 *Chee-chee-chee* as it takes flight.

✓ Beautifully marked; usually seen in small groups; approachable.

Black-headed plover
Vanellus tectus

🐦 Tussocky grassland.

🦅 Common in semi-arid areas, eg Fajara golf course, and in eastern Gambia.

🎵 Sharp *kiarr* or, when alarmed, high-pitched *kir*.

✓ Active at night, resting in the shade by day; staring, golden eyes.

Senegal thick-knee
Burhinus senegalensis

🌴 Riverbanks and creeks.

🦅 Common throughout The Gambia.

🎵 Staccato wailing call that rises and falls.

✓ Shelters in shady mangroves by day, active at dawn and dusk.

Senegal coucal
Centropus senegalensis

🌴 Bush and gardens.

🦅 Common throughout The Gambia.

🎵 Sonorous, guttural *ouk-ouk-ouk* or pigeon-like *who-who-who*, like water glugging out of a bottle.

✓ Largish, and strikingly coloured in black, chestnut and cream, seen on perches or creeping through undergrowth.

Verreaux's eagle owl
Bubo lacteus

🌴 Thickets and dry savanna.

🦅 Reasonably common throughout The Gambia.

🎵 Loud, grunting *whuuk-whuuk-whuuk*.

✓ Large owl, with pink eyelids and horn-like ear-tufts; seen roosting in trees; nests once every two years in baobab cavities; eats rats and hedgehogs, which it "peels", discarding the spiny pelt.

Pied kingfisher
Ceryle rudis

🌴 Beaches, cliffs, estuaries, rivers, creeks and pools.

🦅 Common in aquatic habitats.

🎵 Very vocal, squeaky, chattering call.

✓ Africa's only black-and-white kingfisher, strikingly marked; unusually, hovers over water before diving for fish; approachable.

🌴 HABITAT 　　🦅 DISTRIBUTION 　　🎵 SONG 　　✓ SIGHTING TIPS

Giant kingfisher
Megaceryle maxima

🌴 Coastal inlets, streams and ponds.

🐦 Common in aquatic habitats in western Gambia, eg at the Bambo pool, Abuko, especially in the rainy season.

🎵 Loud crow-like *kek-kek-kek*.

✓ Large, heavy-billed kingfisher; favours particular perches, returning daily.

African pygmy kingfisher
Ceyx picta

🌴 Thickets near pools and puddles.

🐦 Common, especially during rainy season.

🎵 Thin, squeaky *seet-seet* or *chip-chip*.

✓ Tiny; seen on low, shady perches or splash-bathing in pools; eats insects.

Abyssinnian roller
Coracias abyssiniica

🌴 Open bush and grassland.

🐦 Common, especially up-country in the dry season.

🎵 Raucous, guttural *kra-kra-kra*.

✓ Gorgeously coloured, with long tail streamers; conspicuous, often seen perched on trees, telephone wires or termite mounds by the roadside.

Little bee-eater
Merops pusillus

🌴 Grassland, shrubbery and marshes.

🐦 Common, the most widespread bee-eater.

🎵 Soft *sip* on taking flight; *siddle-iddle-ip-djee* on greeting.

✓ Contorts its body in order to sun its feathers; approachable.

Red-throated bee-eater
Merops bullocki

🎋 Riverbanks (freshwater reaches), quarries and gardens.

🐦 Reasonably common up-country, abundant in some areas, eg at Bansang quarry; often seen on high riverside perches.

🎵 Frequent *wip* call.

✓ Highly gregarious; breeds in closely packed colonies of burrows in vertical banks.

Northern carmine bee-eater
Merops nubicus

🎋 Riverbanks, up-country mangroves and dry grassland.

🐦 Reasonably common in central and eastern Gambia, especially during the rainy season.

🎵 Short *tunk* on taking flight, or *chip-chip-chip*.

✓ Large, strikingly coloured bee-eater.

Violet turaco
Musophaga violacea

🎋 Forests and orchards.

🐦 Reasonably common, endemic to West Africa.

🎵 Resonant, guttural *kourou-kourou-kourou*.

✓ Glossy purple plumage, with stunning red wing-feathers conspicuous when in flight; nearly always in pairs; eats figs.

Grey plantain-eater
Crinifer piscator

🎋 Bush, dry open savanna and tall trees.

🐦 Common throughout The Gambia.

🎵 Loud, distinctive, laughing *kow-kow-kow* and *kalak-kalak-kalak*.

✓ Grey, with a large conical yellow bill and a shaggy crest, which it raises when alarmed; white wing stripes conspicuous in flight; eats fruit and flowers.

🎋 HABITAT   🐦 DISTRIBUTION   🎵 SONG   ✓ SIGHTING TIPS

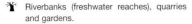
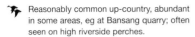

Rose-ringed parakeet
Psittacula krameri

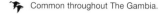 Woodland savanna, thickets and gardens.

Common throughout The Gambia.

Noisy screeches and whistles.

✓ Slim, long-tailed bird, all green with (in the male) black chin and pink collar; eats fruit and flowers; often seen in baobabs.

Red-billed hornbill
Tockus erythrorrhynchus

 Open woodland, burnt savanna and large gardens.

Common throughout The Gambia.

Chuckling *kok-kok-kok-kokok-kokok-kokok*, rising in tempo and volume.

✓ Smallest Senegambian hornbill; found in pairs or flocks, often sunbathing on the ground; builds mud-nests in trees in the late rainy season; the entrance is plastered up with the female inside; characteristic "beak-heavy" flight.

Abyssinian ground hornbill
Bucorvus abyssinicus

Open bush.

Reasonably common.

Deep, booming, repeated *uuh-uh-uh* from prominent bare branches.

✓ Huge black bird often seen walking through grassland; throat skin is pink in male, blue in female; conspicuous white primary feathers only visible in flight.

Bearded barbet
Lybius dubius

Woodland and gardens.

Common especially in western Gambia.

Occasional crow-like *kaw* or bark.

✓ Large barbet with a massive yellow bill and bare eye-patches; heavy flight; eats ripe figs and pawpaws.

🌴 HABITAT   🦅 DISTRIBUTION   🎵 SONG   ✓ SIGHTING TIPS

Fine-spotted woodpecker
Campethera punctuligera

🐦 Woodland and palm groves.

🦅 Common throughout The Gambia.

🎵 Loud ringing *wik-wik-whew-wee-yeu wee-yeu*.

✓ Often seen feeding on oil palms or on termite mounds; sometimes forages on the ground.

Beautiful sunbird
Nectarinia pulchella

🐦 Farmland, bush and gardens.

🦅 Common throughout The Gambia.

🎵 Reedy chirps, then a shivering tumble of quick notes.

✓ The male is shiny emerald, with yellow- and red breast, and long tail streamers; the female is drab olive; drinks nectar from flowers like a humming bird, often hanging at odd angles, even upside down.

Yellow-crowned gonolek
Laniarius barbarus

🐦 Woodland, shubbery and gardens.

🦅 Common throughout The Gambia.

🎵 Pairs call in unison, a liquid whistle and rasping rattle *too-lioo ch-chacha*.

✓ Unmistakable black, red and golden plumage; often seen low down in shrubs; pairs are territorial.

Purple glossy starling
Lamprotornis purpureus

🐦 Savanna, woodland and open bush.

🦅 Common throughout The Gambia.

🎵 Squeaking, bubbling and wittering notes, or a scolding *shree*.

✓ One of several gregarious and noisy shiny- plumaged Senegambian starlings; short tail and yellow eyes; perches high in trees.

🐦 HABITAT 🦅 DISTRIBUTION 🎵 SONG ✓ SIGHTING TIPS

Village weaver
Ploceus cucllatus

🌴 Village trees, farms; breeds in colonies of knot-like nests in silk cotton trees or palms.

🦅 Very common throughout The Gambia.

🎵 Noisy, squabbling chirps.

✓ Yellow and olive plumage; the breeding male (Jun–Dec) is black-headed, with a chestnut nape; the head of the female and non-breeding male is yellow; very gregarious.

Northern red bishop
Euplectes franciscanus

🌴 Millet and sorghum fields, and open bush.

🦅 Common throughout The Gambia.

🎵 Constant stream of high-pitched squeaky notes.

✓ The breeding male (Aug–Dec) has spectacular scarlet and black plumage, which it puffs up when displaying; the female and non-breeding male are an inconspicuous straw-brown.

Red-cheeked cordon-bleu
Uraeginthus bengalus

🌴 Woodland, scrub and gardens.

🦅 Common throughout The Gambia.

🎵 Thin-toned piping call, or more elaborate *wit-sit-diddly-diddly-ee-ee*.

✓ Small, gregarious finches, often seen feeding on the ground with red-billed firefinches; the female lacks red cheek spot.

Exclamatory paradise whydah
Vidua interjecta

🌴 Dry savanna woodland.

🦅 Reasonably common in up-country Gambia.

🎵 Simple *chip* calls.

✓ The breeding male (Nov–Dec) has an extraordinarily long black tail, three times its body-length; perches high in leafless trees; the female and non-breeding male are drab brown.

Contents

Using the Rough Guide

We've tried to make this Rough Guide a good read and easy to use. The book is divided into five main sections, and you should be able to find whatever you want in one of them.

Colour section

The front colour section offers a quick tour of The Gambia. The **introduction** aims to give you a feel for the place, with suggestions on where to go. We also tell you what the weather is like and include a basic country fact file. Next, our authors round up their favourite aspects of The Gambia in the **things not to miss** section – whether it's great food, amazing sights or a special hotel. Right after this comes a full **contents** list.

Basics

The Basics section covers all the **pre-departure** nitty-gritty to help you plan your trip. This is where to find out which airlines fly to your destination, what paperwork you'll need, what to do about money and insurance, about Internet access, food, security, public transport, car rental – in fact just about every piece of **general practical information** you might need.

Guide

This is the heart of the Rough Guide, divided into user-friendly chapters, each of which covers a specific region. Every chapter starts with a list of **highlights** and an **introduction** that helps you to decide where to go, depending on your time and budget. Likewise, introductions to the various towns and smaller regions within each chapter should help you plan your itinerary. We start most town accounts with information on arrival and accommodation, followed by a tour of the sights, and finally reviews of places to eat and drink, and details of nightlife. Longer accounts also have a directory of practical listings. Each chapter concludes with **public transport** details for the region it covers.

Contexts

Read Contexts to get a deeper understanding of what makes The Gambia tick. We include a brief history, articles about society, religion, wildlife and music and a further reading section that reviews **books** relating to the country.

Language

The language section gives useful guidance for speaking Wolof and Mandinka and pulls together all the vocabulary you might need on your trip, including a comprehensive menu reader. Here you'll also find a glossary of words and terms peculiar to the country.

Index + small print

Apart from a **full index**, which includes maps as well as places, this section covers publishing information, credits and acknowledgements, and also has our contact details in case you want to send in updates and corrections to the book – or suggestions as to how we might improve it.

Map and chapter list

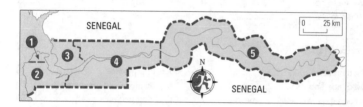

Contents

Contexts   231–268

Language   269–280

Index and small print   281–294

Map symbols

maps are listed in the full index using coloured text

CONTENTS

▬▬▪▬	International border
▬ ▬ ▬	Chapter division boundary
═══	Major tarred road
▬▬▬	Major clay road
══	Minor road
··········	Unpaved road
- - - - -	Path
⑉⑉⑉⑉⑉	Steps
▬ ▬	Ferry/boat route
▬▬▬	Waterway
↯	Point of interest
⸙	Custom post
🕌	Mosque
♟	Fort
▬▬▬	Wall
❖	Stone circle
⚘	Baobab tree

✕	Airport
★	Bus/taxi stop
⛽	Petrol pump
◉	Accommodation
◲	Eating/drinking
ⓘ	Tourist office
⊠	Post office
ℭ	Telephone
⛳	Golf course
▰	Building
⊞	Church (town maps)
⊹	Cemetery
▨	Park
⌁	Mangrove
⣿	Beach/sand

Basics

Basics

Getting there

The Gambia is around six hours' flying time from the UK and Europe, with little or no change in time zones. Visitors have a choice of buying just a flight, or buying a flight plus accommodation package with airport transfers and other extras thrown in; this can be a very inexpensive way to spend time in Africa.

The Gambia's **tourist season** runs from mid-October to late May; off-season, the choice of flights is relatively limited. The highest airfares are around Christmas and New Year, with lesser price hikes over Easter and during the British half-term holidays in November and February. You'll get the best prices during the low season, June to October, which roughly coincides with the rainy season.

Most short-term visitors from Europe travel to The Gambia by **charter flights**, which are generally cheaper than any of the available scheduled flights, but have fixed departure and return dates; withdrawal penalties can be high. While a few specialist sources offer charter flights on a flight-only basis, flight-plus-beach-hotel **package deals** are far more common. Even if you're planning on travelling independently during your visit, you may find it cheap and convenient to pick up a bargain package from one of the tour operators listed on p.12–13. If you're flexible enough about dates, you may even find a package for less than the price of a flight on its own. You're under no obligation to actually stay in the hotel included; you could use it instead as a launch pad for finding other accommodation or exploring further afield.

The cheapest package deals tend to be aimed squarely at people looking for a relaxing tropical beach holiday; others cater for those wishing to explore beyond the resort areas. As a special interest **safari destina-tion,** West Africa is little visited in comparison with East and southern Africa. Nonetheless, The Gambia is extremely attractive to ornithologists, and there are a number of specialist **birdwatching trips**; you'll also find some holidays for West African music and dance aficionadoes, plus a few "Roots" and **African heritage tours** aimed principally at African-Americans. Some of these, and some of the group treks organized by adventure travel companies, include neighbouring West African countries as well as The Gambia.

If you're looking for **scheduled flights**, you can sometimes cut costs by going through a **specialist agent** – either a consolidator, who buys up blocks of tickets from the airlines and sells them at a discount, or a **discount agent**, who in addition to dealing with discounted flights may also offer special student and youth fares.

The Gambia is within easy reach, either overland or by air, of Senegal, Mali, Guinea-Bissau, Guinea and Sierra Leone, and as such makes a useful, as well as low-cost, **entry point into West Africa**. Banjul is also a good exit point from a long-haul African trip: conveniently, it's possible to get a one-way ticket on a charter flight *back* from The Gambia to the UK (one of the best hubs for air travel from The Gambia), bookable either before you leave or after arrival in The Gambia, through specialist agent The Gambia Experience (see p.11). This allows you to get to The Gambia overland, then leave by direct flight from Banjul to Gatwick, Manchester, Bristol or Glasgow.

If you have the time, and sufficient sense of adventure, covering all or part of the distance from Europe to The Gambia **by land and sea** gives rewards of its own – and an unbeatable introduction to the region. If you'd rather go it alone, you could take a mixture of public transport and lifts with

Airport departure tax

The Gambia's airport **departure tax** ($20, payable in any currency) is nearly always included in the price of both charter and scheduled flights out of Banjul – but double check with the airline or their agent.

other travellers, or, with careful planning, set off with your own vehicle, motorcycle or bike.

Booking flights online

Many airlines and discount travel websites offer you the opportunity to book your tickets **online**. Good deals can often be found through discount or auction sites, as well as through the airlines' own websites. Territory-specific sites owned by the same company are usually linked.

Online booking agents and general travel sites

ⓦ **www.cheapflights.co.uk** Scheduled and charter flights, travel agents, plus links to other travel sites.
ⓦ **www.cheaptickets.com** American discount flight specialists.
ⓦ **www.expedia.com** Discount scheduled airfares, all-airline search engine and daily deals.
ⓦ **www.geocities.com/thavery2000/** A useful list of airline websites and toll-free numbers to call from the US.
ⓦ **www.lastminute.com** Offers good last-minute holiday package and scheduled flight deals.
ⓦ **www.travelocity.com** Provides access to the travel agent system SABRE, the most comprehensive central reservations system in the US.
ⓦ **www.travelshop.com.au** Australian website offering discounted flights, packages, insurance, online bookings.
ⓦ **www.travel.yahoo.com** Incorporates a scheduled flight search facility and information about places to eat and sleep etc.

Flights from the UK and Europe

By far the most straightforward way to get to The Gambia **from the UK** is by **charter flight**. There are regular direct services to Banjul International Airport from London Gatwick all year round, and from Bristol, Glasgow and Manchester during the tourist season (Oct–May). Flight prices range from £200–450 return, depending on the season and the length of stay, with full price mid-season tickets typically around £360. Most of these are only bookable through agents and tour operators, rather than through the airlines direct. Special promotions are some-

times introduced to fill seats. There are also direct charter flights to Banjul from **Amsterdam**, **Helsinki** and **Stockholm**, bookable through European travel agents.

There are direct **scheduled flights** from mainland Europe to The Gambia with SN Brussels Airlines, from Brussels; you could fly to Brussels to pick up the connection.

It's also worth investigating scheduled flights via **other West African destinations**, with or without a stopover en route. There are plenty of options for getting to Banjul via Dakar or Accra if you're starting from the Benelux countries, France, Germany, Italy, Scandinavia, Spain or Switzerland. Most major European cities have direct flights to one or two West African capitals which have onward connections to Banjul.

Dakar, capital of Senegal, is close to The Gambia and a fascinating destination in its own right. It's conveniently located for access to Banjul by direct flight (taking forty minutes or less on frequent services) or overland (see p.15). There are direct flights to Dakar from Paris with Air France or Air Sénégal International (which also flies from other French towns and has good connections to Banjul); from Milan with Alitalia; from Madrid or Las Palmas with Iberia; from Frankfurt with Lufthansa; from Lisbon with TAP Air Portugal; and from all over Europe with the charter airline Condor.

Another possibility is to fly direct from London to **Accra**, capital of Ghana, with British Airways or Ghana Airways, and continue to Banjul from there. Ghana Airways doesn't have the best reliability record, but it does have connecting flights to Banjul.

There are no non-stop flights from **Ireland** to West Africa. Your best bet is to fly to Gatwick, Bristol, Glasgow or Manchester, then by charter to Banjul or by scheduled flight via another West African city.

Airlines

The following airlines fly into Banjul from the UK and Europe and accept direct bookings; most charter airlines that serve Banjul are only bookable through tour operators and travel agents.
Britannia Airways UK ☎ 0800/000747, ⓦ www.britanniadirect.com. Charter flights to Banjul, which can be booked as flight-only.
Ghana Airways ☎ 08707/707117. Direct flights from London to Accra, with connections to Banjul.

SN Brussels Airlines UK ☎0870/735 2345, Belgium ☎32/70.35.11.11, ⊛www.brussels-airlines.com. Reliable and relatively frequent flights to Banjul via Brussels.

Travel agents in the UK and Europe

Africa Travel Centre UK ☎020/7387 1211, ⊛www.africatravel.co.uk. Helpful Africa specialists offering packages and overland tours.
Destination Group UK ☎020/7400 7045, ⊛www.destination-group.com. Good discount airfares.
Flightbookers UK ☎0870/010 7000, ⊛www.ebookers.com. Low fares on an extensive selection of scheduled flights.
The Gambia Experience UK ☎023/8073 0888, ⊛www.gambia.co.uk. Mostly deals in Gambian package holidays, but also acts as a charter flight agent.
North South Travel UK ☎ & ℱ01245/608291, ⊛www.northsouthtravel.co.uk. Friendly, competitive travel agency, offering discounted fares worldwide – profits are used to support projects in the developing world, especially the promotion of sustainable tourism.
STA Travel UK ☎0870/1600599, ⊛www.statravel.co.uk. Worldwide specialists in low-cost flights and tours for students and under-26s, though other customers welcome.
Trailfinders UK ☎020/7628 7628, Dublin ☎01/677 7888, ⊛www.trailfinders.com. One of the best-informed and most efficient agents for independent travellers.
Travel Bag UK ☎0870/890 1456, ⊛www.travelbag.co.uk. Discount flights worldwide including a few cities in West Africa.
TravelPoort Gambia Netherlands ☎31-71/589 3200, ⊛www.gambiatravel.com. Flights and packages from the Netherlands and Belgium.
usit NOW Dublin ☎01/602 1600, ⊛www.usitnow.ie. Student and youth travel specialists.

Package holidays

The Gambia is the best-known West African **package destination** from Britain and northern Europe. Most UK travel agents offer winter sun brochures which include the Gambian resort area (departures Nov–May), while specialist tour operator The Gambia Experience also features year-round up-country accommodation options.

Gambian package holidays are generally aimed at those looking for a relatively cheap tropical winter holiday. Until the late-1990s, there was very little **luxury tourism** in The Gambia, but the mix is changing, with new top-end hotels opening and others improving their services. Facilities, atmosphere and value for money all vary a great deal.

The companies below offer **standard package tours**, and sometimes have last-minute offers. For information on special interest tours organized by companies worldwide, see pp.12–13.

UK package tour operators
Airtours ☎0870/238 7788, ⊛www.uk.mytravel.com. Large tour company offering trips worldwide, including packages to The Gambia from Gatwick and Manchester.
Cosmos ☎0800/093 3915, ⊛www.cosmos-holidays.co.uk. Offers a few packages to The Gambia from Gatwick and Manchester, but not the cheapest.
First Choice ☎0870/750 0001, ⊛www.firstchoice.co.uk. Package holidays, including a few mid-price options to The Gambia.
The Gambia Experience ☎023/8073 0888, ⊛www.gambia.co.uk. Gambia specialist. Far more Gambian hotels than any other operator and the only one with year-round departures from Gatwick, plus departures Nov–April from Manchester, Glasgow and Bristol.
JMC ⊛www.jmc.com. Package holidays to The Gambia for a variety of budgets.
Panorama ☎0870/759 5595, ⊛www.panoramaholidays.co.uk. Winter sun holidays in The Gambia, with a wider choice of hotels than most.
Thomas Cook ☎0870/752 2960, ⊛www.thomascook.com. Tours include mid-price winter sun packages to The Gambia.
Thomson ☎0870/160 4529, ⊛www.thomson.co.uk. Winter sun packages to better-quality Gambian tourist hotels at keen prices.

European package tour operators
Big X-tra Germany ☎49-89/244 419010, ⊛www.bigxtra-touristik.de. Package deals from Cologne, Munich, Berlin, Dresden and Stuttgart to The Gambia, including off-season departures.
MyTravel Denmark ☎45/7010 2111, ⊛www.mytravel.dk; Netherlands ☎0900/10 20 300, ⊛www.mytravel.nl; Norway ⊛www.mytravelairways.no; Sweden ☎46-771/230230, ⊛www.mytravel.se. Huge operator incorporating Ving, Spies, Marysol and Sunair,

offering flights and package tours to The Gambia from Scandinavia and the Netherlands.
Olympia Netherlands ☏ 31-55/506 6666, ⓦ www.olympia.nl. Package deals to The Gambia from the Netherlands.
Thomas Cook (Belgium) ⓦ www.thomascook.be. Flights and packages to The Gambia from Belgium.
Tjäreborg Finland ⓦ www.tjareborg.fi. Packages to The Gambia from Helsinki.
Travel World Belgium ⓦ www.travelworld.be. Holidays in The Gambia including flights from Belgium and Amsterdam, and a good selection of resort hotels.

Flights from the US and Canada

Currently the only direct flight **from North America** to The Gambia is from Baltimore to Banjul with Ghana Airways (☏ 1-800/404-4262, 212/371-2800 or 410/694-6241, ⓦ www.ghanaairways-us.com) in around six hours. Ghana Airways doesn't have the best record for reliability, so you may prefer to travel **via Europe**, especially if you have time for a stopover. Flying to **London** on a discounted transatlantic flight (from around $300) and then on to Banjul by discounted

Special interest holidays

The Gambian holidays offered by the companies listed below are designed to appeal to **travellers from all countries** who want to join a group in pursuing a special interest, such as birdwatching, fishing, cycling, trekking, or exploring African music, culture and heritage. While few of the long-distance adventure tours that cross Africa visit The Gambia, many pass through nearby Senegal, and their itineraries are often flexible enough to accommodate a detour into The Gambia. Some of these agents and tour companies can put together **tailor-made itineraries**. These type of trips don't generally include flights, but most companies can arrange flights for you on request. They're listed by region, but it's normally possible to join their trips from any point on the globe, either booking direct or through a local agent.

Operators in the UK and Europe
Angling Classics Northern Ireland ⓦ www.anglingclassics.co.uk. Holidays for fishing enthusiasts, including Gambia trips with flights, hotel, boat charters, tackle and fishing guides, from £875 for eight nights.
Avian Adventures UK ☏ 01384/372103, ⓦ www.avianadventures.co.uk. Offers small-group birdwatching trips to The Gambia and Senegal.
Batafon Arts ☏ 01273/605791, ⓦ www.batafonarts.co.uk. Drum and dance holidays in Guinea and the Gambia.
Birdfinders UK ☏ 01258/839066, ⓦ www.birdfinders.co.uk. Special interest tours for birdwatchers, including one- and two-week tours of The Gambia, and custom trips.
Cool Running Tours Germany ☏ 49-33209/72800, ⓦ www.cool-running-tours.de. Drumming and dancing holidays and cultural study programmes based at *Boucarabou* in south Kololi, with excursions up-river.
Drum Doctor Holidays UK ☏ 01373/831171, ⓦ www.realafrica.net. Music-focused holidays, with daily drum tuition and accommodation in a simple Gambian compound a ten-minute walk from the beach in Bakau, with vegetarian meals.
Explore Worldwide UK ☏ 01252/760000, ⓦ www.explore.co.uk. Interesting small-group tours including an easy-going Gambia and Senegal trek by land and river.
Gambia Magic ☏ 01684/568676, ⓦ www.fishgambia.co.uk. Package holidays for anglers, including a programme of sea-, creek- and beach-fishing, from £425 for eight nights, plus flights.
Hidden Gambia ☏ 01527/576239, ⓦ www.hiddengambia.com. Design your own tour of The Gambia by booking your flight, driver, guide and hotels through this imaginative operator.

charter (also from little over $300) is one of the least expensive ways to get to The Gambia from most North American departure points. You could, equally, plan a route **through Brussels**, in order to fly to Banjul by Belgium's scheduled airline, SN Brussels, or **through Amsterdam** or one of the Scandinavian capitals, all of which handle tourist traffic to Banjul by charter plane.

If you'd like to fly into another **West African city** and continue to Banjul by connecting flight or overland, you have a greater choice of European hubs, but not much more choice of direct flights from North America. South African Airways has services from New York to Dakar and Royal Air Maroc flies from Montreal and New York to Dakar via Casablanca.

If you do break your journey in Europe, remember that the "two pieces" **luggage limit** that applies on transatlantic flights becomes a "20kg" (44lb) limit for the rest of the world.

Travel agents

Airtreks.com ☎1-877-AIRTREKS, 1-877/247-8735 or 415/912-5600, ⊛www.airtreks.com.

Milton Keynes Angling Centre ☎01908/374400, featured on ⊛www.gambiafishing.com. One-week guided fishing trips to The Gambia, using the services of the excellent British-run charter company, Gambia Sport Fishing, from £699 including flights.

Nubian Travel UK ☎020/8797 9660, ⊛www.nubiantravel.co.uk. Specialists in cultural tours aimed at travellers of African descent, but open to all. Programme includes a one- or two-week visit to The Gambia's International Roots Festival.

Ornitholidays UK ☎01794/519445, ⊛www.ornitholidays.co.uk. Offers trips to renowned birding destinations, including The Gambia.

Responsible Travel UK ⊛www.responsibletravel.com. Offers recommendations to travellers seeking trips and homestays run on a sustainable tourism basis. Tours reviewed include those organized by Tribes in The Gambia (see below).

The Travelling Naturalist UK ☎01305/267994, ⊛www.naturalist.co.uk. Guided wildlife tours; worldwide programme includes an annual fifteen-day tour of Senegal and The Gambia.

Tribes UK ☎01728/685971, ⊛www.tribes.co.uk. Highly acclaimed reponsible tourism organization offering small-group holidays run on fair trade principles, including eight-day Gambian tours (from £480, plus flights).

Operators in the US

Alken Tours ☎1-800/327-9974 or 718/856-9100, ⊛www.alkentours.com. This company has a specialist division for flights and trips to Africa, including heritage, ecological and cultural tours, plus bespoke itineraries.

Bicycle Africa ☎1-206/767-0848, ⊛www.ibike.org/bikeafrica. Easy-going small-group cycling tours that visit many West African countries including The Gambia between October and December, in two-week chunks.

First Person Journeys ☎1-800/670-0467, ⊛www.firstpersonjourneys.com. Small-group tours, including a ten-day tour of up-country Gambia by river and road from $1000.

Palace Travel ☎1-800/683-7731, ⊛www.palacetravel.com. African tour specialist, offering an eight-day tour of The Gambia (from $1795 including flights).

Spector Travel ☎617/338-0111, ⊛www.spectortravel.com. Roots and culture tours of The Gambia and Senegal.

Turtle Tours ☎888/299-1439, ⊛www.turtletours.com. Organized and tailor-made tours to many West African countries, with a focus on cultural events.

Victor Emanuel Nature Tours ☎1-800/328-8368, ⊛www.ventbird.com. Runs an annual two-week birdwatching expedition in The Gambia (from $4395).

Round-the-world specialist that can provide multi-stopover flight tickets including Banjul.
Educational Travel Center ☎1-800/747-5551 or 608/256-5551, 🖳www.edtrav.com. Student/youth discount agent.
STA Travel ☎1-800/781-4040, 🖳www.sta-travel.com. Worldwide specialists in independent travel.
Travel Cuts Canada ☎1-866/246-9762, US ☎1-800/592-2887, 🖳www.travelcuts.com. Canadian student-travel organization.

Flights from Australia and New Zealand

The only direct flights to Africa currently on offer **from Australia or New Zealand** are the Qantas or South African Airways flights from Sydney or Perth to Johannesburg. From there you can pick up connections to West Africa, but nothing direct to Banjul. The easiest option is to get yourself to Europe and pick up a flight to Banjul from there.

Travel agents

Adventure Travel Company New Zealand ☎09/379 9755, 🖳www.adventuretravel.co.nz. New Zealand agent for overland companies such as Explore.
Africa Bound Holidays Australia ☎08/9361 2020, 🖳www.africabound.com.au. Travel consultant covering the whole of Africa.
Flight Centre Australia ☎133133 or 02/9235 3522, 🖳www.flightcentre.com.au, New Zealand ☎0800/243544 or 09/358 4310, 🖳www.flightcentre.co.nz.
STA Travel Australia ☎1300/733035, 🖳www.statravel.com.au, New Zealand ☎0508/782872, 🖳www.statravel.co.nz.
Student Uni Travel Australia ☎02/9232 8444, New Zealand ☎09/300 8266, 🖳www.sut.com.au.
Trailfinders Australia ☎02/9247 7666, 🖳www.trailfinders.com.au.

Flights from other African countries

Banjul is well connected with other **West African countries**, with direct flights from Dakar (Senegal), Conakry (Guinea), Freetown (Sierra Leone), Accra (Ghana), and Lagos, Abuja and Port Harcourt (Nigeria). All other West African capitals have connections to Banjul via Dakar.

If you're starting your journey to the Gambia from **North, Central, East or South Africa**, you will not be able to fly to Banjul direct. Ghana Airways has flights to Accra that connect with their Accra–Banjul service. Other options include flying to **Dakar** with South African Airways or Royal Air Maroc, and continuing to Banjul with another airline or overland. South African Airways fly from many African cities to Dakar via Johannesburg, and Royal Air Maroc flies to Dakar via Casablanca.

Airlines

Air Guinée 🖳www.mirinet.com/airguinee. Flights to Banjul from Dakar and Conakry.
Air Sénégal International 🖳www.air-senegal-international.net. Flights from Dakar to Banjul five times a week.
Bellview Airlines 🖳www.bellviewair.com. Flights to Banjul from Abuja, Freetown, Lagos and Port Harcourt.
Gambia International Airlines 🖳www.gia.gm. Flights to Banjul from Dakar and Freetown.
Ghana Airways Ghana ☎21/221901, South Africa ☎11/331 1256, Zimbabwe ☎4/75166. Flights to Accra from Johannesburg and Harare with connections to Banjul.
Sierra National Airlines ☎397551. Weekly flights to Banjul from Freetown.

Travel agents

Africa Travel Centre South Africa ☎021/423 4530, 🖳www.backpackers.co.za. Local branch of the London-based Africa specialist.
STA Travel South Africa ☎011/447 5551, 🖳www.statravel.co.za. Good for youth and student airfares.

Overland travel

With careful planning, sufficient time, and some determination it's feasible to get all the way from Europe to The Gambia **overland** via the Mediterranean, Morocco, Western Sahara, Mauritania and Senegal. This is an excellent way to travel if you want to become fully immersed in the identities and landscapes of West Africa en route. Other land routes into The Gambia include approaching from Ziguinchor, Casamance, or from Mali and Senegal into eastern Gambia.

Driving yourself

Civil conflict in Algeria and banditry in the Central Sahara have effectively closed the old routes across the middle of the Sahara; instead, vehicles hug the **Atlantic coast** on the way south from Morocco. Although scenically less impressive than the Algerian desert pistes, this route is relatively easy on vehicles, and many people with no prior experience complete the journey in unmodified cars or motorbikes.

Taking into account fuel, maintenance, insurance, the inevitable bribes and equipment such as a GPS system, driving yourself can be a fairly **expensive** business. Even if you have someone aboard who knows your vehicle inside out, any serious breakdown can be costly and tedious. Travelling in a **convoy** of at least two vehicles cuts down on the chances of getting stranded. You'll also need time: a minimum of two weeks moving fast, or a month at a more comfortable pace.

The outstanding advantage of taking your own vehicle is that you can get right **off the beaten track**, if the vehicle is sturdy enough. A good way to recoup at least some of the costs is to **sell up** on arrival in The Gambia, or on the way through Senegal; with the right type of vehicle, you could make a profit, but be prepared for a certain amount of red tape when selling any vehicle. For more information on driving to West Africa, consult *The Rough Guide to West Africa* and a desert-driving manual.

Local transport and hitching

Public transport on the overland route to The Gambia is nonexistent for much of the way until Senegal. Without your own vehicle, you could cover the distance by **hitching**, if you're willing to accept the associated dangers.

Once in Dakar, it's straightforward to continue to The Gambia by **bush taxi**. Shared Peugots drive from Dakar's *gare routière* (taxi garage), via Kaolack, to the Senegalese border at Karang in 3–4 hours. Normally, you then have to change to another vehicle to take you to the Gambian border at Amdallai, where you change again to continue towards your destination in The Gambia. There's a direct (but badly potholed) road route from Amdallai to Barra, where you can take the passenger and vehicle ferry across the mouth of the River Gambia to Banjul, or make the crossing by passenger *pirogue* (see pp.86–87).

It's also easy enough to enter The Gambia overland from the south. The road from **Ziguinchor** in Casamance, southern Senegal, takes you to the hassle-free border post of **Séléti**, not far from Mandina Ba and Brikama. Frequent bush taxis run from Ziguinchor's *gare routière* to Séléti, where you need to change onto a Gambian bush taxi.

Travelling overland **from Mali**, the route to Banjul via eastern Gambia is more enjoyable, though slower and more expensive, than the dreary highway through Senegal to Dakar. Break your journey at Tambacounda, then make your way into The Gambia either via Vélingara, or the less-used crossing near Fatoto, and pick up a bush taxi to Basse; from here, you can take a bus to Banjul (two each morning), or bush-taxi-hop your way down the river.

Cycling

Cycling to The Gambia from Europe takes considerable time. If you cross Europe in the summer and Morocco in the autumn, then load your machine on a lorry for the hardest part of the Sahara crossing; you can arrive in The Gambia during the dry season, when the going is firm even on the backroads.

The Plymouth–Dakar Challenge

Inaugurated in December 2002 and set to become an annual event, this slightly batty amateur **trans-Saharan race** was inspired by the famous Paris–Dakar Rally. It follows a different – rather straighter – route across the desert. Participants have to follow a few idiosyncratic rules – notably, no car may be worth more than £100 at the outset, and all must be auctioned for charity at the end. This auction takes place in The Gambia, where all the banger-drivers gather for a triumphal celebration. For online information, visit Ⓦ www.plymouth-dakar.co.uk.

A **tourer** is much faster on the main roads than a mountain bike, significantly so over the long distances involved in this journey: a fit cyclist could cover 120km a day or more. But with a **mountain bike**, broken spokes and punctures at unexpected potholes are less likely and you're freer to leave the highways. More cycling practicalities are detailed on pp.33–34.

Red tape and visas

All visitors to The Gambia require a full ten-year passport, valid for at least six months beyond the end of the trip.

Citizens of the UK, Belgium, Denmark, Finland, Germany, Iceland, Ireland, Italy, Luxembourg, The Netherlands, Norway, Spain, Sweden, the Commonwealth and the Economic Community of West African States (ECOWAS) do not require a visa to enter The Gambia on a trip not exceeding 90 days. On arrival in The Gambia, your passport will normally be stamped with a **tourist visitor's pass** that allows you to stay in the country for fifteen days, unless you request a longer stay – the maximum allowed on entry is 28 days. This can be easily be extended by a month at a time for up to three months (D200 per month) at the Immigration Office in Banjul.

French, Swiss, US and Japanese passport-holders are among those that need a **visa**, available for around $25 from any of The Gambia's embassies and consulates; enquire at a British consulate if there's no Gambian representative in your home country. Visas are normally issued for thirty days and can be extended like tourist visitor's passes.

Only under special circumstances can you organize your visa at Banjul International Airport **on arrival** (assuming your airline allows you to fly without a required visa); you're likely to be issued with a temporary stamp giving you 24 hours to get a visa from the Immigration Office. It's far preferable to get a visa in advance. If applying by post rather than in person, you should allow at least two weeks, plus transit time, for processing.

All West African countries, including The Gambia, require a **yellow fever vaccination certificate** if you arrive from an area classified by the World Health Organization as infected; many African countries come into this category (information online at ⓦ www.who.int/en). Possession of a **cholera vaccination certificate** is not an entry requirement for The Gambia, but there have been rare cases of border officials demanding to see one.

Gambian diplomatic missions abroad

Gambian embassies and consulates generally open from Monday to Friday, and usually close on Gambian national holidays.

UK Gambia High Commission, 57 Kensington Court, London W8 5DG, UK ☎44-20/7937 6316.
USA Embassy of The Gambia, 1115 15th St, NW, Washington, DC 20005, USA ☎1-202/785-1399; 11718 Barrington Court 130, Los Angeles, CA 90077, USA ☎1-310/274-5084.
France Ambassade de Gambie, 117 rue Saint-Lazare, 75008 Paris, France ☎33-1/42.94.09.30.
Japan Consul General of The Gambia, Hyana Building 504, 3-14, 1-Chome Hiroo, Shibuya-Ku, Tokyo, Japan ☎81-3/444 7806.
West Africa Gambia High Commission: 11 rue de Thiong, Dakar, Senegal ☎221/821 1440; 6 Wilberforce St, Freetown, Sierra Leone ☎232-22/5191; 162 Awolowo Rd, Ikoyi, Lagos, Nigeria ☎234-1/682192.

Visa services

If there's no Gambian consulate in your home country, it may be worth considering a commercial **visa service**: for a set fee, you sign the application forms and mail them your passport and they do all the legwork. A visa service can be extremely practical in the **US**, where the only Gambian missions are in Washington DC and Los Angeles, and personal applications by mail can be slow. Agencies can generally get visas in about a week; count on another two to three weeks to send the applications back and forth through the mail and have your passport returned.

AAT Visa Services 3417 Haines Way, Falls Church, VA 22041 ☎703/820-5612.
Embassy Visa Service 1519 Connecticut Ave NW, Suite 300, Washington, DC 20036 ☎202/387-0300.
International Passports and Visas 205 Beverly Drive, Suite 204, Beverly Hills, CA ☎310/274-2020.
Travel Agenda 119 W 57th St, Suite 1008, New York, NY 10019 ☎212/265-7887.
Travisa ☎1-800/222-2589, ⊛www.travisa.com. Offices in Washington DC, Chicago, San Francisco, Detroit and New York.

Information, websites and maps

The best way to get up-to-date information on the country is to keep an eye on news websites and talk to tour operators, hoteliers, and independent organizations with interests in Gambian tourism. For more in-depth background reading, try the libraries of universities running African Studies courses.

The **Gambia Tourism Authority** is a policy-making body that's not really geared up for providing advice for tourists on demand. Its branch in London, **The Gambia National Tourist Office** (57 Kensington Court, London W8 5DG ☎020/7376 0093, ⊛www.gambiatourism.info), downstairs from the Gambia High Commission offices, has limited facilities, but can supply a few brochures and handouts. There's also a new office in Sweden (Gambias Turistbyrå, Drottninggatan 35 1tr, 4114 Göteborg, ☎031/136650, ⊛www.gambiainfo.com).

Websites

The Gambia's **Internet** industry is still in its infancy, and some of the most interesting online information about the country is presently generated in Europe and the US. This situation is likely to change, as Internet literacy begins to gather pace locally. One or two Gambian newspapers are trying to assert an online presence, but their websites are invariably unreliable. By far the best source of online news is AllAfrica (see p.18).

General information on The Gambia

Asset ⊛www.asset-gambia.com. Site of The Gambia's Association of Small Scale Enterprises in Tourism, with features and information about member hotels and other tourism services.
Columbia University Libraries African Studies Internet Resources
⊛www.columbia.edu/cu/lweb/indiv/africa/cuvl /Gambia.html. Comprehensive academic resource.
Gambia Daily ⊛www.gambiadaily.com. West African news from the World News network and links to Gambian sites.
Gambia Gateway
⊛www.gambiagateway.tripod.com. Gambian portal with links to small business sites and a photo gallery.
Gambia Net ⊛www.gambianet.com. Gambian news portal, with a few oddities such as traditional Gambian recipes.
Gambia Resource Page
⊛www.africanculture/dk/gambia. A mixed bag of general information on the country.
Gambia Tourism Authority
⊛www.visitthegambia.gm. Official tourist board site.

Gambia Tourism Concern ⓦ www.subrosa .uk.com/tourism. News and features from this campaigning organization supporting sustainable tourism in The Gambia.

Gambia Tourist Support
ⓦ www.gambiatouristsupport.com. Excellent and informative general interest site from a highly committed charitable organization.

Office of the Gambian President
ⓦ www.statehouse.gm. Official news and reports. **Nijii Gambia** ⓦ www.home3.inet.tele.dk/mcamara. Personal pages created by a Gambian enthusiast with general information about the country.

Travel advice

Australian Department of Foreign Affairs
ⓦ www.dfat.gov.au. Advice and reports on unstable countries and regions.

British Foreign and Commonwealth Office
ⓦ www.fco.gov.uk. Constantly updated advice for travellers on circumstances affecting safety in over 130 countries.

Canadian Department of Foreign Affairs
ⓦ www.dfait-maeci.gc.ca/menu-e.asp. Country-by-country travel advisories.

US State Department Travel Advisories
ⓦ travel.state.gov/travel_warnings.html. Provides consular information sheets and travel warnings for most countries.

Online news and general information on Africa

The Africa Guide ⓦ www.africaguide.com. Informative general-interest site covering the whole African continent.

Africa on Roots World ⓦ www.rootsworld.com /rw/africa.html. Features about the African music scene and audio clips.

Afrol ⓦ www.afrol.com. News and links. **AllAfrica** ⓦ www.allafrica.com. Excellent searchable database of news from the African press, covering the whole continent; it also publishes extracts and articles from Gambian newspapers. **BBC Africa** ⓦ www.news.bbc.co.uk/1/hi/world /africa. Daily news from Africa and audio bulletins. **Contemporary Africa Database** ⓦ www .africaexpert.org. Information about prominent Africans.

Magazines

Travel Africa ⓦ www.travelafricamag.com. Excellent features; strong on wildlife and safaris. **West Africa Review** ⓦ www.westafricareview .com. Features, essays and interviews.

Wildlife

Bird Studies Canada ⓦ www.bsc-eoc.org/links. Links to reports on birdwatching in The Gambia. **BirdTours** ⓦ www.birdtours. co.uk/tripreports/gambia. First-hand birdwatching information.

Chimpanzee Rehabilitation Project
ⓦ www.chimprehab.com. News and information from the River Gambia National Park's rehabilitation project.

The Gambia Birding Group ⓦ www .gambiabirding.org. Excellent bird information from a British association.

Maps

There's presently a shortage of accurate, up-to-date **maps** of The Gambia. The most useful general interest map for touring the country is Macmillan's *The Gambia Travellers' Map* (1:400,000, 1996), which is clear and reasonably comprehensive, although The Gambia's ongoing road-building programme means that it's now out of date. Less accurate alternatives are the *Gambia Road Map* (1:400,000, 1999) published by Freytag and Berndt and the *Gambia International Travel Map* (1:350,000) published by ITMB, Vancouver. All these are available in Europe and from a few bookshops and souvenir shops in The Gambia.

For more **detailed maps** of The Gambia, you need to get hold of the Directorate of Overseas Surveys 1:50,000 series (1982) based on aerial photographs, that show roads, tracks and streams. These can be ordered from map specialists such as Stanfords (12–14 Long Acre, London WC2E 9LP ☏020/7836 1321, ⓦ www.stanfords .co.uk, ✉sales@stanfords.co.uk), or, if you have the patience to sift through the acetate originals and order (pricey) copies, from the Gambian Department of Lands and Surveys in the Offshore Marina area of Banjul, near Arch 22. There's also a 1:250,000 sheet (1980) covering the whole country in the same series. All these are now very out of date; new surveys are underway.

For wider travels in **West Africa**, the single most useful item to take is the 1:4,000,000 Michelin map 741 *Africa North and West* (ⓦwww.viamichelin.com), which covers most of North and West Africa. ITMB (Vancouver) publishes a useful 1:800,000 *Gambia and Senegal International Travel Map*.

Insurance

It's essential to take out an insurance policy before travelling to cover against theft, loss, illness or injury. Before paying for a new policy, however, it's worth checking whether you are already covered: some all-risks home insurance policies may cover your possessions when overseas, and many private medical schemes include cover when abroad. Students will often find that their student health coverage extends during the vacations and for one term beyond the date of last enrollment.

After exhausting the possibilities above, you might want to contact a specialist **travel insurance company**, or consider the travel insurance deal we offer (see below). A typical travel insurance policy usually provides cover for the loss of baggage, tickets and – up to a certain limit – cash or cheques, as well as cancellation or curtailment of your journey. Most of them exclude so-called dangerous sports unless an extra premium is paid. If you do take **medical coverage**, ascertain whether benefits will be paid as treatment proceeds or only after return home, and whether there is a 24-hour medical emergency number. When securing **baggage cover**, make sure that the per-article limit – typically under £500 – will cover your most valuable possession. If you need to make a **claim**, you should keep receipts for medicines and medical treatment, and in the event you have anything stolen, you must obtain an official statement from the police.

Rough Guides travel insurance

Rough Guides offers its own low-cost travel insurance, especially customized for our statistically low-risk readers by a leading British broker, provided by the American International Group (AIG) and registered with the British regulatory body, GISC (the General Insurance Standards Council).

There are five main Rough Guides insurance plans: **No Frills** for the bare minimum for secure travel; **Essential**, which provides decent all-round cover; **Premier** for comprehensive cover with a wide range of benefits; **Extended Stay** for cover lasting two months to a year; and **Annual multi-trip**, a cost-effective way of getting Premier cover if you travel more than once a year. Premier, Annual Multi-Trip and Extended Stay policies can be supplemented by a "Hazardous Pursuits Extension" if you plan to indulge in sports considered dangerous, such as scuba-diving or trekking.

For a policy quote, call the Rough Guide Insurance Line: toll-free in the UK ☎0800/015 0906 or ☎+44 1392/314665 from elsewhere. Alternatively, get an online quote at ⓦwww.roughguides.com/insurance

Health

There's no reason to expect to get ill in The Gambia if you are careful. The most likely hazards are stomach problems and sunburn; malaria is a real danger, but can be avoided with proper precautions.

For serious medical treatment, you're advised to return home: The Gambia suffers from a shortage of facilities. The Royal Victoria Hospital in Banjul is undergoing a programme of improvement, and up-country there are new **hospitals** at Farafenni and Bwiam as well as the older one at Bansang, but in all cases standards and equipment are limited. Moderate injuries and illnesses can be treated locally, however. The coastal urban area has a choice of **private medical and dental clinics** (see p.126), and, in remote districts, **there are** rudimentary **community clinics** where treatment is normally proficient and charges are low.

Vaccinations

If you're visiting The Gambia for a couple of weeks or so and don't plan to spend time staying in rural villages or poor urban neighbourhoods, or travelling by local transport, then no pre-departure **vaccinations** are necessary. A few are recommended though – contact your doctor for advice specific to your personal circumstances. For longer stays involving significant time in places and situations in which there's a significant chance of exposure to infection, the following vaccinations are currently recommended: meningitis, polio, yellow fever, typhoid, tetanus and hepatitis A. Your doctor will be able to advise whether your particular itinerary necessitates all or just some of these.

Plan ahead – some first-time inoculations need to be administered well in advance of your travels, and some can't be taken together. A complete course may need to be spread out over a few weeks.

Immunization against meningitis is a good precaution if you're planning extensive travels – although there have been no recent outbreaks in The Gambia, other West African countries are affected from time to time. Polio is now more or less eliminated in the region, but it's still worth checking that you're covered.

Yellow fever jabs are good for ten years and confer high immunity. A yellow fever certificate becomes valid ten days after you've had the shot. Yellow fever is a monkey disease but it can be spread by mosquitoes to humans. Once contracted, there are no specific drugs to cure the illness, which takes a few days to develop into liver failure and kills about fifty percent of its victims. Epidemics are very rare, but the jab is nonetheless a wise precaution – recent outbreaks in Senegal and Guinea led to massive vaccination campaigns. On arrival in The Gambia, you'll be required to show a yellow fever certificate if you're coming from an infected area.

You shouldn't consider major travels without a **typhoid** vaccination (which lasts three years) or a **tetanus** booster (ten years). Nor is there any reason not to get Havrix shots which protect you for up to ten years against **hepatitis A** which can be spread by contaminated food and water. It's a lot nicer having the jabs than catching the disease, which seriously damages your liver and can leave it permanently scarred. The only problem with Havrix is the fact that you need to have the first shot at least two weeks before departure. Whether you have the hepatitis A shots or not, be extra careful about cleanliness and watchful about contamination of water – tap water is usually safe to drink, but in a few remote locations domestic water supplies may be of poor quality.

Hepatitis B, like **HIV**, is caught through unprotected sexual contact and through the transfer of blood products, usually from dirty needles; combined immunization against hepatitis A and B is available.

Many doctors no longer recommend the **cholera** jab; it's ineffectual, and the risks of contracting cholera are negligible unless you're living in the middle of an epidemic. Some doctors will quite willingly provide a cholera certificate discreetly indicating you *haven't* had the jab. It seems to do the job on those odd occasions when up-country border officials are checking absolutely everything.

Malaria

Malaria is caused by a parasite carried in the saliva of *Anopheles* mosquitoes. Although curable, it causes more deaths than any other tropical disease, killing over a million people annually, of whom over ninety percent are Africans, mostly children under five. Malaria has a variable **incubation period** of a few days to several weeks, so you can become ill long after being bitten. If you go down with malaria, you'll probably know: the fever, shivering and headaches are like severe flu and come in waves, usually beginning in the early evening. Malaria is not infectious but it can be highly dangerous if not treated quickly.

Protection against malaria is absolutely essential in The Gambia, where the disease is endemic. Despite a long-term programme of research into the disease, not least at the Medical Research Council in The Gambia, a vaccine has yet to be developed. As well as taking common-sense measures to avoid being bitten (see p.22), it's vital to be prepared with a course of **preventive tablets**. We've outlined below some of the drugs available, though it's important to discuss the various options with your doctor before deciding which one or combination to take. It's worth noting here that the strain of the malarial parasite commonly found in West Africa, **falciparum**, is especially severe and often resistant to treatment with chloroquine. **Pregnant women** are at particular risk from the complications of falciparum malaria and need to explore the issue especially carefully with their doctor when planning a trip.

Malarial **mosquitoes** prefer to bite at dusk and at night. Their prevalence varies between seasons and from location to location. As a rule of thumb, there are more mosquitoes in humid areas than in arid areas; the banks of the River Gambia and the mangrove creeks have far more mosquitoes than the beaches; Banjul has more than Serrekunda; shady woodland areas (including hotel gardens) have more than open areas. If you choose to stay in air-conditioned hotels and don't go out much, your risk of exposure is lower than if you camp or stay in bush lodges. Throughout the country,

the worst time for mosquitoes is the **rainy season**: most incidences of malaria in The Gambia occur between June and December. By the end of the dry season, the insect population has dropped to a minimum.

It's possible for a single mosquito bite to infect you with malarial parasites, but, because the effects can be **cumulative**, your chances of going down with a fever increase the longer you spend in an area where it's hard to avoid being bitten.

Antimalarial drugs

The range of antimalarial drugs available includes **chloroquine**-based tablets (such as Nivaquin, Aralen and Resochin), **proguanil**-based Paludrin and **pyrimethamine**-based Daraprim and Fansidar. Depending on where you live, you can buy some or all of these without a prescription at a pharmacy before you travel. In The Gambia, they can be bought in small shops and from street vendors (the more modern drugs – Lariam, doxycycline and Malarone – are only occasionally available in The Gambia). Chloroquine and proguanil have minimal side effects but are the least efficacious option as protection against Gambian strains of malaria, so are only really worth considering for trips to a low-risk part of the country at a low-risk time of year.

Mefloquine (sold as Lariam) is worth asking your doctor about as it's efficient protection against the strains of parasite found in The Gambia and it's taken only once a week, though there is widespread evidence of neuro-psychiatric side effects. Alternatively, you could consider **doxycycline**, if you're not concerned about taking an antibiotic as a prophylaxis. Taken daily, it's almost the only choice if you've left the decision to the last minute – the course is still effective if started just one day before you enter a malarial region. Another useful benefit is the protection it can offer against traveller's diarrhoea; on the downside, it can make your skin more susceptible to sunburn. Probably the best option is **Malarone**, a relatively new drug, which also can be started a day before you travel and can be discontinued just a week after you leave the malarial zone. It's recommended by many doctors, as it has no significant side effects and is extremely effective; however, it's the most expensive option (the combination of chloroquine and proguanil is the cheapest), and not suitable for babies or for trips of over a month.

No tablets are completely **effective** in preventing malaria, and all have side effects – but the chances of these causing you more harm than a bout of malaria are extremely small. They don't prevent infection by malaria parasites, but they do help destroy any entering your bloodstream. Malarone also destroys parasites that lodge in the liver, minimizing the chances of recurrent malaria. To optimize the effectiveness of the tablets, keep a **routine** and cover the correct period before and after your trip.

Mosquito nets and repellents

Sleep under a **mosquito net** when possible – it's worth bringing a small, lightweight net with you, as locally bought ones tend to be bulky. Other precautions include burning mosquito coils at night (also on sale locally) and spraying your room with insect-killer (hotel staff will do this for you on request). It's worth getting into the habit of applying a reliable mosquito repellent such as Deet before dusk. If you're staying in cheap accommodation, try to choose a reasonably bug-proof room: make sure the windows have mesh screens and that the door fits well in its frame.

Treatment for malaria

If you think you might be getting a fever, the priority is to seek **treatment**. Delay is potentially risky; overly casual travellers die of the disease every year. Ideally, confirm your diagnosis by getting to a doctor and having a blood test to identify the strain. If this isn't possible, take an appropriate remedy, which should be a different drug from the one you're taking as an anti-malarial. If you're taking chloroquine and proguanil, try three **Fansidar** tablets in a single dose, followed by two **quinine** tablets (600mg) twice daily for seven days. If you're taking Lariam, doxycycline or Malarone as an anti-malarial, take one of the others as a cure. The recommended doses are: two Lariam tablets, followed by another two, six hours later; or one doxycycline capsule twice a day for seven days plus two quinine tablets thrice daily for the first three days; or four Malarone tablets in a single dose per day for three days.

Be aware that the symptoms of malaria can be cyclic – after a day or two of improvement you may be knocked out again.

Schistosomiasis

Schistosomiasis – also known as bilharzia – is potentially very dangerous, though easily curable. Bilharzia comes from tiny flukes that live in freshwater snails and which, as part of their life cycle, leave their hosts and burrow into animal (or human) skin to multiply in the bloodstream. The snails themselves favour only stagnant water, though the flukes can be swept downstream. While it's possible to pick it up from one brief contact, the risk of contracting bilharzia is fairly low unless you repeatedly come into contact with infected water. If infected, you'll get a slightly itchy rash an hour or two later where the flukes have entered the skin. If you have severe abdominal pains and pass blood – the first symptoms after 4–6 weeks – see a doctor.

To avoid the disease, the usual **recommendation** is to steer clear of river water that's not been vouched for. Snail-free water that's stood for two days, or has been boiled or chlorinated, is safe, as is salt or brackish water.

Sleeping sickness

Sleeping sickness – trypanosomiasis – is mainly a disease of cattle and horses and, to a much lesser extent, people. It's carried by tsetse flies that crowd streams and riverbanks in deep bush areas. They're determined insects with a painful bite, attracted to large moving objects such as boats or Land Rovers, and often fly in the windows of vehicles driving through game parks.

Infection is rare among travellers – fortunately, because the drugs used to treat it aren't very sophisticated. But a boil which suddenly appears, several days after a tsetse fly bite, might indicate an infection you should get examined. Untreated, sleeping sickness results in infections of the central nervous system and drowsiness.

Sexually transmitted diseases and HIV

The only other real likelihood of your encountering a serious disease in West Africa is if it's **sexually transmitted**. Assorted venereal diseases are widespread, particularly in the larger towns, and in The Gambia the HIV virus which causes AIDS is alarmingly prevalent and spreading all the time, despite its incidence being far lower than in many other African countries. It's very easily passed between people suffering relatively minor, but ulcerous, sexually transmitted diseases, and the high prevalence of these is thought to account for the high incidence of heterosexually transmitted HIV.

Condoms are available from most pharmacies and from some shops, but can be expensive or of dubious manufacture, so bring some with you.

Heat-related complaints

It's essential never to underestimate the power of the tropical sun. Common-sense precautions against **dehydration**, **heatstroke** and **sunburn** include drinking plenty of water, limiting intake of caffeine and alcohol, and wearing a high-protection factor sunscreen, even on overcast days. It's important not to overdose on **sunshine** – at least to start with; the powerful heat and bright light can mess up your system, so a hat and sunglasses are necessities.

Before acclimatizing, many people get a bout of **prickly heat** rash, an infection of the sweat ducts caused by excessive perspiration which doesn't dry off. A cool shower, **zinc oxide powder** and cotton clothes should help.

Water and bugs

You should have no trouble finding safe **drinking water** in The Gambia. Bottled water is widely available for sale; plus, in most places, any unbottled water you drink will have come from a tap and is likely to be clean. Gambian tap water is chlorinated and much safer than the tap water in most other African countries. There's no need to hesitate, therefore, about ordering ice. However, in remote rural areas with no mains supply, you should be cautious of drinking unpurified water, unless you know the source to be free from contamination: bad water is a principal cause of **diarrhoea**.

In truth, **stomach upsets** don't plague many travellers badly, but everyone's constitution reacts differently to unfamiliar food and drink. If you're visiting for a short time only, and want to be able to drink water of uncertain origin, add a few drops of iodine tincture, use purifying tablets and/or boil water. If you want to be absolutely safe, **purification**, a two-stage process involving both filtration and sterilization, gives the most complete treatment.

For **longer stays**, and especially if you're travelling widely, think of re-educating your stomach rather than fortifying it. It's virtually impossible to travel in West Africa without exposing yourself to strange bugs from time to time. Take it easy at first, don't overdo the fruit (and wash it in clean, safe water before peeling), don't keep food too long, and be wary of salads. Ironically, if you're travelling on a shoestring budget and rarely eat restaurant meals, your chances of picking up stomach bugs are considerably reduced; the worst culprits are restaurants that don't take proper care over freezing and thawing food. The most popular simple local restaurants and street food sellers generally use fresh ingredients, and cook them well.

If you do have a **serious attack**, 24 hours of nothing but plain tea, flat Coke, or just boiled water may rinse it out. While most upsets resolve themselves, it's vital to replace lost fluids; you can make up a **rehydration mix** with four heaped teaspoons of sugar or honey and half a teaspoon of salt in a litre of water. If the diarrhoea seems to be getting worse, or you have to travel a long distance while stricken, any pharmacy should have brand name anti-diarrhoea remedies. These shouldn't be overused; restrict yourself to a day's worth.

Avoid using **antibiotics** at the first sign of trouble. They annihilate your gut flora and will not work on viruses; it's better to seek a doctor. If you have blood in your diarrhoea and it's impossible to see a doctor, take a course of ciprofloxacin – arrange this on prescription with your GP before leaving home. Antibiotics and anti-diarrhoeal drugs shouldn't be used as preventatives.

Lastly, two common gynaecological problems. **Cystitis** can be relieved, if not eradicated, with plenty of water, vitamin pills and acidic fruit juice: oranges and pineapples are available in abundance during the dry season. As a last resort, the broad-spectrum antibiotic amoxycillin, available on prescription, is useful against this (and many other infections). **Thrush** responds well to a good dose of yogurt, both eaten and applied.

Injuries, rashes and bites

Take more care than usual over minor **cuts** – in the tropics, the most trivial scratch can become a throbbing infection if you ignore it. As for animal attacks, Gambian **dogs** are usually sad and skulking and pose little threat, though like captive **monkeys** they may carry rabies: if bitten, see a doctor without delay.

Apart from mosquitoes, insects are less of a problem here than in many other tropical countries, but **tsetse flies** and **sandflies** can sometimes be a nuisance, and you should pack insect bite relief cream, since scratching may lead to dangerous infection. If you wake up with a neat row of small, red, very itchy bites then **bedbugs** (which occasionally lurk in cheap accommodation) may well be the cause – the best solution is just to change hotels. **Scorpions** and **spiders** abound, but are hardly ever seen unless you go turning over rocks or logs. Scorpion usually need considerable goading before they'll bring their tail into attack; their stings are almost never fatal, and spiders are mostly quite harmless. **Snakes** are common but, again, the vast majority are harmless and rarely seen – walk heavily and they obligingly disappear. **Sea anenomes**, **sting rays** and **jelly fish** are occasionally found in shallow tidal water; the varieties found in The Gambia are not dangerous, but it still pays to be vigilant.

Medical resources for travellers

Websites

ⓦ **www.fitfortravel.scot.nhs.uk** UK NHS website carrying information about travel-related diseases and how to avoid them.
ⓦ **www.istm.org** The website of the International

Society for Travel Medicine, with a full list of clinics specializing in international travel health.
ⓦ **www.tmvc.com.au** Contains a list of all Travellers Medical and Vaccination Centres throughout Australia and New Zealand, plus general information on travel health.

In the UK

The first source of advice and probable supplier of jabs and prescriptions is your **GP**. Not all NHS practices are able to provide yellow fever shots, however, and you may have to visit a specialist clinic, often in a county town health authority headquarters.
British Airways Travel Clinics Central London ☏ 0845/600 2236, ⓦ www.britishairways.com /travel/healthclinintro). Vaccinations, tailored advice from an online database and a complete range of travel healthcare products.
Communicable Diseases Unit Glasgow ☏ 0141/211 1062. Travel vaccinations including yellow fever.
Hospital for Tropical Diseases Travel Clinic Central London ☏ 020/7388 9600 (recorded Health Line ☏ 09061/337733; 50p per min). Immunizations and advice on hygiene and illness-prevention.
Liverpool School of Tropical Medicine Liverpool ☏ 0151/708 9393. Travel vaccinations including yellow fever.
MASTA (Medical Advisory Service for Travellers Abroad) ☏ 0870/606 2782; pre-recorded 24-hour Travellers' Health Line ☏ 0906/822 4100 (60p per min). Written information tailored to your journey by return of post. 40 regional clinics offer vaccinations.
Nomad Pharmacy London WC1 ☏ 020/7833 4114 and London N8 ☏ 020/8889 7014 (telephone helpline ☏ 09068/633414; 60p per min). Vaccinations, dispensary and medical kits. Very helpful free advice if you go in person.
Trailfinders Travel Clinic London W8 ☏ 020/7938 3999. Immunizations and supplies.

In Ireland

Dun Laoghaire Medical Centre Dublin ☏ 01/280 4996, ⓕ 01/280 5603. Advice on medical matters abroad.
MASTA (Medical Advisory Service for Travellers Abroad) Prerecorded 24-hour Travellers' Health Line ☏ 01560/147000 (75p per minute), for written information tailored to your journey by return of post.
Travel Health Centre Department of International

For a book on your health in tropical countries, you couldn't do better than *The Rough Guide to Travel Health* or Dr Richard Dawood's *Traveller's Health*. If you plan to live in The Gambia, get hold of the classic *Where There is No Doctor* by David Werner.

Health and Tropical Medicine, Royal College of Surgeons in Ireland, Dublin ☎ 01/402 2337. Expert pre-trip advice and inoculations.
Travel Medicine Services Belfast ☎ 028/9031 5220. Offers pre-trip medical advice and help in the event of a tropical disease.
Tropical Medical Bureau Dublin ☎ 01/671 9200, ⓦ tmb.exodus.ie. Nine clinics in Ireland.

In the US and Canada

North American travellers should not immediately head for expensive specialist travel clinics, where the cost of various jabs can easily run into hundreds of dollars. Local county or city health departments across the country offer inoculations at a far lower rate.
Canadian Society for International Health Ottawa ☎ 613/241-5785, ⓦ www.csih.org. Distributes a free pamphlet, "Health Information for Canadian Travellers", listing travel health centres in Canada.
Centers for Disease Control Atlanta ☎ 1-800/311-3435 or 404/639-3534, International Travelers Hotline ☎ 1-877/FYI-TRIP, ⓦ www.cdc

.gov. Publishes outbreak warnings, suggested inoculations, precautions and other information for travellers.
International SOS Assistance Trevose, USA ☎ 1-800/523-8930, ⓦ www.intsos.com. Members receive pre-trip medical info, plus overseas emergency services designed to complement travel insurance coverage.
Travel Medicine ☎ 1-800/872-8633, ⓕ 1-413/584-6656, ⓦ www.travmed.com. Medical kits, mosquito nets and health-related travel products.
Travelers Medical Center New York ☎ 212/982-1600. Consultation service on immunizations and treatment of diseases.

In Australia and New Zealand

In Australia and New Zealand you can usually get vaccinations from your GP or at a local health centre, but you're likely to find more specialized information from the privately run Traveller's Medical and Vaccination Centres (☎ 1300/658 844, ⓦ www.tmvc .com.au), which have clinics in 23 cities.

Costs, money and banks

Rapid inflation has become a fact of life in The Gambia. With exchange rates and prices changing almost daily, it's essential to keep tabs on the situation if you're in the country for more than just a short stay. There's a black market for foreign currency that, while not strictly legal, is sufficiently overt for both bank rates and "parallel rates" of exchange to be published in Gambian newspapers. Visitors with hard currency in cash have most to gain from shopping around for an exchange deal; the difference between the rate offered by hotels for changing travellers' cheques into local currency and the street rate for cash can be as much as fifteen percent.

Costs

It's perhaps surprising to find that, in general, West Africa can be an **expensive** part of the world, and the cost of living in The Gambia is high for the region. Mere survival can be dirt cheap, but anything like a Euro-American lifestyle costs as much, if not more, than in Europe or America.

If you're visiting The Gambia on a flight-

plus-hotel package, and plan to minimize costs by using cheap transport, eating market food or at local restaurants, and possibly spending a few nights away from your hotel either camping in the bush, staying with people, or in budget hotels, it should be just about possible to get by on **£75/$120 a week** (though £150/$240 split between two gets you more value for money). It's clearly much harder to keep costs down in the resort areas, where tempting comforts and consumables are available, and it would be easy to get through double the above amount. If you arrive on a flight-only deal and choose to stay in a **tourist hotel**, the cost of accommodation is likely to be your biggest single expense: typically £20–45/ $32–72 per night for a double room.

If you'd like to see more of the country than just the resorts, a good way to keep costs really low is to **cycle** (see p.33), which not only saves on fares but also enables you to seek out inexpensive accommodation or tent space. A cycle tour of The Gambia need not cost more than £6.50/$10.50 a day.

As a very general guideline to budget planning, a twin room in a cheap hotel can usually be had for under £10/$16, often under £7/$11 and very occasionally under £5/$8. Short hops by **shared taxis** in urban areas have fixed fares of around 10–20p/15–30c; **local taxi** hire starts from under £1/$1.60; and long-distance road transport by **bush taxi** works out, on average, at £1–2 /$1.60–3.20 per 100km, though it varies with the quality and speed of the vehicle. River trips tend to be more expensive. As for **food and drink**, you can eat your fill for well under £1/$1.60 if you eat street food or sit at a market or taxi garage chop house. Main courses at the more reasonable tourist restaurants are around £2–3/$3.20–4.80). A 1.5-litre bottle of water is 25p–£1/ 40c–$1.60, a 330ml bottle of Julbrew beer is 40p–£1/65c–$1.60 and a soft drink is 15–65p/25c–$1. You'll quickly discover that prices vary a great deal between the tourist places and those with a more local clientele, and that small shops and supermarkets are much cheaper than hotels and bars.

Travelling on a higher budget, **tourist taxi fares** are relatively steep (starting at £2.50/$4 for a short hop), **car rental** rates can be high at £17–90/$27–145 per day, and the **top flight hotels** are expensive at over £100/$160 per night for a double room. The cost of fuel – in mid-2003, D15/38p/60c per litre – is rising all the time.

Bargaining

You'll need to get into **bargaining** quickly, as it's the normal way of conducting business. Moreover every time you pay an unreasonable price for goods or services you con-

tribute to local inflation. There's a danger, however, that by bargaining over-hard you could cause offence, so if you're in any doubt about what constitutes a fair price, ask a disinterested local, and remember that good humour counts for much.

Bitikos (small general stores) and supermarkets invariably have **fixed prices**, as do the itinerant sellers of fruit, nuts, bags of water and suchlike who mainly sell to locals. Fares on shared **transport** are subject to state control and are fixed, but baggage fees can be haggled over. Tourist taxi fares are officially fixed but in practice there may be some room for negotiation. Fares for "town trips" by local taxi (see pp.30–31) are more flexible. Pretty much every other item or service (including, sometimes, hotel rooms) can and should be bargained for. Don't make any offer you're unwilling to commit to, though, as to refuse to pay once an offer has been accepted can cause grave offence.

In **negotiations** there's generally a "last price" which the seller has in mind from the outset. You can assume the one you're quoted is more, but a few good-natured offers will establish the fact. Don't automatically assume you're in the clutches of a rip-off artist: concepts of **honour** are very important. Try offering a bulk price for several items or services at once, or ask for some "presents" to be added to the thing you're negotiating over. You could consider throwing items from home into the deal as well – bartering is accepted practice, particularly in tourist markets.

Most importantly, men should make **physical contact** – clasping hands with the trader is usually enough to emphasize a point. Be as jocular as possible and don't be shy of making a big scene – the bluffing and mock outrage on both sides is part of the fun. Women can't pursue these negotiating tactics in quite the same way, except when buying from women – invariably much tougher.

Try to delay the moment when you have to name your first price. The seller's price may drop way below your expectation before you've made any **offer**, so forget the standard "offer-a-third-come-up-to-a-half" formula. If you do arrive at an impasse you can always drop the matter and come back later. With stalemates, a disinterested companion tugging your sleeve always helps.

Tipping

If you stay in tourist hotels, and go on organized excursions, you will be expected to **tip** staff, but it can be a problem to know how much to give, and when. Many staff will only be paid around £1/$1.60 per day, while those in business for themselves, such as taxi drivers, might make ten times this. For most **minor services**, a small-denomination banknote is adequate – about the price of a soft drink or a packet of green tea from a shop. For **waiters** in tourist restaurants, around five percent of the bill is fine. For hotel waiters and domestic staff who look after you evey day, think about giving something up to £1/$1.60 at the end of each week. Many tourist hotels have a staff box, so gratuities are shared equally. If you'd like to give a special gift to somebody, it's a good idea to enclose a note explaining it's a present from you, so there's no chance of misunderstanding.

In the humblest establishments, tipping is not very common, so the owners of **local restaurants** will be delighted if you tip them. Gambian **taxi drivers** do not normally expect tips. On organized excursions, the **guides** and **drivers** consider tips at the end almost as part of their pay: everyone on a group trip should give something under £1/$1.60 per day for each crew member.

Currency

The Gambian currency is the **dalasi**, which comes in 5, 10, 25, 50 and 100 dalasi notes, and one-dalasi coins. Various denominations of bututs exist (there are 100 bututs to the dalasi), but are now rarely used.

The days of the dalasi may well be numbered, since Ghana, Nigeria, Sierra Leone, Guinea and The Gambia are in discussion over the formation of a new monetary union, the **West African Monetary Zone**, with a common currency. The new currency could be introduced as early as 2005, and is likely to behave similarly to the **CFA franc** (pronounced "seffa"), which you will encounter in The Gambia from time to time. The CFA franc is the common currency of eight West African countries including Senegal, and is a hard currency with a fixed exchange rate pegged to the euro.

> Because exchange rates are presently climbing to unrealistically high levels, a few services (especially hotel accommodation and excursions) may be payable only in hard currency.

In mid-2003, the following **official exchange rates** (approximate) apply: £1 = D40; $1 = D25; €1 = D28. You can check current exchange rates and convert figures on ⊛ www.xe.com/ucc/full.shtml.

Cash and travellers' cheques

While a few European exchange bureaux deal in dalasis, you'll get better rates in The Gambia. If you're spending more than a few days, you're best off carrying funds in sterling, dollar or euro **travellers' cheques**, each of which is equally widely accepted. Danish and Swedish kronor are also often accepted in the resort areas. For the best rates over a period of more than a week or two, change money in stages, as the current trend is for the dalasi to weaken almost daily.

Hotels and some shops and traders will take travellers' cheques as payment, but it's essential to have some sterling, dollars or euros in **cash** as a stand-by. If you're in The Gambia for a short stay and you're on a budget it's worth considering carrying all your hard currency in cash and changing money as often as suits you. You will get a better exchange rate for cash than for travellers' cheques.

Denominations of travellers' cheques and cash should be as small as you can manage, bearing in mind the bulk that a large sum of exchange will amount to. A small stash of low-value hard-currency notes (£5, US$1 or €5) is always useful.

The usual **fee** for travellers' cheque sales is one or two percent, though this may be waived if you buy the cheques through a bank where you have an account. Keep the purchase agreement and a record of cheque serial numbers safe and separate from the cheques themselves. Some banks may not cash your cheque without the original receipt. In the event that cheques are lost or stolen, the issuing company will expect you to report the loss immediately to their nearest office; most companies claim to replace lost or stolen cheques within 24 hours. **American Express** and **Thomas Cook** are the most widely recognized brands, and also the fastest to replace lost cheques.

It's wise to keep cash, travellers' cheques and airline tickets in **small plastic bags** (to protect them from sweat) somewhere secure and invisible. Tourist hotels usually have room safes rentable by the day.

Credit and debit cards

Credit and **debit cards** are a handy backup source of funds, and can be used either in ATMs (if you can find one that works) or over the counter in banks, some shops, and in payment for tourist services such as major hotels, restaurants, tours, car rental and flights. Visa, American Express and MasterCard are the most recognized.

Don't count on **cash advances** against credit cards on demand – you'll have to find the right local bank. Remember that all cash advances are treated as loans, with interest accruing daily from the date of withdrawal; there may be a transaction fee on top of this. It's more cost-effective to make withdrawals from ATMs or over the bank counter using your debit card, which is not liable to interest payments, and the flat transaction fee is usually quite small – your bank will able to advise on this. Make sure you have a personal identification number (PIN) that's designed to work overseas.

A compromise between travellers' cheques and plastic is **Visa TravelMoney**, a disposable pre-paid debit card with a PIN which works in all ATMs that take Visa cards. You load up your account with funds before leaving home, and when they run out you simply throw the card away. You can buy up to nine cards to access the same funds – useful for couples or families travelling together – and it's a good idea to buy at least one extra as a back-up in case of loss or theft. The card is available in most countries from branches of Thomas Cook and Citicorp. For more information, check the Visa TravelMoney website at ⊛http://usavisa.com/personal/cards/visa_travel_money.html.

Banks and exchange bureaux

The most useful **bank** is Standard Chartered, most branches of which have ATMs. Other banks you'll come across include Trust Bank and IBC. The charges for foreign exchange differ from bank to bank. In the Kombos, there are banks in Banjul, Serrekunda, Bakau, Fajara, Kololi, Brikama and at the airport, not all of which have ATMs. Up-country, Farafenni and Basse are currently the only towns with banks.

If you have essential bank business to conduct, try to arrive early in the day and bring your passport. Never start a transaction without checking the **rate of exchange**, the commission and any other charges.

If all you need to do is change money, and you don't want to suffer the premium rates set by the hotels but you're not comfortable with the idea of the parallel market either (see below), it's worth seeking out an **exchange bureau**, generally found only around the resort areas. Bureaux are quicker and more efficient than the banks, and generally offer rates somewhere between bank and parallel market rates, usually with no commission. Their rates are not always fixed, so it's worth striking up a friendly relationship with one and seeing how far negotiations can take you.

The parallel market

An unofficial, **parallel exchange rate** (effectively a black market) exists wherever there's a local demand for hard, foreign currency that can't be met through official channels. Gambians can't always walk into a bank and buy sterling, euros, dollars or other hard currency over the counter, and hard currency is sold to private individuals reluctantly, with all sorts of conditions. Dalasis are more or less worthless outside The Gambia and local people have difficulty obtaining hard currency to travel abroad, conduct business or support relatives. Consequently, the parallel market in hard-currency cash and travellers' cheques is thriving, and travellers can, if they choose, benefit from higher than bank rates. Such rates are negotiable to an extent, but are typically at least five percent above bank rates.

The parallel market is far from secret: **moneychangers**, easily identified by their calculators and wads of notes, are found in all the major towns, and *The Point* newspaper publishes a table of parallel market rates alongside bank exchange rates every Saturday.

You should exercise extreme caution if you change money **on the street**. Although such transactions are pretty routine in certain areas such as the airport, the Westfield Junction end of Kairaba Avenue in Serrekunda, and the market areas in Serrekunda and Banjul, police are beginning to crack down on moneychangers; furthermore there is a risk that you will be skilfully ripped off. You don't need to change money somewhere hectic and exposed: any shop or other business which trades in imported goods may be interested in buying your cash.

Wiring money

Having money **wired from home** using one of the companies listed below is never convenient or cheap, and should be a last resort. Even faxed or telexed draft orders can take weeks to reach you at the counter – though the normal delay should be only four or five working days. Money is only paid out in dalasis. It's far better to bring with you on your trip all you'll need, and more, in travellers' cheques, or to make a cash withdrawal with a debit or credit card, even if this means waiting for somebody back home to pay the funds into your account first.

Money-wiring companies with connections in The Gambia include: Bayba Express (🌐 www.bayba.com), which is relatively efficient and has good rates, and Western Union (🌐 www.westernunion.com), which has many agents, but can be pricey and slow.

Getting around

The Gambia has no rail network and no internal flights, except by private arrangement. The most common way to get around is by road, which is often a slow, dusty and bumpy experience. The most satisfying ways to get around the country are by rented Land Rover (if you can afford it), by bicycle (if you have time) or by double-decker *pirogue* on the river.

Internal communications within The Gambia are severely hampered by the state of the country's **roads**. The major artery which runs all the way along the south bank of the River Gambia from Banjul to Basse, via Serrekunda, Brikama and Soma, was sealed in the 1970s, then neglected so badly that a few stretches (most notoriously the 100km or so west of Soma) are currently a nightmarish mess of potholes. Meanwhile, on the north bank of the river, very little of the main road from Barra to Kerewan, Farafenni, Kau-ur, Kuntaur, Lamin Koto and Basse has ever been sealed, though graded laterite can be more comfortable to drive on than potholed tarmac.

A much needed programme of **highway resurfacing** is underway, due for completion in 2005. For now, the smoothest journeys by road are mostly around the resort areas, with good tarmac stretching from the airport to the coast, then up to Fajara and Bakau, and right down to Kartong in the south. The Banjul–Serrekunda–Brikama road is mostly in excellent condition, as is the road from Barra to Kerewan on the north bank. The section from Soma to Basse is a blessed relief after the rigours of the stretch west of Soma.

Hitting the **backroads** can be a relaxing and rewarding way to travel. By vehicle, even in the dry season, you'll need a **4WD** to tackle the tougher laterite and sand tracks; in the rainy season many backroads become impassable.

If you're thinking of **hitching** around The Gambia for free, think again. The majority of rural people in West Africa get around by waving down vehicles (not thumbing, which may be considered rude), but they invariably pay. Private vehicles are scarce up-country, and there's a reluctance to deny trade to the bush taxi drivers; off their routes, you may get lifts but you'll usually end up paying a contribution to the driver.

If you're hardy and not tied to any schedule, you could simply **walk**. All over the region, you'll come across local people walking vast distances because they have no money at all to pay for transport. Many schoolchildren have to walk several kilometres to and from school every day. If you're hiking for a few days you can fall in with them, they'll enjoy trying out their English on you.

By tourist taxi

Tourist taxis are painted green, with white diamonds on the sides and bonnet. They're fully insured and have to pass an annual inspection. They offer trips at **fixed prices**, including waiting time and a return journey if required, and these prices are posted up on boards at the taxi ranks in the resort areas, so you know exactly where you stand. There may be room for a little negotiation. They also have access to the (few) restricted areas within the resorts that are out of bounds to local taxis.

The main **disadvantage** of tourist taxis is that their prices are way above those of local taxis (roughly three times as much as "town trips", see p.31). As they're beyond the means of most Gambians, you'll have only limited contact with local people if you always choose tourist taxis over equivalent local transport.

By bush taxi

The alternative to taking a tourist taxi is to take a **local taxi** or **bush taxi**, which will cost just a few dalasis if you're happy to get on and off at points along a standard route, or a little more if you'd like to hire a car for a "town trip" to a specific address (see p.31).

The **bush taxi** is the classic form of West African public transport, providing an essential public service in both urban and rural areas. Bush taxis are cars, minibuses, vans and carts that function like buses, in that they follow standard routes and are shared between a number of passengers who each pay a fixed price for their seat and, usually, their luggage, according to how far they're travelling; unlike buses, however, they don't normally run to a timetable, and passengers can get on or off anywhere along the fixed route.

In urban areas bush taxis are usually either small **minibuses**, converted to squeeze in the maximum number of passengers, complete with narrow benches and lino on the floor, or **yellow** and green four-door saloon cars, shared between up to four passengers.

Up-country bush taxis can vary from a reasonably comfortable **Peugeot estate** (station wagon) seating five, six or seven plus driver in reasonable comfort, to the same thing seating nine or ten in discomfort, to a converted **pick-up truck** (known as a *tanka-tanka*) with slat-wood benches and a canvas awning jammed with fifteen people or more. A basket of chickens stuffed under the bench, and maybe a goat or two tied to the roof are regular fare-paying additions. Brightly painted **passenger vans** (known as *gelleh-gellehs*), big enough for 15–25 passengers, are no less zoo-like, though padded benches or seats help, as does the extra ventilation. Most vehicles have roof-rack luggage carriers and one or two much-coveted seats at the front, next to the driver. In rural areas, **carts** – basically wooden platforms on two wheels, drawn by horses, donkeys or oxen – operate as bush taxis.

The chaos that seems to accompany bush taxi journeys is an illusion. They are nearly all licensed passenger vehicles, serving approved routes at fixed rates. In busy areas they run frequently all day. On quieter routes, however, there may well be only a couple of vehicles a day, and these won't leave their starting point (generally an open area or section of roadside known as a bush taxi garage: see opposite) until they have a full complement of paying passengers. There may be occasions when you want to pay for more than one seat, either to give yourself extra room, or to get the taxi on the road if it's taking a long time to fill up. There's no point in trying to pick up a bush taxi down the road from the garage on a route like this as they will all cruise past you full.

To flag down a bush taxi, hold out your

arm and wave up and down. Bush taxis with spaces to fill may well try to flag *you* down, by decelerating and hooting as they approach. Once you're near your destination, the driver (if it's a car) or fare-collector (if it's a minibus or van) will collect the fares – *pass* in Wolof. You're very unlikely to be overcharged. When you want to get off, indicate to the driver or fare-collector. If the taxi is crowded and it's hard to get their attention try yelling *"Fi!"* ("here!" in Wolof). There are some places, such as certain junctions, where taxis may not stop; otherwise you can get off anywhere

All bush taxis are available for **private hire**, and if you get into an empty taxi, the driver may assume you want to charter the whole vehicle unless you say otherwise. A journey to an address you specify (which may be off the standard bush taxi routes) is known as a **town trip**; you have the car to yourself. Taxis are unmetered, so you negotiate **fares** in advance. Ask the advice of a local you trust if you're not sure what you should be paying;

some tourists pay far too much because they don't realize that town trip fares are far lower than tourist taxi fares (see opposite). As a guide, work out how much a similar distance by shared taxi would cost if you paid for all the seats – this is the absolute minimum you can expect to pay, though in practice you may end up paying double this. It's best to equip yourself with directions to your destination as the driver may have no clue. If you find a good driver based in a convenient location, it's worth taking his mobile phone number for future bookings.

Bush taxi garages

Most towns have a **taxi garage**, not a building but an area where vehicles assemble to fill with passengers. Some large towns, like Banjul, Serrekunda and Soma, have several garages, each serving different destinations and usually conveniently located for the appropriate route out of town (though not always conveniently located for you). They

Bush taxi survival

Travelling by bush taxi can be a feat of endurance, your comfort dependent on the vehicle, the driver and the state of the roads. Give some attention to the **condition** of the vehicle before embarking. It's rare to undertake any journey over 20km in West Africa without encountering a posse of uniforms at the side of the road. A neatly turned-out Peugeot with a well-tied load and quite possibly some persons of influence inside is likely to pause for a greeting and move on. Conversely, a bruised and shaken *tanka-tanka* with a cosmopolitan crowd of passengers, no lights and the contents of someone's house on the roof may be detained for some hours.

Bush taxi **drivers** are generally competent and experienced, but their vehicles are among the most dangerous on the roads. Don't be afraid to make a big fuss if the driver appears to have lost all sense. Ask and then shout at him to "Slow down!" and try to enlist the support of fellow travellers – though to many Gambians being hurtled along in a rickety vehicle is a routine experience. You'll be in close bodily contact with fellow passengers throughout. On long distance journeys, sharing some kola nuts goes down well (see p.64). As ever, it's a good idea to bring **water** with you, but there are always plenty of fruit-, nut- and drink-sellers keen to strike a deal through the windows whenever taxis make routine stops.

You won't have much opportunity to enjoy the scenery, unless you're in one of the prized **front seats**: the windows inside the minibuses and vans are often curtained against the sun. Nor is this the most flexible way to travel – up-country, you may be reluctant to get off a taxi anywhere that doesn't have a bush taxi garage, for fear of getting stuck.

On the plus side, travelling by bush taxi can be a colourful, even enjoyable, experience, allowing you to meet ordinary Gambians in an ordinary context. It's up to you whether to chat or just lose yourself in your own private space – a relief for anyone weary of the intrusive attention foreigners often attract elsewhere.

sometimes double as, or adjoin, market places, and they're good places to pick up street food; they're also noisy, grimy places, often full of action and energy.

The **smaller taxis** generally sell their places and drive straight from A to B, if possible without stopping. They often do the trip in half the time it takes a more beaten-up minibus, *gelleh-gelleh* or *tanka-tanka*, which may drop people off and take fares en route. But the latter options are often the only way to get to more obscure destinations, or to travel on the roughest roads. Not surprisingly they're cheaper.

In the busiest taxi garages, such as those in Serrekunda and Barra, you'll find you're quickly surrounded by **taxi touts** trying to get you into their vehicle, which can be a hassle. It pays to behave robustly and to know exactly where you're going, plus the names of any towns en route or beyond, as you may have to change vehicles.

Up-country, the ideal **time to travel** is early in the morning. By a couple of hours after sunrise the best vehicles have gone, and on some routes, there won't be another that day.

Before long, you'll run into a situation where you seem to be the only passenger in a **stationary vehicle** you were assured was about to leave. When this happens, it's better to forget over-ambitious travel plans (especially after midday) or to take a shorter journey with a vehicle that's nearly ready to go. In order to guarantee you'll stay and attract others, drivers, owners and scouts will often try to get you to pay up front. Your luggage tied on the roof generally ought to be sufficient sign of your good faith and, unless you see others paying, it's always best to delay. Make sure you pay the right person when you do.

The only occasion on which you're in danger of being **overcharged** is when you're only travelling part of a long-distance route,

when you might be asked for the full fare. The charges made for hoisting your **luggage** onto the taxi roof may be up for debate, too, and you might have to argue about how small, light and streamlined it is – don't be afraid to make a scene, but remain good-humoured. You shouldn't have to pay more than one-third of your fare for a backpack or large bag. It's normally much less.

During **long waits**, keep an eye on your luggage. Anything tied on the roof is safe, but bags very occasionally get grabbed through open windows. Don't worry unduly, however, if the vehicle, while waiting to fill, and with booked passengers scattered around, suddenly takes off with all your gear on top. While it's obviously a good idea to make a mental note of the vehicle registration, you should avoid appearing suspicious or you may cause offence. They've probably gone to fill up with fuel, and will be back.

By bus

Buses, when you have the option, are usually slightly more comfortable and less expensive than bush taxis. Bus travel also tends to give you a better view of the passing scene. One big advantage of the buses is being able to buy tickets in advance for seats on a (reasonably) definite departure at a (more-or-less) set time. If you make a booking, you are, in theory, guaranteed a seat; if you just turn up at a stop you may end up standing.

Gambian buses are run by a state-controlled corporation, **GPTC**, and their service, once extensive, is presently severely depleted. This is partly because the most decrepit vehicles have had to be taken off the road, while others have been requisitioned as school buses or used for private hire. There's a daily service which runs between the GPTC depot in Kanifing and Basse, but only two vehicles run in each direction each day.

Choosing your seat

Whether travelling by bus or bush taxi, it's worth considering your general direction through the trip and **which side to sit on** for the shadiest ride. This is especially important on dirt roads when the combination of slow, bumpy ride, dust and fierce sun can be horrible. On a busy dirt road with lots of other traffic, try to avoid sitting on the left of the vehicle, or you'll be inhaling fumes.

Bush taxi seats vary greatly in legroom, and the best **views** are from seats at or near the front, which is also the safest place.

There are also two northbound buses every day from Barra to Dakar in Senegal. Though in reasonable condition, these buses are not particularly comfortable, and long delays and breakdowns are common.

By truck

Although it's against Gambian transport regulations, you can hitch rides on **lorries** in villages or up-country roads: because of its illegality, you'll rarely find a truck ride in a large town. You can expect the lorry to stop at every checkpoint to pay bribes, which makes for slow progress.

It's unusual to be offered a lift on a truck for free. It helps to know the equivalent bush taxi or bus fares and distances or you might find yourself being asked for a **payment** that's way over the odds.

There's sometimes a spare seat or two in the cab, but more often space in the back. Travelling in the back of panelled vehicles is pretty miserable, but many older trucks are open with wood-frame sides. When loaded with suitable cargo, these can be surprisingly comfortable, with great views. However, avoid getting the driver in trouble with the police by being conspicuous or foolhardy.

Travelling in an **empty goods lorry** on bad roads can be intolerable. They go much faster unladen and you're typically forced to stand and clasp the sides as the vehicle smashes through the potholes. Lorries often drive late into the night, so you'll need something warm to wear.

By car

Car rental is not highly developed in The Gambia. You can pick up a car at the airport or in the resorts (see p.126), but elsewhere in the country the possibilities are effectively zero. Rates including mileage and insurance start at around £17/$27 per day for a car, and £28/$45 for a 4WD, but can be astronomical. Petrol costs D15 (38p/60c) per litre, and rising; fuel shortages are a regular occurrence.

There are several general points to bear in mind. First, rented cars cannot, as a rule, be driven out of The Gambia into Senegal. Some firms insist on **four-wheel-drive** if you'll be departing from surfaced highways, even in the dry season. It's normal to have a **driver** (self-drive is less common), and it's

important to be clear in advance about his daily pay, lodgings and subsistence. If you're driving, you'll need an **international driving licence**, and will normally need to be over 23.

An alternative is to simply rent a **taxi** each day. Buy the fuel separately, and settle every other question – the driver's bed, board, cigarettes – in advance too. However good the price, don't take on a vehicle that's unsafe, or a driver you don't like and can't communicate with.

Driving

Don't automatically assume the vehicle is roadworthy. **Before setting off**, have a look at the engine and tyres and don't leave without checking water, battery and spare tyre (preferably two and the means to change them) and making sure you have a few tools. Except on the main highways, it's important to keep jerry cans of water and fuel on board. As for breakdowns, local mechanics are usually excellent and can apply creative ingenuity to the most disastrous situations. But spare parts, tools and proper equipment are rare outside the Kombos.

When **driving**, beware of unexpected rocks, ditches and potholes – not to mention animals and people – on the road. It's usual to honk your horn stridently to warn pedestrians and cyclists. Never pass a roadside checkpoint or barrier without stopping and waiting to be waved on, and don't drive anywhere without all your documents.

All of West Africa drives **on the right**, though in reality vehicles keep to the best part of the road until they have to pass each other (potholes account for many head-on collisions). Right- and left-hand **signals** are conventionally used to say "Please overtake" or "Don't overtake!", but you shouldn't assume the driver in front can see that the road is safe for you to pass, and many drivers never look in their mirrors. Don't assume anything about the behaviour of other drivers – road death statistics are horrifying, especially considering how few vehicles there are in the country.

By bicycle

In many ways **cycling** is the ideal form of transport in The Gambia. It gives you total independence; you can camp or take your bike into hotel rooms with you. If you get tired of pedalling you can transport your bike on top of a bush taxi or bus (reckon on paying about half-fare for it).

A bike allows you to explore well off the beaten track. Routes that can't be used by motor vehicles because they're too rough, or involve crossing rivers, are all accessible. With a tough bike, you can follow **bush paths** – though remember to give ample verbal warning to people walking ahead of you, who may otherwise be frightened by your sudden arrival behind them. If your tyres are up to it you can also ride along the beach at low tide (leaving the bumsters standing).

Bike practicalities

You can **rent** bicycles from a number of bike rental stalls in the Kombos, mostly near major hotels. The quality varies hugely. The going rate is reasonable at around £2/$3.20 per half-day or £3/$5 per day, with discounts negotiable for longer periods.

Hire bikes are not usually well adapted for long-distance touring, although they often have carriers. For long trips you could bring a bike from home to The Gambia, or buy one there: there are dealers in most towns. Serrekunda has the greatest choice, with good secondhand machines from about £50/$80 and new ones for under £120/$190. Remember to take powerful battery-powered **lights** – the front light can double as a torch and getting batteries is no problem. A rear-view mirror is very useful for main roads but, when it comes to predicting the movement of the traffic around you, don't take anything for granted. Cycle locks, and sturdier padlocks and chains are sold in markets.

Spares for mountain bikes are rare in The Gambia, although ingenious mechanics are easy to find. Take only what you might need in an emergency – spare tubes, replacement spokes and a good tool kit. If you need to do anything major, you can always borrow large spanners and other heavy equipment. Don't bother with spare tyres if you're going to be on the road for under six months. On a long trip, it's worth having the contact details of a reputable dealer so that, in an emergency, they could sent out parts by courier service.

Finding and carrying **water** is a daily chore

on a long cycle trip. Ideally you should have one five-litre container per person (more if you're camping out and want to wash), but you'll rarely need to carry it full. You'll also need good **sun protection**, even though you're unlikely to want to cover much distance while the sun is strongest.

Lastly, a word about **distances**: depending on your fitness and enthusiasm, expect to cycle around 50km in a day. The going in The Gambia is generally flat and gentle and, with breaks, you could cover the whole country from west to east and back again in a fortnight.

By ferry, river cruiser and pirogue

While it's unbeatable for sightseeing, the **River Gambia** has no regular up- and downstream public services. In practical terms, it can't be considered a significant transport route, and what should be one of The Gambia's major transport arteries is instead a hindrance to north–south communications. There is a plan to build a bridge between Bambatenda and Yelitenda near Farafenni and Soma, providing a crucial link in the Trans-Gambian highway, but at present there are no bridges, and only small, hand-hauled or spluttering **diesel ferries** pulling people and vehicles across the river at key points up and down the country. The most significant of these is the vehicle ferry across the mouth of the river from Banjul to Barra (see box on pp.86–87). There are also **vehicle ferries** linking Janjanbureh Island to the north and south banks of the river at Lamin Koto and Sankulay Kunda; a Bambatenda–Yelitenda ferry; and ferries at Bansang, Basse and Fatoto. Elsewhere, the river can be crossed by **hand-paddled passenger boat**.

You can also travel on the river by small motorized fishing **pirogue** (a long, narrow traditional wooden canoe), motorized launch, larger *pirogue* or powerboat. These are excursions rather than public transport services. Enjoyable trips include Banjul to Jinack Island, or from Denton Bridge, at Oyster Creek, near Banjul, into the mangrove creeks of the Tanbi Wetlands, or upstream to *Lamin Lodge*, James Island and Juffureh; or as far as Tendaba. For sightseeing, birdwatching and sheer relaxation, an up-river cruise by double decker tourist *pirogue* is unforgettable. For more details on excursions, see pp.53–58.

By microlight and light aircraft

The Gambia has no internal flights and no up-country airports – just a few landing strips. It is, however, possible to get around **by air**, though only by private arrangement.

Madox Microlights (☎374259, mobile ☎918576), primarily a microlight and light aircraft training centre, take people out as passengers on request – an unforgettable way to experience the country. Based at the airport, they are in easy flying distance of all points on the Kombos. By **light aircraft**, you can be flown up-river to Tendaba or Janjanbureh in a fraction of the time it takes to bump along by road.

Accommodation

Most tourist visitors to The Gambia have hotels pre-booked for the duration of their stay, as part of a flight-plus-accommodation package, but it's perfectly possible to take an ad-hoc approach to finding accommodation, allowing your itinerary to be flexible. At certain times of year (particularly at the peak holiday times of Christmas, New Year and Easter) the busiest tourist hotels are all booked in advance – and the most popular places may be completely sold out throughout the season – but it's always possible to find somewhere to stay if you're happy to look a little off the beaten track, and not limit yourself to the hotels used by the tour operators.

The availability of accommodation reflects the extreme localization of The Gambia's tourist industry. The vast majority of **tourist hotels** are concentrated in the resort area in the northern **Kombos**, west of Banjul and Serrekunda. Despite this high density of accommodation, even the busiest resort areas are, for the time being, low-key and uncrowded, and development has, for the most part, been sympathetic to the environment. The Gambia doesn't have any towering concrete monstrosities; even the largest hotels (accommodating well over four hundred people each in the high season) are low-rise and well landscaped with tropical trees and flowering shrubs.

The area of fastest tourist development outside the resort areas is the **southern coast** – the stretch of empty beaches running from Bijilo down to Kartong, near the Senegalese border. Even here, development has progressed at a gentle pace, with rustic **guesthouses** and **lodges**, their sophistica-

tion partly limited by the shortage or lack of services in this area. This is now changing, and options are likely to increase greatly.

Gambian hoteliers are becoming increasingly aware of the tourist appeal of the up-country districts, and particularly of the River Gambia itself; there are a small but growing number of **riverside lodges** and **up-country hotels** catering for adventurous, ecologically aware visitors.

At the budget end, there are, on the fringes of the resort areas and up-country, **tourist guesthouses** catering for backpackers and independent travellers looking for a down-to-earth place to stay which feels distinctively African.

It's also possible to find informal **lodgings with local people**, useful if you're really travelling on a shoestring, and a good way to experience local life. If you have appropriate connections (or are prepared to make some), you can also stay in mission houses and NGO or volunteer rest houses.

Accommodation price codes

Accommodation prices in this book are coded; the prices refer to the rate you can expect to pay for a double or twin room for two people. Single rooms, or single occupancy, will normally cost at least two-thirds of the twin-occupancy rate. Bear in mind that there's often a chance to negotiate a better deal.

In the resort area, you can often get a fairly basic place, usually without air-con and certainly without hot water, for about £5–10/$8–16. For a simple but decent twin room with clean sheets, air conditioning and private shower room, expect to pay £15–20/$24–32. A night at a tourist hotel with a/c and good facilities is likely to start at £20/$32. The top-end places, at well over £50/$80 per night, offer international-class luxuries – Gambian style. Up-country, prices are lower across the board.

- ❶ under £5/$8
- ❷ £5–10/$8–16
- ❸ £10–15/$16–24
- ❹ £15–20/$24–32
- ❺ £20–30/$32–48
- ❻ £30–40/$48–64
- ❼ £40–50/$64–80
- ❽ over £50/$80

Finally, **camping** is a viable option if you're fully equipped, although there are virtually no campsites as such.

Major tourist hotels

Most of The Gambia's **major tourist hotels** are designed to appeal directly to European holidaymakers visiting for a week or two's relaxation in the tropical sun. As such, they're fun, informal places, where the rooms themselves may be nothing special but plenty of thought has gone into creating appealing pool, bar, restaurant and beach areas – the places where most of the guests spend most of their waking hours.

Facilities and levels of service tend to be modest by international standards, so tour operators use their own locally specific grading systems to distinguish between the top-end, mid-range and budget hotels. All have swimming pools, restaurants, bars and rooms with private bath or shower rooms. In some, extras such as a/c, TV and the use of a safe are not automatically included without additional payments.

The **atmosphere**, style and nationality mix of the hotels varies greatly. One subtle factor to bear in mind is how "African" you'd like your stay to feel. Some hotels have gone so far to cater for Western tastes that they've lost all sense of their surroundings, while others have a distinctively African atmosphere, in their decor and the attitude of the staff.

If you're booking a short break in The Gambia, it's worth considering just going for the **cheapest possible option**, staying there for your first night, then, if it's not to your taste, writing off the cost of the other nights and moving on somewhere else, possibly to a small independent hotel or an up-country lodge.

Some tourist hotels are **block-booked** by tour operators, but others are available to independent travellers. They're expensive, unless you land a **special deal**, possibly by calling at least a day or two in advance and asking whether there are discounts available. Tourist hotels that stay open off season (June–Oct) generally operate lower tariffs at these times.

Small independent tourist hotels

If you're travelling independently, rather than booking a cut-price package, you'll discover that most of the tourist hotels ignored by the tour operators are much more affordable than those splashed across the glossy brochures. Some of the small **independent tourist hotels** in Bakau, Fajara, Kotu and Kololi are among the most pleasant and interesting places to stay in the whole country. Sometimes tour operators don't send their package tourists to these places merely because their pool is small, or they're not right on the beach.

Small independent hotels tend not to have extensive activity programmes but they're generally much more **tourist-oriented** than urban hotels and hostels. They make a very good choice if you're looking for a place that's relatively quiet, and attract a mixture of locals, expats and discerning independent travellers.

Self-catering accommodation

Self-catering accommodation is really taking off in the resort areas. Some have a pool, restaurant and bar; others are aimed at those for whom the extras laid on by the tourist hotels have no great appeal. A self-catering mini-apartment tends to be much more spacious than a hotel room, and even if you end up eating out all the time rather than cooking for yourself, having a fridge is useful. When choosing self-catering accommodation, check how close it is to shops, markets, restaurants and local transport routes.

Tourist guesthouses

The Gambia's **tourist guesthouses** cater for independent travellers looking for a good-value, down-to-earth place to stay which feels distinctively African. They tend not to be located in the prime resort areas, but are mostly found on the fringes of the resorts, a walk away from the beaches, or on the less-developed southern Atlantic coast.

Some guesthouses are in **blocks** like West African urban compounds, or in **thatched roundhouses** in a garden compound. Furnishings are simple (a mattress on a built-in platform for a bed, possibly some locally made cane chairs and batik fabrics). You may or may not have private washing facilities and electricity. Hot water is rare, but at most times of year you're unlikely to miss it.

Urban hotels

Every sizeable Gambian town has simple **urban lodgings** aimed at locals rather than foreign tourists; standards vary a great deal but the good ones can be excellent places to stay and offer a much more grass-roots experience of The Gambia than the tourist hotels.

Outside Banjul and the resorts, there's not much local demand for Western-style hotels. **Small-town hotels**, particularly the cheapest dives, are usually equated with drinking and prostitution. Rooms are often taken for a few hours only, and there may well be a gang of women and toddlers permanently in residence. Don't be put off unduly; these can be lively places, and by no means all are intimidating for female travellers – though you may have to pick a room carefully for anything like a quiet night.

Although there are no internationally affiliated youth hostels in West Africa, you'll find a YMCA **hostel** in Kanifing.

Up-country riverside and bush lodges

It's much easier to find people and places unaffected by tourism up-country than on the coast. If you have time, an up-country stay is highly recommended. You can enjoy the River Gambia to the full by staying at one of the **up-country riverside lodges** catering for birdwatchers, fishing enthusiasts, and anyone keen to spend time in the wilderness. There are also **bush lodges** away from the river; their facilities vary from simple to luxurious, but all have bags of character, and can be memorable places to stay.

At present, the **choice** of up-country tourist accommodation is very limited; this should change as the road network improves and The Gambia's popularity as an ecotourism destination takes hold.

Rest houses

In English-speaking West Africa a network of government **rest houses**, for the use of offi-

---

Cheap hotel practicalities

- Ask to **see the room** first. Check the essentials, such as the mosquito screening on the windows and state of the bathroom, and keep asking to see more rooms until you're satisfied.
- It's worth **haggling** over the price of a room. If there's air-con or a fan but no electricity, or if you'll be staying for a few days, ask for a discount. Check there'll be no tax on top. You usually pay on taking the room and may have to leave your passport with the person in charge if there's no registration card to fill out.
- During the **cold weather** of the *Harmattan* (generally Jan–Feb), ask for a bucket of hot water to supplement the cold tap.

cials on tour, is theoretically available to travellers when rooms aren't occupied. In fact, these places are often unused for long periods and need a good airing; water and electricity are often turned off or disconnected, and you'll need to find the caretaker to open up. Some aid and development organizations based in The Gambia operate rest houses, as do voluntary organizations and various missions. It's generally only possible to stay as an invited guest, but in some cases there's a special tariff for "outsiders".

Staying with locals

If you have friends in The Gambia, or are happy to scout about for an invitation, **lodging** in a family compound is a great way to experience Gambian daily life. As a holiday option, such experiences can vary enormously, and depend as much on the outlook and expectations of the guests as on the hosts. All over the country you'll run into people who might want to put you up for the night. A warm but, more noticeably, *dutiful* **hospitality** characterizes most of these contacts: to Gambians it would be unthinkable not to treat a stranded traveller royally. Single travellers who get into conversation on public transport are most likely to receive invitations. Your hosts are typically a low-income family, and you'll be expected to correspond later and send photographs.

It's sometimes difficult to know how to **repay** such hospitality, particularly since it often seems so disruptive of family life, with you set up in the master bedroom and kids sent running for special things for the guest. In the resort areas it would be normal to offer a daily payment roughly equivalent to the price of a room in a basic local guesthouse in exchange for bed and board; in rural areas you might like to offer the whole family something special. While it's impossible to generalize, for female guests a trip to the market with the woman or women of the household is an opportunity to pay for everything. Men can't do this, but buying a sack of rice (get it delivered by barrow or porter) makes a generous gift.

Camping

Away from the coastal resorts, **pitching a tent** is unproblematic if you have your own transport. Despite a fairly high population density, you can find secluded spots off the main road where you can camp for a night and enjoy the bush. Don't assume you can always do this anonymously, though, particularly with a car: a vehicle in the deep bush is unusual and noisy and people will flock round to watch you.

Bush-camping is easier if you're cycling or walking. Bring the lightest tent you can afford. For safety's sake, always get right away from the main road to avoid being accidentally run over or exciting the interest of occasional motorized pirates. You may still be visited by delegations of machete-wielding villagers, but satisfaction that you're harmless is usually their first concern. Some cigarettes or a cup of tea breaks any ice.

In more heavily populated or farmed districts it's best to **ask someone** before pitching a tent. It's safe to assume that every plot of land belongs to somebody; approaching them may well lead to an invitation to stay in their compound. Out in the wilds, hard or thorny ground is likely to be the only obstacle. Fill your water bottles from a village before looking for a site.

If you're travelling by **public transport**, it's a lot harder to camp. Vehicles go from town to town and it's hard to arrange to be dropped off at just the right spot in between. Heading out of town to find a place to camp, you could end up walking for miles.

Eating and drinking

If you're staying in the resort area for most of your time in The Gambia, you'll find no shortage of places to eat and drink, but you may have to search around to find traditional Gambian cooking.

Most of the **tourist restaurants** aim to appeal to the broadest possible clientele by offering "international" menus, and the results are often disappointing. By far the best way to sample authentic Gambian food is to be invited to a Gambian home. Alternatively, you could do as the locals do when they're away from home in the daytime, and eat at one of the inconspicuous **local restaurants** or streetside stalls found in the commercial districts of every town. It helps to know where to look and what to ask for, so going with a guide or a Gambian friend can help you find very inexpensive food that's fresh, tasty and nutritious.

The Gambia lacks a well-defined **cuisine**, partly because supplies can be erratic, and recipes aren't written down, so no two meals ever taste quite the same. Even so, there's a considerable variety of culinary pleasures, and a huge range of intoxicating drinks.

The resort area **bar scene** is growing rapidly, with many different tastes catered for, from conventional hotel bars and relaxed poolside bars, to English-style pubs, intimate cocktail bars and pre-club joints with loud music and a flashy clientele.

Traditional Gambian food

The great thing about Gambian food – if you're hungry – is its massive calorific value. Although less bulky alternatives are usually available, most meals consist of a pile of the staple diet plus a sauce or stew. By far the Gambians' favourite **staple** is **rice**, but **couscous**, tiny grains of durum wheat flour known locally as **coos**, is also common, as are root crops such as **cassava**.

Sauces can be based on **palm oil** (thick and vermillion- or copper-coloured, harvested from the oil palm trees found all along the Gambian coast and in the better watered areas up-country), on **groundnut paste** (local peanut butter), **okra** (five-sided, green pods with a high slime content which is much appreciated), various **beans**, and the **leaves** of sweet potatoes and cassava among others. All are usually spiced, often with **chillies,** and seasoned with stock cubes.

The more expensive, or festive, "sauces" contain **fish**, **beef**, **chicken** or **mutton**. Beef and chicken, being relatively pricey, may be reserved for special occasions; **eggs** are always available. Various kinds of **"bush meat"** are widely eaten except in the most devoutly Muslim regions; in some areas monkeys and antelopes are becoming endangered as a result of this practice. Wild boar ("bush pig") and large, herbivorous rodents ("bush rat") are the commonest varieties of bush meat and usually delicious, if carefully prepared.

Most tourist hotels have a weekly buffet evening which is a great opportunity to try out a range of Gambian specialities. One standard is **chicken yassa** – chicken marinaded with onion, lime, garlic and chilli served with rice – delicious when prepared well, but sometimes just casseroled fowl with a searing sauce. **Domodah** (in Mandinka) or **mafe** (in Wolof) is invariably good, a rich peanut stew often made with palm oil, bitter tomatoes and chicken or beef, again served with rice.

Jollof rice is a rice and palm oil dish usually cooked with beef (or sometimes fish), tomato puree and vegetables – peppers, aubergine, carrots and squash. **Benachin** (which means "one pot" in Wolof) is a chunky fish stew, essentially fish and rice, sometimes with vegetables. **M'bahal rice**, another Wolof rice dish, is made with dried fish mashed together with groundnuts and peppers – dry, hot and spicy. **Plasas** is an okra- or cassava-leaf and palm-oil sauce with dried fish and sometimes meat.

The best feature on the coast is quantities of fresh **fish and seafood**: shrimps, ladyfish (like sole), butterfish, meaty barracuda if you're in luck, and excellent chowders and bisques in a few places. Gambians are keen on grilling food over charcoal, and some of their most delicious meals are the simplest – such as grilled barracuda steak with salad, or seafood kebabs. The commonest Gambian fish is the **bonga**, which doesn't often appear on tourist menus because it's so bony, but, once smoked, can be ground to make a delicious paté.

You'll find quite good French-style **bread** all over, the two commonest varieties known locally as *tapalapa* and *senfour*. **Pies** – resembling Britain's Cornish pasties, but fried like samosas – seem to be a leftover of colonial influence; they're found in meat and fish varieties, and are often surprisingly tasty. **Fruit** you can get just about everywhere (see p.42).

Where to eat

Bakau, Fajara, Kotu and Kololi all have a variety of **restaurants**; Fajara has the greatest concentration of quality places, and the Senegambia area of Kololi is the busiest, brashest strip. Each of the major hotels, and many of the small independent places, have at least one restaurant.

There's a far greater choice of eating places in the Gambian **resort area** than anywhere else in the country. If you leave the coast and head up-river, you will find virtually no tourist restaurants except at the hotels (which are few in themselves). Even Banjul has very few restaurants, since eating out does not figure prominently in typical Gambian family or business life. Every town has **local eateries** that are cheap enough for the pockets of most Gambians, but these are aimed largely at people on the move, and local workers who don't have the opportunity to go back to their compound for lunch.

An alternative source of quick and tasty calories when you're in a town is to eat **street food**, which is sometimes superb. But if you're ever invited to eat in a **family compound** then all previous experiences of Gambian food are likely to pale into insignificance – home cooking can be truly excellent.

Tourist restaurants

Few Gambian **hotel** and **tourist restaurants** qualify as anything better than mediocre, but a few are excellent. In the Kombos, you'll never be more than a short taxi ride away from the better places, most of which are in Fajara and Kololi. Styles of food represented – with varying success – include American, Chinese, Thai, Japanese, Indian, Lebanese, Italian, traditional international and modern international. Most concentrate on tried-and-tested standards like steaks, pizzas, curries, grilled fish, salads and chips. Very few tourist restaurants make a big feature of traditional Gambian food.

A main course at a modest tourist restaurant is likely to be priced around £2–3/$3.20–4.80; the most expensive places charge £6–10/$10–16.

Beach bars

Beach bars tend to be rustic, bohemian places serving simple, fresh **food**, typically grilled fish and chips. In a country where the vast majority of meals served to tourists use at least some frozen ingredients, it's refreshing to go to a beach bar and know that you can order fish that was caught only hours earlier. You may, of course, have to wait a while for it to arrive.

For more about beach bars in the Kombos, see pp.114–115 & pp.144–145. A plate of fish and chips is likely to set you back less than £2.50/$4.

Local restaurants

Most towns, even the smallest, have at least one or two **basic restaurants** or **chop shops**. However unpromising these may look from the outside, it's definitely worth checking some of them out. Some are inconspicuous, others more obvious with jaunty hand-painted signs, but they all offer a genuine African experience, with simple, but often excellent food at rock-bottom prices – typically less than £1/$1.60 for a plate of whatever is on offer that day.

If they have a **menu** at all, it might be a blackboard with a list of choices of which most are not available on the day of your visit. But don't be put off – it's normal for such places to just serve one or two dishes of the day, and they do them well. It's natural to feel hesitant over what you eat in small restaurants where you can't be certain of the freshness or provenance of your food, rather than at street stalls where it's all cooked before your eyes. But it's worth consoling yourself with the fact that if a place has neither a working fridge nor a freezer than it has to buy its ingredients very fresh and cook them immediately. Places packed with locals are usually a good bet.

Local restaurants sometimes have a few **tables** in a courtyard, or **benches** outside at the front, but Gambians in general prefer to eat in seclusion rather than in public, so it's normal to be seated on a bench inside one of these hot, dark, smoky boxes, at a shared, oilcloth-covered table.

The Gambia has local **fast-food** joints, too. Some are as forgettable as fast-food joints anywhere (though the international chains are, to date, still absent), but some are pretty good. **Lebanese places**, providing snacks and sandwiches, especially *chawarma* – spit-grilled mutton in pitta bread – are almost as common as burger franchises in the US.

Afra barbecues

Uninterested though they generally are in eating out, Gambians all over the country love **afra**. It's a simple formula common to many African countries – you choose a cut of meat from a joint hanging from a hook in the shop, and it's chopped up in front of you, seasoned, flung on a grill to sizzle over hot embers in a wood-fired furnace, then, when done, doused with mustard and/or sauce and wrapped up in brown paper, for you to eat in your fingers, with fresh *tapalapa* bread. The price depends on the quantity of meat you order, typically starting at under £1/$1.60. Though essentially fast food, there are *afra* places that have benches and tables and something of a restaurant feel. *Afra* is almost exclusively a **late-night** habit for Gambians, especially after a night out clubbing.

Street food

Gambian street food is certainly worth trying, but you won't normally find much in the resorts. The best hunting grounds are the busy commercial and market areas of any town.

The secret is to **eat early** (11am–noon) and at dusk (5–6pm), when most people eat and food is fresh. Street food isn't usually a takeaway – there's often a table and benches, plastic bowls, spoons and cold water.

Sometimes, though, you'll just find women with covered enamel bowls waiting by the roadside or in the market for customers. They may well have a different type of **stew** or **sauce** every day, to pour over rice or into bread to make a sandwich. You'll also find little **fritters** made from millet or rice flour, sometimes spicy, sometimes sweet. One snack that's pretty well universal is sticks of kebabed meat, often eaten as a sandwich in a piece of bread. Everything is extremely cheap: just a few dalasis. Anything extra you want – soft drinks, instant coffee – can be fetched for you from nearby.

If you're travelling you're likely to adopt the habit of eating **breakfast** in the street. At roadside coffee stands you'll get excellent hot Nescafé, shaken up to give it a cappuccino-style froth, with bread and margarine or omelette. But be ready to say so promptly if you want your coffee black or – big shock to local people – without sugar. As it's sometimes made with sweetened condensed milk, white-no-sugar can be a problem.

Vegetarian food

Traditionally, The Gambia makes no concessions to **vegetarians**, for whom eating ready-prepared food, whether on the street or in all but a few restaurants, is unrewarding. Animal protein is the focus of most dishes, and even where it's apparently absent (for example, in vegetable *domodah*) there's likely to be some meat or fish stock somewhere – rice is often cooked in it. This means, if you're strictly vegetarian, you're mostly going to have to choose your resturants carefully, or stick to eggs, market fruit and veg and any food you cook for yourself.

Peanuts, boiled or roasted, and locally ground peanut butter are a good source of vegetable protein. **Cheese** is hard to find, except, imported, in supermarkets, but even when you're away from the resort areas, where the supermarkets are concentrated, bread, margarine, canned **milk** in various forms (and milk powder) and **hard-boiled eggs** are always easily obtainable, as are, often, delicious **sour milk** and **yoghurt**.

Vegetarians who are the **guests** of Gambian families have a hard time – with such status attached to meat, vegetarianism is regarded as an alien philosophy.

Communal eating

If you're lucky enough to be staying **with a family,** or just visiting for the day or for a special ceremony, you're likely to experience well-prepared and tasty food – though according to their means this may depend on how much you contribute. In homes or at work, people eat around a **communal dish.** In strictly Islamic families it's always males at one, females at another (although foreign women tend to be treated as honorary men). Everybody **washes their hands** first, generally with water poured from a kettle, and the bowl or bowls are placed on a mat on the floor. These will contain mounds of rice or couscous with sauce poured on top and vegetables, meat or fish balanced in the middle.

Take off your **shoes** (it's polite to do this before stepping onto any mat in a Gambian home) and sit down by the bowl, following the example of your hosts. Even if you're not hungry, it's impolite to refuse an offer of food, so you should at least taste a little. You may be offered a spoon; if not, you eat with your right hand only (this is a strict rule), helping yourself from the part of the bowl nearest you, mashing some rice or couscous into a ball in your fingers and rolling it in a little sauce. You may find that your hosts politely nudge the choice bits of meat or vegetables from the centre of the bowl towards you.

It's normal to **eat in silence** (punctuated by the occasional polite belch and compliments to the host, remarking how wonderfully "hot" or "sweet" the food is), and for everyone to finish in order of age, the eldest first. You get up and leave the bowl as soon as you're finished.

Communal eating is such an integral part of Gambian social interaction that it's no great surprise that restaurants, where someone goes and buys a meal for themselves and eats separately from their companions, are not all that common away from the tourist areas.

Fruit and nuts

Fruit and **nuts** make for satisfying eating in The Gambia. Most hotels make a big feature of fruit at breakfast time, but, unfortunately, only a few bars serve fresh juices, sticking instead to bottled soft drinks or imported juice from cartons. There are plenty of juice-sellers serving made-to-order concoctions from stalls on the resort beaches, but these are all too often watery and over-sweet.

It's very easy to find fruit, peanuts and cashews at **markets** and **on the street**, from itinerant traders with trays on their heads, and on the beach at stalls. Some stalls sell coconuts, in slices or whole, with the top lopped off for you to drink the juice. Locally grown bananas, coconuts and paw-paws are available all year round, but other fruit is seasonal: mangoes are everywhere from June to September, and most other fruit ripens in the dry season.

Local **bananas** come in several varieties, all wonderfully flavoured, including the thin-skinned dwarf ones sometimes called "apple bananas". **Pawpaw** trees are common although Gambians don't eat pawpaws

much. They're very good (and good for you) with lime juice. Gambian **mangoes** are gorgeous and come in many varieties, but most tourists miss them as they ripen in the rainy season. African varieties of **citrus fruit** are very sweet, particularly grapefruit and limes. From December to the end of the dry season, **oranges** (bright green when ripe) are abundant and available for next to nothing from women with trays or men with barrows and sharp knives. Gambians like them peeled with the pith left on so they can suck out the juice. Also easy to grow in the Gambia are **watermelon** – you'll see mountains of them for sale by the roadside from November to January – sweet and thirst-quenching. **Pineapples**, however, are usually imported from other West African countries.

You'll come across several different grades and varieties of **dates**, especially during Ramadan, when they're a favourite part of breaking the fast after sunset. You'll also come across fruit which is more often used to make juices and cordials than eaten. There's the **ditah**, a little brown fruit with tasty, bright green juice, and the **tamarind,** available from January to March, and crushed to make *daharr* juice, which has a dark, treacly, slightly bitter flavour, and is sometimes added to *benachin* (see p.39).

Wonjo, not actually a fruit, but the flower-like crimson pods of the sorrel plant, is commonly cultivated in fields and gardens, and sold fresh or dried, to be steeped in water with sugar and (sometimes) mint to make a refreshing bright red cordial. The fruit of the **baobab** tree, ripe from around January, contains white seeds, which, when dried, are used as a sherbet for making *bwi* cordial or sorbet. The juice, naturally tart, is sometimes sweetened with sugar and flavoured with vanilla or banana essence.

Known locally as groundnuts, **peanuts** are harvested from November, when you'll see stacks of plants piled up in the fields. They can be eaten raw, fresh from the field, but are more commonly shelled and boiled or roasted then sold by the tin cupful (wrapped in paper) or small bagful as a snack. They're a primary ingredient in Gambian cooking. Look out for Gambian peanut brittle, sometimes sold by market, street and beach vendors.

Cashew nuts are sold in little bags by vendors everywhere, and cashew fruit are available in June and July. A single nut grows at the apex of each cashew "apple" which is too bitter to eat, but can be chewed for its delicious, light juice. In some parts this stuff is made into a potent hooch. It's best not to feast off cashew trees – they only have a small number of valuable nuts each and owners get very upset. Beware, too, of the staining properties of the juice.

Drinking

Gambian **tap water** is safe to drink (see Health p.23), though tour reps may try to convince you to drink nothing but **bottled water**. Supermarkets and some general stores carry large bottles of mineral water – The Gambia has its own quality brand called *Naturelle*, which is filtered, ozonized and bottled in Kanifing – but it's less common to find this in village shops.

Probably the most widely consumed beverage in The Gambia – after water – is **green tea**, known locally as *attaya* (see box below). Apart from Nescafé, which is

Attaya

Brewing and sharing **attaya** (green tea) is a quintessentially West African ritual. It's a procedure that demands a certain amount of artistry and skill, giving the tea-maker an opportunity to show off and share a little downtime with companions. *Attaya*-drinking does not form part of a meal, but is an **event** in its own right. The sharing involved expresses appreciation and cements and reinforces friendships, and the whole ritual takes time, constituting a lengthy but hotly defended break in any working day. *Attaya*-making is particularly big with youths; friends take it in turns to brew, and tease each other as to who's the expert.

The *attaya* ritual traditionally has three rounds. The **recipe** is a packet of tea (always bitter Chinese Green Gunpowder), boiled up over a charcoal burner with a small amount of water and a large amount of sugar in a little enamel teapot. Brewers with flair may add something extra, like fresh mint or vanilla. The brew is poured repeatedly, and with a flourish, between two small Maghrebian-style glass tumblers until the glasses contain half liquid, half foam. It's then sipped, loudly, as a mark of approval.

For the **second round**, more sugar and water is added before steeping; the third round is even sweeter. Supposedly, the **third round**, sweet and mild, is for children and the elderly, the second, full-bodied, for women, and the first, strong and bitter, for "real men". But, as in everything Gambian, form doesn't have to be followed. As a **hot tonic**, it has a real kick, which explains why it's apparently required drinking for night watchmen – you'll spot the glow of charcoal burners on compound doorsteps when you're out at night.

Attaya is so **popular** that whenever you're in Banjul you're likely to see merchants unloading crate after crate of the stuff, freshly imported from China. A packet of *attaya* and a bag of sugar, found at any *bitiko*, makes a good small gift.

ubiquitous (the variety available in West Africa is strong and good), **coffee** is less popular, and real coffee rare except in some tourist hotels and a few cafés in the resort areas. Various tea-like **infusions** are locally common. If you're drinking at a local coffee stand, you might come across one which is widely popular in West Africa (as a base for mixing in a lot of sweet concentrated canned milk): *kinkiliba*. It's reasonable on its own straight from the hot bucket or kettle, but don't mistake it for water and have Nescafé added (this would, however, raise no eyebrows as Gambians sometimes drink it this way).

When you can't get cold water, **soft drinks** (known as "softs") – especially Fanta orange, Sprite lemonade and Coke, all manufactured and bottled locally – are permanent standbys. In remote areas any establishment with electricity is almost bound to have a fridge of battered bottles (bottles are always returned to the wholesaler: *never take the bottle away* – this is serious theft!). Less-regularly available bottled sodas include fruit cocktail (which contains some fruit juice), Vimto, VitaMalt, tonic water, bitter lemon, soda water and Malta (a very sweet non-alcoholic beer).

On the street, particularly in market and bush taxi garage areas, you'll often see vendors carrying trays of cold tap water in sachets, and locally made **fruit juices** (cordials) and **ices**, also in plastic bags, sold by children from cooler buckets. They're all made with tap water: ginger (light brown) is refreshing, as too are *wonjo* (red) and *bwi* (white), made from the sherbet of baobab fruits.

Beer and spirits

The most obvious drink in The Gambia is **JulBrew lager**, which is 4.7 percent proof and fairly palatable. Although many Muslim Gambians don't drink, they are tolerant of those who do, and alcohol is widely available in the resort area and in major towns. However, this European-style beer is extremely expensive to the majority of local people and it can therefore sometimes be difficult to find in smaller villages.

Most of the time, JulBrew is served cold, in 330ml bottles, as is **Guinness**, also brewed locally. It's worth tracking down the bars which serve JulBrew on **draught**, particularly those with a high enough turnover to keep it fresh.

Palm wine, a coastal West African speciality, is produced from palm sap which, after tapping, ferments in a day from a pleasant, mildly intoxicating juice to a ripe and pungent brew with seriously destabilizing qualities. The flavour is aromatic and slightly acidic. It can also be distilled to produce a colourless firewater with various jokey names including "Kill-me-quick". The most common palms tapped are oil and raffia palms. Palm-tapping is a speciality of the Manjagos, a non-Muslim ethnic group, who sell palm wine from informal drinking dens known as palm wine ghettoes – either a compound, or just a clearing in the bush.

Imported spirits are common enough in the resort area bars, restaurants and supermarkets, some of which also sell **imported beer and wine**, often at very reasonable prices.

Communications

Mail and telecommunications in The Gambia have improved enormously over the last ten years. Ordinary letters sent from main post offices rarely go astray, and postage from The Gambia to Europe or North America still costs less than domestic mail in the West. Receiving mail is a little more variable, however; residents use post boxes at post offices. As for phoning, international calls are easy enough, and mobile phones are becoming increasingly common. Meanwhile, Internet cafés are springing up all over the place, and email is rapidly gaining in popularity.

Mail

Gambian **post offices** are called the GPO (General Post Office), a remnant of British colonial days. They usually have separate counters for different services; the Banjul GPO even has a philately desk, where you can buy collectors' sets of the country's attractive stamps.

It's easiest and most secure to use postage-paid **aerograms** for writing home; these should arrive in Europe or North America seven to ten days after posting. If you have **urgent mail** to post abroad, the best place is Banjul International Airport; the small post office here can often send mail out on the next flight. For similar reasons, if you're sending slightly heavy or valuable items, it's worth doing so with a friend or contact who's flying (leave it unsealed for customs). A lot of ordinary mail is sent this way too – it's always quicker.

Poste restante

If you're staying at a reliable **hotel** in the Kombos, you could have your mail sent there; otherwise, have it sent to a friend with a **PO Box** in the Kombos, or to the Banjul **GPO Poste Restante**. It can take some time for post to find its way up-country. Note, too, that some post offices only hold mail for a few weeks before returning it to the sender.

To **collect mail** from the poste restante desk at the Banjul GPO, write out your name as you'd expect it to appear on the letter, and bring your **passport**, without which you'll rarely be allowed to collect mail. If in doubt, ask the assistant to check under both your first and second names.

Ask **senders** to put their own address on the back and to write your address in this form: GREGG Emma, Poste Restante, GPO, Russell Street, Banjul, THE GAMBIA. Mail posted from Europe is likely to be in transit for two weeks before you can collect it from Banjul; three days longer from the rest of the world.

Telephones

Gambian telephone numbers have six digits and no area code. To make a phone call on a land line in the Gambia, you can choose between using a **phonecard** (the cheapest option), using a commercial **telecentre** (more expensive), or calling on a **hotel phone** account. Some hotels will charge a reasonable fixed rate for local calls, but those who allow you to call abroad direct mark up the cost considerably.

The most economical way to make local or international phone calls is to buy a **Kachaa card**, only available from Gamtel offices, in various denominations. This is a charge card which gives you an access code to make calls from any landline. Other brands of phonecard, which operate similarly, are sold at supermarkets.

Without a card, you can call locally or abroad from booths in **Gamtel offices** (the state-run telecom company) or any of the private telecentres which are numerous in every town, both in the Kombos and up-country. Check that the meter for your booth is set to zero before you start, then make the call and pay afterwards. You will see **public call boxes** designed for coins or charge cards all over the country, but most don't work.

Useful local numbers

Ambulance ☎16
Police ☎17
Fire ☎18
International operator assistance
☎100
Directory enquiries ☎151

International phone calls from The Gambia sometimes take a while to connect, as do calls to mobile phones – you'll often get a message saying all lines are occupied. **Reverse charge** or **collect** calls are possible from landlines, but expensive; it's better to arrange in advance to receive a call at a certain time and number. The Gambia's **international dialling code** is +220.

To **call abroad** from The Gambia, you dial the international access code (00) followed by your country code, then the area code (without the initial "0" if there is one) and then the number.

Mobile phones

If you want to use your **mobile phone** in The Gambia, check with your phone provider whether it will work abroad, and what the call charges are. At the time of writing, there were no international roaming agreements in place allowing mobile phone owners with foreign accounts to make or receive calls in The Gambia, but this is likely to change.

One solution is to buy a Gambian SIM card and pay-as-you-go **scratch cards** from either Gamcel or Africell (The Gambia's two rival GSM networks) in order to use your non-Gambian mobile in The Gambia. SIM cards cost around £7.50/$12 and scratch cards come in various denominations starting from D50. This can be a convenient, though expensive, way to stay in touch, and very practical if you receive local calls in The Gambia. You'll automatically have the benefit of **voicemail** retrievable from any Gambian landline – useful when you're out of mobile range.

Mobile **coverage** is generally excellent in all Gambian towns, with a few rare exceptions (Janjanbureh residents have been known to climb trees in search of a reliable signal). The signal drops off sharply to zero on the fringes of urban areas. Despite their expense, mobiles are rapidly becoming essential accessories for urban Gambians.

If your phone is programmed to be used exclusively on your home mobile network it will need to be **unlocked** – many Gambian mobile phone shops offer this service from around £4/$6.50. If your phone is a very new model, they may not have the necessary software, and you'll have to get it unlocked before you leave.

Email and Internet

Internet cafés are opening in every Gambian town, and proliferate in the Kombos. Charges are reasonable but vary a great deal from place to place, as does the quality of the hardware and the speed and reliability of the service. Gamtel offices often have the lowest rates (less than £1/$1.60 per hour), and the highest rates are up-country, where computers are much rarer and everything – mains power supplies, generator fuel supplies and phone connections – less reliable.

The media

English tends to predominate over Gambian languages in public life: education and parliament operate almost exclusively in it, and the media uses it heavily. Although there are TV and radio broadcasts in Wolof, Mandinka and, occasionally, other African languages, Gambian newspapers are in English. The Gambian press is pretty lively, though very parochial; for international news and sport, CNN, the BBC, and European sports stations are increasingly available on satellite TV, and you can find imported newspapers in the Kombos.

Gambian **newspapers** and radio and television **news bulletins** are not only overwhelmingly Gambia-centric, they're also constrained by government attempts to muzzle reporters by setting up a National Media Commission with the power to silence writers who won't reveal their sources, and to shut down unlicensed media operations.

For all this, Gambian **journalists** can be intrepid and forthright, and the country has a thriving press. Gambian newspapers are far from sycophantic towards the government and they are stridently opposed to what they perceive as infringements of press freedom. Their **news coverage** may be patchy, with occasional lapses into grandiose prose, but they're still an excellent window onto local preoccupations and concerns. They sometimes carry adverts for **forthcoming events** (the *Daily Observer* is best for this). All are flimsy tabloids, which can sometimes be hard to track down, especially upcountry. There are usually vendors selling copies at the Kairaba Avenue traffic lights in the mornings. Shops in the Kombos that stock newspapers include Timbooktoo bookshop in Fajara and a few supermarkets and hotel shops.

The availability of **imported English-language newspapers** and magazines is slowly improving, but again you're unlikely to find any outside the Kombos. A few supermarkets regularly stock European titles, plus the *Herald Tribune* and *USA Today* and sometimes *Time* and *Newsweek*. You'll also see *West Africa* and *BBC Focus on Africa* magazines. After every flight in from London, vendors do the rounds with British newspapers.

Gambian radio stations have blossomed in recent years, though like the print media they're subject to harassment. They're a good way to tune into the mood of the country, music-wise, and also act as bulletin boards for local live events. Unfortunately for visitors, most adverts are in Wolof only.

If you're travelling for any length of time, it's a good idea to invest in a small short-wave radio in order to listen to the **BBC World Service** – quite an institution in West Africa.

The Gambia's single national **television channel**, Gambia Television, run by the state-owned broadcasting corporation GRTS (Gambia Radio and Television Service), is still young (The Gambia had no television until 1995). Its comprehensive coverage of presidential goings-on can make it seem like an APRC propaganda vehicle, but it also broadcasts magazine programmes and cheesy imported soaps (which, inevitably, have cult following) plus classified ads (birth, marriage and funeral announcements against a background of tasteful muzak). It's hard to find programme listings anywhere.

The station broadcasts nationwide, with the potential to reach sixty percent of the population. Both up-country and in the Kombos, families which can afford a television often set it up outside in their compound in the evening for themselves and their neighbours to watch – so long as there's electricity. Expats generally prefer **satellite TV** or rented **videos** – video shops abound. Many of the tourist hotels have satellite TV, some tuned permanently to CNN.

Newspapers and magazines

Daily Observer The most popular daily, with unadventurous reporting; good for occasional "what's on" news and ads.

Foraaya Leftish alternative newspaper.

The Gambia Daily Good editing and writing, with well-balanced reporting.

The Independent One of The Gambia's more opiniated papers, pulling no punches in criticizing the government.

Mango News Magazine co-published by Gambia Tourism Concern and the Association of Small Scale Enterprises in Tourism, covering topics of interest to tourists, and sold, *Big Issue*-style, by reformed bumsters.

The Point Rather bland daily; publishes the latest exchange rates on Saturdays.

Radio stations

BBC World Service 6.005MHz (49m), 11.765Mhz (25m), 15.400MHz (19m) and 17.830MHz (16m) at different times of day, ⓦ www.bbc.co.uk/worldservice. General BBC World Service coverage, plus excellent Africa Service programmes including the morning magazine Network Africa (3.30–7.30am GMT) and Focus on Africa (5.06pm GMT).

City Limits 93.6FM. A Dutch-run music and chat station, with similar sounds to the more popular West Coast Radio, and reggae at weekends.

Radio 1 FM 102.1FM. Commercial station broadcasting in Wolof and other languages and playing West African music.

Radio France Internationale 89.0FM. African and international news bulletins and magazines in French, with some items in English.

Radio Gambia 648 AM, 91.4FM. Anodyne national broadcast service from GRTS, in English, French, Wolof, Mandinka and other local languages. News, announcements ("will all members of the national football squad please get in touch with the coach..."), endless request shows and phone-ins.

Radio Syd 909 AM. Long-established station broadcasting in English, German and Swedish.

Sud FM 92.1FM. Senegalese station playing *ndagga* music and current affairs shows in Wolof and French.

Voice of America various short-wave frequencies, ⓦ www.voa.gov. Less wide-ranging output then the BBC and not such good reception.

West Coast Radio 95.3FM. Popular independent radio station, with good reception, mostly broadcasting in English and Wolof, and playing reggae, soul and R&B, plus chat and news of gigs and other events.

Public holidays and festivals

In addition to the main Christian and Islamic religious festivals, The Gambia has its own national holidays and festivals. These are rarely as established as you would find, for example, in Europe. Holidays commemorating no longer respected events are quietly ignored, and new holidays are declared whenever the president deems it appropriate. Traditional Gambian festivals are joyous occasions, featuring plenty of music, dance and song, and the highlight of the secular festival calendar is the unmissable biennial International Roots Festival.

Public holidays

January 1 New Year's Day
January/February (at present) Tobaski
February 18 Independence Day
March/April Easter Sunday
March/April Easter Monday
April/May (at present) Maolud Nabi
May 1 Labour Day
August 15 Feast of the Assumption
July 22 Revolution Day/Anniversary of the Second Republic

November (at present) Koriteh
25 December Christmas Day

Islamic holidays

Like other West African countries, The Gambia has a significant **Muslim** population. Muslim holy days are observed devoutly in strictly Muslim districts, less formally elsewhere. Transport services are reduced during these festivals, and most other services

Islamic festivals – approximate dates

Beginning of Ramadan (1st Ramadan) Oct 27, 2003 Oct 16, 2004 Oct 5, 2005	**Tamharit – Islamic New Year (1st Moharem)** Feb 22, 2004 Feb 10, 2005 Jan 31, 2006
Koriteh – Id al-Fitr (1st Shawwal) Nov 25, 2003 Nov 14, 2004 Nov 4, 2005	**Ashoura (10th Moharem)** Mar 2, 2004 Feb 19, 2005 Feb 9, 2006
Tobaski – Id al-Kabir (10th Dhu'l Hijja) Feb 1, 2004 Jan 21, 2005 Jan 10, 2006	**Maolud Nabi – The Prophet's birthday (12th Rabia)** May 2, 2004 Apr 21, 2005 Apr 11, 2006

grind to a halt, except for tourist restaurants and hotels.

The **principal events** to be aware of are the ten days of the Muslim New Year which starts with the month of Moharem (**Ashoura** on the 10th of Moharem celebrates, among other events, Adam and Eve's first meeting after leaving Paradise); the **Prophet Muhammad's birthday** (known as *Maolud Nabi*); the month-long fast of **Ramadan** and the feast of relief which follows immediately after (sometimes known as *Id al-Fitr* but best known in The Gambia as *Koriteh*); and the **Feast of the Sacrifice** or *Tobaski*, which coincides with the annual *Hajj* pilgrimage to Mecca, when Muslim families slaughter a sheep.

The days surrounding Tobaski can be lively, with clubs and live music venues laying on special events for a few nights in a row. **Ramadan** isn't an entirely miserable time either, although some businesses close during the daytime, service can be slow, tempers short, and you won't hear much music anywhere. **Fasting** applies throughout the daylight hours, and covers every pleasure including food, drink (even water), tobacco and sex. While non-Muslims are not expected to observe the fast, it's offensive in strict Muslim areas to contravene publicly. Instead, switch to the night shift, as everyone else does, with dried dates, iced water, fresh fruit and sweet tea to break the fast at dusk, and applied eating and entertainment through the night.

Both Tobaski and Koriteh are occasions for massive **family celebrations**, with plenty of eating, drinking and parading of new clothes. The pressure can be great to provide a spectacular spread, and to dress fabulously. The weeks preceding major festivals can be tense times, with Gambians from all walks of life trying to up their income however they can, and tailors working shifts round the clock. When the festival arrives, **charity** is expected, and you may be approached for "saliboo" – a gift in honour of the festival.

The **Islamic calendar** is lunar, divided into twelve months of 29 or 30 days (totalling 354 days), thus festival dates shift forward by about eleven days each year, their precise dates dependent on official sightings of the moon. For more about Islam in the Gambia, see Contexts, pp.252–253; for greetings used at festival times, see p.277.

Christian holidays

Christmas and, to a much lesser extent, **Easter** are observed as religious ceremonies in Christian areas and, on a more or less secular, national basis, all over the country. It's business as usual at the markets and even if you can't find a bank or post office open, you'll have no trouble finding street food and some transport.

Festivals

The Gambia's most important cultural event is the **International Roots Festival**, held in various locations over 10–14 days, biennially in June. Inaugurated in 1996, the festival's original target audience were black Americans keen to reconnect with their roots in a joint celebration of African cultural heritage. Now devised with **all nationalities** in mind, but especially individuals of African descent, it attracts Gambians of all ethnicities, resident and expatriate, plus other Africans and people from the African diaspora. Its underlying agenda is to **court foreign patrons** willing to get involved in The Gambia, long-term, by buying property, starting businesses, sharing skills and resources, or contributing to development projects; but everyone, whatever their interests, is welcome to join in the festivities.

The organizers hope to make the Roots festival as big on the world stage as the Notting Hill Carnival; while it's a long way off achieving this kind of fame, it's a superb event.

Festival-goers can choose between attending a few individual events (some of which are free), or paying a **registration fee** for the whole programme of cultural shows, visits, concerts, seminars and parties. The centrepieces of the festival have in previous years been a one-day "Roots pilgrimage" to Juffureh, Albreda and James Island, and a two-day event held at **Kanilai**, President Jammeh's home village. The pilgrimage is similar to standard Roots trips

Christmas and New Year in The Gambia

Christmas and **New Year** are major events in the resort areas, where the Western influence is greatest, and in Banjul, where there's a sizeable population of Akus and other Christians. From early December, hawkers sell tinsel in the streets, and resort hotels really go to town on Christmas lights, music, gala menus and firework displays. Hotel Christmas dinners can be extravagant, while restaurants and clubs also lay on special entertainment.

The Gambia's most idiosyncratic Christmas tradition is its **fanal processions**, unique to the Kombos. *Fanals* are large model boats, often over three metres in length, made from paper lace stuck over a bamboo frame; by night, they are beautifully lit from inside with small lights or candles. They're paraded from compound to compound in urban areas by *fanal* societies, with much drumming and singing. The *fanal* societies collect donations from each compound head, which go towards a big party. The *fanals* themselves end up on display at the compound of their most generous sponsor.

In recent years these processions have to an extent been shelved, with Christmas more or less coinciding with Ramadan. However, The Gambia Tourism Authority is keen to revive the tradition, and has begun organizing *fanal*-making **competitions**. Meanwhile, there's an example of a *fanal* at the National Museum in Banjul.

Another popular and noisy Gambian Christmas and New Year tradition is the hunting devil **kankurang**. Gaggles of singing Mandinka kids or youths with seed-pod shakers, jerry-can drums and other home-made instruments tour the streets collecting money, in the company of the *kankurang*, a masked dancer dressed in a costume made of red rag, sacking and fur fabric, with various gourds and bells hanging down his back, and horns on his head. Similarly, Jola **kumpo dancers** (see box on p.189) also make an appearance at Christmas and New Year. The Wolof contribution to the fun is the **simba** or **zimba** (lion dancers), impressive in their cow-hair headdresses, yellow and black face-paint, and spectacular suits of fur fabric embellished with *jujus* and cowries. The *simba* have a stomping, kicking style of dancing, and fix onlookers with a fierce stare until they dance too; if the *simba* is not satisfied, the victim has to pay a cash tribute, which the dancer clamps between his teeth.

Sometimes there'll be a Christmas street carnival in the northern Kombos, when the whole area explodes with music and dancing – you may even see a Gambian Father Christmas on horseback. Events like this are not always well publicized, so ask around locally to find out what's on when.

(see box on pp.176–177), except that participants are met and entertained by a welcome committee of hundreds including chiefs, *jalis* and local schoolchildren. At Kanilai, "Homecomers" from the diaspora have the opportunity to undergo a scaled-down version of the *futampaf*, the traditional Jola tribal initiation rites associated with circumcision (but without the surgery). Traditional "bush school" is not common nowadays, and traditional values are being eroded, so part of the purpose of the Roots *futampaf* is to serve as a tangible reminder of the past. After their instruction, the initiates are dressed in beads and cloth and presented to the tribe, in a ceremony with much music, dance and noise. Saplings are planted on their behalf, they are presented with a ritual spouse, and a chicken is sacrificed for each of them. Other events at Kanilai include **wrestling** bouts, **fire-eating**, and **cultural shows** of music and dance with troupes from all over The Gambia and beyond.

The range of events staged during the Roots festival changes from year to year but the variety is excellent. Big-name musical stars such as Youssou N'Dour, Viviane and Jaliba Kuyateh may appear onstage at **gala shows** and massive **stadium events** in the Kombos. Outstanding in the past has been the **Banjul regatta**, with rowing teams from fishing communities competing in speed trials, and wrestlers whacking each other with pillows on a greasy pole held horizontally over the dock. Equally entertaining are the stage shows and **carnival processions**; practically every event is accompanied by exuberant singing, drumming and dancing.

For more information, see Ⓦ www.rootsfestival .gm

Other festivals

Independence Day (Feb 18) celebrates The Gambia's declaration of independence from Britain in 1965. Most communities stage events at stadia and football fields. These involve military parades, schoolchildren marching past in impeccable uniforms, military and traditional bands, and cultural troupes.

In The Kombos, where reggae is a way of life for huge numbers of young Gambians, **Bob Marley Day** (May 11) is celebrated with tribute nights at the clubs and bars, decked out in red, gold and green.

Carnival Parade (June) is a spirited one-day carnival of floats, costumed dancers and music in the Kairaba Avenue and Bertil Harding Highway area, culminating in a music and dance show at the National Stadium, Bakau, or the football field, Kololi. In years when the Roots festival is held (see above), the carnival is incorporated into the programme.

Liberation Day (July 22) is the anniversary of the 1994 coup which brought Jammeh to power. In recent years it has been marked as a political occasion, with forthright speeches from the President.

Finally, **National Tourism Week** (Oct/Nov) is held in the Kombos to mark the beginning of the tourist season. The aim of the festival is to promote cultural tourism, including music, dance, traditional Gambian cooking, stage shows and visual arts.

Sports and entertainment

The Gambia's national sport is traditional wrestling, although in recent years football fever has been sweeping the country. With no film industry and very little theatre of any sort, The Gambia's entertainment programmes tend to focus on live music and dance.

Spectator sports

Visitors are welcome at the **Senegambian wrestling** tournaments that are staged in various locations from time to time. Unfortunately, popular interest in the sport has declined somewhat. Bouts used to be held regularly in many Gambian towns and villages, especially in the arena on the outskirts of Serrekunda, where enthusiastic crowds of onlookers gathered to enjoy the show every weekend in the dry season. Today, Kanilai is the usual venue for international events (see p.190).

The Gambia is too small a country to have much international sporting success, and, when it comes to **football** (soccer), Gambians tend to support the successful Senegalese national side as much as their own. The game is enormously popular, especially among young Gambians, both as a pastime and as a spectator sport, and now that more Gambians (in the Kombos at least) have access to satellite television, the international football scene has become a favourite topic of conversation. It has also hit the political agenda – in 2003, President Jammeh declared that the *nawettan* (the annual country-wide rainy season tournament) should be banned, as it distracted people from the crucial business of seasonal farming work, and a passionate public

Music lessons

One way to become involved in Gambian culture is to spend time with a **jali** or *griot* – a traditional musician – learning the art of the *kora*, *balafon* or drums (*djembé* or others), or singing and dancing. Brikama is a good place to make enquiries, especially about *kora* lessons, as this town is home to many talented *jalis*; you may also be able to stay in your teacher's family compound. The following contacts can provide lessons, or put you in touch with musicians:

Boucarabou Kerr Serign Njaga ☎463363; can be booked through Cool Running Tours (see p.12). This pleasant Kololi guesthouse (see p.109) sets up music and dance workshops, plus jamming sessions for individuals and groups.

Drum Doctors UK ☎01373/831171, ⓦwww.realafrica.net. Residential music workshops or daily individual *djembé* tuition in Bakau, with a UK-based musician.

Drum factory Manjai Kunda (no phone). A compound where craftsmen build and carve drums; you can try them out or enquire about lessons here.

Kounta Kinte Association ☎398439; French run classes and workshops in Juffureh, with master musicians from Senegal and Mali.

Alagi M'Bye Nema Kunku ☎950030. The *kora* player who runs Maali's Music School in this village between Serrekunda and Sukuta offers *kora* lessons to visitors. The music school itself is a ground-breaking project whereby the children of non-*jali* familes (traditionally barred from music tuition) can learn music.

Safari Garden Hotel Fajara ☎495887. The hotel can recommend good *djembé* and dance teachers in Fajara, and has Gambian dance-aerobics sessions.

Foday Suso Brufut ☎934760. Talented and charismatic musician, running a new residential music project.

Zinzani Cultural Centre Kololi ⓦwww.zinzani.com. Residential workshops debate ensued. Major **matches** are held at the National Stadium in Bakau, typically at weekends during the dry season, and are noisy, spirited events, with plenty of drumming and chanting. Recent years' **Gambia Football Association League Cup** winners have been Real de Banjul, Ports Authority and the dominant team Wallidan. The most popular fixtures sell out so it's best to arrive well in advance of kick-off.

Live music and cultural shows

While for the majority of visitors entertainment means the hotel formula-mix of "cultural dance troupes" and home-style discos, it's easy enough to escape the dross and find real Gambian **musical entertainment**. To be fair, the hotels do sometimes host worthwhile gigs – some of The Gambia's best *kora* players have played to tourist audiences.

A good time to be in the Kombos for live music is during a festival, or at the end of the month, when people can afford tickets for the bands that occasionally visit from abroad, usually Senegal. Visiting stars may perform two or three gigs on subsequent nights in different venues, the biggest by far being at the **National Stadium**, Bakau. International masters of *ndagga* and *mbalax* (distinctive styles of the Senegambian region) sometimes play here. Arrive early to get a seat or you'll never see the musicians, but don't expect the main act on stage until well after midnight.

Currently the biggest vogue among young Gambians is for **reggae** and **ragga**. The Gambia, however, is more distinguished for its Mandinka **kora musicians**. The most famous talents – Dembo Konteh, his brother-in-law Kausu Kouyaté, Foday Musa Suso, Jaliba Kuyateh, Malamini Jobarteh, Ebrima Jobarteh, Tata Din Din and junior Pa Jobarteh – are as likely to be playing in a British folk festival or with American musicians, as in a compound in Brikama or at a wedding in Serrekunda. Wolof drummers often perform at "private" functions too – keep your ears open and drop in politely.

 # Tours and guides

Organized tours in The Gambia are the equivalent of group safaris in East or southern Africa – you don't have to participate, but if you don't, you might miss out on a great deal of what the country has to offer. They're a great way to get your first taste of the country outside the resorts, and highly recommended if you're new to West Africa. As a way of getting out and about, without the hassle of organizing everything for yourself, the idea can have great appeal.

If you'd like a more tailor-made feel to your adventures, or you prefer to travel in a very small group, talk to one of the **ground tour operators** (local tour companies running organized trips) about arranging a bespoke trip: their guides, drivers and vehicles can be hired by the day for this purpose. There are also **specialist guides** and operators who can accompany you birdwatching or fishing; it pays to select these carefully according to the level of expertise you require. Alternatively, you could hire one of The Gambia's posse of freelance **Official Tourist Guides** (OTGs); this is likely to work out cheaper than hiring a guide from a ground tour operator or a specialist guide, but most OTGs don't have a comparable level of knowledge and experience. Finally, there are **bumsters**: ubiquitous in the tourist areas, these young Gambians make their money by offering various services to tourists on an informal basis. While many are totally unreliable, some bumsters are very good at introducing visitors to off-beat places and people they wouldn't encounter by other means.

Birdwatching trips

Many of The Gambia's native bird species are so brightly hued, noisy and conspicuous that even the most inexperienced birdwatchers can spot them easily. However, if you'd like to study the country's birdlife in detail, or seek out particular species, a professional guide can be invaluable – without their assistance, you may find it hard to spot the birds that interest you most.

Birdwatchers can visit a variety of habitats with the assistance of a professional guide, either by joining a group tour designed specifically for wildlife enthusiasts, or by hiring a freelance bird guide by the day. Most group birding trips organized by special interest tour operators (see pp.12–13) promise sightings of hundreds of species. However, if you prefer just to study the behaviour of a handful of species, a well-run trip can accommodate this.

A good **guide** will know exactly which species are most likely to be feeding or roosting in which location, and how to get you there. Of course, guides with in-depth ornithological knowledge charge higher fees. The best can mimic many bird calls, summoning a particular species within minutes, and can throw calls back and forth with the bird in a conversational manner. Bear in mind when choosing a guide that they have to be able to communicate well with you too – some guides are brilliant birders but poor English-speakers.

Guides sometimes meet and wait for clients on the Kotu Stream Bridge, Kotu, or at the Education Centre at Abuko Nature Reserve. The Gambia Birding Group (ⓦwww.gambiabirding.org) is a good source of information and advice on guides and other ornithological matters, while the detailed reports of bird sightings posted on the Internet by enthusiasts (see p.18) can also help a great deal in planning an itinerary.

Recommended guides include:
Birds of The Gambia ☎936122, ⓔbirdsofthegambia@hotmail.com. Private bird-watching safaris for specialists and keen beginners, run by the renowned British ornithologist Clive Barlow, author of the region's most authoritative field guide, from his base in The Gambia.
Mass Cham c/o *Senegambia Hotel*, Kololi ☎462717.
Wally Faal, Serrekunda ☎372103.
Solomon Jallow based at *Lamin Lodge*, ☎907694, ⓔhabitatafrica@hotmail.com. Works with Habitat Africa, a small network of associate bird guides.

Ground tour operators

Ground tour operators offer programmes of standard tours (see p.56), some of which overlap: several companies run similar excursions to popular destinations, while other trips are unique to individual operators.

Most operators can also tailor-make **private trips** on request. On the simplest level, these can amount to just hiring a Land Rover with a driver and possibly a guide. This kind of travel enables you to get to places that public transport doesn't reach – without the hassle of lugging your bags around on your back – particularly appealing if you're visiting national parks. Getting more detailed, you could ask the company to pre-arrange an itinerary including overnight stops, special events or ceremonies, visits to stone circles or meetings with musicians or healers. The best ground tour operators may be able to **recommend a guide** who knows your target area inside out, and can act as your interpreter, wildlife expert and cultural guru – you're likely to experience far more with their assistance than you could ever hope to on your own.

African Adventure Tours ☎497313, ⓔadventure@gambianet.gm. New company offering some standard itineraries plus a more unusual "Roots by land" trip.
Alkamba Travel & Tours ☎202059, ⓔalkamba@gamtel.gm. Gambian-run operator, often running Roots and heritage tours.
Discovery Tours ☎495551, ⓦwww.discoverytours.gm. Professional outfit with

a good choice of group tours, including "Roots" river cruises and "Bush and Beach" safaris.

Gambia River Excursions ☎497603, 🌐www.gre.gm. One of the most interesting and enlightened ground tour operators, specializing in up-river boat trips. Also runs *Lamin Lodge*, and the "Birds and Breakfast" and "Sunset Cruise" boat trips.

Gambia Tours ☎462601, 🌐www.gambiatours.gm. Large company with a comprehensive list of group excursions, including "Roots", Janjanbureh, Tendaba, and shorter trips.

Gamtours ☎392259, 📧gamtours@qanet.gm. Gambian-owned company with a standard selection of trips.

Paradise Tours ☎494088, mobile ☎920201, 📧trawallyfoday@hotmail.com. Arranges visits to *Madiyana Lodge* on Jinack Island, by *pirogue*.

RM Tours ☎462226, 🌐www.rmtours.gm. Group excursions, including fishing, dolphin-spotting, and a "Gambia By Night" tour, plus tailor-made trips.

West African Tours ☎495258, 🌐www.westafricantours.com. A large, well-established and reliable operator, with excellent drivers and guides. Extensive programme of popular standard group excursions, including Roots, Treasure Island (Jinack), Makasutu, Janjanbureh, and Tendaba, plus some more unusual ones. If you'd like to plan a bespoke trip, they're an ideal first port of call.

BASICS | Tours and guides

Fishing trips

The Gambia is still a top **fishing** destination for beginners and experts alike, even though its waters have been over-fished by illegal trawlers in recent years. The country attracts serious enthusiasts, including the celebrity angler **John Wilson**, and the unofficial world record for the heaviest line-caught Atlantic tarpon (38kg and well over 2m long) was made here. The **Masterline International West African Shore Fishing Festival** is held in The Gambia every year in November, a major competitive event with a £50,000 prize fund; the Masterline International Tarpon Festival is held in July.

For **inexperienced anglers**, a number of tour companies and one-man-and-a-boat operators can arrange **fishing trips** lasting from a couple of hours to a day, usually launching from near Denton Bridge, Oyster Creek, to explore the mangrove-lined waterways near Banjul (see box on p.137). Rods, bait and lures are provided and you stand a good chance of catching some of the commonest fish, such as ladyfish, snapper, catfish or mullet – some trip operators promise "no fish, no fee".

Experienced anglers will probably prefer the assistance of a specialist **fishing charter company**, who can provide fully equipped boats, tackle, bait and expert guides as required. You can choose between high-adrenaline **Atlantic sport fishing** for sailfish, dorado, tuna, barracuda jacks and tarpon (generally on a catch-and-release basis); **creek fishing** in the Tanbi Wetlands (sailing from near Denton bridge) for smaller saltwater species; and **freshwater fishing** up-river (notably at Janjanbureh) for prize species such as tigerfish and arius and clarius catfish. Boat fishing is possible all year round, conditions permitting; tarpon are caught during the rainy season.

You can also fish from the **beaches** anywhere along the Atlantic coast for tarpon, guitarfish (like sand sharks), captainfish, groupers and rays. October to May is the best time of year for this, particularly November and December. When on the beaches you should be prepared to deal with bumsters. Sanyang is a favourite beach-angling spot, as the hassle here is far less than in the northern Kombos, the fishing is decent, and there are some great beach bars.

Recommended fishing charter companies include:

Gambia Sport Fishing ☎908577 or 930329, 🌐www.gambiasportfishing.com. One of the best fishing operators in The Gambia.

Janneh Boating Fishing and Limo Hire Bakau, ☎497630, mobile ☎905894, 🌐gambiafishing.tripod.com. Three fully equipped boats available for private charter.

Standard tours

Off-the-peg group tours from the resorts to The Gambia's attractions run every week (sometimes more than once a week) during the tourist season. They're aimed at the average tourist who wants an interesting and enjoyable trip that's not too arduous, and doesn't require special background knowledge or equipment. You'll be **collected** from your hotel or another prearranged spot, and driven back there at the end of the trip. **Tour groups** vary in size but are typically 12–25 in number; organizers try and plan things so that all the members of a group speak a common language.

These tours are not for everybody of course – they can give you a quick, fun look around, but won't generally give you an in-depth insight into Gambian ecology, tradition or lifestyles. The size of groups makes one-to-one discussion with the guide difficult. Guides are for the most part trained not to be over-pushy, sticking instead to a pre-planned patter, so it's only the most inquisitive groups that end up extracting detailed information from them. The trips will, however, answer at least some of your questions (plus a few that hadn't yet occurred to you), and possibly inspire you to plan your own, more personalized, travels in due course.

Trips **vary in length** from a couple of hours to a few days, and guides will cheerfully announce that all timings are GMT – "Gambia Maybe Time" – preparing you for unexpected delays on route. Having said this, most trips are very efficiently run – the guides and drivers follow tried and tested schedules, and you may, if anything, be left wishing there'd been more time to dawdle. **Payment** for the trip is generally made in hard currency, in advance, but not normally before you arrive in The Gambia. Most tourists **book excursions** through tourist hotel reps – who earn a commission on the sale – but there's nothing to stop you approaching one of the operators direct, particularly if a tour that interests you doesn't feature on your rep's day-by-day programme. You're likely to pay the same price however you book. Depending on the length of trip, meals may be included. Your only **expenses** during the trip will be drinks, souvenirs and tips for the driver and guide. The prices below are approximate.

Abuko Nature Reserve Half-day; £11/$18. A short guided walk around the forest, with time to admire the trees and plants, and hopefully spot monkeys, birds and crocodiles. See pp.133–135.

Birds and Breakfast or **Sunset Cruise** Morning or late afternoon; £17/$27. Enjoyable cruises by dugout canoe and/or double-decker cruising *pirogue* through the mangrove creeks of the Tanbi Wetlands, with a stop at *Lamin Lodge*, a wonderful rickety timber bar/restaurant on stilts. See pp.135–138.

Bush and beach (4WD adventure) Full day; £28/$45. Thoroughly recommended, these trips pack a lot of experiences into a day, driving round the Kombos in a safari truck. You'll get to see a slice of real-life urban and rural Gambia, meet people living in a family compound, and visit a village school; you'll get driven through the bush, have lunch on the beach, and have a visit to the excellent Tanje Village Museum and the village's busy fishing centre. See pp.138–148.

Camel safari and beach barbecue Half-day; £22/$35. A very touristy trip – you'll head down to Tanji where camels will carry you along the beach for half an hour or so, two punters per beast. Humans and camels then lunch and relax before lumbering back again. See pp.146–147.

Champagne and caviar Full day; £27/$43. A luxurious way to explore the Tanbi wetlands near Banjul in a double-decker *pirogue*. The caviar may or may not materialize but you'll certainly be well looked after. See pp.135–137.

Creek fishing Half-day; £17/$27. A chance to mess about in boats and haul something wriggly out of the mangrove creeks near Banjul. See pp.135–137.

Gambia River Excursions One to three days, from £38/$60. Cruising by river from Tendaba to Janjanbureh, or from Janjanbureh to Basse, you travel by rustic double-decker *pirogue* past lush riverside jungle, stopping at remote villages and markets. Nights are spent mid-river, sleeping on deck under the stars on mattresses with mosquito nets. Highly recommended. See chapters 4&5.

Janjanbureh Two days and one night; £75/$120. A whistlestop visit to Janjanbureh Island. Groups usually stay at either *Janjang Bureh Camp* or *Bird Safari Camp*, both good bases for birdwatching and river-swimming, with campfire entertainment from local drummers and dancers. See pp.214–220.

Jinack Island (Paradise or Treasure Island) Full day; £28/$45. After taking the ferry to Barra on the River Gambia's north bank, you visit a remote rural village near the Senegalese border, then cruise the waterways of the southern Saloum Delta to Jinack Island, with lunch on the beach. See pp.176–180.

Juffureh, Albreda and James Island "Roots" Full day; £30/$48. Very popular excursion. Most tour groups get to Albreda, Juffureh and James Island by river cruise from Banjul, but it's also possible to cross from Banjul to Barra by ferry and continue overland. You visit the village, meet members of the Kinte family (made famous by Alex Haley's novel *Roots*), and visit the slave trade museum and Fort James. See p.170.–176

Makasutu Culture Forest plus Brikama craft market or jam-making centre Full day; £29/$46. Includes a guided woodland stroll and quiet cruise

Bumsters

The Gambian term **"bumster"** refers to touts, fixers, chancers, gigolos, wheeler-dealers, informal guides and guardian angels – you'll find them wherever you find tourists, unless they've been specifically banned or driven away. Their **services** range from showing you around, fixing up deals on taxis, trips and foreign exchange, and general chaperoning, to being your best friend (and more) throughout your stay, barely leaving your side.

Gambian bumsters tend to be a dignified lot, with a highly developed sense of self-worth: they believe they are offering an honest and useful service, and as such should have the same rights as any tourism workers. The truth is that most are **school drop-outs** who are smart enough to realize that there's far more money to be made out of offering services to tourists than from any of the other options available to them. Some see "bumstering" as a way to accumulate enough capital to enable them to start their own business; others hope that it's only a matter of time before they meet the European or American benefactor who will make their dreams come true; others are simply desperate for quick cash to fund a drug habit.

The classic **bumster–tourist relationship** is the partnering of young, attractive rastas with middle-aged white women. Some of these liaisons are innocent and completely genuine, but some are founded on a basis of prearranged mutual exploitation, for sex and money. The Gambia has plenty of stories of European women who have fallen in love with Gambians and arranged their passage to Europe, only for them to turn abusive or disappear without trace, or of young Gambians (male and female) who have been promised the world by a tourist, who in the end fails to deliver.

If you take on a bumster, you're guaranteed an adventure of sorts. Sometimes their **assistance** can be useful; they can be great company, and you won't be hassled by others. Yet, however friendly a bumster may be, some completely fail to deliver, and they're all in it for the money. Get all the **negotiation** done in advance to avoid misunderstandings later – not all bumsters are as honest as they make out.

Tourists can find them **intimidating**, especially at night. Bumsters on the make will barge up to tourists, butt into conversations, and start hustling, using a catalogue of standard chat-up lines. Some visitors have said that they will never return to The Gambia because they found the hassle from bumsters so enervating. Furthermore, many bumsters are worse than useless as guides. However, bumsters are **rarely dangerous**, and it doesn't take long to devise your own strategy for dealing with them. If one invades your space, tell him plainly that you didn't invite him: in Gambian society it's rude to impose yourself on somebody uninvited. Tell him you have no work for him – you may have to harden yourself to a little verbal abuse, but it almost certainly won't lead to anything.

With passions boiling about the threat to the Gambian tourist industry posed by bumsters, the government embarked on a **major crackdown** in the 2002–3 tourist season. Their controversial tactics were heavy-handed in the extreme – raiding parties of paramilitaries rounded up suspected bumsters on the beaches and in the main tourist areas, in full view of tourists, abused them verbally and physically, dumped them in trucks and threw them in jail for a day or longer. Rastas have had their hair cut off, and some individuals have been packed off to up-country agricultural projects. At the time of writing, the bumsters, though defiant, have not fought back. Some are operating more covertly, while others have retreated to Senegal, allegedly to grow marijuana – there's plenty of money in that.

by dugout pirogue along the beautiful Mandina Bolon. After an African buffet lunch, there's spirited singing and dancing from local women. The visit to Brikama is basically a souvenir stop. See pp.155–158.

Orientation and city tour Half-day; £11/$17. A brief introduction to Banjul and the northern Kombos, the idea being that you can come back under your own steam later for a longer look at anything that appeals. Stops include Banjul's Arch 22, National Museum and Albert Market, plus possibly a local school, Banjul Brewery, a batik "factory", and the Katchikali crocodile pool. See chapter 1.

Sport fishing Full day; £25/$40. Aimed at experienced anglers, sport fishing trips take you out into the mouth of the River Gambia or to the Atlantic reefs, fishing for jacks, ladyfish, butterfish, red snapper and barracuda.

Tendaba Two days and one night; £60/$96. A trip to *Tendaba Camp*, a large riverside lodge with a swimming pool, around four hours' drive from the coast along bumpy roads, with opportunities to visit Kiang West National Park and Bao Bolon Wetland Reserve. See pp.191–195 & pp.201–202.

Official tourist guides

Official tourist guides (OTGs) are badged and uniformed freelance guides who have gone through a selection and training procedure, and also abide by a code of conduct. The OTG scheme arose partly as a solution to the bumster problem (see p.57); a number of bumsters were selected to be trained up to be OTGs, thus "legalizing" a role they had already adopted for themselves.

You can book one for a simple assignment like showing you around the local market, to something more involved such as accompanying you on an up-country trip lasting several days. Not all **prices** are fixed, so you may need to negotiate fees and expenses in advance; £2.50/$4 is a reasonable daily rate.

Guides can be invaluable, taking you to places you may not otherwise have discovered, introducing you to local customs, and acting as a **translator**. On the other hand, going around with a uniformed OTG makes it all too obvious you're a tourist. Furthermore, their training is not exhaustive – your guide's knowledge of history and culture may be as sketchy as the average untrained bumster's.

Most OTGs are based at the **OTG station** in Kololi (near the *Kairaba* and *Senegambia* hotels). There's another station in Juffureh/Albreda, and more are planned for elsewhere in the country.

National parks and reserves

The Gambia is not a safari destination in the same league as Kenya, Tanzania, or South Africa: it doesn't have huge reserves teeming with game such as zebra, elephant, wildebeest and lion. It does, however, have vast stretches of unspoilt wilderness, and a number of national parks that are worth taking in if you're interested in seeing West African birds and animals.

There are a number of good wildlife-watching locations, such as the protected areas at Abuko and Bijilo, within **walking**, **cycling** or **taxi-ride distance** of the resort hotels. Elsewhere, you'll need your **own transport**, or to be part of a **guided tour group**, to reach the best areas. Once you're there, there are plenty of opportunities for exploration without a vehicle (avoiding disruption and noise), either on foot, walking through the bush, or by boat, exploring the river or the miles of mangrove creeks.

Growing awareness in the 1960s and 1970s of the long-term detrimental effects of hunting and deforestation led to the establishment of The Gambia's first **reserves**. None of the reserves have much in the way of tourist infrastructure, and only Abuko

For information on guides and organized wildlife tours, see pp.53–58. For more on habitats and species, see pp.xv–xxiv, 73 & 258–261 receives more than a trickle of visitors. However, each reserve has a distinctive character, and visitor numbers are likely to increase when the roads are improved, making them more accessible.

All Gambian protected areas have the same fixed **entrance fee** (D31.50), and all are open daily from 8am to 6pm; special permission may be requested to visit outside these hours (visiting at dawn, at dusk and at night yield different experiences). For further information on parks and reserves, contact the Department of Parks and Wildlife Management, ☎472888, ✉wildlife @gamtel.gm.

Abuko Nature Reserve The Gambia's first protected area. It's close to the resorts and small enough at well under two square kilometres to be explored comfortably on foot, and it includes dense evergreen gallery forest and Guinea savannah, with an impressive population of birds, monkeys and reptiles (see pp.133–135).

Bao Bolon Wetland Reserve At around 220 square kilometres, this is The Gambia's largest protected area. It's also one of the least-visited, but it has a fascinating range of habitats, including desert-like salt marshes and beautiful, bird-rich creeks forested with towering mangroves. It can be visited by boat from Tendaba, or by private vehicle from the Kerewan–Farafenni road (see pp.201–202).

Bijilo Forest Park Very close to the Senegambia area hotels and easily strolled around on foot, this tiny park (half a square kilometre) is a good place to spot wild (but fearless) monkeys (see p.118).

Kiang West National Park Riverside woodland habitat, 115 square kilometres in extent, with wild baboons and bush pig, commonly explored by vehicle from Tendaba (see pp.193–195).

Niumi National Park Situated on The Gambia's northern Atlantic coast, and including Jinack Island, this Ramsar-recognized park is noted for its untouched stands of mangroves, explored by boat from Banjul or Jinack (see pp.176–180).

River Gambia National Park Formerly known as Baboon Island's National Park, this is a group of five lushly forested, protected islands mid-river downstream from Janjanbureh. The islands house a rehabilitation centre for chimpanzees which is closed to the public; you may catch a glimpse of the primates as you pass by boat, and you may also spot hippos on this stretch of the river (see pp.213–214).

Tanji River (Karinti) Bird Reserve In a country famed for its birdlife, this walkable area of just over six square kilometres is the only officially protected bird reserve, and it includes the offshore Bijol Islands, an important breeding colony for birds and turtles, which can only be visited by DPWM boat (see p.146).

Crime and personal safety

It's easy to exaggerate the potential hassles and disasters of travel in The Gambia. Many visitors feel safer in The Gambia (which has the lowest crime rate in sub-Saharan Africa) than in their home country. True, there are a few urban locations, easily enough pinpointed, where snatch robberies and muggings occur from time to time. But most of the country carries minimal risk to personal safety compared with Europe and North America. The main problems are sneak thieving, "bumstering" (see box on p.57) and corrupt people in uniforms. The first can be avoided; the second is more an irritation than a danger; and dealing with the third can become a game once you know the rules.

Obviously, if you flaunt the trappings of wealth where there's **urban poverty**, somebody may want to remove them. There's always less risk in leaving your valuables in a securely locked hotel room or, judiciously, with the management. If you clearly have nothing on you (this means not wearing expensive-looking jewellery or wristwatches), you're unlikely to be threatened.

On arrival in The Gambia, it's wise to be cautious at first day. It's important to distinguish harmlessly robust, upfront interaction from more sinister preludes that might lead to you being "bumstered". In the resort areas, **scams** include people spinning you a hard-luck story in order to cadge money. Don't feel unnecessarily victimized, but be rationally suspicious of everyone until you're more confident. Lastly, remember that impoverished **fellow travellers** are as likely – or unlikely – to rip you off as anyone else.

Apart from the standard of driving, Gambian **public transport** is fairly safe – The Gambia has none of the banditry that makes some parts of the developing world hazardous to travellers.

Theft

Hotel room **burglaries**, car break-ins and **muggings** do occur, but they're rare, and vary with the seasons: the rainy season and the weeks before major festivals, when people need cash, are the most likely times for opportunistic thieving. If you shout "Thief!", be swift to intercede once you've retrieved your belongings: robbers and pickpockets caught red-handed are usually dealt with summarily by bystanders, who generally assume the culprit is a foreigner who deserves swift punishment.

Pickpocketing can happen anywhere – usually the work of kids hanging around in markets, ferry terminals or other crowded places. Make sure your valuables are secure.

More serious attacks are rare, but sometimes take place in specific areas of the Kombos. Black spots change regularly so to listen to local advice. The least threatening districts include bush taxi garages (full of tough young transport workers on the lookout for threats to their passengers) and, surprisingly perhaps, the lower income suburbs and slums where people aren't used to travellers.

If you're **walking** in an area you're not sure of, keep a destination in mind and stay alert: look ahead and don't dawdle. Steer clear of creepy looking street sharks in jeans and running shoes (every robbery ends in a sprint). And never allow yourself to be steered down an alley or between parked cars.

The police

Unless, you've lost a lot of money or irreplaceable property, think twice about going to the **police.** They rarely do something for nothing – even stamping an insurance form may cost you. While Gambian police can be among the nicest in West Africa, their treatment of suspects can be pretty brutal. Even so, you will inevitably come into a fair amount of contact; **checks** on the movement of people (police, security services and immigration officers) and goods (customs officers) take place at junctions and along highways. Never go anywhere without **identification** – you don't have to carry a passport at all times, but a photocopy of the first few pages in a plastic wallet is very useful.

Be warned that failure to observe the following points of general **public etiquette** can get you arrested or force you to pay a bribe. Never destroy banknotes, no matter how worthless they may be. Stand still on any occasion the Gambian national anthem

---

Drugs

Drug possession can easily land you a large fine or worse, and possibly deportation. Don't expect to buy yourself easily out of this kind of trouble. **Grass** (marijuana, cannabis, *djamba*, *niamo*, *kali*) is the biggest illegal drug in The Gambia, much cultivated (clandestinely) and as much an object of confused opprobrium and fascination as anywhere else in the world. Many social problems are routinely attributed to smoking the "grass that kills" and it's widely believed to cause insanity. The usual result of a fortuitous bust is on-the-spot fines all round. An altogether different state of affairs exists with **heroin** and **cocaine**, which are smuggled though West African airports en route to Europe (often inside hapless female "swallowers"). Some of the consignments get on to the streets, however – stay well clear.

is played or a flag raised or lowered; if you see others suddenly cease all activity, do the same. Pull off the road completely, or stand still if motorcycle outriders, armoured vehicles and limos appear.

Finally, the police and security forces will often hassle you if they see you filming or taking **photographs** – usually on the pretext that you are taking pictures of them, or of "sensitive" buildings. You shouldn't take photos of anything that could be construed as strategic or military – including army or police buildings, vehicles and uniforms, prisons and, in theory, the President. Officially, this is seen as a "risk to state security". In practice, the president is far from camera shy and you're likely to get the chance to take a snap if you see him at a festival or state occasion. For more on camera etiquette, see p.65.

Bribery and corruption

If you find yourself confronting an implacable person in uniform, you don't have to give in to tacit demands for gifts or money; the golden rule is to **keep talking**. Most laws, including imaginary ones, are there to be discussed rather than enforced. If you haven't got all day, a **"small present"** – couched in exactly those terms – is all it usually takes. If you're **driving**, you'll rarely be forced to pay bribes, except sometimes on entry to or exit from the country. If you're travelling by lorry or bush taxi, it's the driver who pays. Be polite, patient and good-humoured; aggressive travellers always have the worst police stories.

Shopping

You'll have no shortage of opportunities to shop for souvenirs in The Gambia if you're staying in the resort area: every tourist hotel has a boutique of some sort, craft markets and hawkers sell locally made bits and pieces, and there are a few gallery shops. Local markets mainly sell produce and household goods but they're good for fabric and are colourful and lively to visit. Up-country there are far fewer places to browse.

European cottons printed with African designs (known as **"wax"**) and plain or patterned **damask** are to be seen everywhere, and can be both high-quality and good value. You'll also see plenty of tie-dye and batik, used for clothing and furnishings – fabulous creations are worn by both women and men, particularly at festivals or celebrations, or just because it's Friday, and Gambian tailors are adept at copying items or creating originals. Cotton is generally sold in six-yard dress lengths. **Bespoke items** of all sorts, not just clothing but also leather bags and shoes, silver jewellery, or items forged from steel or carved from wood, are often the best bargains in The Gambia.

The resort areas have **craft markets** known as *bengdulas*, where you'll find masses of items made specifically for tourists. Don't dismiss these places out of hand – look carefully, and you may spot some gems among the hastily carved wooden elephants (supremely un-Gambian) and cheap bangles made from wire and plastic strips.

Gambian **jewellery** and **belts** have always featured leather, beads and cowrie shells, so it's surprising that Gambians haven't latched on to the fact that these are fashionable in Europe and the US, and jazzed up their designs accordingly. If you'd like a genuine *juju*, rather than just a bit of stitched leather with a cowrie shell fixed on it, then you'll need to visit a *marabout* or one of the market medicine men. **Basketware**, woven not only into baskets but also trunks, lamp

Craft shopping in The Gambia

Africa Living Art Centre Bakau. Fabulous, eclectic collection of art, antiquities, textiles, jewellery and designer clothing. See p.116.

African Heritage Gallery Bakau. A good selection of old masks and bronzes, clothing and books. See p.111.

Albert Market Banjul. Wax prints, damask, souvenirs, musical instruments, bootleg cassettes, antique West African masks and carvings – plus vast quantities of food and household goods. See pp.93–94.

Atlantic Road Craft Market Bakau. Watch carvers at work making *djembés* and wooden animals; also plenty of batik clothing and souvenirs. See p.111.

Bamboo, Samory and African Art Collection Serrekunda. A trio of shops selling musical instruments, antique masks and beads, and Malian *bogolan* (mud cloth). See p.119.

Senegambia Craft Market Kololi. Clothing, shoes and bags made from batik, tie-dye and leather. Dolls dressed in Gambian costumes. Beads, carvings, jewellery and souvenirs. See pp.117–118.

Traditions Basse. Local weaving and West African artefacts. See p.227.

Woodcarvers' Market Brikama. The biggest concentration of woodcarvers in The Gambia. See pp.153–154.

shades, fruit bowls and other items, is generally good quality; craftsmen work on the beach and at roadside stalls.

If you hunt about in the *bengdulas* and in the shops on Sayerr Jobe Avenue in Serrekunda, you'll find a few places selling **antique African carvings** and **masks**, imported from as far afield as Mali, Togo and Côte d'Ivoire. It's very unlikely these objects will ever have been used for ritual purposes (those that are, and have not been destroyed in the process, are guarded jealously by their owners), and their antiquity may be entirely artificial (a combination of rough treatment and judicious application of cobwebs and dust), but you may well find something made to a traditional design and with far more spiritual resonance than the shiny new teak objects churned out by the Gambian carvers. Similarly, beads described as **"trade beads"** are almost certainly not the genuine article – the beads that the eighteenth-century European explorers exchanged for slaves and other commodi-

ties have long since been sold, lost or consigned to museums – so judge them on their aesthetic appeal.

Places selling antiquities often also sell **musical instruments**, including *djembés*, *koras*, *balafons* and all sorts of percussion. However, if you're taking music lessons (see p.52) during your stay in The Gambia then your tutor, or his associates, are likely to be the best source of instruments; you can have the pleasure of watching an instrument being made for you to your own specifications.

Some *bengdulas* and hotel boutiques local sell **honey** and jam packaged as souvenirs, and the National Beekeepers Association of The Gambia, in Banjul Nding, near the airport approach road, sells honey, beeswax candles and royal jelly beauty products.

While you'll hear fabulous **music** everywhere in The Gambia, CDs are hard to find – music is generally distributed on cheap, low-quality cassettes. Be aware that pirating is rife (see p.72 & p.276).

Cultural hints

You can't hope to avoid social gaffes completely in The Gambia, but humour and tolerance abound, so you won't be left to stew in embarrassment. Getting it right really takes a West African upbringing but people are delighted when you make the effort. Gambians are generally swift to include strangers into their lives with smiles and salutations, and you'll have to get used to saying hello countless times a day.

Greetings

Greetings have a crucial part to play in everyday social interactions: no conversation starts without one. This means a handshake followed by polite enquiries, even as you enter a shop. A simple "Hello, how are you?" before you launch into your request is the very least you should say. Ideally, in English or an appropriate local language, you should swap something like "How are you?", "Fine, how's the morning?", "Fine, how's business?", "Fine, how's the family?", "Fine, thank God". Questions about your name, where you're from, and where you're going are all standard elements of routine greetings. Traditionally, such exchanges can last a minute or two, and you'll often hear them performed in a formal, incantatory manner between two men. While someone is speaking to you at length, it's considered polite to murmur in the affirmative, or say thank you at short intervals. Breaks in conversation are filled with more greetings. For local language examples, see pp.272–274.

Shaking hands is normal between all men present, on arrival and departure. Foreign women, in most social situations, are likely to be treated by Gambians as honorary men. Gambian women shake hands with each other, but not normally with men. Soul brother handshakes and their variations are popular among young males. Less natural for Westerners (certainly for men) is an unconscious ease in **physical contact** between members of the same sex, but a studied lack of public contact between men and women. Male visitors need to get used to holding hands with Gambian men as they're shown around the compound, or guided down the street.

Social norms

Be aware of the left hand/right hand rule. which, like many "rules", is sometimes broken. Traditionally the **left hand** is reserved for unhygienic acts so to give something with the left hand amounts to an insult. Never use your left hand when eating from a communal bowl. Don't be put off by apparent shiftiness in **eye contact**, especially if you're talking to someone much younger than you. It's fairly normal for those deferring to others to avoid direct looks. **Hissing** ("Tsss!") is an ordinary way to attract a stranger's attention. You'll get a fair bit of it, and it's quite in order to hiss at the waiter in a restaurant.

Answering anything in the negative is often considered impolite. Try to avoid asking yes/no questions, and avoid phrasing things in the negative ("Isn't the taxi leaving?") because the answer may well be an ambiguous "Yes…" Be on the look out, too, for a host of **unexpected turns of phrase** which often pop up in Gambian English, and can be amusing. "I am coming", for example, is often said by someone just as they leave your company – which means they're going, but coming back. Confusingly, "he" and "she" are used interchangeably when referring to either males or females, since Mandinka and Wolof do not have separate pronouns for the genders.

Gifts

It's a great privilege to be invited into a Gambian family compound, especially to join in a celebration, and if you accept an invitation, it's normal to take your hosts a **gift**. While money is always appreciated and a major celebration might merit a major gift such as a bag of rice, it's also very useful to

Kola nuts

Giving and receiving **kola nuts** is a traditional exchange of friendship and respect. They also have a crucial ritual function as a symbolic gift in social and business transactions such as marriages and the purchase of land.

Kola nuts are the pink and white chestnut-sized fruit from the pods of an indigenous tree, cultivated and traded on a grand scale throughout West Africa. Before the arrival of tobacco, cannabis, tea and coffee, kola, an appetite depressant and a mild stimulant when chewed for the bitter juice, was the main non-alcoholic drug of the region.

Buy a handful for **long journeys**, as much to share among fellow passengers as to stay awake. If you're visiting a village, a little bundle of nuts makes a **good present** to offer the *alkalo*, or village chief, when you first meet him or her.

have some tokens to give to people. **Postcards** of sights from home and pictures of you and your family are appreciated by Gambians who are generally passionate about photos of friends and family but may only have a few of their own. School kids are also delighted with school materials – exercise books or paper and pencils (more useful than ball-point pens if paper is scarce, as pencil can be rubbed out).

When **visiting villages**, think carefully about how you are going to distribute any gifts you may have brought, and to whom. For example, it's better to give gifts for children to a parent or teacher, who knows who needs what, than to hand stuff out at random, which usually means it's the pushiest that end up with the most. You might also consider making an appointment to **visit a school**, to get a first-hand opinion of what would be most useful to the majority of students. Never **throw gifts** to children for them to scrabble over – even if you see Gambians do this – and never give gifts from vehicles, as this encourages chidren to tear after the wheels of cars and trucks, heedless of the hazards.

Time-keeping

People and things in West Africa are often late and Gambians like to joke about "GMT" (Gambia Maybe Time). That said, if you try to anticipate **delays** you may be caught out. Scheduled transport does leave on time at least some of the time – or even early if it's full. Even planes have been known to take off before schedule. Outside the urban areas, however, notions of time and duration are pretty hazy: dusk and dawn are the significant markers. Note also that in remote areas, if a driver says he's going somewhere

"today", it doesn't necessarily mean he expects to *get there* today. Always allow extra time – there's no better way to ruin Gambian travel than to attempt to rush it.

Appearance

West Africans set great store by their style of **dress**, and find it hard to respect those who, in their opinion, dress inappropriately or shabbily. Traditional Gambian dress for both men and women is long and loose, covering the torso, legs and head, and often the shoulders and arms as well. Covering up with cotton is generally cooler than exposing bare skin to the African sun.

While **topless sunbathing** (though not nudity) is acceptable around hotel pools and on the tourist beaches (as opposed to the fishing beaches), **beachwear** is entirely inappropriate elsewhere in The Gambia, particularly in traditional rural areas. Women should cover their legs, at least down to the knee, and men shouldn't go bare-chested.

Religious practice

The vast majority of Gambians are **Muslim**, and a well-balanced, tolerant attitude to religious differences characterizes the country. Gambians generally find it far harder to empathize with an atheist than with those with non-Muslim beliefs.

One of the requirements of Islam is that Muslims should **pray** five times a day, so you should take this into account if you're spending a day in the company of Muslims. Prayer may take place in a public place. On Fridays, Gambian Muslims wear their best traditional clothes for (in the case of men) their visit to the mosque for Friday prayers, or (for most women) prayers at home. Prayers normally take place around 2pm. If visiting a **mosque** you should take off your shoes. Women should be modestly dressed, with body and head covered. Some mosques are closed to women, and menstruating women cannot enter any mosque. Non-Muslims are never allowed in during prayer times.

Muslims are forbidden from eating **pork** or drinking **alcohol**. Some choose not to abide by this rule, but it's still advisable to be judicious about drinking in strict Muslim areas. During the lunar month of Ramadan a fast is strictly observed by Muslims during daylight hours. Another requirement of Islam is the giving of **alms**, and many people give to the same beggar regularly.

For more information on Islam in The Gambia, see pp.252–253.

Photographing people

The Gambia is immensely photogenic, but to get good pictures takes great cultural sensitivity. If you want to get **photos of people**, you can take pictures before anyone knows it's happening. However, such behaviour will almost inevitably cause offence or get you into trouble – it's far better to ask people first, and to accept refusal with good grace. Shooting with a **digital** or **polaroid** camera or means you can show your subjects their picture as soon as you've taken it; many people are delighted by this, especially if they have never had a photo of themselves.

Be prepared to **pay** a small something or to send a print if your subjects have addresses. Or you could have a lot of photos of you and your family printed up with your address on the back, which should raise a few laughs at least when you try the exchange. A family you've stayed with is unlikely to refuse a photo session, and may even ask for it. The same people might be furious if you jumped off the bus and immediately started taking photos, or took pictures through the bus window.

Toubab! Toubab!

Nobody really knows how white people came to be known as "*toubab*" in West Africa – some say it's a corruption of a word meaning "doctor"; others (less plausibly) that it's derived from "two-bob", meaning two shillings, a tip paid to Africans by Europeans for errands run. These days the label *toubab* is applied indiscriminately in referring to any non-black. It's not a racist term, although, in some Gambians' eyes, it's a defining term – long after a Gambian has learnt a white individual's name, or professsion, or country of origin, they'll still be calling them the *toubab* rather than the American, or the engineer, or John.

Children can get totally hyperactive when they spot a white visitor, particularly in rural areas – they run full tilt towards tourist vehicles, regardless of the danger, screeching "Toubab! Toubab!" at the tops of their voices. Black tourists get similar treatment as well, as soon as the kids rumble them. Visitors to The Gambia quickly discover that behind all the smiles, yells and rapt attention, the local children can often be shameless **beggars**. Children teach toddlers the catchphrase, "Any pen?" quickly followed by "Any mintie?" and, more aggressively, "Gimme money!", and some kids bunk off lessons in order to harangue passing tourists. However, don't encourage begging by dishing stuff out in the streets like Santa Claus – if you want to help children who are genuinely in need, give your gifts direct to a school or a recognized charity (see p.74).

Of course, some children and adults have less mercenary intentions, and simply want to **chat** – many Gambians are genuinely interested in people from other countries. You will frequently be bombarded by a string of questions: "Hello – what is your name? – where is your husband/wife? – from which country? – from which hotel?" and so on. Remember that these are standard forms of address Gambians use on each other (see p.63), and the kids are just trying out sentences learnt during their English lessons at school. Bear with them – as more and more youngsters begin to speak English with as much confidence and flair as they speak multiple African languages, the brighter the future of The Gambia is likely to be.

Working in The Gambia

In general it's not easy for foreigners to find paid work in The Gambia, unless you have skills that can't be matched by a Gambian candidate, and you're prepared to work for a local salary. The sizeable expatriate volunteer community, however, is cosmopolitan, active and committed.

Bed and board in return for your help is sometimes available on development projects, in schools or through voluntary agencies, but such arrangements are often entirely informal and word-of-mouth. A direct, personal approach to the appropriate ministry might open some doors. Under-employment is a serious problem and work permit regulations make your getting a wage without pulling strings almost impossible. It's normally a condition of entry into the country that you won't seek work. **Volunteering** is more feasible, if you have appropriate skills, and sufficient time to devote to a project; details of organizations to contact are given below.

Teachers, medical personnel, agriculturalists and engineers have the best chances of finding openings, paid or unpaid. The Gambia is going through a period of rapid structural and agricultural development and appropriate skills are in demand; the health service is badly under-resourced. **English language tuition** is of great value to Gambian schools, particularly up-country where there is an acute shortage of qualified teachers. Even children whose parents are fluent in English may have insufficient language practice at home, where everybody chats in Mandinka, Wolof, Fula, or whatever, rather than English. The Gambian education system rules that all lessons be conducted in English, rather than in African languages, so students' progress in other subjects such as maths or science can be severely hampered if their command of English isn't up to scratch.

Voluntary work and study programmes

Some universities which run courses in African studies offer study-abroad

progammes to The Gambia. The following are independent organizations that run volunteer programmes.

Gambia Tourism Support Kololi ☎00220-462476, ⓦwww.gambiatourismsupport.com. Imaginative and committed Anglo–Gambian organization which raises funds to support Gambian children through school, and can find work placements and study placements in The Gambia for gap year students and other self-funded volunteers.

International House UK ☎020/7518 6999, ⓦwww.ihlondon.com. Head office for reputable English-teaching organization offering TEFL training leading to a Certificate in English Language Teaching to Adults (CELTA); also recruits for teaching positions.

Mondo Challenge UK ☎01604/858225, ⓦwww.mondochallenge.org. Organizes placements for a small number of self-funded volunteers with the National Beekeepers Association of the Gambia, which aims to help alleviate rural poverty and to encourage careful husbandry of the natural environment by providing Gambian villagers with the training and equipment they need to start beekeeping businesses. Also places volunteers in rural teaching posts.

Peace Corps USA ☎1-800/424-8580, ⓦwww .peacecorps.gov. Accepts applications from US citizens over 18 for voluntary field work in developing countries, including The Gambia. They recruit people with knowledge of agriculture, education, engineering or health care; to be sent to a specific country, you must have skills required by that country.

VSO (Voluntary Service Overseas) UK ☎020/8780 7200, ⓦwww.vso.org.uk. Respected charity that sends professionals qualified in key fields to spend two years or more working for local wages on projects beneficial to developing countries. The Gambian division is very well established and efficiently run. Applicants can state their preferred country, but the organization's prime concern is to find the right people for the posts available.

Travellers with disabilities

Although by no means easy, travelling around The Gambia does not pose insurmountable problems for people with disabilities. For wheelchair or frame users, facilities are non-existent, but most hotels are single-storey or have ground-floor rooms. Access ramps are rare, however, and travel within and between towns requires even more time and determination than usual. You'll at least have no problems recruiting local help and you can expect overwhelming consideration.

Attitudes to disabled people in The Gambia are generally good, though government provision for disabled needs is almost completely absent. **Getting around** in a wheelchair on half-paved or unpaved roads, or over soft sandy streets, is extremely hard work, and no forms of public transport are wheelchair-adapted.

Visiting national parks and historical sites is problematic. Historical and archeological sites are often barely maintained, or at least require some climbing of steps or hiking through a bit of bush. In the case of the parks, it's not only difficult to reach them, but hard to get around them when you arrive. Guided tours in safari vehicles with good springs are rare.

Despite the difficulties, the effort is worthwhile if you count yourself a very outgoing individual, and are prepared to be carried repeatedly. The Gambia is sufficiently low-key, accessible and accustomed to visitors to make the hassles bearable.

Contacts for travellers with disabilities

In the UK and Ireland

Irish Wheelchair Association Blackheath Drive, Clontarf, Dublin 3 ☎ 01/818 6400, ℻ 01/833 3873, ℮ info@iwa.ie, ⓦ www.iwa.ie. Useful information provided about travelling abroad with a wheelchair.
Tripscope Alexandra House, Albany Rd, Brentford, Middlesex TW8 0NE ☎ 08457/585641,/ ℻ 020/ 8580 7021, ⓦ www. tripscope.org.uk. Registered

charity with a national telephone information service offering free advice on international transport for those with a mobility problem.

In the US and Canada

Access-Able ⓦ www.access-able.com. Online resource for travellers with disabilities.
Directions Unlimited 123 Green Lane, Bedford Hills, NY 10507 ☎ 1-800/533-5343 or 914/241-1700. Travel agency specializing in bookings for people with disabilities.
Mobility International USA ☎ 541/343-1284, ⓦ www.miusa.org. Information and referral services, access guides, tours and exchange programmes.
Society for the Advancement of Travelers with Handicaps (SATH) ☎ 212/447-7284, ⓦ www.sath.org. Non-profit educational organization that actively represents travellers with disabilities.
Wheels Up! ☎ 1-888/389-4335, ⓦ www.wheelsup.com. Sells discounted flights for disabled travellers; also publishes a free newsletter.

In Australia and New Zealand

ACROD (Australian Council for Rehabilitation of the Disabled) Australia ☎ 02/6282 4333 or 02/6282 4333, ⓦ www.acrod.org.au. Provides lists of travel agencies and tour operators for people with disabilities.
Disabled Persons Assembly New Zealand ☎ 04/801 9100, ⓦ www.dpa.org.nz. Resource centre with lists of travel agencies and tour operators for people with disabilities.

Travelling with children

Wherever you go in The Gambia, the reaction of local people to families and their children is exceptionally welcoming. However, travelling with young kids can be extremely hard work. The following is aimed principally at families with babies and under-5s.

Children's health

Health issues figure prominently in most parents' minds. With the exception of malaria, however, you can discount fears about your children getting tropical diseases in The Gambia, assuming they've been adequately immunized.

Breast-feeding babies will be as protected against malaria as their mother, but it can be very difficult to persuade small children to take **pills** under any guise. With toddlers you may have to choose between ramming pills down their throats or giving in and risking it. In the latter case, the coast is much safer than up-country riverside Gambia, but you should be extremely careful to cover them with Deet repellent early each evening and be sure they sleep under secure nets (take small nets for babies). For more on malaria, see pp.21–22.

You can buy **disposable nappies** (diapers) in The Gambia, but they are expensive and hard to find except in the Kombos. **Baby foods** are also available in supermarkets in the Kombos. You'll have few catering problems if you're staying in hotels: there's usually a good variety of fresh food and staff, given some warning, will be happy to prepare it to infants' tastes.

Unless you're visiting during the rainy season, bring some **warm clothing** for chilly mornings and evenings. Temperatures can drop considerably in December and January and hotels are not heated. Swimming pools, focus of attention for most children, are invariably unheated too and are often very cool in the mornings until the sun warms them up.

Probably the most important health concern is the **sun** – in the tropics, the effects of ultraviolet on delicate skin can be severe. Keep children covered in sunblock and insist they wear hats; they should also wear T-shirts when swimming. Sunglasses, too, are a good idea, even for babies, to reduce the intense glare – you can always find little novelty ones that will fit. Also, make sure they drink plenty of clean **water**.

Travelling

Air travel with under-2s (who get no seat for their ten-percent fares) can be a nightmare. Make every possible effort to get bulkhead seats and a baby bassinet (hanging cradle). When you reconfirm 48 hours before flying, double-check you still have them. If you have lively children who won't easily settle, consider sleeping tablets; trimeprazine can be obtained on prescription and your children will sleep right through the flight.

For a young family, standard group excursions are probably not on. Renting a **private vehicle** is quite feasible, however, and gives you the flexibility and privacy you need for changing nappies, toilet stops and so on. For babies and children too small for seat belts, you'll need a car seat which, if you have the right model, also works as an all-purpose carrier, pool-side recliner and picnic throne. If you have a light, easily collapsible **buggy**, bring it; many hotels and lodges have long paths from the central public areas to the rooms. A **child-carrier backpack** is also useful. For flying with all this baggage, remember you have a full **luggage allowance** for every passenger with a seat.

Accommodation

Only a few **hotels and lodges** specifically exclude children of any age. The most child-friendly hotels are those situated on good sandy beaches, such as at Cape Point, Bakau. Very few places make provision for **babysitters**, but, with a few hours' notice, the management can usually find somebody local to come in, and they're likely to leave the question of payment up to you. Alternatively, if the children are asleep, speak to the manager about arranging for a night watchman to sit outside.

Sex and gender issues

Sexual attitudes in West Africa are liberal, with sexual expression an important part of the social fabric in most communities, even though you'll rarely see public displays of physical affection between partners. Sex is openly discussed except in the presence of children, and it's rarely the subject of personal hang-ups. You're likely to be treated as a sexually available person even if you travel with a companion of the opposite sex, although being seen as half a couple may insulate you from advances to some extent.

Flirting and sexual encounters

Flirting is universal in the Gambia and in order to avoid it you'd have to be very selective where you go. This is particularly true for female travellers, who may find the frank scrutiny from men unnerving. If a man asks a woman to "come and see where I live", he means you should come and see where you are going to sleep together. Of course, sexual interest is by no means exclusively one-sided, which can make things awkward for women not out for adventures.

Both men and women are likely to have no shortage of friendly amateur **offers** while visiting The Gambia. These are usually easy to turn down if you refuse as frankly as you're asked. Unwanted physical advances are rare. But it always helps to avoid offence if you make your intentions (or lack of them) clear from the outset. If you're not with a partner, a fictitious spouse in the background can be useful; having a photo with you might help. This may, of course, be met with responses such as "But you're here on your own? In that case, I'd really like us to know each other...", so bulk up your arsenal of rejoinders.

All this can be fun – there's no reason you can't spend an evening dancing and talking and still go back to your bed alone and unharassed. However, if you're uncomfortable, don't be afraid of **causing offence** by being over-cautious, as long as you're polite at all times. Women should be wise to the tactics of bumsters (see p.57) and be wary of big men in small towns. Don't accept an invitation to the disco from the local chief of police unless you're on very firm ground, and don't feel obliged to meet someone as arranged if you've had serious second thoughts. Always lock your door at night.

For **male travellers**, questions of personal safety and intimidation don't arise in quite the same way. However, it's common for Gambian women, and especially unmarried girls, to flirt with strangers, and many town and resort bars and hotels are patronized by **prostitutes**. This is not the secretive and exploitive transaction of the West and pimps are generally unknown. There are plenty of cheap hotels happy to rent out rooms by the hour, and this even happens in some tourist hotels from time to time. However, premises suspected of operating as brothels, and women suspected of being sex workers, have recently been the subject of a sweeping clampdown by the Gambian government, enforced by the military police, as part of Jammeh's crusade to make his country a morally irreproachable Muslim nation.

Sexually transmitted diseases, and the AIDS virus, are on the increase, although their incidence in The Gambia is far lower than in many African countries. Attitudes are beginning to wake up to this reality, but you should be aware of the very real risks – and prepared for the occasion – if you accept any propositions. Both men and women should always carry, and use, **condoms** – the chances are, local men won't have any.

One final word of warning: in the light of recent unearthing of what are alleged to be **child prostitution** rings in The Gambia, it's imperative that you make sure any friendships you strike up with Gambians and their children could never be in any way misconstrued.

Gay life

Beyond the urban areas, **homosexuality** in The Gambia is more or less invisible. People

69

from a more traditional African background usually deny it exists, find the notion laughable, or describe it as a phase or a harmless peculiarity; others are more condemning. Gay sex is still illegal in The Gambia – though prosecutions are extremely rare.

For gay male visitors, you're most likely to find like-minded company in the resort areas, where there are a few low-key hangouts. Contacts, however, tend to be rather exploitive on both sides. **Gay women** can't hope to find any hint of a lesbian community anywhere.

Women's issues

Travelling solo or with a female companion, you'll usually be welcomed with generous hospitality in The Gambia. You might suffer occasional hassle because of your gender, but fully fledged machismo is rare, and women travel widely on their own or with each other without major problems. Women's groups flourish and are concerned more with improvement of incomes, education, health and nutrition than with social or political emancipation.

Women travellers

On rural **public transport** a single woman traveller may cause quite a stir. Fellow passengers won't want to see you badly treated: they'll speak up on your behalf and get you a good seat or argue with the driver over your baggage payments. Male passengers may assume protective roles. This can be helpful but is sometimes annoyingly restrictive, and can lead to misunderstandings – it's best to speak your mind, be polite but direct, and nobody will take offence.

In **up-country** towns and villages, foreign women travelling alone are a rare sight and a source of curiosity. Women get offers of accommodation in people's homes more often than men, most without strings attached. If you're staying in less reputable hotels, there'll often be female company – employees, family, residents – to help you.

The **clothes** you wear and the way you look and behave get noticed by everyone – they're more important if you have no male escort. Long, loose **hair** is seen as extraordinarily provocative; doubly so if blonde. Women can avoid sending out the wrong messages in strictly Islamic areas by keeping hair fairly short or tied up (or wearing a scarf) and wearing long skirts or loose trousers.

In the heat it can be hard to be that disciplined, but if you wear **shorts** make them long loose ones. If you find it's too hot to wear a **bra**, nobody will mind; if you'll be travelling much on rough roads, however, you'll need a bra for support. Seriously.

Meeting other women

It's easy to **meet women** in The Gambia, but it's often very difficult to get to know them well. Unless your first meeting has been professional – they have a job at your hotel, say, or in a shop or office you have visited – most contact is mediated, at least initially, through their male relatives, with whom you'll take on the social role of honorary man. In small towns and villages women are usually less educated than men and often don't speak English. They don't hang out in bars and restaurants either (Gambian women almost never drink or smoke), and are much more often to be found in their compounds, fields or vegetable gardens working hard. Their fortitude as **housewives** is something to behold – always in total control of the family's food and comfort, from chopping wood to selling home-made produce in order to make ends meet. The extended family and the use of younger girls as helpers is a major contribution. Men are away a great deal of the time.

For their part, Gambian women will try to picture themselves in your position, traipsing around *your* homeland – a scenario that most find hard to imagine. **Family obligations** are everything. Conveying the fact that you, too, have a family and a home is a good way of reducing the barriers of incomprehension but, assuming you're over 15, explaining the absence of husband and children is normally impossible. You can either invent some or expect sympathy – or even the offer of fertility medicine.

You might want to take cosmetics in small containers, or earrings and necklaces, to give as **small presents** to female friends (every woman has pierced ears).

Gambian women's rights

Despite widespread paper commitments to **women's rights**, and a few women holding prominent positions in government and commerce, The Gambia remains a powerfully **male-dominated** country. Women do the vast proportion of productive labour and there are non-governmental women's organizations working to improve the lot of mothers, agricultural labourers and crafts workers. Professional market women usually run their own informal unions in towns. In The Gambia, current major women's issues, apart from labour rights, are primarily concerned with legal inequalities, and prescriptive religious and traditional cultural practices.

The Gambia has three parallel **legal systems**: modern sector law (based on English common law); customary law (based on ethnic tradition) and personal law (based on Islamic shari'a law). Both customary and personal law may be applied to cases regarding divorce and inheritance, and both tend to favour men over women. While mildly violent disciplinary behaviour towards women and children is socially accepted practice in The Gambia, harmful violence of any kind is a criminal offence. It can be assumed that abuse of women is as prevalent here as anywhere else, but actual prosecutions for violence against women are extremely low.

Probably the most controversial traditional practice in West Africa is **female circumcision**, also known more bluntly as female genital mutilation (FGM). It's widespread in The Gambia: around eighty percent of women have had it performed. There have been worldwide campaigns to ban it, but in The Gambia President Jammeh has been unwilling to outlaw what he sees as a element of unimpeachable cultural tradition. Also controversial is **polygamy**, a common practice in Muslim communities – while it sometimes brings benefits to the women concerned, the more usual net result is emotional and financial hardship. For more on traditional practices, see pp.248–257.

All these issues are complex and sensitive and it's wrong to make **assumptions** about Gambian women's own perceptions of their status and rights, or to attempt to raise any of these issues in casual conversation.

Ethical tourism

Although The Gambia has been welcoming tourists since the 1960s, its holiday industry is still very much in the developing stages. The country's decision-makers are therefore in a good position to learn from mistakes made elsewhere, and encourage growth which minimizes cultural disruption and is socially and environmentally sustainable. At the same time, tourists themselves have an important role to play in shaping the country's future as a holiday destination.

The Gambia Tourism Authority has expressed a hope that the country will be welcoming a million tourists a year by 2010, ten times the present number, and President

Jammeh himself has substantial personal investment in tourism projects. With the country's ambitions running high, campaigners are working to encourage **environmentally responsible** and **culturally sustainable** development. Sadly, however, to many tourism stakeholders, ethical tourism is something they either ignore or bandy about as a buzzword, but fail to address with long-term practical policy-building. Meanwhile multinational **package tour operators**, which allow only minimal trickle-down of the benefits of tourism to the Gambian people, have a stranglehold over the whole Gambian holiday industry, making it hard for small, independent hotels and tour companies to survive.

The best hope for the future of tourism in The Gambia is that **tourists themselves** exert sufficient pressure to ensure that future development is sympathetic both to the natural environment and to the long-term interests of the Gambian people. If you're con-

Guidelines for responsible tourism

• Respect local **culture and customs**. Read "Cultural hints" on pp.63–65, and try to be alert to messages, spoken or unspoken, from Gambians you encounter. Dress appropriately, be aware of a few key points of Gambian history (such as the slave trade, colonization, independence and the coup), respect Muslim sensibilities, and try to learn a few phrases in the local languages – greetings are a good start.

• Go **up-country**. At present, rural areas reap few of the benefits of tourism – the Kombos get the lion's share. By visiting up-country communities you assist the process of alleviating rural poverty.

• Visit **national parks and reserves**. By doing so you are contributing to their upkeep and helping safeguard Gambian fauna and flora.

• Think about visiting **off-season**. Staggering the influx of tourists throughout the year would greatly improve The Gambia's tourism cash flow – many Gambian holiday industry workers are jobless during the rainy season.

• Consider travelling on a **flight-only** basis, rather than booking a package. Choosing your accommodation independently gives you complete freedom to move around the country, and more of the money you spend will go to local businesses. Gambian hotels sell rooms to foreign package-tour companies at a huge discount, little of which is passed on to the customer – the multinationals benefit most from package tourism.

• If you buy a **package**, don't buy a full-board or all-inclusive one. There has been a semi-successful campaign in The Gambia to have these banned, as they eliminate fair competition from local providers such as restaurants and bars. They also isolate tourists, culturally and physically, from the real Gambia. If you're on a tight budget, an all-inclusive package is not the best option anyway – local restaurants and bars are very cheap.

• Choose products and services from **local suppliers**. Some tourist restaurants import ingredients to make international-style dishes. Many places use cheaper Dutch eggs (usually quality-control rejects), even though Gambian eggs can be excellent, and some supermarkets sell imported goods even when good Gambian alternatives are available. Seek out the places that sell and use Gambian produce – local (rather than tourist) restaurants use fresh ingredients straight from the nearest market.

• Don't buy **CDs** or **cassettes** from hawkers, "recording studios" or market stalls – they will almost certainly be pirate copies, which deny local musicians royalties.

• Don't flaunt your relative wealth, and respect the Gambians' right to expect locals and tourists to pay **different rates** for the same things, such as museum entrance fees. Taxi drivers are well known for trying it on, but don't automatically assume that others are out to rip you off. Remember also that some workers, such as musicians and guides, rely on **tips** as a principal form of income.

• Don't break **promises** – if you take a photo of somebody and say you'll send them a copy, don't forget to do so; if you say you're going to raise funds for a village school when you get home, follow your pledge through.

cerned about the impact of tourism, contact the organizations listed below.

Contacts

Association of Small Scale Enterprises in Tourism (ASSET) Gambia ☎ 462057 or 946925, ⓦ www.asset-gambia.com. Gambian organization representing small tourism service providers such as guesthouses, ground tour operators and juice-pressers. Provides information about these and about sustainable tourism issues, and publishes *Mango News* (see p.48).

Gambia Tourist Support (GTS) UK ☎ 01256/356342; Kololi ☎ 462476, ⓦ www.gambiatouristsupport.com. Non-profit charitable fundraising organization which can provide information and advice on many issues relating to tourism in The Gambia, including responsible and sustainable tourism, and has an informative and refreshingly candid website.

Tourism Concern UK ☎ 020/7753 3330, ⓦ www.tourismconcern.org.uk; Gambia c/o *Bakadaji Hotel*, Kololi ⓦ www.subrosa.uk.com /tourism. Campaigns for the rights of local people to be consulted in tourism developments affecting their lives. The Gambian branch of Tourism Concern co-publishes *Mango News* with ASSET.

Environmental awareness and ecotourism

The Gambia is a small country with a rapidly expanding population, and awareness of the fragility of the **natural environment** is just beginning to hit home. Human requirements – for farming land, firewood and food – can sometimes appear to be in direct conflict with accepted conservation practice, and education programmes are seeking to encourage Gambians to explore ecofriendly ways of running their lives.

There's visible evidence of The Gambia's losing battle against environmental degradation everywhere in the country. **Refuse** is

poorly managed, with beaches suffering from the litter washed up by the Atlantic breakers, and deliberate dumping on waste ground is a major problem. The Gambia has no heavy industry, and traffic is not yet heavy enough to cause major **air pollution**, but rubbish fires emit toxic gases in residential districts. The Atlantic beaches are badly eroded in some areas (see box on pp.114–115) and, up-country, wind erosion has left chunks of deforested land barren. Bush fires, some of them started deliberately by farmers to clear land for crops, degrade the environment further every season.

As a visitor, you can do your bit to combat **environmental damage**. Try not to create litter, and try to take home everything you brought with you. Minimize your electricity consumption, and think about whether you really need your room to be air-conditioned – if the answer is yes, don't leave it on when you're out, or when you have the door or windows open. Think, too, about your water consumption, and don't request items such as towels to be laundered if they've barely been used.

Consider your means of **transport**. Travelling on foot or by bicycle can be preferable to travelling by taxi. Never drive or permit yourself to be driven on the beach – Gambian beaches were once home to breeding turtles but human disturbance of their natural habitat has almost wiped them out.

Gambian tour operators are fully aware of the pulling power of the label "**ecotourism**", and not all of them follow ecologically sound practices as a matter of course. Check your tour operator's commitment to conservation issues carefully before committing to an excursion on the basis of its supposed eco-friendliness. If you're concerned about the behaviour of any hoteliers, tour operators, drivers or guides, consider making a formal complaint.

Charity projects

Many charitable organizations work in The Gambia, most of them primarily concerned with poverty alleviation, education and healthcare. Gambian tradition fosters a culture of self-help within the family, and Gambians aspire to being totally self-sufficient. Nevertheless, The Gambia is a developing country and it welcomes help from charities and NGOs, which in turn depend to a great extent on donations.

Apart from cash, skills and training, charities also welcome **donations** of medical supplies, old but useable crutches, spectacles and wheelchairs, school supplies (exercise books, text books, readers, encyclopaedias, computers, pencils and pens), sports equipment like footballs and tennis balls, and children's clothing.

If you'd like to distribute your own donation of skills, funds or supplies to Gambians in need, rather than channel it through a charity, it's essential to seek local advice first, in order to make sure your contribution ends up in the most appropriate hands. The non-profit Anglo–Gambian organization **Gambia Tourism Support** (GTS) is an excellent source of advice on this (see below).

If you book your holiday through The Gambia Experience (see p.11) you will automatically trigger a small contribution to their school-building fund by filling in one of their holiday questionnaires. They can also advise about making your own donations.

Charitable organizations

Action Aid UK ☎01460/238000, Ⓦwww.actionaid.org. NGO concerned with reducing poverty worldwide, with long-running practical projects in up-country Gambia.
Concern Universal UK ☎01432/355111. Has been working in The Gambia since the early 1990s, specializing in sustainable agricultural and

horticultural development, enabling communities to be self-sufficient.
The Essau Project (contactable c/o GTS). Christian nursery school project.
Friends of Gambian Schools (FROGS) (contactable c/o GTS). Raises funds to send primary school materials to The Gambia.
Friends of The Gambia Association UK Ⓦwww.fotga.org.uk. Organizes child sponsorship.
Friends of the Gambian Organisation for the Visually Impaired UK ☎01493/721506, Ⓦwww.friendsofgovi.org.uk. Tackling blindness and sight-impairment in The Gambia.
Gambia Tourism Support (GTS) Kololi ☎00220/462476, Ⓦwww.gambiatourismsupport .com. Information about schoolchild sponsorships and a point of contact for various initiatives including a small-scale paper recycling project that creates employment and training opportunities. Also raises funds to sponsor the education of needy children.
Go Gambia UK Ⓦgogambia.org.uk. Raises funds for Gambian hospitals, and sponsors kids' school fees and expenses.
Makasutu Wildlife Trust Makasutu ☎00220 /782633, Ⓔdrumohq@qanet.gm. Aims to protect and preserve wildlife in The Gambia and raise awareness of conservation issues (see p.157).
SOS Children's Villages Sponsorship office (Vienna) ☎43-1/3682-4570, Ⓦwww .sos-childrensvillages.org; Gambia: Ⓦwww .sosgambia.org. Offers shelter and support for orphaned and destitute children.

Directory

ADDRESSES Mail is sorted into PO Boxes. Your own address is likely to be much in demand – a stack of small address labels is very useful.

BOOKS Literacy levels in The Gambia are low, and books do not play much part in most people's lives. The country has only one bookshop that merits the name – the well-stocked Timbooktoo (see p.116) in Fajara, which has a sub-branch at the airport. Some hotel shops have a few books, but most Gambian "bookshops" are in fact stationers which also sell school textbooks. There's a small library of paperbacks at the Fajara Club (see p.116).

DUTY FREE ALLOWANCE You can bring the standard quantities of one litre of wine, one litre of spirits and 200 cigarettes into The Gambia, duty free. Watch out for customs officials who may try to convince you otherwise.

ELECTRICITY When there is some, it is 220V AC, and sockets may be either European-style two-pin, or UK-style three-pin type. If you're bringing a mobile phone, it's worth having a travel adapter with your phone charger so you can use either. Only some resort hotels have shaver points or outlets in the rooms. Resort hotels have back-up generators to cover power cuts; elsewhere it's wise to be prepared with candles and a torch.

EMERGENCIES Ambulance ☏16; Police ☏17; Fire ☏18.

LAUNDRY In rural areas, washing is done by hand, usually in a stream. You won't find public laundries, but there are plenty of people willing to do the job. It's considered bad form to give your underwear to somebody else to be washed. *Bitikos* (small shops) sell cheap washing powder. Ideally, dry your clothes indoors, and avoid spreading them on the ground – they may become infested by Tumbu fly which lays its eggs on wet clothes. Ironing kills the eggs.

OPENING HOURS Most Gambian shops and offices close on Friday and Saturday afternoons, and all day Sunday. Government offices open Mon–Thurs from 8am to 3pm or 4pm, and Fri–Sat 8am–12.30pm. Banks generally open Mon–Thurs 8am–1pm and 4.30–6.30pm, Fri 8–11am. Telecentres and Gamtel offices generally open 8am–10pm daily. Post offices generally open Mon–Thurs 8.30am–12.15pm and 2–4pm, Fri 8.30am–12.15pm and 2.30–4pm, Sat 8.30am–12noon. Shops and businesses open Mon–Thurs around 8am–5.30pm, sometimes later, and sometimes with a break for lunch, and Fri–Sat 8am–noon. Supermarkets have longer hours, which may include Sundays. Daily markets are generally open from 8am till dusk.

PHOTOGRAPHY Insure your camera, and keep it in a dust-proof bag. Bring spare batteries, and all the film you'll need – it's very pricey here. Keep film cool by stuffing it inside a sleeping bag or roll of clothes. Local print processing is hit and miss – If you'll be away for some time, post it home, or send it with someone flying back. Early morning and late afternoon are the best times for photography; the contrast between light and shade can be huge, so expose for the subject and not the general scene. A flash is useful to fill in shade, even in bright sun. Dark skin needs extra exposure: think of people as always back-lit – a half stop is normally enough.

SPELLING Confusingly, there are no universally accepted spelling rules in The Gambia. Mandinka, Wolof and the other African languages used in the country are primarily spoken languages, so many African words – including proper nouns – have several alternative spellings.

SPORTS The Gambia's only 18-hole golf course is at Fajara's sports complex the Fajara Club (see p.116), which, like some of the resort hotels also offers tennis, squash and table tennis. Watersports on the Atlantic coast are limited due to dangerous currents; body boarding is sometimes possible, but even swimming here can be dangerous at times. For parascending, waterskiing and banana boat rides, contact the Gambia Watersports Centre (☏765765), based at the *Atlantic Hotel*, Banjul.

What to pack

• Binoculars are essential for birdwatching; small ones with good lenses are most practical.

• A multipurpose penknife is useful, but avoid ones with blades longer than a palm-width which could be misconstrued.

• A torch.

• Plastic bags are invaluable – carrier bags to keep dust off clothes, small sealable ones to protect cameras, film, tickets and documents.

• If driving or hiking in remote areas, take a compass or a GPS gadget.

• A lightweight mosquito net: nets are cheap to buy locally, though often bulky.

• Disposable razors (available only at import supermarkets), or preferably an old-fashioned razor blade holder.

• Condoms are best brought from home. Tampons are expensive and only easy to find in supermarkets and shops in the Kombos (they're very scarce up-country).

• The best material for clothes is cotton; for dusty up-country roads, dark colours are best. For the resort areas you'll want beach wear and smartish light clothes. Pack at least one warm jacket or sweater, and take the lightest, toughest, airiest footwear you can afford.

STREET NUMBERS The numbering of buildings is erratic in The Gambia – even if a house has a number, it may not be clearly marked. If in doubt, ask for directions.

TIME Most of West Africa, including The Gambia, is on Greenwich Mean Time (GMT). The twelve-hour clock is generally used. Although The Gambia lies some distance north of the equator, it has roughly the equatorial twelve hours of daylight – a little more in summer, a little less in winter, with sunrise always between 6.30am and 7.30am, and sunset between 6.30pm and 7.30pm.

TOILETS Except in tourist hotels and restaurants, where the facilities are generally good, paper is usually provided by the user rather than the owner; Gambians prefer to use water. In such cases, the facilities are usually a hole in the ground, or a "long-drop" toilet built into a cubicle. A bucket or kettle of water for washing will be provided.

WEDDINGS Many tourist hotels can lay on garlands of flowers, music, dance and "complimentary" cakes.

Guide

Guide

Banjul and the
northern Kombos

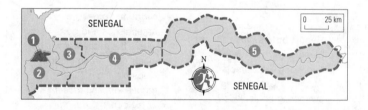

CHAPTER 1 # Highlights

* **Arch 22** Banjul's monument to President Jammeh's regime looks pretty monstrous, but the top floor balconies give you fantastic views of the whole capital. See pp.92–93

* **Albert Market** One of the country's most accessible urban markets, brimming with colour, noise and pungent produce. See pp.93–94

* **Resort hotels** There's plenty of accommodation along the Gambian Atlantic coast, offering swimming pools, kids' entertainers, sumptuous African buffets or just a secluded retreat. See p.88–89 and pp.105–110

* **Beach bars** Sunshine, sand and sparkling sea, with fresh fish on the barbecue and cold beer in the icebox. See p.115

* **Microlighting** Get a whole new perspective on the Kombos from the back seat of a motorized kite. See box on p.97

* **Nightlife** Forget the hotel discos and go where the in-the-know locals go – urban garden clubs playing mellow reggae, rippling *mbalax* or high energy *ndagga* music. See pp.120–126

Banjul and the northern Kombos

Most visitors to The Gambia, and the vast majority of expatriate residents, spend most of their time in the northern corner of **the Kombos**, as Banjul's hinterland is universally known. The Kombos are a collection of districts occupying a peninsula of around nine hundred square kilometres, edged by the mouth of the River Gambia to the northeast and 50km of tropical beaches to the west. Concentrated in the vicinity of the northernmost beaches are most of the hotels in the country, some of them in enclaves catering solely for foreign visitors.

Banjul, the capital, is a small city, with a population that's actually decreasing. Hot and hemmed in by mangroves, river and sea on a small, flat island jutting into the mouth of the River Gambia, this low-rise town is not attractive in the conventional sense. To a significant extent, it's a daytime centre only – at dusk, workers by the minibus-load pour back over Denton Bridge to the mainland and down the highway to their suburban homes.

Banjul is not really geared towards tourists, despite having a few noteworthy attractions such as the National Museum, an excellent market and a rich architectural heritage. Most visitors choose instead to enjoy the hotels, restaurants, bars and clubs of the **coastal resort areas**, where there are ample opportunites to chill out in the sun: the facilities here are unmatched anywhere else in the country. The main resorts of Bakau, Fajara, Kotu and Kololi each have their own distinctive character; some are upbeat holiday centres, while others are swish residential neighbourhoods or large African villages that happen to be near the ocean. The area's credentials as a **beach resort** are, to some extent, under revision, since natural tidal erosion has been wearing away the sand for some years. However, its attractions as a **tropical sunshine** destination are still huge, with plenty of hotel guests content to relax and do nothing, pottering from pool to restaurant to bar. For the slightly more adventurous, tour companies offer excursions that showcase the northern Kombos' most interesting features, such as Banjul's landmarks and the sacred crocodile pool in Bakau.

At the heart of the area, close to but very distinct from the tourist areas, is The Gambia's largest town, **Serrekunda**, which houses about fifteen percent of the total population, and constitutes the country's commercial nerve centre. It's sometimes overlooked by beach-mad tourists, but it's a living, breathing, cacophanous West African town that's intriguing to explore.

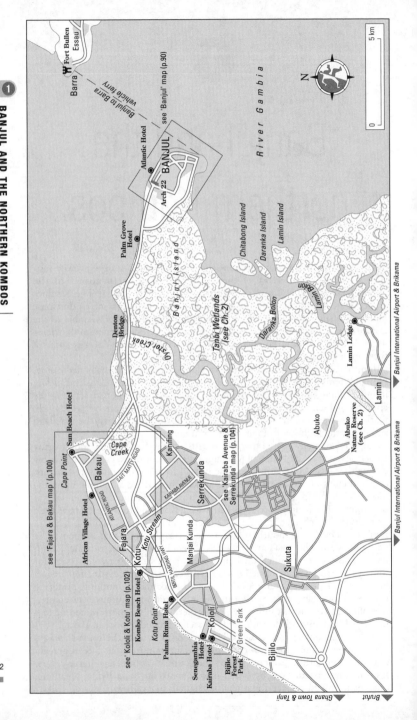

Independent travel in the northern Kombos is straightforward once you get too know transport types, departure points, routes and prices. The hotel areas are served by taxis and some public transport routes, and none of the Atlantic beaches are more than a few kilometres from the nearest surfaced road. The area is also a convenient starting-point for travels further afield, on foot, bicycle, by bush taxi or rented car.

For **naturalists**, especially ornithologists, the area offers opportunities to explore a rich variety of habitats, home to numerous species. If you're staying in one of the many hotels with a large garden, then spotting exotic species is as easy as stepping onto your verandah, and there are bird-rich stretches of beach and countryside within walking distance of most accommodation options. You'll also see small, colourful lizards sunning themselves on rocks, and possibly a few wild monkeys.

Arrival

Most visitors to the area first arrive at **Banjul International Airport** near Yundum, south of Serrekunda, and 24km from Banjul city (it's actually closer

Banjul International Airport

Three decades ago, The Gambia's international airport was no more than a shed next to an airstrip. Now there's an impressive terminal building with a modern, sculptural silhouette, and a runway registered with NASA as an emergency space shuttle landing site. The terminal, designed in 1997 by renowned Senegalese architect Pierre Goudiaby, has a bright, lofty interior, with soaring white pillars and subtle friezes depicting Gambian artisans, farmers and fishermen.

Arrival formalities are low-key and straightforward. At **passport control**, you're given an entry stamp (see p.16), and you're required to pay a **tourist tax** (£5/$10/€10) at the Gambia Tourism Authority desk. Customs officials have been known to angle for bribes, so hold your ground if you suspect the rules are being bent, and ask the advice of a tour rep. Rates for **porters** are fixed at D10, £1 or $1, and there'll be a scramble for your stuff; luggage trolleys are free. For **currency exchange**, the Trust Bank at the airport (Mon–Fri 9am–5pm, Sat 9am–1pm) offers rates similar to hotels – not great. You can also change money with one of the calculator-wielding moneychangers who make themselves very obvious. There's also a **post office** (Mon–Sat 8am–4pm or until after the last flight, an **Internet café**, public telephones and an outlet for mobile phone SIM cards and scratch cards. For details of flight arrivals and departures, the **information desk** (☎473000) is to the left as you exit the arrivals hall. Other facilities in the main hall of the terminal include a a Hertz vehicle rental desk and a Gambia Tourism Authority office, which offers very basic tourist information.

Transport from the airport

Tour guests pre-booked into the package hotels are normally driven there by complimentary **coach**. For independent travellers, fixed **tourist taxi** fares from the airport are posted on a board outside the arrivals area (D200 to Banjul or the resorts); you'll be approached by plenty of touts. You should be able to negotiate a lower price if you seek out a **yellow local taxi** – there may be a couple out in the car park. Otherwise, it's a three-kilometre walk to the main road where, during the day, you can pick up a **bush taxi** to Brikama, or to Banjul via Serrekunda – change at Serrekunda for Kotu, Kololi, Fajara or Bakau.

to the coastal resorts than to the capital). A sleek, newly surfaced road leads from the airport to the main south bank highway that runs up-country. A branch leading off the highway serves the resorts and connects to another new road, the Kombo coastal highway, which follows the coast south to Kartong. The road from the airport to Serrekunda should also, by the end of 2003, be newly resurfaced, and this connects with the dual carriageway leading direct to Banjul. For information on arriving by road from Senegal, see p.15.

To get around Banjul and the northern Kombos by **public transport**, you can choose between chartering a green **tourist taxi**, hiring a **yellow taxi** for a "town trip", or flagging down a **bush taxi** (or "local taxi"), which could be either a shared yellow taxi or a minibus, for a trip along a fixed route (see pp.30–32). In the resorts, especially in high season, there's stiff competition among the tourist taxi drivers, and some may offer you better prices than the fixed rates displayed at the taxi ranks near the hotels. Note that tourist taxi drivers pay a premium to be allowed to work in the tourist areas, and confrontations between your driver and the police may result if you persuade a bush taxi to carry you to or from a tourist taxi zone.

Banjul

Sweltering, confined and at times seething with mosquitoes, The Gambia's capital **BANJUL** is not an obviously appealing town for most visitors. Its tarmac streets seem to pump out heat in the dry season, and its alleys become a chaos of red mud and puddles during the rains. The dilapidated assemblage of corrugated iron, peeling paint and, deep in the backstreets, open drains with no slopes to drain them, complete a somewhat melancholy picture. With a population of less than 50,000, Banjul is too small to offer any of the ordinary facilities and diversions of a capital, and nightlife is all but nonexistent. Most city workers make an understandable exodus after business hours; few choose to live here.

To be won over by Banjul you need a little patience, or perhaps a specialist interest in West African history or architecture. More than any other Gambian town, the capital conveys a strong sense of the country's **colonial past**. Elements of this are being lost almost daily, as streets are renamed, and new buildings replace old, but there are still interesting details and architectural juxtapositions to seek out. Banjul's architecture tells the story of its history and development, with visible remnants of building styles spanning nearly two hundred years, from early nineteenth-century *kirinting* houses (similar to wattle and daub) to late-twentieth-century banks and law courts. The city is ripe for regeneration – with some judicious preservation, improvement and investment it could feel vibrant rather than drab, intimate rather than claustrophobic.

More immediately, Banjul has a few attractions which are worth a brief visit by any standards: the **National Museum** for its small but enlightening collections relating to local and regional history and ethnography; the **Atlantic Hotel**, for its attractive swimming pool and watersports centre; **Albert Market**, for its colour, verve and range of commodities; and **Arch 22**,

President Jammeh's vainglorious monument, for its inspiring rooftop views.

Though a capital, Banjul has an idiosyncratically relaxed **small-town atmosphere**. If you have business to get on with, whatever you need to accomplish here can usually be done in reasonable safety – and at less than three square kilometres, the town can easily be covered on foot. You may be warned by some Gambians that Banjul is unsafe after dark, but it's wrong to mistake the quietness of the place for any undue threat. The **security** presence is low-key: when recently the local police were issued with bicycles, it was seen as a great innovation, as previously the only way they could get to a crime scene was to walk or take a taxi. Even so, it's a town with people constantly in transit, so take the same precautions as in any urban area at night.

Some history

The expansion and development of Banjul, known to the colonial British as **Bathurst**, was from the outset hampered by the serious drawbacks of its site. The British built Bathurst on St Mary's Island, a small, insect-infested landmass separated from the mainland by a band of creeks and swamps prone to flooding. Kankujeri Road (formerly Bund Road) forms a dyke that constrains the city on its present small patch, making further expansion impossible.

The early settlers, however, were probably not thinking beyond their immediate ambition of safeguarding British commercial interests in this corner of West Africa. St Mary's Island, which at the time seems to have had no permanent inhabitants, was acquired by Britain in 1816 to defend the River Gambia from **slavers** and to control trade with the interior. A detachment of the British Royal African Corps led by **Captain Alexander Grant** equipped the island with a battery of cannon to intimidate rogue traders from France, Spain and Portugal. The island itself was now secure enough to function as a trading base, and a number of British merchants moved their businesses from the Senegalese island of Gorée to the new town of Bathurst. The population then quickly grew, with an influx of Wolofs from Gorée and St Louis, and freed slaves from Freetown in Sierra Leone. Grant is generally credited with making a significant contribution to eliminating the slave trade on the River Gambia once and for all. One of his honours was to have a street named after him – most of the other streets of Bathurst were named after generals who served at the Battle of Waterloo, and prominent merchants.

Bathurst grew from a fort and **collection of villages** to a city in the space of a century. With a basin deep enough to dock ocean-going vessels, the port became one of the Senegambia region's principal trade gateways, with Wellington Street (now Liberation Street) the focus of commercial activity. In 1889, the city was declared capital of the newly created British "Crown Colony and Protectorate of The Gambia", as present-day Gambia was first named, and the twentieth century saw a steady increase in trade as the country's population expanded.

In 1973, eight years after independence, Bathurst was renamed **Banjul**. At this time, great optimism in the country's commercial future led to the expansion and modernization of the docks; however, the city itself had nowhere to grow, and Serrekunda took over as The Gambia's largest town. By the mid-1980s, an air of despondency and neglect had settled over the capital, its streets mostly unpaved, its colonial buildings crumbling, and its citywide network of drainage ditches choked with reeking refuse. Things went from bad to worse in 1986, when Albert Market was destroyed by fire. In the late 1980s, derelict buildings began to be replaced, and the change in government in 1994 brought with it a number of development initiatives, including improvements to the

The **Barra ferry** is one of Banjul's lifelines, a crucial link in its line of communication to The Gambia's nearest neighbouring capital, Dakar. The service runs between Banjul's Liberation Street terminal and the wharf at Barra, on the opposite side of the mouth of the River Gambia. There are no bridges across the River Gambia, so the smooth operation of the ferry has a critical part to play in Banjul's activities as an import–export centre; unfortunately, the service is often erratic.

There are presently two boats in operation – *Johe* is relatively new, and crosses the river in as little as thirty minutes, while *Barra* is older and slower (45–60min). A third, *Niumi*, is undergoing lengthy repairs. Each one can carry two large trucks, three or four smaller ones, or an equivalent number of cars, plus foot passengers (daily 7am–11pm, hourly on the hour in each direction; vehicles D145, foot passengers D5); contact the Port Authority ☎228205 for information on any delays.

Limited space on board means that vehicles sometimes have to queue for several hours, even when the ferries are running to timetable. Acute **delays** are fairly common – sometimes for trivial reasons such as "the crew are eating" – although often they are unavoidable, such as when unfavourable tides and strong currents stretch the journey to two hours. At the end of the dry season (May–June) the ferry may not even run at all except around high tide, as the Gambia estuary is prone to silting up. Further delays can be expected in the few days before and after major festivals (see p.48), when the whole country seems to be on the move, and Liberation Street becomes one big ferry queue.

In order to buy a vehicle **ticket** at Banjul, you drive into the yard containing the slipway and report to the ticket office; all tickets are basically till receipts. From the north bank, however, you need to get a ticket before you can enter the terminal, from the Port Authority ferry office just south of Essau. On either side of the river, Port Authority security staff in Day-Glo shirts can assist you. If you're travelling as a **foot passenger**, in either direction, then having bought your ticket you make your way to the waiting room, a hot concrete bunker with a gate like a cage door, through which everybody surges at once when it's time to board. If you're with a tour group, you're generally spared the waiting room and can board ahead of the crowd.

It's worth remembering that it can be surprisingly cool and breezy on the river. Watch out for pickpockets on the ferry and in the jostling crowds in both terminals.

Royal Victoria Hospital, road surfacing and, more controversially, the construction of Arch 22. In the late-1990s came the near-total eradication of the old British street names from the map of Banjul. Today, **city renewal** appears to be gathering pace, with long-neglected buildings being torn down to make way for new. Unfortunately, historical structures are being lost in the process, and there's every chance that Banjul's cityscape will be barely recognizable within a few decades.

Arrival, orientation and transport

Banjul is not the first stop for most people flying into The Gambia – visitors staying in the resort hotels head straight for those instead (for information on arriving at Banjul International Airport, see pp.83–84). Arriving **by road**, there are two approaches to Banjul. If you're coming from northern Gambia or northern Senegal, you arrive on the north bank of the River Gambia at the small port of Barra (see pp.165–168); from here, the regular **ferry** (see box above) brings you straight to the terminal in Banjul town centre. The fastest

There are plenty of hustlers, some of them fairly intimidating, touting currency exchange or transport on the Barra side, particularly in the stampede for buses and bush taxis. The pedestrian gateways through which you leave either terminal on arrival are narrow and crowded, and can feel claustrophobic.

The crossing itself is an experience that's much more authentically Gambian than travelling by tourist transport. You'll see passengers crowd on board with all manner of stuff, from sheep on ropes and chicken held upside down by the ankles, to wardrobes manhandled by two or three people. Some women carry huge headbundles, others may be chatting on the hands-free of their mobile phones. As well as transporting traders and trade goods, the ferry is a trading place in its own right, with hawkers peddling everything from natural remedies to plastic toys, and shoe menders busily cleaning and stitching up shoes whether invited to or not. From mid-river, there are good views of the Banjul skyline, and of Barra.

Early morning is a pleasant time to make the crossing, with a good chance of seeing dolphins plunging in the bow-wave. The 7am ferry from Banjul is the slow one, and it sometimes holds up the 8am one outside Barra, but the 8am one can't overtake, so if you want to dash for onward transport then the first ferry gets you ahead.

An alternative way to cross the river is to take a passenger **pirogue**, but these are only worth considering on calm days, and not after dark, when the crossing is more dangerous and prices higher. They're faster than the ferry (20–30min) and more flexible, running not to timetable, but when full (bush taxi style), and so can be preferable to a long wait if the ferry's delayed. The fare is normally the same as the foot passenger fare on the ferry. The pirogues have been tightly regulated since a fatal accident in early 2002 when an overloaded boat tipped over mid-river, drowning around sixty of its passengers and crew. Now everybody has to wear a lifejacket, and there are strict load limits of 20–40 people, depending on the size of boat. Deep decking means there's little chance of falling out, but the boats can be rather leaky and boys with buckets bale out from time to time. You're always close to the water, so if you sit on the ocean side you'll get mildly drenched – it's drier on the riverward side, and driest in the middle. You'll also get wet if you have to wade to get on and off the boat, particularly at the Barra end. If you'd like a burly Gambian to fireman's lift you onboard, that's extra.

route from the ferry terminal out of town is to take Kankujeri Road (also known by its former name, Bund Road) to the Banjul–Serrekunda highway. The second approach to Banjul is from the **south bank**, along this highway, which passes dense banks of mangroves before Oyster Creek, separating the island from the mainland. The creek is crossed by Denton Bridge, after which the highway follows the coast of the island, passing beach cemeteries on the way, until forking into Independence Drive, Marina Parade and Wallace Cole Road at Arch 22. No vehicles (apart from the president's) are allowed to pass under the arch, so you'll probably turn down Marina Parade, one of Banjul's more pleasant and shadier streets, fringed with somnolent government buildings and terminating, after the *Atlantic Hotel* and the Royal Victoria Hospital, at the guarded gates of State House. Independence Drive is graced with the impressive Court House and House of Representatives.

Despite its compactness, Banjul's **layout** can initially be disorientating, as all the streets look much the same; to add to the confusion, some addresses still use the old British street names. The **Gamtel Tower** is a good landmark to navigate by, visible from many different angles and taller than all the surrounding buildings. You're likely to spend most of your time in the **commercial**

Travelling from Banjul to Dakar

To get **from Banjul to Dakar**, the capital of Senegal, you need first to take the ferry or a *pirogue* to Barra (see box on p.86–87), and then take either a bus or a bush taxi. GPTC runs two **buses** a day from Barra to Dakar, the first leaving around 8am and the second around 10am, or sooner if all the pre-booked passengers are on board. The buses wait just inside the Barra ferry terminal exit gate. Count on four to seven hours for the three-hundred-kilometre journey. It's possible to buy a ticket (D150) on board, but to be sure of a seat you need to book in advance at the GPTC depot in Kanifing, Serrekunda (☎394776). The ticket office opens at 7am; if you're there first thing and make an immediate dash for the Barra ferry, you should catch the second bus. Due to a dispute with the Senegalese authorities at the time of writing, Gambian buses are forced to drive back from Dakar empty, so if you're planning a return journey you'll need to use another mode of transport.

By **bush taxi**, you travel to the Gambian border post of Amdallai by *gelleh-gelleh* van (D15) or shared Peugeot car (D18) from Barra's taxi garage adjoining the ferry terminal; you then change vehicles to get to Karang, the Senegalese border post (D5), and again to be driven on to Dakar via Kaolack (CFA5000). There are border formalities at both Amdallai and Karang.

There are regular **flights** (£30/$50) from Banjul International Airport to Dakar.

district around July 22nd Square and Liberation Street down by the waterfront, where Albert Market, the post office and banks are all located.

Banjul has two **bush taxi garages**: one with minibuses serving Bakau (15-20min; D5), opposite the National Museum, and the other, serving Westfield Junction in Serrekunda (20min; D5), the main taxi garage near Serrekunda market (25min; D5,) and Brikama (1hr; D10), near the Gamtel Tower. **Green tourist taxis** are found outside the *Palm Grove* and *Atlantic* hotels, and **yellow taxis** can be flagged down for short hops, or hired for town trips (from D20), all over town. GPTC buses no longer serve the city.

Accommodation

Despite its idiosyncratic appeal, The Gambia's capital city is not everybody's idea of the perfect base for a holiday. It has only two **tourist-class hotels**, the *Atlantic* and the *Palm Grove*. There's also a clutch of fairly down-at-heel **smaller hotels** and **guesthouses** in the town centre, catering mainly for travelling Africans. The best of these are a little shabby, while the worst rent out rooms by the hour – but even some of these are worth investigating for a low-cost experience of Banjul.

Apollo Hotel Tafsou Ebou Samba St ☎228184. Stuck in a 1970s timewarp, this is a characterless place, but a reasonable choice if you're looking for something vaguely resembling an international-style self-contained room, on a budget. ❸
Atlantic Hotel Marina Parade ☎228601, ⓦwww.corinthiahotels.com. Recently renovated, comfortable hotel geared towards wealthy business travellers and the high-end tourist market, situated right on a narrow but attractive beach, but within walking distance of the centre of Banjul. The grandly proportioned bar and restaurant areas

are popular with local movers and shakers. The two hundred plus rooms are a little small, but well furnished and equipped. Most have views of the pool, the ocean, the flower gardens, or a jungly bird garden that attracts over 150 bird species and has a viewing platform. You can parasail or jet-ski here with The Gambia Watersports Centre (see p.127), based in the hotel. ❻
Banjul Ferry Guest House 28 Liberation St ☎222028. The best choice in this price range, located right in the thick of things near the Barra Ferry terminal, with a communal balcony great for

watching the incessant activity in the street below. It looks unpromising from the outside – you enter through a dingy yard and climb some back stairs to the first floor – but the fifteen rooms are well-kept and a good size; some are self-contained with a/c, and a few on the higher floors have private balconies. ❷–❸

Carlton Hotel 25 Independence Drive ☎228670, ⓕ227214. Old-fashioned four-floor, forty-room hotel with a slightly formal atmosphere. The rooms are self-contained and decently furnished; some have a/c, and some just about have views of Arch 22. At street level the outdoor terrace is leafy and cool. ❸–❹

Duma Guest House 1 Jallow Jallow St ☎228381. Friendly guesthouse deep in a residential quarter, but not the easiest to find – look for a three-storey yellow and white building with a brown gate. Unfortunately the building is crumbling and the decor has definitely seen better days. Four of the thirteen rooms are self-contained. ❶

Palm Grove Hotel Mile 2, Banjul–Serrekunda Highway ☎201620, ⓦwww .gambia-palmgrovehotel.co.uk. Tourist hotel with a pleasant location next to a lagoon and a quiet stretch of beach. Unfortunately, it's way outside the town centre, and guests mostly have to rely on costly green tourist taxis to get around – it's difficult to flag down bush taxis hurtling along the busy highway outside the hotel. It's an attractive place to spend time, though; the 120 self-contained rooms are stylish, with optional a/c, and the decor includes works by local artists. ❺

Princess Diana Hotel 30 Independence Drive ☎228715. Twelve-room hotel with, plain self-contained rooms with fans or a/c. It's clean and adequate, but a little soulless, with narrow corridors. ❷

The Town

Banjul's commercial bustle, centred around its **docks** at the city's eastern limit, makes an immediate, vivid impression on most visitors. Small though the port is, it's an important gateway for imports and exports, and the streets around the harbour are regularly clogged with fume-belching lorries waiting to pick up new consignments as fabric, tea and rice are disgorged from ocean-going vessels by the container-load – some commodities are destined for the shops and stalls of Liberation Street and Albert Market, others get moved on up-country and to other West African states.

The area just inland from the docks is Banjul's **shopping district**. The town can be a diverting place to shop, but don't expect to find any department stores, supermarkets or even boutiques with window displays – trading is done very informally on the street corners, in the market or in the shops that are little more than market stalls with walls and doors, crammed together along the colonnaded shopping streets. Banjul's trading community is dominated by Gambian Lebanese, but you'll also find Mauritanians here, hazel-skinned and instantly recognizable in their long blue robes. You'll see Gambian and Guinean tailors, too, at work on the pavements, their treadle-powered machines whirring away. An ever-present element of Banjul street life is the travelling traders, many of them Senegalese, hawking trays of fake designer sunglasses, cartoon-character toothbrushes or bootleg CDs.

Banjul is at its most appealing in the residential quarters in the west and southwest of town, in the golden light of late afternoon or at weekends. Once the frenetic crowds of wheelers and dealers have packed up for the day, the place lends itself to exploration on foot, when there's time to stop and look at the **architecture** with less danger of being bumped by an orange-seller's barrow or butted by a goat-seller's goat. Good areas to wander include Rene Blain, Hannah Forster and Rev William Cole streets southwest of the Serrekunda taxi garage where, side by side, you'll see examples of *kirinting* houses, with bamboo-weave walls sometimes daubed with plaster, and timber houses, faced with planks. The *kirinting* houses, quick and cheap to construct,

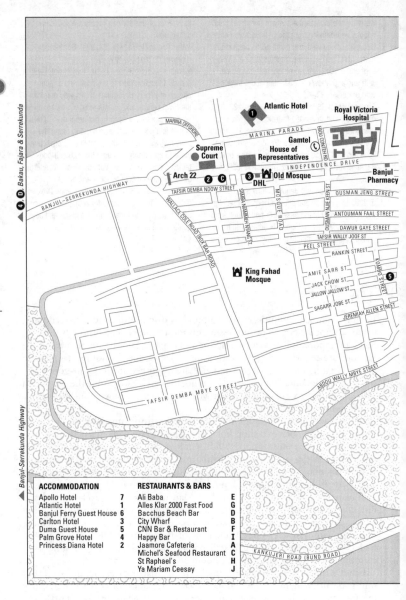

ACCOMMODATION		RESTAURANTS & BARS	
Apollo Hotel	**7**	Ali Baba	**E**
Atlantic Hotel	**1**	Alles Klar 2000 Fast Food	**G**
Banjul Ferry Guest House	**6**	Bacchus Beach Bar	**D**
Carlton Hotel	**3**	City Wharf	**B**
Duma Guest House	**5**	CNN Bar & Restaurant	**F**
Palm Grove Hotel	**4**	Happy Bar	**I**
Princess Diana Hotel	**2**	Jaamore Cafeteria	**A**
		Michel's Seafood Restaurant	**C**
		St Raphael's	**H**
		Ya Mariam Ceesay	**J**

are among Banjul's oldest buildings, originally home to the less well-off African settlers on the island in the early nineteenth century. The next architectural wave – the timber houses – dates from the 1840s, built and owned by more affluent Aku settlers. Later in the nineteenth century, when Bathurst was a thriving trading post, the Portuguese, British and French merchants built the commercial houses that still line Russell Street, Liberation Street and ECOWAS

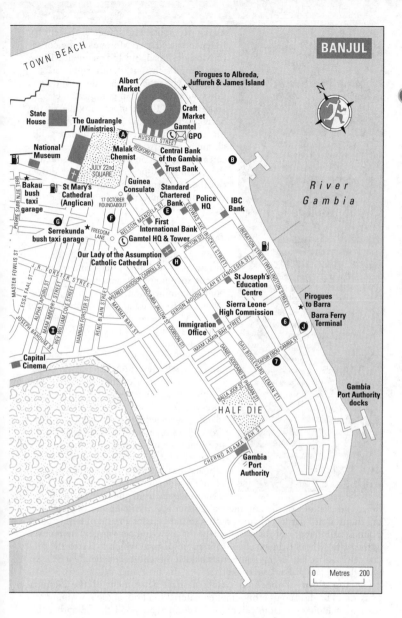

Avenue, with arched colonnades at street level and roofed-in verandas on the first floor.

Banjul has an interesting collection of **mosques**, the principal of which is the King Fahad Mosque, built in 1988 and named in tribute to the Saudi Arabian monarch, and huge enough to be visible for miles around; if you fly over Banjul, the mosque's enormous sandy praying area is one of the easiest land-

Birdwatching around Banjul

Kankujeri Road, formerly known as Bund Road, passes through a variety of bird-rich habitats, and a few sessions spent here can easily yield sightings of over a hundred species. On the west side of the road are mangroves and the tidal mudflats of the estuary, with the rusting hulks of wrecked ships sunk into the mud, the roosts of pelicans and cormorants. At low tide, the mudflats are well populated with gulls, terns, herons and waders. To the east is reclaimed land, some of it cultivated, some of it wild and dotted with tamarisk and mangrove. Here you are likely to see little grebs, Senegal thick-knee and black-headed plovers. The roadside itself is to a varying extent a vehicle scrap yard, so you have to make your way carefully, and it's also preferable to pick a time when there aren't too many lorries thundering past, so weekends are best.

marks to spot. The nineteenth-century Independence Drive Mosque on the corner of Mosque Road and Independence Drive was Banjul's first; it stands right on the street, so when the gate-like doors and windows are open you can glimpse the elegant arches inside. Right in the middle of the Serrekunda bush taxi garage is a miniature mosque with jaunty green minarets like chimney-pots. At prayer times the drivers spread their mats on the tarmac outside, and the blaring loudspeakers manage to drown out the car horns. Non-Muslim visitors can enter the mosques if they're suitably attired (see pp.64–65).

Arch 22

Arch 22 (daily 8am–10pm; D25), a ten-storey, cream-coloured, free-standing monument spanning Independence Drive, was built to commemorate the coup of July 22, 1994, and to herald a new era in Gambian history. Completed in 1996, it's something of a monstrosity, and totally at odds with the rest of Banjul.

The best reason to visit Arch 22 is the unobstructed **view** from the top-floor balconies – rare in a country as flat as The Gambia, with so few tall buildings. From here you get a good sense of Banjul as an island city, ringed by river, ocean and mangrove. You might also be struck by the relative grandeur of the buildings that serve as reminders that this small town is the nation's capital: the circular Supreme Court, the House of Representatives and the huge mosque. Even from the halfway level, the noise and clamour of the commercial district is diminished, and the over-riding impression – far less obvious on the ground – is of a maze of family compounds, palms and baobabs, the elements of any Gambian village. The **terrace** at the halfway level is an excellent vantage point from which to watch the official celebrations and events sometimes held at this end of Independence Drive, with the Arch as a dramatic backdrop.

The **top floor** of the Arch houses a small department of the National Museum. The displays of ethnographic material (traditional tools, weapons and textiles, including gorgeous ceremonial costumes) are good, though rather thin on explanation. The first exhibit you come to is easy to miss since it's so incongruous: the small, very ordinary stool on which Jammeh sat when he announced the AFPRC had taken over The Gambia.

The architect responsible for the Arch is Senegalese **Pierre Goudiaby**, whose work has become closely associated with the Jammeh regime (other commisions have included Banjul International Airport and the Farafenni and

Bwiam hospitals). At a cost of US$1.15 million – an astronomical sum in local terms – Arch 22 is not Goudiaby's finest achievement, despite Jammeh's desire for a massive structure that would inspire patriotic pride. The Arch's formula of decorated pediment upon Doric columns (eight of them, big enough to house staircases and lifts) has nothing to do with modern Gambia. While Goudiaby is noted for capturing the spirit of traditional Africa in his modern buildings, here his only nod towards ethnic idiom seems to be the viewing balconies, which African architecture buffs describe as "curved like calabashes". Technically, it's a bit of a disappointment, too – soon after it opened, one of the lift shafts became unuseable due to the twisting of the structure as it settled into the soft ground. As a symbol of progress within the capital, its message rings a little hollow for many Banjul residents.

At the foot of the Arch is a gilded **statue** of a soldier holding an infant, supposedly representing the rescue of the nation by the military coup, although critics have remarked that the soldier looks more like a kidnapper than a rescuer. On the opposite side, the area where ceremonies are sometimes held is adorned by equally tacky statues of traditional musicians and elders, the work of Goudiaby's brother, Tony.

National Museum of The Gambia

The **National Museum** on Independence Drive (Mon–Thurs 8am–4pm, Fri & Sat 8am–1pm; D25), though small, poky and badly lit, contains some gems – you just have to be patient to find them. Some visitors don't make it beyond the ground floor, where the worthwhile twentieth-century displays include a collection of **Oku marabout** oddments (including *jigida* waist beads, a *shukoo* bridal basket, like a big colourful laundry basket, and an *igba* engagement calabash, which would have contained the bride's dowry, engagement ring, kola nuts and spices). There's also **colonial ephemera**, including a first-class ticket for a passage from Bathurst to the UK "on or about 30 August 1959" aboard the MV *Apapa*, a banana boat which, pitching and rolling, would have taken about a week to make it to Liverpool.

If you take time to peer into some of the darker corners, you'll find, among the mouldering ethnographia, a few prehistoric artefacts, some illuminating maps, documents and generally informative stuff about the wars and migrations of the Senegambia region, and a good display on **Islam** in The Gambia. Kids used to interactive displays will be yawning within minutes at the yellowing notices against the exhibits; they might pause at the **traditional musical instrument** collection downstairs, but just for long enough to discover that you're not allowed to touch anything. Also downstairs are some interesting old photos of *jalis* playing at ceremonies and gatherings.

The building that presently houses the Museum used to be the **Bathurst Club**, a Europeans-only establishment, and it still has an appropriately quirky, old-fashioned atmosphere. Its garden, which has a drinks stall, is a green oasis which contains Banjul's last remaining well; the others were all abandoned in the 1930s, when piped water was introduced to the city.

Albert Market and the commercial district

Albert Market (Mon–Sat), a laid-back and unusually tidy version of the everything-under-the-sun kind of market found all over West Africa, is one of Banjul's big draws. It's quite a maze, but the stalls are reasonably well separated by paved paths. The produce stalls sell common West African culinary ingredients such as sticky brown tamarind, lurid scarlet chillies, lumpy tomatoes stacked in neat pyramids, lentil-like locust bean seeds, mounds of groundnut paste and baskets of pungent dried fish, plus all sorts of basic groceries sold in a vast range of quantities, from rice by the sackful to oil by the polythene-bag-ful or macaroni by the spoonful. Barrowloads of **fruit** are sold in season, especially mangoes in the rainy season, watermelon after the rains, and oranges and pineapples in the dry season.

Beyond the produce there are stalls selling **beauty products** such as shea butter (a natural moisturiser), handmade soap and hair extensions, and household goods of every description. There are some great bargains in **clothing**: Chinese-made clothes are especially cheap, as import duty in The Gambia is very low. You may also come across **fetish stalls**, selling cowrie shells, bits of animal horn, bones, kola nuts, small pipes, trade beads and old rusty bangles. The *bantaba* area within the market is a treasure trove of fabric, and one of the best places in the country to buy the latest cottons, including wax prints and embellished damask in a riot of fabulous colours.

Deep inside the general market, among fig-draped trees, is the highly enjoyable **tourist market**. There's a good choice of batik clothing here, plus musical instruments (drums, *balafons*, *koras*, and all sorts of percussion), beads and handmade leather goods. There are also a couple of stalls selling African antiquities including masks from all over West Africa. Many stalls sell cheap and cheerful souvenirs – necklaces, bracelets, bangles and the ubiquitous carvings – be prepared to bargain.

Albert Market overspills into **Liberation Street** and the nearby roads, where shops and stalls sell more cheap, trashy shoes and clothing, plus household oddments and bootleg cassettes. Fabric wholesalers in this area are open to the public, and offer good selections of imported cloth in African designs.

You'll also find handmade clothes, tablecloths and items of knitting, crochet and patchwork in the shop a block back from Liberation Street at **St Joseph's Adult Education and Skill Centre** (ECOWAS Avenue, T228836; Mon–Thurs 8.30am–3pm, Fri 8.30am–noon, closed for two weeks over Christmas and Easter and late July–mid-Sept). The goods are all produced by the centre's talented students, young women aged 16–25, some from underprivileged backgrounds. They're usually happy to give you a tour of the centre so you can watch traditional craft techniques; staff encourage this, as it's a good opportunity for them to practise their English. The classrooms are bright and inviting, and there's an inspiring atmosphere of purposefulness to the whole place.

Eating, drinking and nightlife

Banjul suffers from a serious shortage of **restaurants**, particularly in the evenings, but there is first-class simple food to be had from local eateries and fast-food joints in the daytime. For rice and sauce, there's plenty of choice among the stalls in the Albert Market, where all the traders eat, and you'll find itinerant traders everywhere – especially around July 22nd Square – with fruit, fritters, frozen juices and peanut brittle.

There's not much **nightlife**, either, in the conventional sense. At the time of writing, the last club in town had closed, and the only option was the rather plush air-conditioned disco at the *Atlantic Hotel* (nightly till 3am). Banjul is the kind of place where people prefer to hang out with their mates in the streets, playing table football or checkers, or brewing *attaya* – after dark, the pavements are dotted with glowing charcoal braziers topped with little teapots.

△Banjul (townscape from Arch 22)

Ali Baba Nelson Mandela St. Popular Lebanese place that's highly recommended, even though it's not much to look at, with white plastic tables and a fair few flies. Decent snacks, sandwiches and main meals, including first class *falafel*, delicately spiced *kafta* and juicy burgers, plus mango and guava juice and fresh fruit smoothies. Subtitles itself *"The King of Chawarma"*, but is not to be confused with the less appealing *King of Chawarma Restaurant* a couple of doors down the street. Mon–Sat 9am–5pm.

Alles Klar 2000 Freedom Lane. A grubby little streetside stall selling chicken, spaghetti and pies near the Serrekunda bush taxi garage, only worth visiting if you're running for a minibus and desperate for a few calories.

Bacchus Beach Bar & Restaurant Mile 7, Banjul–Serrekunda Highway, ☎ 227948. Situated on the lagoon behind what used to be the Wadner Beach Hotel (now derelict), this slightly overpriced bar/restaurant is aimed at tourists, with standards like steak and barracuda; it's too out of the way to attract much passing trade, but popular with the guests at the nearby *Palm Grove Hotel*. It's on the beach but indoors, with mosquito screens, and there's a pool table.

City Wharf Restaurant On the beach, off Liberation St, reached by the turning near the IBC bank. A few waterside tables and chairs with sunshades, where you can enjoy a drink and basics like chicken and chips while watching the pirogues and other river traffic.

CNN Bar & Restaurant Rene Blain St. Serving *chawarmas*, chicken and chips, this bar can be near-deserted by day, but is often busy late at night. There's a largeish interior, and a yard that bakes if it's sunny. It's a bit grimy, with once-funky murals that have seen better days and, despite the name, no TV. Open 24 hours.

Happy Bar Rev William Cole St. A tiny hole-in-the-wall drinking place with a very local atmosphere, in a quiet street where kids play table football on the corner.

Jaamore Cafeteria On the corner of July 22nd Square, near Albert market. Pleasant outdoor café, with a few shaded tables in a fenced-off corner of the square, giving a new lease of life to a lovingly preserved 1930s drinking fountain. Excellent meat pies and hot and cold drinks; you can order simple meals, if you can wait while somebody fetches ingredients from the market; there's also a tiny bookstall. Visited mostly by tourists, but not touristy, this is a great place to relax and people-watch. Daily till 8pm.

Michel's Seafood Restaurant 29 Independence Drive, opposite the Court House. Banjul's only relatively formal restaurant outside the hotels, an old-fashioned, functional, rather than romantic place. Serves a good choice of fish and a different West African dish every day, at a very reasonable price. Specialities include tiger prawns, lobster and fresh local juices. Daily 8am–late.

St Raphael's Wilfred Davidson Carroll St, opposite the Catholic cathedral. Low-key place that feels rather like a Catholic family drawing room, serving good-value *benachin*, *domodah*, and other West African dishes such as *chew-kong* (catfish) and *foofoo* with soup.

Ya Mariam Ceesay Bar & Restaurant Liberation St, by the Barra ferry terminal. The only bar in this busy street, and worth dropping in for a drink if you're waiting for a ferry.

The Atlantic resorts and Serrekunda

The Gambia's principal **tourist strip**, which accommodates virtually all the country's package holidaymakers, covers just over ten kilometres of the Atlantic coast west of Banjul. This area is an appealing place to unwind, with its easy-going restaurants, low-key nightspots, and clusters of clifftop and beachside hotels. It provides many tourists with all the distractions they need, and it's common for visitors to return again and again without venturing further up-country.

The Gambia by microlight

The Gambia is more or less flat, so elevated views of the countryside are rare. By **microlight** you get a unique perspective on the Gambian landscape, covering large distances in a matter of minutes. There's also the physical thrill of being airborne at five hundred metres in a small craft, with no fuselage separating you and the breeze. Plus, if you're up for it, your pilot can take you through some stunt manoevres that will really get your pulse racing; you feel very exposed, so the experience is not for the faint-hearted, but microlights have an excellent safety record.

The Gambia has one microlight base, Madox Microlights (☎374259, mobile ☎918576), in the grounds of Banjul International Airport. It's primarily a small-scale training centre with a CAA authorized examiner – you can become an internationally qualified microlight or light aircraft pilot here. The Gambia is a good part of the world for clocking up flying time, since weather conditions are very favourable most days throughout the dry season. The instructors will also take visitors out on tours, for an hourly fee (you can arrange to be collected from one of the resort hotels for no extra charge). In this case, you'll be the passenger in a two-seater microlight, with a communication link from your helmet to the instructor's so you can talk during the flight. After taking off from the airport's main runway, within minutes you can be soaring over Makasutu or Serrekunda, or cruising from bay to bay along the Atlantic coast. The snaking mangrove creeks of the Tanbi Wetlands, in particular, are extremely beautiful when viewed from the air.

There are four main **resort** areas, strung along the coast. **Bakau**, the most significant coastal community after Banjul itself, is long established, and it has a large enough population to assert an identity of its own that's far from swamped by the presence of visitors. Despite the ravages of tidal erosion, the sandy beaches at its northern limit, Cape Point, are still among the best in the area. Bakau's "old town", east of Sait Matty Road, is a swarming village of dirt streets and noisy compounds and home to many of the hotel staff, while the "new town", west of Sait Matty Road, has more villas and lawns. **Fajara**, adjoining Bakau on the coast, is one of The Gambia's most desirable neighbourhoods, with bougainvillea draping decoratively over walls enclosing large private houses. To the southwest, Fajara merges into **Kotu**, where a high concentration of tourists pack into a clutch of established hotels, at the debouchment of the small Kotu stream. Finally, further south, **Kololi** and its neighbouring villages of Manjai Kunda and Bijilo make up a very mixed area where some of the most upmarket hotels, the most bohemian guesthouses and the trashiest tourist traps in The Gambia are found. At the hub of the resort area, and indeed of the whole country, but scarcely registered by many of the sun-worshippers, is **Serrekunda**, The Gambia's largest town, a seething, cacophanous commercial centre that's on the go 24 hours a day.

The Gambia's holiday industry is extremely localized in this corner of the Kombos; as a result, the area's atmosphere and relative affluence makes it quite unlike anywhere else in the country. There are more newly surfaced roads in the resort area than in the rest of country put together, and far more vehicles cruising them, many of them taxis, Land Rovers and coaches exclusive to foreign visitors. There are also better (though far from perfect) supplies of water and electricity – not that any hotelier would consider operating without private generators and water tanks.

Some hamlets in the resort area are practically tourist ghettoes, populated entirely by visitors, tourism workers and bumsters. The towns and villages where Gambians actually live have expanded hugely since the first plane-loads of winter sunseekers arrived from Sweden in the 1960s, while up-country villages have been emptied of whole generations of school-leavers (and school dropouts) as youngsters get swept up in the coastward drift. Meanwhile, the coastal Kombos' old rural economy of planting, fishing and palm-wine-tapping is fading fast.

Since tourism has had such a strong foothold in this area for so long, it's an accepted element of contemporary life for the Gambians living in the northern Kombos. Most residents, remarkably, have retained an equable regard for the visitors who pay them such scant attention. Inevitably, where locals and tourists interact, the question of patronage sometimes creeps in, and even wise village elders here believe that a major benefit of tourism is the opportunities it presents for Gambian youngsters to make their families' fortunes by marrying foreigners. Nonetheless, it's still perfectly possible to strike up lasting friendships with northern Kombos residents that have no hidden agenda.

Arrival, orientation and transport

A new tarmac road covers the 10km between the airport (see p.83) and the new coastal highway that serves the resort areas, and most visitors enter the area by this quick and easy route. The Kombo coastal highway runs from the resorts all the way down to Kartong, near The Gambia's southwestern limit. Leading from Kololi and Kotu, north towards Fajara, the same road is known as **Bertil Harding Highway**.

Serrekunda, 7km from Banjul and 13km from the airport, is connected to Fajara by **Kairaba Avenue**, The Gambia's four-kilometre commercial artery. At Kairaba Avenue's southern end, it meets the Serrekunda–Banjul dual carriageway at the landmark Westfield Junction. At its northern end, Kairaba Avenue connects with Bakau's main roads, and meets Bertil Harding Highway at a junction marked by a Shell garage and the only set of **traffic lights** in The Gambia.

Bush taxi (or "local taxi") rides around the northern Kombos are all short hops of 10–20min (D4–5). Serrekunda is the hub, with many routes turning around at the main bush taxi garage north of the market, causing huge traffic jams. Banjul–Serrekunda minibuses run from Banjul's Gamtel Tower bush taxi garage, along the Banjul–Serrekunda Highway, to Westfield Junction, and on to Serrekunda's main garage. Banjul–Bakau minibuses run opposite the National Museum, along the Banjul–Serrekunda Highway, then along either

---

Moving on from Serrekunda

Serrekunda is The Gambia's main terminus for public transport services. **GPTC buses** running along the main south bank highway to Basse and serving Brikama (40min; D10), Soma (4hrs; D45), Sankulay Kunda for Janjanbureh (6hrs; D75), Bansang (7hrs; D80) and Basse (8hrs; D85) start from and finish at the depot in Kanifing district, Serrekunda (reservations ☎394776, from 7am daily). **Bush taxis** covering the same route, plus the routes to Banjul, the resorts, the southern coast, most other villages in the Kombos, and to Senegal, operate out of Serrekunda's several bush taxi garages and stops. Minibuses from Serrekunda to Abuko (20min; D5), Lamin (25min; D7) and Brikama (40min; D10) leave from the stop on Kombo Sillah Drive at Westfield Junction. For points along the south bank highway beyond Brikama, such as Soma (3.5–4hrs; D50), Sankulay Kunda for Janjanbureh (5–6hrs; D80), Bansang (6–7hrs; D85) and Basse (7–8hrs; D90), gelleh-gelleh vans leave from the garage near Bundung police station, further south.

Sait Matty Road or Old Cape Road to Bakau's main turnaround on Atlantic Road near the market. Westfield–Bakau and Serrekunda–Bakau minibuses and cars run from near Gamtel at Westfield Junction or from outside Serrekunda's main garage, along Kairaba Avenue, Garba Jahumpa Road and Sait Matty Road to Atlantic Road. Cars sometimes run along Atlantic Road between Bakau and Fajara. Serrekunda–Kololi and Serrekunda–Kotu cars run from London Corner on Sayerr Jobe Avenue in Serrekunda, to either the Badala Park or the Palma Rima junctions, then on to the Senegambia area (Kololi) or the *Bungalow Beach* area (Kotu). Ask for "Senegambia" or "*BB*". **Town trips** by yellow taxi start from D20, and **tourist taxis** and **car rental** are also available (see p.126 & p.127).

Bicycles can be rented outside most major hotels, giving you the freedom to explore the back-country near the resorts, the best beaches further south, or the bush tracks on the north bank of the River Gambia (accessible by ferry, see pp. 86–87).

Accommodation

With the exception of the pricier places, most of the **tourist hotels** along the coastal strip are quite basic by international standards, but they all have a swimming pool, restaurant and bar, and most have a garden. While many are built on the beach, or very close to it, sea views are by no means guaranteed. Booking a flight plus hotel package through a tour operator gives you at least a small discount, with special offers reducing the price even further. In season, the Kotu to Kololi stretch becomes the heartbeat of the tourist industry, while Bakau and Fajara hotels are somewhat quieter.

Independent travellers looking for somewhere reasonably cheap to relax for a few days will find several friendly, **small independent hotels** and **guesthouses**, a few of which have pools and restaurants, a short distance away from the coast in Bakau, Fajara, Kololi or Serrekunda.

Birdwatching in hotel gardens

It's not unusual for tourists to come to The Gambia for a beach holiday and go away with a brand new interest in birds, just through watching jewel-bright little creatures hopping around outside their hotel window. If you choose a hotel with a large, leafy garden you could spot a couple of dozen different species within an hour of arrival.

Just about every well-planted hotel garden is visited by gems like the tiny red and brown firefinch and its frequent companion the red-cheeked cordon-bleu, which looks much the same but with a different paint job – this time sky-blue with a jaunty scarlet spot on each cheek. Dipping into the hibiscus flowers will be sunbirds, West Africa's answer to the humming bird, tiny with delicate curved beaks and beautiful plumage. Hanging from tall bamboo stands or palm fronds may be the knot-like nests of weaver birds, scruffy, gregarious black and yellow birds of which The Gambia has several species. Then there are the raucous gaggles of long-tailed glossy starlings, which look a bit like common starlings dressed up for a night out, with fabulous iridescent blue-green wings and show-off tails. Senegal coucal, common bulbul and yellow-crowned gonolek are also frequent garden visitors.

Good tourist hotels for birdwatching in the resort area include the *Kairaba*, the *Senegambia*, the *Bakotu* self-catering apartments and the *Badala Park*.

Self-catering accommodation is taking off in a big way – there are enough produce markets, supermarkets and restaurants in the resort area to make catering straightforward. Finally, if you are interested in staying as a house guest in **a Gambian compound** (something which many in Bakau and Serrekunda are happy to offer, as they can charge, daily, the equivalent of a week's wages),

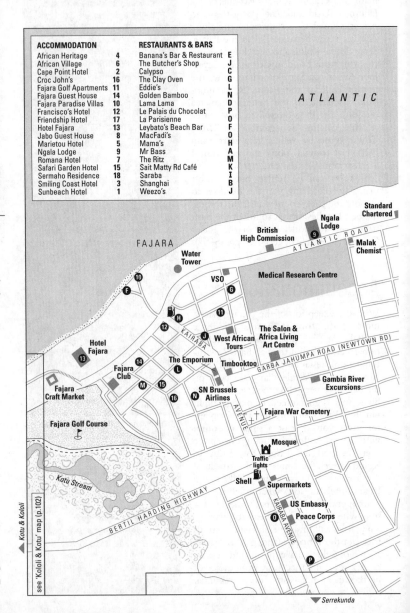

ACCOMMODATION
African Heritage	4
African Village	6
Cape Point Hotel	2
Croc John's	16
Fajara Golf Apartments	11
Fajara Guest House	14
Fajara Paradise Villas	10
Francisco's Hotel	12
Friendship Hotel	17
Hotel Fajara	13
Jabo Guest House	8
Marietou Hotel	5
Ngala Lodge	9
Romana Hotel	7
Safari Garden Hotel	15
Sermaho Residence	18
Smiling Coast Hotel	3
Sunbeach Hotel	1

RESTAURANTS & BARS
Banana's Bar & Restaurant	E
The Butcher's Shop	J
Calypso	C
The Clay Oven	G
Eddie's	L
Golden Bamboo	N
Lama Lama	D
Le Palais du Chocolat	P
La Parisienne	O
Leybato's Beach Bar	F
MacFadi's	O
Mama's	H
Mr Bass	A
The Ritz	M
Sait Matty Rd Café	K
Saraba	I
Shanghai	B
Weezo's	J

ATLANTIC

Standard Chartered

Ngala Lodge

British High Commission

ATLANTIC ROAD

Malak Chemist

FAJARA

Water Tower

VSO

Medical Research Centre

The Salon & Africa Living Art Centre

KAIRABA

West African Tours

GARBA JAHUMPA ROAD (NEWTOWN RD)

Hotel Fajara

The Emporium

Timbooktoo

Gambia River Excursions

Fajara Club

SN Brussels Airlines

Fajara Craft Market

AVENUE

Fajara War Cemetery

Fajara Golf Course

Mosque

Kotu Stream

Traffic lights

Shell

Supermarkets

KAIRABA AVENUE

US Embassy

Peace Corps

BERTIL HARDING HIGHWAY

see 'Kololi & Kotu' map (p.102)

Kotu & Kololi

Serrekunda

then just ask around and take pot luck; you should expect to be asked anything from £2/\$3.20 to £4/\$6.40 per person per day, with meals included, depending on the season. It's easiest to find this kind of arrangement if you already have a base, even just a cheap hotel, so you won't feel under pressure to rush into any deals you're uncertain about.

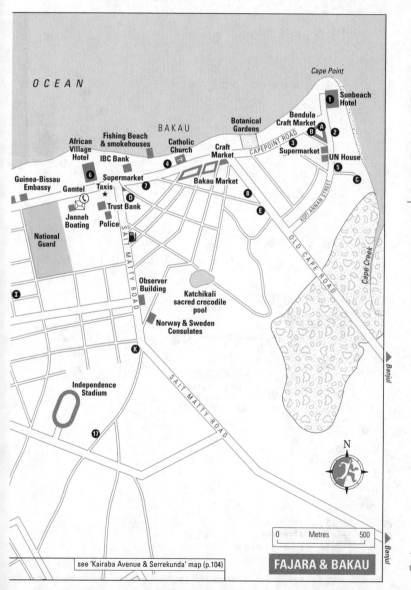

FAJARA & BAKAU

see 'Kairaba Avenue & Serrekunda' map (p.104)

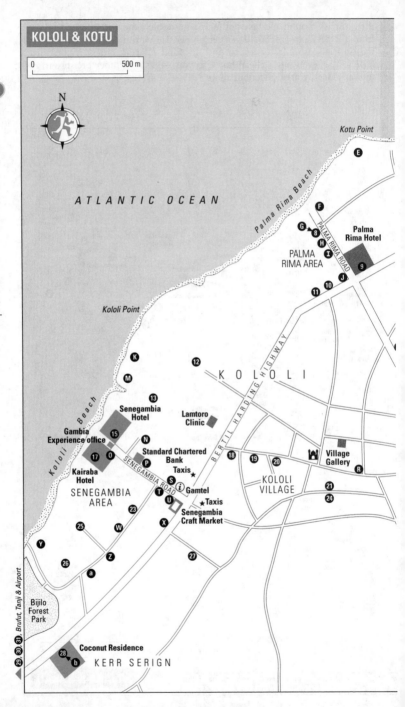

KOLOLI & KOTU

0   500 m

N

Kotu Point

ATLANTIC OCEAN

E

Palma Rima Beach

F

G   8

H

PALMA
RIMA AREA

I

Palma
Rima Hotel

9

J

11 10

Kololi Point

K

M

12

K O L O L I

13

Senegambia
Hotel

Lamtoro
Clinic

Gambia
Experience office

15

N

Standard Chartered
Bank

17 O

P

Taxis

Kairaba
Hotel

S

Gamtel

i

Taxis

SENEGAMBIA
AREA

T

U

Senegambia
Craft Market

23

18   19   20

Village
Gallery

R

KOLOLI
VILLAGE

21

24

25   W

X

Beach

Kololi

Y

26   Z

27

a

Bijilo
Forest
Park

Brufut, Tanji & Airport

29

30 31

28   b   Coconut Residence

KERR SERIGN

BERTIL HARDING HIGHWAY

SENEGAMBIA ROAD

PALMA RIMA ROAD

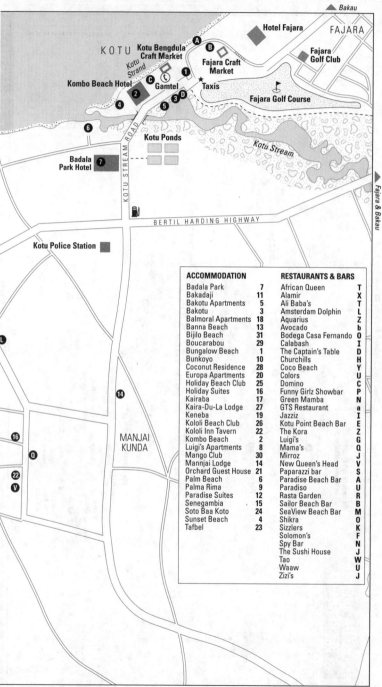

ACCOMMODATION

Badala Park	7
Bakadaji	11
Bakotu Apartments	5
Bakotu	3
Balmoral Apartments	18
Banna Beach	13
Bijilo Beach	31
Boucarabou	29
Bungalow Beach	1
Bunkoyo	10
Coconut Residence	28
Europa Apartments	20
Holiday Beach Club	25
Holiday Suites	16
Kairaba	17
Kaira-Du-La Lodge	27
Keneba	19
Kololi Beach Club	26
Kololi Inn Tavern	22
Kombo Beach	2
Luigi's Apartments	8
Mango Club	30
Mannjai Lodge	14
Orchard Guest House	21
Palm Beach	6
Palma Rima	9
Paradise Suites	12
Senegambia	15
Soto Baa Koto	24
Sunset Beach	4
Tafbel	23

RESTAURANTS & BARS

African Queen	T
Alamir	X
Ali Baba's	T
Amsterdam Dolphin	L
Aquarius	Z
Avocado	b
Bodega Casa Fernando	O
Calabash	I
The Captain's Table	D
Churchills	H
Coco Beach	Y
Colors	U
Domino	C
Funny Girlz Showbar	P
Green Mamba	N
GTS Restaurant	a
Jazziz	I
Kotu Point Beach Bar	E
The Kora	Z
Luigi's	G
Mama's	Q
Mirroz	J
New Queen's Head	V
Paparazzi bar	S
Paradise Beach Bar	A
Paradiso	U
Rasta Garden	R
Sailor Beach Bar	B
SeaView Beach Bar	M
Shikra	O
Sizzlers	K
Solomon's	F
Spy Bar	N
The Sushi House	J
Tao	W
Waaw	U
Zizi's	J

Bakau

Fajara & Bakau

Sukuta & Serrekunda

KAIRABA AVENUE & SERREKUNDA

N

0   500 m

ACCOMMODATION
Adiyata Guest House   2
Camping Sukuta   6
Douniya Motel   3
Green Line Motel   5
Praia Motel   4
YMCA   1

RESTAURANTS & BARS
Afra Citizen Mosdolly   C
Alliance Franco-Gambienne   D
Come Inn   B
Jokor   H
Lana's Bar   J
Marandy's   G
Marie's Pub   I
Samuja Fast Food   A
Westfield Junction Café   E
Willy's Disco   K
Youth Monument Bar   F

Banjul

Traffic lights & Fajara (see 'Fajara & Bakau' map, p.100)

Manjai Kunda, Kotu & Kololi

Sukuta & Brufut

Lamin & Brikama

JIMPEX ROAD

KANIFING

BANJUL–SERREKUNDA HIGHWAY

BANJUL–SERREKUNDA HIGHWAY

Jimpex

GPTC Bus Station

Bush taxis to Banjul

Serrekunda Post Office

Bellview Airlines & IPC Travel

Malak Chemist

Bush taxis to Bakau

Gamtel

WESTFIELD JUNCTION

Banjul Pharmacy & Westfield Clinic

Bush taxis to Brikama

JESWANG

KOMBO SILLAH DRIVE

Senegal High Commission

Gambia International Airways

Footbridge

KAIRABA AVENUE

Africell

Supermarket

KAIRABA AVENUE

Standard Chartered Bank

SAYERR JOBE AVENUE

SERREKUNDA

MOSQUE ROAD, LATRIKUNDA

Big silk cotton tree

LATRIKUNDA

Batik Factory

Serrekunda Market

Police Station

Main bush taxi garage

Aisa Marie Cinema

Samory Bead & Craft Shop

Bamboo Craft Shop

African Art Collection

Banjul Pharmacy

Wrestling Arena

LONDON CORNER

Bush taxis to Kotu & Kololi

Bremen Clinic

Total

Shell

BAKOTEH

Bakau and Cape Point

Bakau is a good choice of neighbourhood if you'd like the sense of staying in an African community, but don't want to be too far from the beaches and tourist facilities. The hotels and guesthouses here are refreshingly down-to-earth, and the village is a good place to start asking around if you're keen to stay in a family compound. The **Cape Point** hotels are tucked away in a quiet tourist enclave with very good, though narrow, beaches. Unfortunately, strong currents make these beaches unsafe for swimming. Cape Point is likely to liven up soon when two new or newly refurbished hotels start taking guests.

African Heritage 114 Atlantic Rd, Bakau ☎496778. Two excellent self-contained upstairs rooms, one overlooking Bakau market, the other overlooking the busy fishing beach, give you a real sense of involvement in your surroundings at this guesthouse, restaurant and gallery shop. Both rooms have the use of a fridge, TV, and a small but lovely garden. Four new rooms in an annexe provide down-to-earth budget accommodation. ❷

African Village Atlantic Rd, Bakau ☎495384, ✉europrop@qanet.gm. Conveniently located in the heart of Bakau, this tourist hotel perched on Bakau's low cliffs is a little scruffy but recommended for its distinctly African atmosphere. There's a brilliant pool bar, a very reasonable restaurant with great Atlantic views and a man-made terraced beach. Accommodation with fans in roundhouses, crammed tightly into a leafy compound, and blocks, some with sea views. ❸

Cape Point Hotel Kofi Annan St, Cape Point ☎495005, ✉capepointhotel@qanet.gm. A little faded, this tourist hotel is close to Cape Point's good beaches; there's also a tiny pool. Rooms vary in size; some have a/c, and all 35 are spotless. ❹

Friendship Hotel Off Stadium Rd, Bakau ☎495830. Good-value choice, designed for sports teams, students and conference delegates, the four-storey blocks here have an institutional feel. It's definitely not a tourist hotel, and lies some distance from the sea and from Bakau and Fajara's bars and restaurants. However, the self-contained rooms are comfortable and clean, with hot water and TV; there's also a good-sized swimming pool plus a dining hall. ❷

Jabo Guest House 9 Old Cape Rd, Bakau ☎494906, ✇www.jabo-enterprises.com. A down-to-earth, reasonably priced place which feels more like a family compound than a guesthouse, with six simple, self-contained rooms with fridge, and the use of a well-equipped kitchen. The beach at Cape Point is within walking distance. ❷

Romana Hotel Atlantic Rd, Bakau ☎495127, ☏496042. Unpromising exterior, but inside this is a good, basic, small urban hotel. The eleven rooms have fans, and the easy-going bar and restaurant are very reasonable. ❷

Smiling Coast Hotel Cape Point Rd, Cape Point ☎497653 or 494653, ✉smilingcoast28@hotmail.com. Fourteen plain rooms with basic self-catering facilities and either fans or a/c, in a two-storey house. Guests can use the small pool at the *Cape Point Hotel* down the road. ❸

Sunbeach Hotel and Resort Kofi Annan St, Cape Point ☎497190, ✇www.sunbeachhotel.com. One of the better tourist hotels, recently refurbished, and a good choice for young families, offering an excellent pool and play area, with sack races, treasure hunts and other games. For bigger kids there's table tennis, beach volleyball, swimming pool games, and nightly discos and live music. The restaurant serves safe European choices; the rooms, though not huge, are comfortably furnished, with a/c and satellite TV. It's a large hotel, with nearly two hundred rooms, but the whole site blends with its surroundings – one of the best beaches in the resort area, a picturesque curve of fine white sand with thatched umbrella shades. ❽

Fajara and Kairaba Avenue

Fajara is a quiet, relatively affluent residential neighbourhood at the north end of **Kairaba Avenue**. Many of The Gambia's best restaurants are found here, and the accommodation options are often excellent value, with a measure of character and style that's all too often lacking in the other resorts.

Croc John's Off Atlantic Rd ☎496068. Clean, good-sized self-catering apartments in a compound that feels homely, secure and un-touristy; it is popular with volunteers and long-term visitors

as well as independent travellers who don't need the facilities of a tourist hotel. The apartments have fans and good beds with mosquito nets. Located in a quiet residential district, with a charming courtyard garden with plenty of places to relax, and you can use the nearby *Safari Garden Hotel* pool if you eat there. ➍

Fajara Golf Apartments Off Kairaba Ave, Fajara ℡ & ℻495800. In a pair of compounds made bright and colourful by the work of a local artist, these eight self-catering apartments are spotless, spacious and very well equipped, with useful extras like CD and cassette players and free mountain-bike hire. Not the closest accommodation to the golf course, and not just for golfers, but caddies and/or tuition can be organized. Recommended. ➍

Fajara Guest House Signposted off Kairaba Ave, near the Fajara Club ℡496122, ℻494365. A peaceful haven with eight small, simple, clean rooms with fans and mosquito screens, around a bright white-pillared courtyard that looks faintly Greek. More rooms, a roof terrace and restaurant are under construction. ➌

Fajara Paradise Villas Off Atlantic Rd ℡494725, ✉fajaraparadise@qanet.gm. Upmarket block of fourteen self-catering apartments, superbly located with gorgeous ocean views and a small pool. ➑

Francisco's Atlantic Rd ℡495332. A clutch of eleven tatty but clean rooms with fan, a/c, fridge and TV, in a small but gorgeous, very African, tropical garden setting, with a popular restaurant. There's no pool, but Fajara beach at *Leybato's* is five minutes' walk away, and you can use the pool at the nearby *Safari Garden Hotel* if you eat there. ➎

Hotel Fajara Atlantic Rd ℡494576, ℻494575. Designed on a grand scale, but showing signs of neglect, this tourist hotel fails to capitalize on its spectacular oceanside location. The pool, surrounded by concrete, has a view of the sea through wire fences beyond dusty tennis courts. Some rooms have a/c and self-catering facilities, but all need redecorating. The reception area and bar, with leatherette sofas, is a good place to watch CNN on TV, but the restaurants are overpriced and lack atmosphere. ➏

Leybato Guest House Off Atlantic Rd ℡497186, ℻497562. Known and loved for its beach bar and hammocks, *Leybato's* has a few basic guest rooms – good if you want to be on the beach, but there are better-value places elsewhere. ➌

Ngala Lodge 64 Atlantic Rd ℡494045 or 497429, ✉info@ngalalodge.com. A former ambassador's residence in a tranquil clifftop garden with towering palms, converted into a hotel with six luxurious suites. There's a small swimming pool and a superb restaurant; the suites and outdoor areas are decorated with quirky pieces of scrapyard art. Likely to appeal to anyone with a sense of the unusual, looking for somewhere secluded and serene, this is expensive but worth it. Bookings through The Gambia Experience only (see p.11). ➑

Safari Garden Hotel Off Atlantic Rd, near the Fajara Club ℡495887, ☺www.safarigarden.com. Very good-value and thoroughly recommended independent hotel. There are a dozen simple rooms around a colourful garden courtyard, a small but excellent pool, a good restaurant and extremely friendly staff. Pleasantly situated in a quiet neighbourhood of sandy residential streets, the warm atmosphere attracts discerning independent travellers, plus volunteers and other expats. The beach, and some of Fajara's best restaurants, are within walking distance. The owners are committed to sustainable tourism, and are developing a new eco-lodge in Kartong. ➍

Sermaho Residence Off Kairaba Ave ℡397786, ☺www.sermahoresidence.com. Small enough to feel exclusive, this reasonably priced self-catering hotel on a quiet sandy backstreet a taxi ride from the beach has six European-style mini-apartments, with good bathrooms and fans or a/c. There's a restaurant and an attractive garden courtyard. ➍

Kotu

In the high season, everything about **Kotu** feels crowded – the hotels, the craft market and supermarkets are often swarming with customers. However, it's a fun place to be if you're into the gregarious package-holiday scene, and there are some very good birdwatching sites within walking distance. The accommodation options are all medium or large tourist hotels owned or backed by major tour operators, either on, or very close to, Kotu Strand, a decent stretch of beach; while most have a low-rent feel, they're not cheap.

Badala Park Hotel Kotu Stream Rd ℡460400, ℻460402 Popular with young independent travellers and birdwatchers, this is one of the cheapest hotels offered by the package tour companies.

Many Gambians are customers, so the atmosphere is distinctively African. Set in gardens so dense with trees and shrubs that insects can be a nuisance, some of the two hundred rooms are shabbily furnished – the ones furthest from reception are quieter. A pleasant beach is a short walk away. ④

Bakotu Hotel Kotu Stream Rd ☎465555, ⓕ465959. An attractive but rather cramped tourist hotel, a couple of minutes from the beach. The main compound has a small swimming pool and 88 characterful rooms with fans in blocks or octagonal buildings; the best are upstairs, away from the road and with a balcony. The hotel also has eight small self-catering apartments – they're a little tired, but have private balconies with fabulous views over Kotu Stream: excellent for bird- and monkey-watching. Rooms ⑥, apartments ⑦

Bungalow Beach Hotel Kotu Stream Rd ☎465288, ⓔbbhotel@qanet.gm. Self-catering tourist hotel with friendly staff and a loyal clientele, mostly of retired Europeans and young families. The 110 mini-apartments in white-painted blocks are well equipped, with optional a/c, but they're a little small; better-value options exist elsewhere. The pool is nothing special, but the site is right on a reasonable beach. There's a restaurant and plenty of other facilities, including a hair salon and Internet café. ⑦–⑧

Kombo Beach Hotel Kotu Stream Rd ☎465466, ⓔinfo@kombobeach.gm. Popular with young European package tourists, this is a lively hotel with plenty of activities, set on a reasonable stretch of beach. The atmosphere is mass-market, with block after block of rooms – 250 in all – designed to a familiar international formula; huge crowds congregate in the bar to watch football on satellite TV. ⑦

Palm Beach Hotel Kotu Stream Rd ☎462111, ⓕ460402 (c/o *Badala Park Hotel*). Sister hotel to the *Badala Park*, and with a similar atmosphere (much more Gambian than the other places in Kotu), but more upmarket. The accommodation – 120 rooms with TV and a/c – is in two-storey villas in jungly gardens. The pool area feels very tropical, and is close to the pleasant beach. ⑥

Sunset Beach Hotel Kotu Stream Rd ☎496397 or 463876, ⓦwww.sunsetbeachhotel.gm. Newly refurbished tourist hotel in a good location on a well-kept stretch of beach that's relatively secluded for Kotu, adjacent to Kotu stream. There are a good pool and two restaurants, one with a rooftop terrace; the food is excellent. Most of the 108 rooms are in utilitarian bungalows in regimented rows, but the place is clean and well furnished. ⑥

Kololi: Palma Rima area

The huge *Palma Rima* resort hotel dominates this area. Since the other accommodation options are limited, the attractive stretch of beach here is rarely overcrowded, and an added bonus is the *Farida's Arcade* (see p.123), a collection of original and excellent dining and drinking places.

Bakadaji Hotel Bertil Harding Highway ☎462307. Basic but pleasant and tranquil Gambian-owned place, with simple self-contained rooms with fans in large scruffy gardens that tend to attract mosquitoes, a few minutes' walk from the beach. ③

Bunkoyo Hotel Bertil Harding Highway ☎463199, ⓕ463199. Small highway hotel that receives mixed reports for standards and service; no restaurant. ④

Luigi's Apartments Palma Rima Rd ☎460280, ⓔluigis@qanet.gm. Well-furnished rooms with self-catering facilities and access to a pretty garden with an open-air jacuzzi, 50m from the beach. ⑤

Palma Rima Hotel Bertil Harding Highway ☎463380 or 463381, ⓕ463382. A brash, mega-touristy resort hotel, famous for its huge swimming pool, this is one of the few places that still offer an all-inclusive option. The 152 rooms are in grounds shaded with palms a short distance back from the beach. The packed entertainment programme includes karaoke, water polo and aerobics, an open-air theatre for show nights, a choice of restaurants and bars (some guests never venture out, preferring to get rowdy here) and the *Moon Light Disco*, a tame but busy club cranking out Europop every night. ⑥

Kololi: Senegambia area

With a hint of Vegas, Benidorm and Blackpool, all with a rather ramshackle Gambian accent, the **Senegambia area** is the country's ultimate tourist strip. It's a mixed bag: once you've made it through the crowds of hustlers and hedonists you'll find yourself at two of the country's best-established and most dignified tourist hotels, the *Kairaba* and the *Senegambia*. Unfortunately, the beach here is completely ruined by tidal erosion; you can still swim at low tide but most tourists stick to the hotel pools.

Banna Beach ☎461217 or 461255, ☎461277. An unglamorous, hundred-room tourist hotel, close to the beach just north of the Senegambia area. ❸

Holiday Beach Club ☎460419, ✉amatagae@hotmail.com. Right on the beach, and a little cramped, but relaxed and down-to-earth with a decent pool and reasonable rates for its simple rooms with fans. Not highly regarded for its food. ❹

Kairaba Hotel ☎462940, ⓦwww.kairabahotel.com. The Gambia's top large hotel – and prime honeymoon territory – with wide-ranging facilities including a choice of good restaurants. Pleasant rooms, 140 in all, with direct dial phones, excellent bathrooms, safes, TV – the lot. Loyal customers return again and again. The once-splendid beach is now practically non existent, but the pool and grounds are good compensation. ❽

Kololi Beach Club ☎464897, ⓦwww.kololi.com. Started life as a timeshare, but now operates as an expensive hotel, with accommodation in self-catering villas in well-tended grounds, including a small golf course, and a pleasant pool edged by low palms. ❽

Paradise Suites Hotel ☎463429, ☎463415. North of the main Senegambia area, and set in small but beautifully planted gardens, this self-catering accommodation is comfortable and well furnished, with attractive options from small apartments to large villas. ❹–❺

Senegambia Beach Hotel ☎462717, ⓦwww.senegambiahotel.com. Gigantic tourist hotel, recommended for its good service and impressive tropical gardens – great for birdwatching, but dusty between February and the rains. The 320 rooms, with either a/c or fans, are cool and clean; some are newly furnished but others are rather tired. The standard rooms in the garden blocks are quieter than the de luxe rooms in the main building. Like the *Kairaba*, it's suffered from the devastation of the beach. ❽

Tafbel Hotel ☎460510, ✉tafbel@qanet.gm. Unpretentious tourist hotel, with a good pool in an attractive central courtyard. A reasonable choice, but the 98 rooms (with optional a/c) are pretty basic, with uncomfortable beds; unless you fly in on a special offer, there are better value places elsewhere. ❺

Kololi Village and Manjai Kunda

Despite being part of the resort area, **Kololi Village** really does feel like a village, and it's a good place for budget accommodation if you don't mind forgoing a few creature comforts. Neighbouring **Manjai Kunda** is a gritty but generally relaxed suburb of Serrekunda with a couple of mid-range hotels that have a more African atmosphere than most beach hotels. All the options here are 1–2km from the beach.

Balmoral Apartments Kololi Village ☎461079 (UK ☎01556/650296), ⓦwww.balmoral-apartments.com. Apartment block with a small garden, a short walk from the *Senegambia Hotel* area. Good standard rooms with adequately equipped kitchen diners, popular with long-stay guests. ❹

Europa Apartments Kololi Village ☎460479, ✉europa@gamtel.gm. Attractive, friendly and reasonably priced, eight self-catering apartments in a compound with a small swimming pool and bar. ❸

Holiday Suites Manjai Kunda ☎461075, ☎461077. Comfortable a/c suites with satellite TV, not particularly geared to tourists but often used by business people on longer stays. ❻

Kaira-Du-La Lodge Kololi Village ☎460529, ✉kaira.du.la@qanet.gm. Smartly equipped self-catering apartments in roundhouses set in a small, well-kept garden; each has a living room and a

small patio. ❸

Keneba Hotel Kololi Village ☎460093. Very basic budget rooms in a small village compound. ❷

Kololi Inn Tavern Kololi Village ☎463410, ☎460484. Budget option that's shabby round the edges but still a good place to unwind in cool, African surroundings. There are seven rooms in a block and six in simple roundhouses; the garden compound has a bar and barbecue. ❷

Mannjai Lodge Manjai Kunda ☎463414 or 463417, ✉manlodge@gamtel.gm. Attractive hotel about 1.5km from Kotu beach, with 53 plain but neatly furnished rooms arranged around a courtyard with a thatched bar area and small swimming pool. The place has a local feel, and sometimes hosts live music sessions at weekends, hugely popular with a smart Gambian crowd. ❹

Orchard Guest House Kololi Village ☎460399 (ask for Alex) or ☎902649. A few simple rooms

with basic self-catering facilities in a leafy village compound. ②
Soto Baa Koto Kololi Village ☎460399, ℮renate-thomas@web.de. Budget accommodation in shabby but appealing thatched roundhouses with a

shared cooking area, in a dusty, shady garden. You'll need your own mosquito net. The excellent and inexpensive two-storey bamboo-and-thatch *bantaba* bar/restaurant is worth visiting even if you're staying elsewhere. ②

South Kololi and Bijilo

South Kololi and **Bijilo** still have something of a frontier feel; accommodation options, though very good, are limited for now, but new tourist developments are likely to fill in the gaps soon, particularly along Bijilo beach. Kerr Serign, the southern fringe of Kololi village, is a quiet neighbourhood set back from the coastal highway, 1km from the beach.

Bijilo Beach Hotel Bertil Harding Highway, Bijilo ☎426706, ℮bijilobeach@airtip.gm. A new tourist hotel with ten mini-apartments and ten double rooms with optional a/c, all small but bright and finished to a high standard, European-style. The roof terrace of the restaurant block has fabulous views over gardens sloping down to the Atlantic. The pool is open to non-resident customers of the restaurant and bar. ④–⑤

Boucarabou Hotel Kerr Serign Njaga, midway between Kololi Village and Bijilo ☎463363, ℮ovl.caputh@t-online.de. An innovative hotel offering simple accommodation, with twin rooms with fans and large, clean shared washrooms, in a delightful environment of gardens, orchards and vegetable plots. The location is a quiet residential neighbourhood, where you'll be woken in the morning by beautiful music from the local mosque. Horses are stabled on site, and dogs, cats and chickens complete the menagerie. The hotel also

sets up music and dancing lessons and sessions. ④

Coconut Residence Bertil Harding Highway, Kerr Serign ☎463377, ℮coconut@qanet.gm. A truly luxurious hotel, with 36 dreamily decorated suites: some have four-poster beds, all have huge bathrooms. There are two swimming pools in the main part of the hotel, surrounded by a lush garden full of mature trees. For total seclusion there are two villas with private pools tucked away in gardens behind the main buildings. The reception areas are a mishmash of African and Asian colonial styles; the atmosphere is suave, and the restaurant is one of the best in the country. Hardly the "real" Gambia, but a very appealing place to indulge. ⑧

Mango Club Kerr Serign. ☎940290, ℮mangoclub@hotmail.com. A newly opened, Belgian-run boutique hotel, with beautifully furnished mini-apartments, and a pool and bar in a small attractive courtyard. ⑥

Serrekunda and Sukuta

Serrekunda's budget accommodation options feel as close to real-life urban Africa as you can get in this corner of the country. The more central places are noisy day and night, but there are also a few appealingly simple options a little way out of the thick of things in Kanifing and Latrikunda, residential neighbourhoods that see few tourists. Like Bakau, the quieter areas of town are good places to look for lodgings with Gambian families. **Sukuta** is a suburb that merges with Serrekunda's southern fringes and has The Gambia's only commercial campsite.

Adiyata Guest House Well signposted off Kairaba Ave, Latrikunda ☎395510, mobile ☎925537. An excellent choice if you want to experience a villagey neighbourhood of Serrekunda, away from the bustle of Kairaba Ave. Simple rooms with large beds, nets and fans in six characterful roundhouses around a small courtyard planted with trees and shrubs; there's also a very reasonably priced outdoor bar/restaurant. ②

Camping Sukuta Bijilo Rd, Sukuta ☎917786, ℮wwwcampingsukuta.de. Well signposted from

Bertil Harding Highway and from Serrekunda, this camping site and lodge is very popular with European overlanders. There's plenty of shade to park and camp, accommodation in simple huts, and good shared kitchen and washing facilities. If you've crossed the Sahara by vehicle and are thinking of selling up and flying off, this is a good place to be put in touch with potential buyers. The much-travelled owners are also a prime source of information on overland routes and travel issues. ①

Douniya Motel Serrekunda ☎370741 A large,

barrack-like urban compound with around twenty simple rooms in long blocks, some with a/c. ❷
Green Line Motel Sayerr Jobe Ave, Serrekunda ☎394015, ⓕ393888. Right in the heart of town, opposite the cinema. You enter through a grimy restaurant into a dim reception area, but upstairs the motel is surprisingly bright, clean and decent-looking, given that the rooms (self-contained, with fans) can be rented by the hour. ❷
Praia Motel 3 Mam Youth St, Serrekunda ☎394887. A modest but comfortable Gambian-owned place in a quiet backstreet of Serrekunda

with secure parking. There are twelve self-contained rooms with TV and either fans or a/c, and a bar and restaurant. ❷
YMCA Off Kairaba Ave, Kanifing ☎392647, ⓦwww.ymca.gm. Adequate and well-managed hostel accommodation with 34 single and double rooms with fans, and either private or shared bathrooms. Features a basketball court, table tennis tables and an inexpensive restaurant (daily 9am–midnight), plus a computer centre next door. ❶–❷

Bakau and Fajara

Brimming with life, its population doubling every decade or so, **BAKAU** is an overgrown village that's part shantytown, part desirable suburb and part coastal resort. Spread over the northernmost point of the northern Kombos, twelve kilometres from Banjul, Bakau includes busy, noisy Bakau Old Town, the salubrious Cape Point area, the leafy streets of Bakau New Town, and the elegant oceanside properties of Atlantic Road, which continues into **FAJARA**, home to politicians and prominent businessmen, plus diplomats and other well-off expatriates.

This is a part of the resort area where you can stay in comfort in either a package tourist hotel or a small independent hotel, but feel part of a vibrant mixed local community at the same time. You could also stay in a simple urban guesthouse or a family compound, and possibly take some West African music lessons. Although some visitors to Bakau and Fajara look no further than the craft stalls, restaurants and supermarkets, the residents are well used to tourists, and the residential streets are conducive to pottering about on foot or bicycle. While Fajara is generally pretty dignified, Bakau is livelier and you'll encounter some persistent bumsters; however, the general hassle is mild compared with the nearby resorts of Kotu and Kololi.

Bakau Old Town

For visitors, **Bakau Old Town**'s focal points are the areas around the junction of **Atlantic Road and Sait Matty Road**, with its banks, post and telephone offices, supermarkets and *bitikos*, and the tourist-oriented *bengdula*, or **craft market**, of Atlantic Road. Take a step or two off the main road here and you're immediately in urban Africa. Near the batik stalls and drum-makers of the *bengdula*, and almost directly behind the stalls selling well-scrubbed imported fruit and vegetables to tourists and expats, is Bakau's **village market**, where flies buzz between rickety stalls stacked with pyramids of knobbly local tomatoes and chillies, hung with bags of rice, couscous and powdered spices, and piled with whatever fruit is in season. Butchers chop up steaks and offal with cleavers in a blur of flies, and fishermen's wives sell buckets of greasy-yellow bonga fish, fresh from Bakau's busy fishing beach.

The **residential quarter** is a tight jumble of sandy lanes, urban compounds and small neighbourhood mosques just inland from the moorings and smoke-houses of the fishing beach. It was originally settled by ocean-going fishermen and their families; more recently, as tourism has taken over from fishing, there's been an influx of hotel and restaurant workers, guides and drivers. The neighbourhood, with its cement block houses, battered corrugated iron fences and reeking drainage ditches, is desperately overcrowded; however, there's little enough traffic here to make it far easier to explore on foot than similar areas in Serrekunda. Bakau Old Town's backstreets also have a few good local chop houses, simple places serving the big plates of Gambian food that are hard to find in some of the resort areas.

For **shopping** in Bakau Old Town, the Atlantic Road *bengdula* is a good one, where you can watch craftsmen at work under the trees by the roadside. Also along Atlantic Road, there are a number of tourist-oriented clothing shops selling West African-style dresses, trousers and skirts, and stalls selling batik hangings. For more batik and tie-dye, visit the brilliant workshop, *Gena Bes* (T 495068), near the old Katchikally Cinema in Bakau. Batiks and crafts are reasonably priced, and you can see the whole process in action, or even join a one-day workshop. Opposite the market in Atlantic Road, the highly recommended *African Heritage Gallery* has crafts and curios from all over West Africa, including ritual masks, small bronzes once used as weights for measuring commodities, and traditional wooden stools.

Katchikali Crocodile Pool

You'd be forgiven for doing a double-take when Bakau's bumsters ask you if you're "looking for Charlie". Charlie is, in fact, a wild but placid crocodile, and something of a local celebrity, generally found playing host to an adoring public at the **sacred crocodile pool** of Katchikali (also spelt Katchikally) on the south side of the Old Town. The pool is a low-key, innocuous tourist trap, often featuring on group guided tours of the Banjul area.

On foot, you can get to the pool in ten minutes from either Atlantic Road or from Sait Matty Road. The most direct route is the path leading almost straight to it from the junction of Atlantic Road and Old Cape Road, near the craft market; alternatively take the road leading off Sait Matty Road at the Norway and Sweden Consulate and turn right at the large tree after about 300m. Once you're away from the main roads it's easy to get lost in Bakau's maze of alleyways, so if you don't already have a guide, ask one of the local kids to show you the way to the crocodiles (*bambo* in Mandinka). On arrival at the site, visitors are asked for a standard donation of D15; the Bojang family, the pool guardians, are forbidden by family lore from exploiting the place for financial gain, lest it lose its sacredness, but feel justified in asking for money for "expenses".

The pool at Katchikali, like The Gambia's other sacred crocodile pools (see box on p.112), is traditionally considered a magical place, where bathing in the water can cure infertility and generally bestow good fortune. Sacred **rituals** are still occasionally held here; if your visit coincides with one, the atmosphere will be highly charged, with accompanying drumming and dancing. Most of the time, however, the only visitors are tourists.

Past the site entrance, you approach the pool itself by way of a path flanked by mature trees frequented by birds and monkeys. You're unlikely to see much of the sacred water, choked as it is by a dense covering of water lettuce (a type of floating arum lily), but you'll almost certainly see at least a dozen of the hundred or so crocodiles said to inhabit the area. None of them are particularly big – all but the most mature are under two metres long – and they look singularly docile, either lurking in the water or lounging on the bank. No one fears these crocs unduly – you can approach quite close even when they're out of the water, but the only one you should get within striking range of is

Sacred crocodile pools

The **crocodile** is a recurring image in traditional Gambian iconography. A single grinning crocodile features on the one-dalasi coin; the watermark on all Gambian banknotes is a crocodile's head, and stylized crocodiles are worked into the designs of textiles and jewellery. Believed by some to have supernatural powers, crocodiles appear in many Gambian folk tales, including Mandinka stories of the crocodile in the moon – the Gambian counterpart to the Western man in the moon. Gambian tradition reveres the crocodile as an intermediary between the living and the dead, communicating with human ancestral spirits; for example, the Bojang family of Katchikali claim that whenever Charlie the crocodile leaves the Katchikali pool and makes his way to their family compound, he has a message from their forebears.

Crocodiles are particularly associated with **fertility**, and the sacred crocodile pools at Katchikali near Bakau (see p.111), Berending (see p.169), and Follonko near Kartong (see pp.150–151) are places of pilgrimage and prayer for childless women from The Gambia and Senegal. The pilgrims bring offerings of kola nuts, cloth and cash; half the kola nuts are thrown into the pool as a ritual sacrifice to the crocodiles and everything else is shared among the elders of the families that guard the pools. Pilgrims undergo a ritual bathing in sacred water brought to them by the women of the pool-keepers' clan. They are then counselled in piety and fidelity by the elders, and given more water to take away and apply to their bodies morning and night. Fertility rituals are open to foreign visitors with a genuine wish to take part. The crocodile pools are also visited by those with other special requests, such as wrestlers hoping to win a championship, or businessmen trying to secure a new contract, and even leading Gambian politicians during election times.

Charlie and his co-residents at Katchikali are **Nile crocodiles**, The Gambia's commonest crocodile species. Preferring fresh water to salt, these reptiles are fairly widespread along the River Gambia, and in freshwater pools, where they breed. They are also sometimes found in the saltwater *bolons* and on the coast. Nile crocodiles have been known to live for over a century, and can in theory grow to a length of 7m, but in practice Gambian crocodiles have little chance of making it to such a grand size. Although they're protected under international law, they can be culled if they appear to pose a threat to human life, and it's rare to encounter one more than 2m long.

Charlie. There have been a few Charlies over the years; the current incumbent is a laid-back character who seems unperturbed by visitors patting his back and having their photo taken with him.

Despite being so close to the coast and the salt wetlands of Cape Creek, the water in the pool is fresh, with a healthy population of frogs, snacked on by the crocodiles between meals of bonga fish, Bakau's speciality, provided by the Bojangs. The water level is low, however, and, every few seasons, the Bojangs call a working party together to dig the pool a little deeper, and sometimes to introduce new crocodiles. The croc population is highest in the rainy season, when they breed here.

Cape Point and the Botanical Garden

North of the Old Town is **Cape Point**, and this area, also known as Cape St Mary, is a secluded part of town with a quiet, cul-de-sac atmosphere, home to diplomats, businessmen and United Nations employees. At its heart is a tourist village, with a supermarket, a couple of restaurants, a recently refurbished *bengdula*, an exchange bureau with terrible rates and a row of fruit stalls with identical stock. This is one of the tidiest of the resort areas, and the beach here is clean and pleasant, too, though another victim of severe natural erosion. Cape Point marks the southwestern limit of the River Gambia where it meets the Atlantic, and the pale sands on the river side are caught by peculiar cross-currents, with waves lapping diagonally against the timber groynes. Round the point on the Atlantic side is the start of Bakau's softly crumbling russet laterite cliffs; the beach here is only accessible at low tide, and is swept clean by the ocean every high tide.

Between Atlantic Road and Cape Point is Bakau's **Botanical Garden** (closed Sun, D5), a small and rather beautiful, though neglected, hideaway just off the main road, near the clifftop. It's naturally greenest and most impressive after the rains – by the middle of the dry season everything is rather dusty. Particularly noteworthy are the fairy-tale teak tree and the prehistoric cycads. Few of the trees and shrubs are local and many need serious attention, so don't come here with high expectations. Even so, it's a pleasant place to relax, and you will see plenty of garden birds, such as bulbuls, red-cheeked cordon bleu, bronze mannikins and Senegal firefinches.

Bakau New Town

Bakau New Town is a residential area shaded by mature trees that burst gloriously into flower in the rainy season. Its main thoroughfare, Garba Jahumpa Road (more commonly known by its old name, New Town Road) runs between Kairaba Avenue and Sait Matty Road and has a few shops, offices and workshops, plus some vicious speed bumps. Bakau New Town is overshadowed by the **Independence Stadium**, The Gambia's principal sports venue, a large open arena surrounded by steeply banked seating. The whole district reverberates whenever there's a major sporting fixture or a live music event – big names from the Senegambian music scene sometimes play here to sell-out crowds.

Fajara

There are no formal boundaries between **FAJARA** and Bakau, along the coast to the northeast. Even so, Fajara has a distinctive atmosphere, with quiet sandy streets of elegant villas, semi-hidden behind high fences and flower-draped walls. It's first and foremost a residential district, with just a few shops, hotels and restaurants, but among these are some of the finest places in the country.

Birdwatching around Bakau

While Bakau's gardens, cliffs and beaches play host to a great variety of bird species, the most interesting areas for birdwatchers are around Cape Creek, which is crossed by Old Cape Road southeast of town, and Sting Corner, at the junction of Sait Matty Road and the Banjul– Serrekunda highway. Old Cape Road is a pleasant place to walk at any time of day, passing a lightly wooded area of oil palms, rhun palms, baobabs and tamarisk. Cape Creek is flanked by mudflats and mangroves; this area yields sightings of red-cheeked bee-eaters, various rollers, starlings, swallows and parakeets, plus, on the mudflats, plovers and thick-knees. In the creek you may see fish-eating birds such as pied kingfishers, reef herons, long-tailed shags and ospreys. On the way from Bakau to Sting Corner along Sait Matty Road you pass the vegetable plots worked by Bakau's women's cooperatives and, particularly in the rice season, this is a good area to see lily-trotters, squacco herons and cattle egrets.

At low tide, it's possible to walk between the major resorts at the water's edge; even in the ten-kilometre stretch of beach between Cape Point and Bijilo there's considerable variation in the landscape along the way. Probably the most pleasant beaches in the resort area are at **Cape Point**. Clean, quiet and with soft white palm-shaded sand, it's a miracle that these have survived the ravages of coastal erosion, though they used to be much broader. In the wake of the erosion, there's little beach development here, so the area is reasonably unspoilt, and the newly refurbished *SunBeach Hotel* and *Resort* (see p.105) has done its best to landscape its part of the beach attractively with loungers and thatched umbrellas under the palms. Unfortunately, cross-cutting tidal and river currents make the water here unsafe for swimming.

It's possible to swim at **Bakau**, round the point to the southwest, but this is principally a working beach. Fishing *pirogues* land at the jetty near the local marketplace to haul out the catch (mostly *bonga*), some of which is destined for the market, while some is taken straight to the smokehouses on the shore. It's a colourful scene, although the combined smell of woodsmoke and drying *bonga* can be overpowering.

Fajara's beaches, down the coast from Bakau, are dramatically located at the foot of russet-coloured laterite cliffs, strewn with tide-washed rocks. The view of the broad sweep of the Atlantic ocean from the cliffs is spectacular, making this one of the best places in the country to enjoy the sunset, or the rainy season's dramatic electrical storms. There are a few hotels on clifftop plots, but most of the plots are privately owned, so access to the beach here is limited; in any case, it's not recommended near high tide, when the few chunks of sand that are not swallowed by the sea may be cut off. The currents and undertow here are treacherous at certain times of year, and the rocky area near *Leybato's*, at the Kotu end of the Fajara beaches, is one of the more dangerous places to swim. Every year several swimmers drown in the Fajara and Kotu area, and there's now a privately funded lifeguard scheme, Beachwatch – it's wise to pay heed to their warning flags.

Southwest of Fajara, the landscape flattens out and the beach becomes an open curve backed by Kotu, Kololi and Bijilo's tourist strip, plus some endangered scraps of coastal forest. You can reach **Kotu Strand** either from Kotu's main drag (Kotu Stream Road), or from the steps which lead from the end of Atlantic Road, Fajara, down past the Fajara craft market to the beach below. This area is hugely popular with young Gambians who come here in droves at the end of the afternoon and at weekends for picnics, impromptu football matches and drumming sessions. It's definitely the most touristy of all the beaches, with hotels backing onto the sands and plenty of beach bars, fruit stalls and juice-pressers' stands. The **fruit stalls** are an innovation – fruit sellers used to wander the beaches with trays of fruit on their heads, touting for custom. Now that they've been allocated regulated stalls, they report an upturn in business – even though customers are faced with a row of stalls all selling exactly the same stuff. The juice-pressers are similarly regulated, and have price lists; they provide a brilliant service in a country where very few conventional bars serve fresh juice, though watch out for how much sugar and water the presser adds to your glass. Most of the Kotu beach hotels and beach bars offer free sun loungers, and some hire out watersports equipment such as bodyboards and windsurfers.

The beach at **Kololi** has, unfortunately, been wrecked by erosion, suffering more apparent damage than elsewhere on this stretch of coast. Beyond here, **Bijilo** beach, presently on the very fringe of the resort area, has suffered from the decimation of its palm trees and from sandmining crews raiding the beach to supply the construction industry. Further south, the beaches are emptier and more attractive, with fishing centres punctuating the broad empty stretches of sand (see box on p.144). It's possible to walk or cycle along the beach all the way from Bijilo to Kartong in the far south of the country, a glorious way to appreciate the ocean scenery. The further south you go, the quieter it is and the fewer bumsters you'll encounter (see p.57).

Beach bars are a colourful part of the Gambian beach scene, and some visitors spend their whole stay moving happily from one to the next, or even just setting up camp at one. They cultivate a laid-back alternative to the inland tourist restaurants and bars, with reggae on the sound system and local live music from time to time; many serve excellent **fresh food**, notably prawns, grills and fish baked in foil. Gambian beaches are simply too hot to lie out for long periods, so beach bars provide a shady haven, with grass-thatched umbrellas and canopies woven from palm fronds. You have to allow time to enjoy the experience, as food tends to be prepared to order (sometimes even the shopping is done to order). Opening times can be unpredictable, although some stay open at night and during the rainy season.

The Kombos beach bar scene has gone through some **major changes** over the last few years. Some places have been literally swept away by coastal erosion, their remains scattered in the Atlantic. Others were closed down in a massive "clean sweep" campaign by the government-run Gambia Tourism Authority in 2000; the government associated the bars with with bumsters and drugs, and, even worse, they weren't paying their taxes, so in went the bulldozers. Allegedly, hoteliers also had a hand in the campaign, to eliminate competition. It's taken a few years for the beaches to recover from these closures, but new places are now at last opening.

Coastal erosion

Coastal erosion is a big problem all along the West African coast. Its **causes** are complex and little understood; cyclical changes in tidal patterns and ocean currents seem to play a part, but industrial-scale mining of sand from Bijilo and Kartong beaches (now outlawed) has exacerbated the situation. Ironically, massive construction projects like Banjul International Airport, built in the late-1990s and intended to raise The Gambia's profile as a world-class tourist destination, have contributed to the near-destruction of some of it's greatest tourist assets. The visible consequences of erosion amount to an unfortunate character change in the beaches – in the worst-affected areas, once-broad gold or silver sands have become narrow, grubby grey-beige ones, and chunks of the soft laterite cliffs behind the sands have tumbled into the ocean. In the Cape Point area, high tides stripped the sand and washed away the beach bars, though the beach itself is still attractive. In Fajara, the climb up to *Leybato Beach Bar* gets steeper every couple of months, and during particularly high tides you may get your feet wet whilst eating at *Paradise Beach Bar* in Kotu. Kololi's beaches have been particularly badly affected, and what little visible sand remains here is completely submerged at high tide. Ill-fated attempts to counter the natural progress of the erosion have ruined the beaches outside the *Kairaba Hotel* (known, in happier times, as the *Kairaba Beach Hotel*) and the *Senegambia*. For most of a decade, these beaches have been scarred with ugly, toppling sandbags and concrete blocks, while experts puzzle over a suitable remedy.

A new phase of more **constructive action** is planned, possibly following the example of the reasonably attractive terraced beach at the *Atlantic Hotel*, Banjul, which, though narrow, is both reasonably attractive and well defended. More concerted efforts, such as creating artificial reefs or off-shore islands, would seem to be the only real way forward, but nothing has yet been done.

The beaches that have suffered least, such as those near Sanyang, Gunjur and Kartong, are south of the main tourist area and little-developed at present. It seems increasingly likely that tourist development will be mushrooming out of the northern Kombos and down the coast long before the northern beaches are restored to their former glory as a major tourist attraction. In the meantime, you have to look a little harder than before for beaches that conform to the sun-kissed ideal of broad, clean sand, sparkling ocean and graceful, over-arching palm trees.

The **Fajara War Cemetery**, on Kairaba Avenue northwest of the traffic lights, is immaculately kept by the Commonwealth War Graves Commission. During the Second World War, The Gambia, like other British colonies in West Africa, was used as a military base and a staging post for aircraft heading towards the middle east and the North African front, and ships bound for India and the near and far east via South Africa. Over two hundred casualties of the war, mostly West African, but also British, Canadian and others, are buried here, their graves laid out in neat rows under flame trees and frangipani, and there's a monument to 33 Gambians buried elsewhere.

Also in Fajara is the **Fajara Club** (☎495456, daily 8am–8pm), an old sports club that's seen better days, well known for its eighteen-hole golf course that has more dust bowls than grass in the dry season. With its main rooms a cross between an English church hall and a run-down country club, it's not an appealing prospect at first glance. But there's quite a range of facilities here: squash courts, tennis courts (lit after dark), a hall for badminton and table tennis, plus a programme of keep-fit with aerobics and yoga classes. The local Hash House Harriers have their notice board in the clubhouse (meetings on Mondays, ☎495054). Drinks and simple meals are cheap from the clubhouse bar, and the clean pool at the back has sunbeds and is popular with children. There's also a small lending library of dog-eared paperback fiction.

The **African Living Art Centre** on New Town (Garba Jahumpa) Road (☎495131) is unique in The Gambia, a lofty, light-drenched concrete-and-glass gallery space that's a work of art in itself, hung with textiles and crammed with a vibrant, eclectic collection of exhibits and merchandise: beads, statues, antiques and some of the most original and creative clothing to be found anywhere in the country. There are also paintings by the owner Suelle, some featuring his trademark *kanaga* symbol, sacred to the Dogon people of Mali. The shop is also part-library and part-café/bar, and is a great place to enjoy *attaya*, Lebanese coffee, or a cocktail.

For other **shopping** in Fajara, on the corner of Kairaba Avenue and New Town (Garba Jahumpa) Road is *Timbooktoo*, The Gambia's only good bookshop, with an excellent selection of fiction and non-fiction, including good material on and from Africa, plus local newspapers and magazines. Nearby on Kairaba Avenue (but possibly moving to the Senegambia area), Gaya sells ethnic gifts including some African masks and carvings. The restaurant at *Ngala Lodge*, Atlantic Road, doubles as a gallery space, with good quality interesting and original contemporary art for sale. Fajara's *bengdula* on the beach, close to Kotu Strand, sells the usual assortment of batiks, wood carvings, musical instruments and jewellery.

Kotu and Kololi

The neighbouring coastal communities of **Kotu** and **Kololi** constitute the epicentre of The Gambia's extremely localized tourist industry. Most of the package tourists, and a good number of independent travellers, choose accommodation here, and if you fly over the area on your way in to Banjul International Airport, you'll see a generous scattering of hotel swimming pools dotted among the palm trees, rice fields and sandy paths. You won't, however, see many Gambian family compounds, except inland in the oldest quarter of Kololi village – tourist facilities predominate. During the four months of the off-season, when many of the hotels, bars and restaurants are closed, both Kotu and Kololi are sleepy and directionless, only stirring into life in early October when the hoteliers and restauranteurs set about their annual programme of repainting and repairs after the rains. As soon as the first peak-season visitors arrive in late October, they're transformed into busy, brash resorts once again.

Kotu

KOTU is a tourist village on the beach, with the Fajara golf course and the Kotu Stream wetland area just behind. It's an area busy with tourist taxis, bumsters and itinerant traders. Supermarkets, telecentres, Internet cafés and a *bengdula* are all within very easy walking distance of each other, and the hub of the action is pretty much right on the beach.

The tourist-trap atmosphere in Kotu may be too intense for some, but there are some excellent **bush walks** and **cycle rides** close by. The track that runs from Kotu Stream road, past the access road to the *Palm Beach Hotel*, and on towards Kololi, is a pleasant 2.5km walk. The Kotu Stream area is particularly beautiful during the rice-growing season (Aug–Nov), when the fields are emerald green. By the end of the dry season, the stream is almost dry, but at any time of year there are birds and beautiful mature palm trees to admire, and sometimes monkeys. You'll often see plastic bottles clustered round the tops of the oil palms, and palm wine tappers shinning up to collect the fermenting sap. You may also be invited to sample some (there's a palm wine "ghetto" near the Fajara golf course), but watch out for con-merchants who try to overcharge.

Kololi

Once an inconsequential coastal village, set back from the sea, **KOLOLI** has been transformed by tourism, expanding considerably and spreading right down to the beach at what are now known as the **Senegambia** and **Palma Rima** resort areas, where many major tourist hotels are found. The original settlement, Kololi Village, now houses as many tourism workers and affluent professionals as rice farmers and palm-tappers; it's also a popular hangout for young independent travellers.

The **Palma Rima area** is a small collection of hotels (the massive *Palma Rima* and a couple of others), restaurants and clubs between the coastal highway and the sea, about 1km southwest of Kotu Stream. Though inescapably touristy, it's low-key compared to the Senegambia area, 1.5km further southwest, and the beach is much better.

The **Senegambia area** – Kololi's main beach resort, named after The Gambia's largest hotel, the *Senegambia* – is the hub of tourist activity in The Gambia, with a busy, fairly tacky strip of restaurants, bars and clubs, and an assortment of tourist hotels. Nobody actually lives here; the area exists solely for tourists. It's by far the most bumster-infested area in the country, and there's an odd ghost-town feel to the place whenever the military police have made a round of arrests. The area's range of facilities makes it a convenient place to stay, but it's not particularly attractive, and you have to escape the area to discover the country's real charm. Happily, there has so far been little large-scale development, even here, but you can find some architectural oddities, such as the plastic-looking **pagoda** that houses an Asian restaurant. There's also a bank, some exchange bureaux, a Gamtel office, The Gambia Experience resort office, and a few supermarkets.

One of the Senegambia area's greatest assets is its newly constructed, up-beat **craft market**, with a good range of local crafts including quality batik clothing and homewares, jewellery and beads, handmade leather shoes (which can be made to order) and bags, and fresh produce such as honey and cakes from

Birdwatching around Kotu

The Kotu tourist hotels are within easy reach of a variety of habitats, making this an excellent base for birders. The Fajara golf course is a good place to start – here you're practically guaranteed sightings of black-headed plovers, bee-eaters, blue-bellied rollers, glossy starlings, doves and wood hoopoes. The wetlands and rice fields around Kotu Stream are frequented by many species including egrets, herons, kingfishers, waders and palm-nut vultures. Another rewarding area to explore (unappetizing though it may sound) is Kotu's sewage ponds, reached by a path on the opposite side of the road from the Badala Park Hotel. The rich pond life here attracts many bird species; you may see common greenshanks, black-winged stilts, white-faced whistling ducks, rose-ringed parakeet and various sandpipers, or even rarities like white-winged black terns, tufted ducks and red-necked phalaropes. The beaches are visited by shore birds; you will have to visit in the quiet early hours to see them in large numbers.

local women's cooperatives. The traders share an agreed code of conduct, which precludes hassling tourists for business.

Kololi Village, on the opposite side of the Bertil Harding Highway from the Senegambia area, is a quiet residential area of family compounds and sandy streets that is distinctively African, in marked contrast to the tourist area close by. There are a few cheap local-style guesthouses here, and it's popular with budget travellers and people studying music and dance; there's also a population of the kind of expats who can't afford to live in Fajara, or don't appreciate its relative rarefication. The area is well known among visitors and locals alike for the *Rasta Garden* (see p.125) one of The Gambia's favourite reggae clubs, with a dance floor and a bar in a garden courtyard, deep in the village. Kololi also has its own gallery, the *Village Gallery* (T463646, daily 10am–late; free), which displays paintings, photography and sculpture by West African artists. In a country where it's difficult to track down local art, this is an excellent exhibition space; displays change regularly, and everything is for sale. There's also a restaurant and bar.

Bijilo Forest Park

Bijilo Forest Park and Nature Trail (daily 8am–6pm; other times by arrangement; D25), sometimes known locally as the Monkey Park, is a half-square-kilometre woodland reserve near the beach at the south end of the Senegambia area, near the *Kololi Beach Club*. It's managed by the Gambian–German Forestry Project. The reserve contains one of the country's last remaining stands of striking **rhun palms**. The Gambian coastline was once bristling with these trees, but they have been decimated by builders and developers.

There are good chances of seeing red colobus and vervet **monkeys**, squirrels, large monitor lizards and a galaxy of **birds**. Trails are marked clearly, with a choice between long and short circuits of the park. Weekly tickets are available, a good idea if you're a birdwatcher lodging nearby and plan to come and go at different times of day. Unscrupulous guides encourage tourists to feed the monkeys in the park; as a result, they are extremely tame, affording great photo opportunities. However, feeding wild animals makes their behaviour unpredictable; the tamer they become, the more they damage crops.

Serrekunda

SERREKUNDA, the largest town in the country, lies just 3km inland from the resorts. Spending a little time here is an excellent way to get close to the heart of Gambian life; the centre of town gives you a strong flavour of modern, urban West Africa – a choking racket of diesel engines, with music blaring from hundreds of cassette players and radios, and streets lined with half-collapsed wooden trolleys and bricolaged stalls selling a riot of dust-covered imports. The focus of all this is the town's central lorry/taxi garage and market – though you'd be forgiven for thinking that central Serrekunda was just one big garage and market. It's a lot of fun, and reasonably safe.

If you stay in Serrekunda, you can take a taxi to the nearest beaches in ten minutes, or cycle there in twenty, and get the best of both worlds: the beach bars and restaurants on the coast, and the chop houses and local dives in Serrekunda. Staying in town doesn't necessarily mean suffering the noise and fumes of the centre – there are a few very pleasant, though simple, places in the residential quarters that will give you a real feel for daily life in this large town.

The thoroughfare that links Fajara and Serrekunda is **Kairaba Avenue**, the former Pipeline Road that, only a couple of decades ago, was a rutted track running through fields and orchards. Today, Kairaba's three-kilometre length is lined with shops, bars, restaurants and offices, and commands the highest rents in the country. It meets the Banjul–Brikama highway at Westfield junction, The Gambia's answer to Piccadilly Circus or Times Square but without the lights.

Serrekunda has few monuments or noteworthy landmarks, and one of the main reasons to spend time here, apart from just enjoying the energy of the place, is to shop. Near the **covered market** at the corner of Mosque Road and Sayerr Jobe Avenue, every inch of streetside space tends to be occupied by traders and pedestrians, and every bit of road is choked with vehicles, bikes, barrows and more pedestrians. A maze of stalls, workshops and eating places stretches from the market building right back to the bush taxi garage behind. The stalls are separated by narrow indoor alleys that all look very similar; it's a good idea to visit with a local friend or guide who can also advise you on prices. The indoor market is the kind of crammed-to-the-rafters place where you can find almost anything, from bicycle locks to flowery foam mattresses to babies' waist beads. There's also a large outdoor produce section, where women sell seasonal vegetables from stalls or enamel bowls and heaps laid out on the ground, while the market building's balconies are great for people-watching.

Beyond the market, the busy **commercial streets** make for interesting browsing, with a huge range of commodities on offer. You'll pass barber shops with hand-painted signs showing examples of the latest styles, plus furniture workshops where craftsmen make elaborately decorated bridal beds, and ironmongery shops, with strings of ladles and stacks of gleaming cooking pots, roughly cast from moulds made from hollowed-out sand. There are also shops selling brightly painted trunks made from recycled oil drums.

Close together on Sayerr Jobe Avenue are three excellent **craft** shops – Bamboo Craft Shop, Samory Bead and Craft Shop and African Art Collection – which sell antique and contemporary masks, carvings, bronzes, beads, musical instruments and textiles from all over West Africa including *bogolan* mudcloth from Mali. For **batik** and tie-dyed fabrics, Serrekunda has a famous "batik factory", Musu Kebba Drammeh's place in Dippa Kunda, signposted off Mosque Road. You can't normally watch craftspeople at work here, but there are plenty of textiles for sale, plus drums and carvings.

Serrekunda is a good place to get a taste of local – as opposed to tourist – **nightlife**, and it's home to The Gambia's most celebrated club, *Jokor* (see p.125). Serrekunda by night might seem an intimidating place to the uninitiated; like every Gambian town, it's poorly lit and, unlike the resort areas, it makes no special concessions to tourists. In reality, however, there's little to fear, particularly if you're with local friends.

The town also used to be very famous for its traditional **wrestling matches**, which still occasionally take place late on weekend afternoons in the arena on Mussa Street, near London Corner in Dippa Kunda. To get there, go west along Sayerr Jobe Avenue (if you pass a bar called *Marie's Pub* on the right you've gone too far). Entrance is cheap, and the advertised time is usually 5pm, though it may take a while for things to get going. For more on Gambian wrestling, see box on p.190.

Eating, drinking and nightlife

As tourism in the northern Kombos has expanded in recent years, so has the choice of **restaurants**, with a huge range of styles on offer, from modern European to Lebanese, from simple barbecues to elaborate Asian banquets. Unfortunately, too many restaurants in The Gambia favour quantity over quality – with enormously long menus of mediocre food. The resort area has the greatest concentration of international-style restaurants in the country – in fact, it's not all that easy to find traditional Gambian food in any of the tourist restaurants. For the real thing, you need to head for the low-key places the locals frequent in the urban centres of Bakau and Serrekunda, where you can eat your fill for next to nothing.

Go to restaurants in a relaxed mood, because you're likely to find that the service is slow, even at the so-called fast-food places. Most of the tourist places have a terrace so you can dine in the sun by day or under the stars by night, but local places may just be a few wooden benches and oilcloth-topped tables inside a hot room that doubles as the kitchen.

The **bar and club scene** here is similarly divided into two camps – tourist places and local places – although there's often a healthy overlap of clientele between the two. Many tourists get their first taste of the resort nightlife on a "Gambia by Night" tour organized by their hotel reps – a coach-driven bar crawl for a flat fee of around £10/$16, where you are driven from bar to bar, sampling a free glass of punch at each, and dancing to what ever sounds they've slapped on to celebrate your arrival. For live music, the local radio, guides and taxi drivers can be good sources of information about forthcoming events – many of which aren't widely advertised. If you're planning a full-on night out, remember that nothing really gets going before midnight here.

Bakau and Cape Point

While **Bakau** has no truly excellent restaurants, it has some great mid-range options with loads of African atmosphere, and a few friendly, intimate bars with a good crossover between tourists and locals. The **Cape Point** area is currently pretty sleepy, but is due for a renaissance with the opening of new hotels.

African Heritage 114 Atlantic Rd, Bakau. With a terrace up on the cliff above Bakau's fishing beach, the breezes here can be pungent, but it's still a quiet, pleasant place to stop, and there's a great gallery shop to browse. The café/restaurant serves an eclectic menu of good-value light meals, including African and Danish specialities and freshly squeezed lime juice. Mon–Sat 10am–6pm.

African Village Atlantic Rd, Bakau. The hotel restaurant, perched on a low cliff, has a terrace with great ocean views – a good choice for lunch – omelettes, sandwiches, kebabs – or cocktails. In the evening there's a varied à la carte menu with tarragon chicken or yellowfin tuna in caper sauce. Prices are very reasonable.

Bananas Bar & Restaurant Old Cape Rd, Bakau. A laidback, cosy place on the edge of Bakau with a European-inspired menu. The only banana-themed option is grilled ladyfish with banana and lime; otherwise the choices are standard tourist restaurant fare, including fish, grills and Gambian dishes, at average prices.

Calypso Beach Bar Off Kofi Annan St, Cape Point. Well-established restaurant on a tide-bitten beach. Despite years of erosion, the spot is still picturesque, with fishing boats pulled up under the palms and a castaway feel. The main restaurant is a brick and thatch *bantaba*; there are also private, romantic mini *bantabas* almost at the water's edge.

Lama Lama Bar and Restaurant Off Atlantic Rd, Bakau. Live music nightly at this bar with a busy local vibe. Daily 8.30am–12.30am.

Mr Bass Kofi Annan St, Cape Point. Street corner bar, on the edge of the craft market, selling beers and soft drinks at well below hotel prices.

Sait Matty Road Café Sait Matty Rd, Bakau. This bright little roadside stop with a courtyard of shells shaded by a mango tree serves drinks at rock-bottom prices, plus chicken and chips, steak sandwiches and great meat pies.

Saraba Off Newtown Rd, Bakau. Don't be put off by the unlikely exterior (it sometimes looks closed): this low-key place, tucked away in a quiet neighbourhood, seves top-notch *afra* to in-the-know locals. There are a few tables in the garden at the back where you can enjoy spicy beef and onions in sauce or grilled chicken with mouthwateringly fresh *tapalapa* from the next door bakery. Nightly 7pm–3am.

Shanghai Chinese Restaurant Cape Point Rd, Cape Point. A small, cheerful place with plenty of Chinese standards and a few more unusual choices, such as squid with spicy sauce, shrimps with pineapple, plus Gambian and international dishes. Nothing special, but decent and reasonably priced. Daily noon–midnight.

Fajara and Kairaba Avenue

Fajara and Kairaba Avenue is the classiest neighbourhood in The Gambia, with some of its most upmarket places to eat and drink. It's also possible to eat well here on a budget at imaginative "boutique" restaurants.

Alliance Franco-Gambienne Kairaba Ave. The garden bar at the back of the centre serves excellent French and Senegalese-style lunches and is very good value.

The Butcher's Shop 130 Kairaba Ave, ☎495069. Fajara's superb butchery, organic greengrocer, delicatessen, bakery and wine shop has an equally fine restaurant on the deck at the front: chic by day and romantic by night, with particularly flamboyant salads and fresh fruit juices. Mon–Sat 8am–late. Prices are above average, but offer excellent value.

The Clay Oven Near VSO and MRC, signposted off Atlantic Rd ☎496600. The Gambia's best Indian restaurant takes itself extremely seriously, and has a loyal local following. The starters can be disappointing, but the main menu includes subtle and inspired variations on familiar South Asian dishes. At the "sizzler night" on Tuesdays you can sample a whole range of specialities. Daily noon–3pm and 7pm–late.

Come Inn 17 Kairaba Ave. Popular with a mixed crowd of Gambian, German, British and Dutch regulars, this *biergarten* with an African twist is a good place to mingle with locals and expats over a drink or a meal – they do steaks, fish, pizza and German

fare. The German owner claims to serve the best draught JulBrew in the country, and it's cheaper here than at the resort bars and restaurants.

Eddie's Off Kairaba Ave (north). In a residential street in Fajara, this very small, informal grill fills the neighbourhood with smoke when there's bush-pig on the barbecue. Excellent chicken and chips; low-priced buffet on Saturday evenings.

Flavours Restaurant *Safari Garden Hotel*, Fajara ☎495887. A charming garden restaurant, with an inspired menu that gives a creative twist to contemporary dishes by including Gambian ingredients wherever possible. Global influences include Thailand (booking is recommended for the highly popular Thai buffet evenings) and England (with bangers and mash and traditional fish and chips sometimes appearing among the choices). Look out for superb special culinary events. Daily 7am–11pm.

Francisco's Atlantic Rd, corner of Kairaba Ave ☎495332. In a leafy tropical garden setting dotted with large West African wood sculptures, this restaurant has a friendly, neighbourhood feel. The menu is standard fare – grilled meat, fish, omelettes – at slightly higher than average prices.

Golden Bamboo Chinese Restaurant Off Kairaba Ave, Fajara. In a country that has no good Chinese restaurants, this is a reasonable one with a long menu of standards.

Leybato's Beach Bar Off Atlantic Rd, Fajara. Long-established beach bar, with hammocks strung over the sand. It's a great place to catch the sunset, or sample home-style African cooking. There's also a long menu of omelettes, fish and grills, including excellent seafood kebabs. Not a place to choose if you're in a hurry.

MacFadi's Kairaba Ave. This Gambian version of an American fast-food joint serves fried food – but not fast. Chicken, chips and burgers available.

Mama's Kairaba Ave (near Atlantic Rd). A reasonable mid-range choice, popular with expats for its *rosti* and its buffet nights, with occasional karaoke.

Ngala Lodge Restaurant 64 Atlantic Boulevard ☎497672. One of the finest places to eat in The Gambia. The evening ambience at this hotel restaurant is particularly seductive, with subtle live music and the sound of the ocean not far away. There's a mouthwatering modern European menu and a good wine list – high prices, but worth it.

Le Palais du Chocolat Kairaba Ave. Authentic-looking French-style café, serving probably the best coffee in The Gambia; the snacks – *croque monsieur* and hot dogs – and service are disappointing, but the pastries are good, while the gorgeously calorific cakes are well worth a splurge. Tues–Sat 8am–9pm, Sun 8am–1pm & 5–9pm.

La Parisienne Kairaba Ave. French-style pastries, ice cream, drinks and sponge cakes frosted in lurid colours; a relaxed place, but outclassed by *Le Palais du Chocolat*.

The Ritz Near Safari Garden Hotel, off Atlantic Rd, Fajara ☎924205. A friendly, casual place in a small courtyard, catering for tourists wanting a change from more formal hotel restaurants. Best-known for its steaks, with over a dozen different options at very reasonable prices. Sevice can take some time. Daily 10am–late.

Samuja Fast Food Kairaba Ave. Sunny by day, strip-lit by night, and with the radio always turned up loud, *Samuja* serves cheap and decent fish or chicken sandwiches, chicken or beef *shawarma*, and meat pies. Daily 9am–7pm, or later if busy.

Weezo's Kairaba Ave ☎496918. Casual but upmarket, well-to-do Fajara's most stylish restaurant has a mixed personality. At lunchtimes it's sleek, with a contemporary European menu, featuring imaginative salads and other light options. In the evenings it's part cocktail bar, with lounge jazz subtle in the background, part Mexican restaurant (the only one in The Gambia, and outstanding), and part gourmet restaurant. There's another total mood change when party animals drop in to dance to corny Europop in the bar, on the Sunday and Wednesday "Gambia-by-night" tour organized by tour operators. Restaurant open Tues–Sun 11.30am–3pm & 7–11pm; bar open till late. Higher than average prices.

Kotu

Kotu's cheerfully touristy image is borne out by its concentration of touristy places to eat and drink. There are also plenty of beach bars, juice bars and fruit stalls. A big new three-storey restaurant, bar and club complex is being built on the beach at the time of writing.

The Captain's Table *Bakotu Hotel*, 2 Kotu Stream Rd ☎466111. Very popular with non-residents, this is a semi-open-air restaurant, with a look that's part African, part Mediterranean. The cooking isn't quite as excellent as the menu suggests, but the fish is pretty good, the bread well chosen and the *bouillabaise* particularly famous. A better-than-average tourist restaurant, but overpriced.

Domino Bar and Restaurant Kombo Beach. West African music, roots and reggae booms out of huge speakers from this beach terrace bar/restaurant, a friendly, down-to-earth haunt of *djembé* players and beach-lizards, serving good-value, decent food including sandwiches, burgers, noodles, omelettes, chicken, fish and African dishes. Open 24 hours.

Paradise Beach Bar & Restaurant Kotu Beach. Right on the sand and a firm favourite with package tourists staying in the Kotu and Fajara areas, some of whom practically live here during their stay, this informal restaurant serves all-day English breakfasts, sizeable sandwiches and generous platefuls of burgers, omelettes, salads and Gambian dishes at reasonable prices. It has a few dozen rickety sunbeds and a motley assortment of sunshades crammed onto the sand between the restaurant and the sea. Service is slow, but this is no hardship for the sun-worshippers who choose to be served at their sunbed. Daily 9am–late; happy hour Mon–Sat 5–7pm; barbecues with live music at weekends.

Sailor Beach Bar and Restaurant Kotu Beach, next to Fajara Craft Market. One of the better beachside restaurants, but not expensive. It's particularly good for fish such as calamari in lime and garlic, or peppered barracuda steak. The menu also includes sandwiches, pizza, omelettes and pasta, plus freshly squeezed juice. Daily

10am–11.30pm; live music every evening except Thurs.

Kololi: Palma Rima area

The **Palma Rima** area is home to Farida's Arcade, an original complex of bars and restaurants designed by local artist Suelle, arranged around a fountain courtyard, roughly opposite the *Palma Rima* on Palma Rima Road. The rest of the area is quite a mixture, with a jazz club, beach bars and an English pub.

Amsterdam Dolphin Bar and Restaurant Kololi. Caters for a European crowd of tourists and expats, with international food at average prices, including *bratwurst*, goulash and a good selection of shrimp dishes. Middle-of-the-road music on the stereo; the TV comes on for British soap operas.

Calabash Palma Rima Rd ☎ 468893. Styling itself as a nightclub for grown-ups, with nightly DJ sets, *Calabash* also has special events such as "Mr Muscle" and "Miss Waistbeads" beauty pageants. Upstairs from *Jazziz*, and close to the *Palma Rima*, the crowd is a good mixture of Gambians and tourists. Tues–Sun 7pm–late.

Churchills Palma Rima Rd. Holiday-resort-style British pub, with English beer and lager, and juicy steaks and other familiar favourites. Football fans pile in when there's a match on TV.

Jazziz Palma Rima Rd ☎ 462175. Ground-floor bar/restaurant and live music venue beneath *Calabash*, with jazz, blues, afrobeat and hi-life on Fridays, and salsa and reggae on Saturdays. Recommended.

Kotu Point Beach Bar and Restaurant Kotu Point, signposted from the back of the *Palma Rima*. One of the most attractive beach bars in the resort area, on a quiet stretch of good sand with a few sunbeds and thatched shades. The restaurant has a terrace with wicker chairs where you can eat the freshest fish around for way below restaurant prices. Beer, soft drinks and palm wine are good value too. Daily 9am–late, happy hour Sun 5–7pm folowed by a barbecue with live drumming.

Luigi's Palma Rima Rd. Busy, established Italian restaurant that's popular with families. The food – pizza, pasta, risotto and jacket potatoes – is overrated, but there's plenty of choice, and big portions. The largest pizzas are gargantuan; the staff will wrap anything you can't manage. There's also a good selection of aperitifs, liqueurs and speciality coffees, and cocktails with a corny beach theme. Daily noon–4pm and 6–11.30pm.

Mirroz Classic Farida's Arcade, Palma Rima Rd. The closest The Gambia gets to a *Cheers*-style bar, this place has three pool tables, a good selection of spirits, a friendly atmosphere, and a loyal expat following.

Mirroz Fooood Farida's Arcade, Palma Rima Rd. Fish and chips with mushy peas, burgers and the like, in a small, super-colourful café with abstract jungle murals and fish paintings. Daily 7pm–3am.

Mirroz Jungle Farida's Arcade, Palma Rima Rd. Gorgeous masks and spears adorn this sleek little bar; good cocktails, plus lager on draught.

Solomon's On the beach at the end of Palma Rima Rd ☎ 460716. Good-value beachside restaurant, serving simple meals like chicken yassa and grilled fish.

The Sushi House Farida's Arcade, Palma Rima Rd. An atmospheric Asian–American restaurant that breaks new ground in The Gambia in serving sushi, grills (*teppanyaki*, *teriyaki*), seafood *tempura* and *shabushabu* fondue; there's also a good wine list. Recommended, despite the above-average prices.

Zizi's Café-Creperie Farida's Arcade, Palma Rima Rd. Intimate American-style creperie and coffee bar – one of the area's most idiosyncratic eating places, with excellent sweet and savoury crepes, salads, good wine, freshly squeezed juices and great coffee. Mon, Thurs & Fri 11am–late, Tues & Wed 5pm–late, Sat & Sun 10am–late.

Kololi: Senegambia area

The Gambia's brashest tourist strip has plenty of **restaurants**, **bars** and **clubs** in an area so small you can walk right round it in minutes. There are one or two gems among the trashier venues, with popularity swinging from place to place.

African Queen Near the Senegambia Craft Market. Scratch *djembé* bands play on the terrace at this informal, inexpensive restaurant and bar.

Alamir Bertil Harding Highway. Large, brightly lit restaurant with gilt decor and waiters in fezes and embroidered waistcoats, serving mid-priced Lebanese standards such as *mezze*, *kafta* and *taboulé*, plus Lebanese wine and mint tea. The service can be slow, but it's worth visiting for the elaborate Friday evening buffet. Daily from 4pm.

Ali Baba's On the corner of Senegambia Rd. Lebanese-run street corner terrace bar and restaurant, a perennially popular tourist hangout that's packed in the high season, but there's better cooking elsewhere. The garden restaurant behind (entrance round the corner) is a much better option – leafy and quirkily decorated, with a good house band every night. Daily till 1am; band 9pm–11.30pm.

Aquarius Near the casino, ☎ 460247. A cocktail bar and disco with an international style. Just about big enough to dance; popular with tourists and smart young Gambian–Lebanese. Daily till 3am.

Bodega Casa Fernando *Kairaba Hotel*. The Kairaba's least formal restaurant has a Mediterranean and Middle Eastern influenced menu, including pizza, tapas, charcoal grills, fresh fish and seafood. Daily 4pm–midnight.

Coco Beach Restaurant *Kololi Beach Club*. A cut above most beach restaurants, elegantly decorated, prettily situated and tranquil. Lunch includes excellent quiches and salads; the evening menu has more elaborate choices, such as spare ribs in honey and black pepper marinade, or *chateaubriant* with *béarnaise* sauce. Recommended.

Colors Near the Senegambia Craft Market. Probably the most stylish of the tourist-strip places, this is a good place to linger over a cocktail and watch the action. The food isn't outstanding, but there are some good choices for breakfast; average-priced European standards at lunchtimes, and grills, salads and pasta in the evenings.

Funny Girlz Showbar Above Wedad's fashion boutique. The most unexpected addition to The Gambia's nightlife scene, this European-style cabaret features a drag artist and a local Elvis impersonator, followed by a 70s/80s/90s disco. Daily 10.30pm–midnight, no entry fee.

Green Mamba Near the *Senegambia Hotel*. The *Spy Bar*'s garden bar offers mini golf, pool tables and cocktails – the latter have a snake theme such as "Little Viper" or "Cobra Spit", and incorporate local juices like *wonjo*, pawpaw and baobab. There's cool electro-jazz and lounge music on the stereo. Daily 2pm–4am.

GTS Restaurant Senegambia Rd. On the edge of the Senegambia action, but definitely worth seeking out, this characterful restaurant is run by

Gambia Tourist Support (see p.18). Relaxed atmosphere and good simple African and European food at extremely reasonable prices.

The Kora Senegambia Rd ☎ 462727. One of the better and more expensive restaurants in the tourist strip, with an international à la carte menu.

Paparazzi bar Near *Senegambia Beach Hotel*. Popular with young tourists and well-dressed locals, this bar has a loud pre-club feel, and is often the last to close. Daily 9.30pm–late.

Paradiso Senegambia Rd. This ordinary-looking place on the tourist strip serves the best pizzas in The Gambia; there's also good choice of salads and the usual standards at keen prices: steak, chicken, seafood, pasta. They do take-aways – perfect for pizza on the beach.

SeaView Beach Bar & Restaurant On the beach near Senegambia Beach Hotel, signposted from Bertil Harding Highway, ☎ 463502. Clinging on to a stretch of beach that's been ruined by erosion, this place is busy late on Fridays with a house salsa band. It's a good place for a drink, but the restaurant is overpriced in the evenings – lunch is much more reasonable. Daily 9am–late.

Shikra *Kairaba Hotel* ☎ 462940. The Kairaba's most expensive restaurant, popular with honeymooners, with an international menu. Mon–Sat 7pm–midnight.

Sizzlers Senegambia beach. Beach restaurant known for its creative cooking, with original combinations such as steak in mango sauce or barracuda with mustard and paprika.

Spy Bar Near the Senegambia Hotel. Once the Senegambia's most happening venue, now in decline after hassle from hustlers. House, garage and West African music; occasional live music sessions. Daily 9pm–4am, entry fee at weekends.

Tao Senegambia Rd. The Gambia's only Thai restaurant, with pan-Asian influences, in a building like a theme park version of a pagoda, with a scarlet and black lacquered-box-style interior. It could so easily be even better: the flavourings are a little heavy-handed, there's nothing remotely Asian to drink, and the staff tend to be brusque. Popular with tourists (less so with Gambians), and busy – book in high season to avoid waiting for a table. Daily 7.30–10.30pm.

Waaw Senegambia Rd, ☎ 460668. A small upstairs club that's something of a pick-up joint, playing soul, funk, ragga, hiphop and old-fashioned disco to a mixed crowd of locals and tourists. Nightly till late, entrance fee at weekends.

Kololi Village and Manjai Kunda

Kololi Village has an eclectic mix of restaurants and clubs, appealing to anyone wanting a break from the mass-tourism atmosphere of Kololi's mainstream places. Some guesthouses in the village serve good food if given enough notice – *Soto Baa Koto* is worth trying for its cool two-storey *bantaba*.

Mama's Kololi Village, on the bush taxi route between Kotu/Kololi and Serrekunda. An excellent local restaurant (not to be confused with *Mama's* in Fajara) with a cheerful, shaded roadside terrace, serving simple food, such as omelettes, spaghetti, steak with peppers and *chicken yassa*, at low prices. Particularly good for breakfasts and for the excellent-value Tuesday evening buffet; the owner makes you feel like one of the family.

Mannjai Lodge Manjai Kunda, ☎463414. The courtyard bar at this hotel is occasionally the venue for live music sessions featuring big names from the Gambian and Senegalese scene, drawing an up-market Gambian crowd. The sound system isn't great, but there's a mellow, appreciative atmosphere to the place.

New Queen's Head Kololi Village, on the bush taxi route between Kotu/Kololi and Serrekunda. British style pub that attracts a male-dominated crowd of local expats with beer, pool, karaoke and more beer. Light meals are available, and there's a happy hour 5–7pm daily.

Rasta Garden On the main road through Kololi Village. Synonymous in the area with rastas, reggae and ragga, this popular open-air club with occasional live music sessions is a great place to dance under the stars or just chill out with the locals in a low-hassle, laidback environment. It's away from the tourist areas on a dark street, so take a taxi. Entrance fee at weekends.

Village Gallery Kololi Village. The garden courtyard outside this interesting art gallery is a restaurant, serving simple, cheap but good daily specials such as grilled chicken or fish.

South Kololi

Choices are limited in **South Kololi** for now, but this is the next expansion hotspot – new restaurants and bars are sure to spring up along the main highway and on the beach.

Avocado Restaurant *Coconut Residence*, Kerr Serign, ☎463377. One of The Gambia's finest restaurants, and an excellent choice for a special occasion – President Jammeh sometimes throws birthday parties here. Imaginative menus with inspiration from all over the world, with careful attention to detail and impeccable service.

Serrekunda

While **Serrekunda** has no tourist restaurants, it has great down-to-earth local eating places, especially around the market, and The Gambia's best club, the legendary *Jokor*. Serrekunda's nightlife is as gritty and energetic as the daytime commercial activity. The action doesn't get underway much before midnight, then carries on until 4 or 5am, when revellers head off in search of *afra*. Many local bars in town see few foreign visitors, but you'll be made welcome.

Afra Citizen Mosdolly Mosque Rd. Cave-like *afra* shop run by Mauritanians; it may look medieval but their barbecued lamb is as good as it gets. Choose a chunk of meat from one of the joints hanging from hooks over the chopping block, and see it cut up in front of you, seasoned, and tossed into the furnace to grill. When it's done, it's wrapped in brown paper with mustard and salt. Daily, eves only, till late.

Alliance Franco-Gambienne Kairaba Ave ☎375418. Also known as the Alliance Française, this French cultural exchange centre has a small outdoor amphitheatre-style performance space, with occasional live music nights, and an excellent garden bar/restaurant serving French- and Senegalese-style lunches. There are also art exhibitions, a library, a recording studio, French language classes, and English and French film nights.

Jokor Westfield Junction. The best club in the Serrekunda and resort area, attracting fast-living Gambians, but the atmosphere is friendly and relaxed, and visitors rarely feel out of place. The atmosphere depends on whether they're playing African, Caribbean or European music, but it's the West African sounds that really get the crowd moving. You dance under the stars in a garden with trees laced with fairy lights, and there's a tiny stage for live bands – big West African stars play here. Sunday night is pretty risqué, when the house band of *sabar* drummers play to electrifying effect, and Gambian and Senegalese women take the floor for an *mbalax* dance competition in which practically anything goes. Nightly till late.

Marandy's Restaurant Off Sayer Jobe Rd, near Westfield Junction. A bright little fast-food place, serving cheap chicken, steak, burgers. Daily except Sun, 9.30am–midnight.

Lana's Bar London Corner. Sandwiches, *shawarma* and cheap beer while watching the busy Serrekunda street life. Open till late, closed Sun.

Westfield Junction Café Westfield Junction. A local spot with rickety furniture on a well-shaded terrace and a signboard that promises plenty of options – however, in practice there's normally only one dish available each day. Cheap, but you're

better off at the nearby Youth Monument Bar and restaurant.

Willy's Disco Near Yundum police station, Lamin, 6km outside Serrekunda. A fun, relaxed local dive with an interior like a circus tent lit with traffic lights. Young Gambians in baseball caps and baggy shirts come here to dance to reggae and ragga; there aren't many females about, but anybody's welcome. Opens irregularly, weekends only.

Youth Monument Bar and Restaurant Westfield Junction. A park that's essentially a traffic island in the middle of one of The Gambia's busiest road junctions may seem an unlikely venue for a restaurant, but this casual, low-key place is excellent. It's a great place for a beer, a simple cheap meal – good kebabs and grills – or a coffee. Open all day, but especially busy as a pre-club venue for *Jokor*.

Listings

Air freight DHL, Independence Drive, Banjul ☎228414; Saga Express (Fedex agent), Kanifing, ☎472405.

Airline offices Air Guinée, 17 OAU Boulevard, Banjul ☎227585, ⓦwww.mirinet.com/airguinee; Air Sénégal International, Ecowas Ave, corner of Mandela St, Banjul ☎202117, ⓦwww .air-senegal-international.net; Bellview Airlines, 16 Kairaba Ave ☎373606, ⓦwww.bellviewair.com; Gambia International Airlines: Satellite House, Banjul ☎223702, Midway Centre, Kairaba Ave ☎374100, ⓦwww.gia.gm; Ghana Airways, 10 Nelson Mandela St, Banjul ☎226913; Sierra National Airlines, ☎397551; SN Brussels Airlines, 97 Kairaba Ave, Fajara ☎496301, ⓦwww.brusselsairlines.com.

American Express agent Gamtours, Kanifing Industrial Estate, Serrekunda ☎392259.

Banks and foreign exchange Standard Chartered: 8 ECOWAS Ave, Banjul; Senegambia area, Kololi; Kairaba Ave, Serrekunda; Atlantic Rd, Bakau; IBC Bank: Liberation Ave, Banjul; Atlantic Rd, Bakau; Sayerr Jobe Ave, Serrekunda; Trust Bank: 3–4 ECOWAS Ave, Banjul; Sait Matty Rd, Bakau; Banjul International Airport; Sayerr Jobe Ave, Serrekunda.

Bicycle rental You can rent bikes from the stands outside most major hotels.

Books Timbooktu, Kairaba Ave, Fajara, on the cor-

ner of Garba Jahumpa Rd, is the most useful general bookshop; it also has a sub-branch at Banjul International Airport. There are small selections of books for sale at supermarkets and hotel shops, and the *Fajara Club* has a small library of paperbacks.

Car rental AB Rent a Car (☎460926, ⓦwww.abrent-gambia.com) is the most reputable of the independent agencies, with an office near the *Senegambia Hotel*. Much pricier is Hertz, with branches at the airport (☎473156) and Bakoteh (☎390041). West African Tours (☎495258, ⓦwww.westafricantours.com) hires out Land Rovers with drivers and guides.

Cinema Alliance Franco-Gambienne, Kairaba Ave, Serrekunda is the best place to watch films, with showings twice a week, at 8.30pm on Mondays (mainstream English language films) and Thursdays (French language films). Aisa Marie, Serrekunda, is a sweltering concrete box showing football from satellite TV or cheap imported action movies; Capital Cinema, Imam Omar Sowe Ave, Banjul, is airier, but has less frequent programmes.

Dentist Swedent, signposted off Bertil Harding Highway on the opposite side from *Palma Rima Hotel* ☎461212.

Doctors The Lamtoro Clinic (☎460934), near the *Senegambia Beach Hotel*, is highly rated but pricey; the Royal Victoria Hospital, Banjul (℡228223) has out-patient facilities. Westfield Clinic, Westfield Rd, Serrekunda (℡392213) is recommended for malaria treatment. Alternatively, try the Momodou Musa Memorial Clinic (Banjul ℡224320, Serrekunda ℡371683); The Medical Research Council, Fajara (℡495442) has a British nurse on duty, while Sheelagh Fowler, the British High Commission nurse, also runs a clinic (℡495133, mobile ℡994785).

Embassies and diplomatic missions Belgium, 14 Liberation St, Banjul ℡227473; Denmark 3 OAU Blvd, Banjul ℡227694; France, Ecole Française, Atlantic Rd, Kairaba Ave end ℡495487; Germany, Independence Drive, Banjul ℡227783; Ghana, 18 Mosque Rd, Latrikunda ℡391599; Guinea, 78 Daniel Goddard St, Banjul ℡226862; Guinea-Bissau, Atlantic Rd, Bakau ℡494854; Lebanon, 26 ECOWAS Ave, Banjul ℡228419; Netherlands, c/o Shell Company, Macoumba Jallow St, Banjul ℡227437; Nigeria, 52 Garba Jahumpa Rd, Bakau ℡495803; Norway and Sweden, off Sait Matty Rd, Bakau ℡492505; Senegal, Off Kairaba Ave, Fajara ℡373752; Sierra Leone, OAU Blvd, Banjul ℡228206; UK, 48 Atlantic Rd, Fajara ℡495133; USA, Kairaba Ave, Fajara ℡392856.

Emergencies Ambulance ℡16; Fire service ℡18; Police ℡17; Royal Victoria Hospital ℡228223; Banjul police station ℡223146; Bakau police station ℡495739; Kotu police station ℡463351.

Golf The Fajara Club (℡495456) has an 18-hole course.

Hairdressing and beauty treatments The best place in the Gambia is The Salon, under the African Living Art Centre, Garba Jahumpa Rd, Bakau ℡495131. They also do manicure, pedicure, reflexology, body-scrub and massage. Many tourist hotels have hair salons, and some have aromatherapy and massage parlours. Recommended hotel hair and beauty salons include those at the *Senegambia* and the *Palma Rima*. Hair braiders work on the beach at Kotu Strand, hotel salons or Gambian salons in towns.

Horse riding Lama Barry (℡776689) arranges horse riding along the Kombos beaches (D250/hr).

Immigration 21 OAU Boulevard, Banjul ℡228611, for visa extensions.

Internet access There are plenty of Internet cafés in the resort area; Gamtel tends to have the lowest rates, and QuantumNet is reliable.

Pharmacy Banjul Pharmacy: Independence Drive, Banjul ℡227470; Liberation Ave, Banjul ℡227648; Sayerr Jobe Rd, London Corner, Serrekunda ℡391053; Kairaba Ave ℡390189; and Kairaba Pharmacy: Independence Drive, Banjul ℡225787; London Corner, Serrekunda ℡290839.

Post office The GPO, Russell St, Banjul (Mon–Fri 8.30am–noon & 2–4pm, Sat 8.30am–noon) is the country's main GPO, and the best place for poste restante. There are other post offices on Atlantic Rd, Bakau, and off Kairaba Ave, Serrekunda.

Quad bikes Quest Quad Trekking, Palma Rima Rd, between Abi's and Churchill's (℡981074), offers one- two- or three-hours self-drive or bush and beach safaris with a qualified instructor on 125cc Yamaha Breezes.

Sports facilities Fajara Club ℡495456. Club house open daily 8am–8pm; bar/restaurant 9am–8pm; swimming pool 9am–7pm; golf course 7am–7.30pm. Temporary membership of D100/day or D400/week gives access to clubhouse, swimming pool, table tennis, badminton, tennis, squash, aerobics and yoga.

Supermarkets The resort area has a multitude of supermarkets along Kairaba Ave, at Cape Point, and in Bakau, Kotu and the Senegambia area, Kololi. Most open Mon–Sat 8.30am–7.30pm, Sun 10am–2pm; some close later. Each hotel zone and many petrol stations have late-opening minimarkets. Banjul has no supermarkets as such, just a couple of small grocery stores.

Telephones The Gamtel offices in Russell St, Banjul; Atlantic Rd, Bakau (opposite the *African Village Hotel*); at the bottom of Kairaba Ave, Serrekunda; and near the *Senegambia Hotel* are all open daily 8am–midnight. Various private telecentres are widely scattered around the urban area, sometimes offering cheaper call rates.

the training and equipment they need to start beekeeping businesses. Also places volunteers in rural teaching posts.

Tourist taxi ranks (green taxis) are found near the *Atlantic* and *Palm Grove* hotels (Banjul); at Cape Point (Bakau); near the *African Village Hotel* (Bakau); near the *Hotel Fajara* (Fajara); near the *Kombo Beach Hotel* (Kotu); near the *Palma Rima Hotel* (Kololi), in the Senegambia area (Kololi), and at Banjul International Airport. Typical prices for a return trip, including a couple of hours' waiting time, include: Banjul to Fajara D400, Senegambia to Tanji D350, Fajara to Abuko D300. Typical one-way fares include: Banjul International Airport to Senegambia area D200, Fajara to Bakau D100, Fajara to Senegambia D200.

Travel agents The Gambia Experience, *Senegambia Hotel*, Kololi ℡463867, acts as agent for charter flights from Banjul to London. For other flight bookings and general flight information, try Banjul Travel Agency, ECOWAS Ave, Banjul ℡228813; IPC Travel, 16 Kairaba Ave, ℡375677, ✉ipctravel@qanet.gm; or Continental Travels, 70B Daniel Goddard St, Banjul ℡224058.

Watersports Gambia Watersports Centre, *Atlantic Hotel*, Banjul (℡765765) offers jet-ski hire, parascending, water-skiing, plus banana boat, catama- ran and power boat rides. If you're not staying at the *Atlantic*, they can collect you by London taxi.

Travel details

Buses

Serrekunda to: Bansang (7–8hrs); Basse (8–9hrs); Brikama (40min–1hr); Sankulay Kunda for Janjanbureh (6–7hrs); Soma (4–5hrs). The express Serrekunda–Basse bus (1 daily) calls at the above towns only; a slower service (1 daily) stops anywhere on the same route on request.

Ferry

Banjul to: Barra (daily, hourly on the hour; 30min–2hrs).

Bush taxis

Banjul to: Brikama (1hr).
Serrekunda to: Abuko (20min); Bansang (6–7hr); Basse (7–8hr); Brikama (40min); Lamin (25min); Sankulay Kunda for Janjanbureh (5–6hr); Soma (3.5–4hr); plus all villages in the Kombos.

The southern Kombos

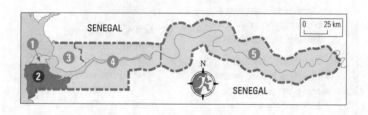

✱ **Abuko Nature Reserve**
This small but fascinating forest park guarantees sightings of tropical birds, monkeys, lizards and crocodiles. See pp.133–135

✱ **Tanbi Wetlands** Best explored by small boat, the mangrove-creeks at the mouth of the River Gambia offer superb birdwatching and angling. See pp.135–138

✱ **Southern Atlantic beaches** Broad, empty and palm-fringed, the best beaches in The Gambia lie between Brufut and Kartong. See pp.142–145

✱ **Tanji** This coastal village has a lively fishing centre, a great little museum of Gambian culture, a camel safari centre and the country's only officially protected bird reserve. See pp.146–148

✱ **Traditional music lessons** Many of the country's greatest *kora* players come from Brikama, making this bustling town the place to get some expert tuition. See p.153

✱ **Makasutu Culture Forest** The Gambia's most celebrated ecotourism project is also the site of its most luxurious lodge. See pp.155–158

✱ **Tumani Tenda** A picturesque rural retreat, where visitors can learn about up-country life as guests in a traditional Jola village. See p.158–159

The southern Kombos

Y ou don't have to travel far from The Gambia's busy resorts and urban areas to find quiet villages, intriguing up-country towns, unspoilt stretches of wilderness and glorious empty beaches. The **southern Kombos** – the clutch of districts to the south of the Kombo peninsula, bounded to the west by the Atlantic, and to the south by the Senegalese border – are so accessible that the region can easily be visited on day-trips from the resorts, particularly if you hire your own transport or join organized excursions. If you'd like to stay deep in the countryside, or if the resorts aren't really your style but you'd still like to spend time near the ocean, it's worth finding accommodation in the southern Kombos for a few days or more – especially if you have a special interest in wildlife or traditional music.

Barely half an hour from the resorts by road is one of The Gambia's finest protected areas, **Abuko Nature Reserve**, a well-preserved small forest park in which birds and monkeys are habituated to visitors, so you stand a good chance of close-up encounters. East of here, and occupying the sixty square kilometres immediately south of Banjul, are the **Tanbi Wetlands**, a maze of mangrove-festooned creeks excellent for birdwatching and fishing. People also come here to enjoy leisurely cruises by traditional *pirogue*, and to visit **Lamin Lodge**, a wonderful rickety timber bar-restaurant built right over one of the broad and beautiful creeks.

To the southwest of the region lie the country's broadest and emptiest **beaches**, and its busiest ones too: those used by local fishermen to moor their brightly painted boats and haul in the catch. The local fishing communities have their village centres a short distance inland. The most visited is **Tanji**, partly because it's close to the **Tanji River (Karinti) Bird Reserve** – an obligatory stop on all birdwatching tours of the region – and partly because it has a unique **museum** of Gambian culture and natural history; it's also the only place in The Gambia where you can ride camels along the beach. Further inland, dozens of small, back-country villages set in an appealing, random patchwork of forest, savannah and farmland are accessible on foot, by bicycle, by bush taxi or by rented car.

At the hub of the region is the district capital of **Brikama**, a staunchly religious town with a vibrant musical tradition, currently being shaken up by the opening of The Gambia's coolest new nightclub. East of here lies **Makasutu**

Culture Forest, The Gambia's best-known ecotourism site, a private nature park with woodland and waterways to explore by guided tour and a new luxury lodge. Further east again is **Tumani Tenda**, a successful experiment in community-managed cultural tourism, where you can experience rural culture from the inside by spending time as a guest in a traditional Jola village. South of Brikama, in the area around **Marakissa** near the Senegalese border, you'll find some of southwest Gambia's most beautiful untamed bush, with mature woodland and savanna that remains lush well into the dry season, perfect for exploring by 4WD vehicle and excellent for birdwatching.

Abuko Nature Reserve and the Tanbi Wetlands

The area around the village of Lamin, about 8km southwest of Serrekunda, draws large numbers of birdwatchers, wildlife enthusiasts and other day-trippers, not for the village itself, which is nothing special, but for **Abuko Nature Reserve** and the **Tanbi Wetlands**. A walk along Abuko's shady paths can yield excellent sightings of birds, monkeys, chameleons and colourful lizards, many of them inquisitive and apparently tame. Exploring the Tanbi Wetlands, the net-

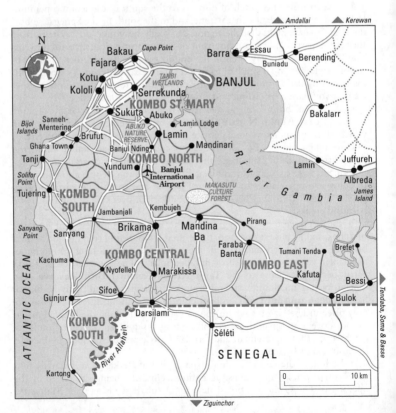

work of mangrove creeks just inside the mouth of the River Gambia, can be equally rewarding for birdwatchers and anglers. A perfect way to end an excursion into the creeks is to relax at *Lamin Lodge*, a charming restaurant and bar built on the banks of the calm and majestic Lamin Bolon.

Abuko Nature Reserve

Abuko Nature Reserve (daily 8am–6.30pm; D31.50) was The Gambia's first protected area, gazetted as a reserve in the 1960s. Rich in flora and fauna, the reserve is justly popular, and at under two square kilometres it's compact enough to explore on foot in a couple of hours. It preserves one of the last surviving examples of **gallery forest** (mature tropical riverine forest) in the country; the variety of healthy trees and shrubs here is excellent, and there are three-hundred-odd bird species and dozens of varieties of small mammals and reptiles.

Not far from the entrance to the reserve there's an education centre; it's not particularly enlightening, but the building itself has fine unobstructed views over the **Bambo pool**, a densely fringed freshwater pool that's one of the reserve's best locations for birdwatching and crocodile-spotting. Exploring the forest can be illuminating – the only real disappointments at Abuko are the Animal Orphanage, essentially a small zoo of bored-looking caged animals, and the tatty craft market at the exit gate.

The founder of the reserve, conservation expert Eddie Brewer, first recognized the unique significance of **Lamin stream** (the tip of Lamin Bolon) and its stunning necklace of forest in 1967, and Abuko was fenced the following year. Apart from pond-dredging, path-clearing and hide-building, the reserve is left more or less as it was found. The strongest impression comes from the magnificent gallery forest trees, spiralling up from the webbed fingers of their buttress roots through a canopy of trailing creepers and epiphytes to create dark cathedrals of evergreen vegetation. The reserve also encloses more thinly wooded Guinea savanna.

Abuko is a narrow rectangular shape, with a single 2.5-kilometre **marked trail**, a crooked path leading up the southeast side towards the

Birdwatching in Abuko

Abuko is the closest patch of tropical forest to Europe, and each winter it attracts thousands of birdwatchers, as well as a host of palearctic migrants (willow warblers, chiff chaffs, black caps and melodious warblers) to swell the numbers of its native species. Most obvious are the water birds – a couple of photo hides overlooking the stream and pools are usually occupied by birders murmuring in raptures over them. Look out for kingfishers (blue-breasted, Senegal, malachite and pied), the "umbrella fishing" black heron, and two great birdwatcher's sights: the painted snipe (the male incubates the eggs) and the stunning red-bellied paradise flycatcher, with its thirty-centimetre tail feathers. You can generally see hammerkops around the pool at the start of the trail; in flight, their swept-back crest of feathers and pointed beaks make them look like miniature pterodactyls, and their huge nests, courtship displays and trumpet calls are remarkable. In the clearings, wait to see fanti rough-winged swallows and the occasional shikra darting through the light and, above the forest canopy, hooded vultures, black kites, swooping bee-eaters and rollers and maybe palm-nut vultures.

Animal Orphanage, then back down the northeast side to the craft market and exit. The whole walk around the marked trail takes a couple of hours, but it could easily turn into half a day or more depending on your interest in the various bird species – more often heard than seen – and your curiosity about the monkeys and the more bizarre life-forms on the forest floor, such as crazy-coloured beetles and seething columns of soldier ants. The path is well maintained, although the distance-marker system needs improving. The one path that branches off the main route is a shortcut to the exit, which reduces the circuit by about three-quarters.

You've a very good chance of seeing all The Gambia's species of **monkey** here – patas, callithrix (sometimes called vervet monkeys) and the particularly attractive western red colobus. There are also plenty of **monitor lizards** which you might spot darting across the paths and clawing their way through the undergrowth. Most monitors here are small, but they can grow as long as two metres. With patience, it's normally also possible to spot **crocodiles** at the Bambo pool from the large lookout veranda at the Education Centre, particularly on cool mornings when they emerge from the water to sun themselves on the banks. Watch for two distinct species: the larger, pale Nile crocodile, and the small, darker, nocturnal dwarf crocodile, critically endangered and very rarely seen. You may also see a **bushbuck** grazing on the banks of the pool. **Snakes** are sometimes seen at Abuko, including green mambas, puff adders, royal and African rock pythons, forest and spitting cobras – but snake phobics should note that there has never been a case of snakebite involving a visitor or member of reserve staff.

The **Education Centre** is a timber building with posters and charts downstairs relating to local wildlife and wider conservation issues. Upstairs there's a one-room museum with a few skulls and other animal relics. The displays probably won't detain you long, but allow plenty of time at the upstairs veranda lookout, as there are plenty of kingfishers, herons, egrets, francolins, sandpipers and turacos in the vicinity of the Bambo pool. It's a gorgeous spot, ringed with fine mature palms and candelabra trees; by the second half of the dry season (March–June) the pool is the only fresh water in the area, so it's a wildlife magnet. There are a couple of **hides** nearby, which allow you to get very close to smaller pools of fresh water frequented by birds.

At the top of the standard circuit is the **Animal Orphanage**, a rehabilitation centre set up by the Department of Parks and Wildlife Management in 1997. Despite its good intentions, it's a rather forlorn place. Monkeys and parrots comprise the vast majority of animals taken in, and those unsuitable for release remain here alongside the orphanage's other permanent residents, lions and hyenas, which swagger round their enclosures or just sprawl despondently in the dust. There are, at least, well-written explanations outside the enclosures.

All the biggest gallery forest trees are in the first quarter of the walk; the rest of the circuit is mostly through more open Guinea woodland savanna, green with foliage all year round. From time to time you have to duck under arches of vines; frustratingly often you will hear scuttling noises in the bush ahead of you, indicating that an animal has disappeared from view just before you've seen it; but equally often you'll be rewarded with very good sightings, particularly of monkeys, who happily outstare visitors from the trees.

Practicalities

To get the most out of your visit, avoid the **Abuko excursions** organized by tour operators (around £11/$18 per person for a morning or afternoon, including return transport from your hotel). These groups tend to visit in the late morning and early afternoon, which are not the best times for wildlife-spotting – shouting guides and chattering crowds of up to thirty people shatter the tranquility, and you'll see far more of your fellow visitors' backs than you will of birds and monkeys.

It's almost as straightforward, and usually more rewarding, to visit the reserve **independently**, either alone or in a small group. The entrance to Abuko is on the main Serrekunda–Brikama road, a busy **bush taxi** route. You can get there from the resorts by making your way to Kombo Sillah Drive, near Westfield Junction, Serrekunda, then taking a minibus **bush taxi** bound for Lamin or Brikama via Abuko (20 min; D5); you get off at the reserve entrance immediately after the weighbridge on the main road. Travelling in this direction, you first pass the exit, conspicuous because of its craft market; the entrance is 500m further south. Alternatively, you could hire a taxi to take you there and possibly wait for the return trip (typically D300 by tourist taxi, less for a yellow taxi).

While it's hard to get lost at Abuko, **guides** are often very knowledgeable and know exactly where to find certain species. Jobbing guides tend to hang out at the Education Centre looking for custom. Park rules forbid them for charging for their services, but they naturally expect a "gift" of some kind – D50 for an hour or two is standard. As elsewhere in The Gambia, early morning and late afternoon tend to yield the most wildlife sightings, and there are spectacular movements of flocks of fruit bats at sunset. Keen naturalists may like to arrange a visit outside normal hours, by paying the gatekeeper direct if you arrive before the ticket booth opens, or letting them know as you go in if you want to stay on late.

It's worth bringing **food** and **drink** with you if you intend to stay a while, although there are drinks and snacks on sale from the booth near the Animal Orphanage within the reserve. There are also a couple of places selling drinks just outside the reserve exit, beyond the very shabby craft market. Bring mosquito repellent, especially during the rains.

The Tanbi Wetlands

Immediately southwest of Banjul, and easily accessible from the resorts of the northern Kombos, the **Tanbi Wetlands** are a wilderness of mangroves, saltwater creeks and mudflats just inside the mouth of the River Gambia. It occupies a total area of about sixty square kilometres, making it one of the largest wetland areas in the country; it's also home to some rare mammals including the marsh mongoose and the West African manatee. A popular area for boat-trips, the wetlands are particularly beautiful at the beginning and end of the day, when the waters are calmest, the air

Birdwatching in the Tanbi Wetlands

You'll almost certainly see several heron species in the creeks, including goliath herons standing sentinel on the muddy banks; you might also see ospreys, pied and malachite kingfishers, white- and pink-backed pelicans, yellow-billed storks and sacred ibis. African darters with their curiously sinuous necks perch on low mangrove branches, while on the topmost branches you're likely to see bee-eaters in candy-bright colours. The dawn chorus is particularly impressive in this environment, as well as the hour before sunset when birds are heading for their island roosts. In the middle of the day, many birds retreat from the heat of the sun, and the glare on the water makes viewing conditions uncomfortable.

Gambian oysters

Gambian oysters are a delicacy, though not a rarity, and when shelled they look and taste rather like juicy mussels. Harvesting them in the mangrove creeks is considered women's work; however, the women who do this, often Jola, have a reputation for being particularly tough and masculine – they even wear trousers, otherwise unheard-of in traditional Gambian society. They work at mid- to low tide, paddling their dugout canoes close to the mangroves where oysters cling to the roots near the water line, cutting them away with a cutlass.

The oysters are later smoked in a barrel, making it easy to separate the flesh from the shell. The **shells** are kept for a year, then burnt and ground to produce a form of lime used to strengthen clay or made into whitewash to paint huts. The shells are also mixed with tar and used like gravel in road surfacing – many Gambian roads, including major ones, have a shell-and-tar surface. Sometimes the shells are simply abandoned in general middens, old examples of which are of great interest to archaeologists. By measuring the rate of growth of shell mounds started in the time of the Gambian Stone Circles, and analyzing their contents, researchers have been able to piece together data about prehistoric societies.

coolest, and the spectacular and prolific birdlife most active. Sunset is a magical time, when you can see pelicans settling down to roost in the baobabs.

The tranquil creeks are best explored by small boat – the smaller the better, to enjoy the narrowest, shallowest creeks to the full. Since every creek is bordered by **mangroves**, with nothing but sky and the occasional baobab on the horizon, and no sounds but the noise of the boat, the cracking and plopping sounds from the mangroves, the occasional bird call, and perhaps the distant pounding of drums, the sense of remoteness is complete, close though you are to the major urban areas. The mangroves are beautiful, eerie and surprisingly tall – up to 20m. Fiddler **crabs** beckon manically on every mudbank, seemingly gathering in silent, jostling droves as boats approach; the quicksilver, dun-coloured hopping things are **mud-skippers** – fish seemingly intent on becoming terrestrial – which always seem to have gone just before you get a good look at them. Occasional inhabitants of the mangroves are **monkeys**, bounding through the foliage, presumably taking refuge from persecutors on the farm plots inland. Sadly, over-hunting in the past means hippos are never seen this far downstream.

The northern limit of the wetlands is in Banjul: **Kankujeri Road** (sometimes still known as Bund Road) runs along the edge of it, and the wetlands hug **Oyster Creek**, the channel separating the capital from the mainland. The southern limit is near **Mandinari**, a village southeast of the Lamin and about 8km from the main highway. The fields between Mandinari and Lamin are a popular place for bird walks, particularly during the rice-growing season – from August to October the fields and nearby foliage are lush, with so many birds they make the creeks look dead in comparison. Ornithologists also come here between November and January specifically to observe Temminck's coursers, which appear while the watermelon- and groundnut fields are being cleared.

The whole wetland complex is a network of tidal channels where oyster-collectors and fishermen make their living, while trying to ward off poachers who over-fish the waters with drag nets, even in the breeding season; illegal sand-miners have been also working clandestinely in the area. Although it's been identified as a site of international importance by the Ramsar Wetlands Convention, the Tanbi Wetlands are not yet officially gazetted as a protected area.

Practicalities

Many visitors to the Tanbi Wetlands get there by **organized tour**. The wetlands can be explored on a number of excursions (see p.56), starting from the resort hotels, then setting off into the waterways by large *pirogue* from Denton Bridge outside Banjul, the waterfront in Banjul or *Lamin Lodge*. These include creek fishing trips, the well-known "Champagne and Caviar" trip and the classic "Birds and Breakfast" and "Sunset Cruise" trips that end up at *Lamin Lodge* for food, drink and entertainment. It's sometimes possible to combine a boat trip in the creeks and a walk round Abuko as part of the same excursion. Enjoyable though these tours often are, they're not recommended for serious wildlife enthusiasts – there'll probably be too many people making too much noise, most of them far more interested in the breakfast or fruit punch than the birds.

It's also straightforward enough to make **independent arrangements**, a good plan if you'd like to travel in a very small group or target a particular location or time of day. You can arrange private **boat hire** with one of the small-scale boat-trip operators at Denton Bridge (see box below), or informally with fishermen on the shore north of the Barra ferry terminal in Banjul. Hiring a boat at *Lamin Lodge* costs around D100 per hour. Take plenty of water and food, binoculars and sun protection. If you're in a motorboat, ask the captain to cut the engine from time to time to enjoy the surroundings at their tranquil best.

Lamin Lodge

A popular destination for creek trips is **Lamin Lodge** (☎497603, ⓦ www.gre.gm), situated on the snaking Lamin Bolon, one of the River Gambia's many saltwater tributaries. It's a large, triple-storey bar-restaurant built on the bank at the creek head, 3km from the village of Lamin, roughly halfway between Serrekunda and the airport, and a couple of hours' lazy cruise from Denton Bridge or Banjul. Everything is made of rustic timber, and there are plenty of seemingly rickety walkways to negotiate and staircases to climb. It's well worth investigating the upper levels, which afford breathtaking views

---

Boat trips from Denton Bridge

The mainland side of **Denton Bridge**, which carries the Banjul–Serrekunda highway across Oyster Creek, is a base for boat-trip operators, covering the Tanbi Wetlands and the River Gambia beyond. Bush taxis travelling along the highway between Bakau or Serrekunda and Banjul will stop at the turning to the Denton Bridge landing area on request. Down on the shore, among the jumble of timber, bamboo shacks and shipping containers used as storerooms, you'll find boat owners willing to discuss tailor-made fishing, birding or sightseeing trips, or just share stories about their adventures.

All approximate rates quoted here are per person. A two-hour local **creek trip** by small boat is likely to cost around £2.50/$4; a half-day to *Lamin Lodge* typically costs £7.50/$12 return. **Sport fishing** costs £15/$24 per day: you've a good chance of hooking red snapper, tapandar, captain fish or angelfish in the environs of Denton Bridge, and metre-long barracuda are a common enough catch. You could also arrange a longer-distance trip, taking you beyond the wetlands, such as **dolphin-spotting** in the Gambia estuary for £10/$16 per half-day, a full day to **James Island** and back for £20/$32, Kemoto for £23/$36 or Tendaba for £25/$40. *Baba's Harbour Café*, near the shore, serves hot and cold drinks and sandwiches, with occasional barbecues, and is usually busy with yarn-spinning sport fishermen.

over this grand sweep of water, mangrove and fields, a special treat in a country where tall buildings are so rare that you hardly ever get to see anything from above. *Lamin Lodge* is also well known as a **birdwatching** base, and it's possible to hire expert birding guides here, in particular members of the recommended Habitat Africa (see p.54) group of guides, who will tailor-make tours on request.

The **food** here is moderately priced and very good, but if you arrive unexpectedly it may take some time to prepare. Specialities include fresh fish and oysters, of course, grilled or lightly fried with limes; they also provide elaborate Gambian-style buffets with all the usual dishes such as *domodah*, chicken *yassa* and *benachin*. Watch out for the bold-as-brass monkeys that operate well-orchestrated raiding parties whenever a group of tourists shows up.

While most people arrive by boat, *Lamin Lodge* is a fine place to come to by road, too, especially early in the morning. Bush taxis running along the main highway between Westfield Junction in Serrekunda and Lamin or Brikama can drop you in Lamin at one of the two access roads for the lodge, one of which is marked by an unmissable sign. From here, it's a pleasant three-kilometre walk along bumpy roads; you wind your way out of Lamin, then continue through more scenic farmland to the lodge. A tourist taxi to *Lamin Lodge* from the resorts costs around D350 return; a town trip by yellow taxi is around D150. It's close enough to the airport (15–20min by taxi or private vehicle) to be an excellent stop for one last drink in The Gambia before you leave; you could check in your luggage way ahead of the queues then head over here to relax for an hour or so before going back to catch the plane.

The southern coast

The Gambia's **southern coast** still feels wild and undiscovered, with swathes of sandy beach where you can walk for hours without seeing another soul. Behind the thirty-kilometre stretch of Atlantic shore are dunes and palms, and a hinterland of thinly populated bush and beautiful tropical woodland that becomes progressively lusher the closer you get to Senegal. Right on the doorstep of the resort areas, it's an excellent area to relax, swim or fish in the ocean, or to sample something of the "real" Gambia of thatched huts and winding country tracks.

The beaches themselves are not entirely undeveloped, and some are extremely busy fishing centres, where fishermen drag heavy traditional *pirogues* up the sand in a flurry of sea birds, and spread out their nets to dry in the sun. Meanwhile, tourist development is proceeding at a gentle pace, with a thin scattering of **beach bars** and simple lodges all along the coast, peaceful hideaways for travellers who don't mind forgoing a few basic comforts. None of these places could be called sophisticated, and some verge on the shabby, with no mains water or power, but some make a virtue of their simplicity, setting themselves up as **ecotourist camps** using solar or wind energy, and keeping consumption of water to a minimum.

Villagers in Kombo South, The Gambia's southern coastal district, live traditional rural lifestyles, and many have no reason to go anywhere near the tourist areas further north from one year to the next. Very few Gambians choose to live within sight of the ocean – even the fishermen prefer to base themselves slightly inland – and the **Kombo South villages** aren't actually on the beach; they're strung out along the newly surfaced Kombo coastal highway, which is the southern extension of the Bertil Harding Highway. Some villages are on the inland side of the highway, more than 5km from the sea. However, several villages lend their name to the beach that's nearest, and the small fishing communities on some beaches are effectively satellite settlements of the farming communities inland. The villages you're most likely to visit, or at least pass through, are **Ghana Town** and **Brufut**, just 8km from Kololi; **Tanji**, with its bird reserve and busy fishing centre; **Tujering**, **Sanyang** and **Gunjur**, all farming and fishing communities; and **Kartong**, 45km from Kololi, and the last coastal village in the Gambia, with a sacred crocodile pool. Inland, the countryside is forested and beautiful, with numerous tiny hamlets which see very few visitors, despite their relative proximity to the resorts.

Until very recently, **getting around** Kombo South was slow, due to the condition of the roads – generally bumpy and dusty in the dry season, often impassable in the rains – and the shortage of transport. However, the situation is changing rapidly: once-remote Kombo South villages are now connected to Serrekunda by the new road, greatly reducing journey times to the northern Kombos, and some settlements are even being connected up with mains electricity and water. Tourist facilities, too, are set to multiply within the next few years, now that the infrastructure is in place. The Gambian authorities seem to be fully aware of the fragility of the marine environment, but they're also wise to the commercial potential of the area – if you like the idea of escaping to an unspoilt coastal wilderness, you'd better move fast.

The Kombo South villages are only served by **bush taxis** (minibuses or *gelleh-gelleh* vans) from Brikama or Serrekunda – most routes haven't yet changed to take full advantage of the new highway. The quickest way to the southern beaches from the northern resorts is therefore by privately hired taxi, straight down the new tarmac; by bush taxi, you have to go to Serrekunda and/or Brikama first and then change. For example, to get to Kartong by bush taxi, you first go to Serrekunda, then from Serrekunda to Brikama (D7), then Brikama to Gunjur (D9), and finally Gunjur to Kartong (D5) – and after this you may still have quite a walk to the stretch of beach you'd like to visit. The same journey by green **tourist taxi** would be much quicker, though costing up to twenty times as much. Driving straight from Kololi to Sanyang takes about fifteen minutes, and from Kololi to Kartong, about thirty minutes.

Most of the **lodges** are located outside the coastal villages, existing in their own microenvironment either on the beach or in the bush, so, unless you're content just to chill out in one place, you may feel isolated without transport. With your own wheels, the whole area is easily accessible, no matter where you're staying, and most visitors therefore choose their lodge for its unique atmosphere, rather than for its proximity to specific attractions. This is a rewarding area to explore by mountain bike, or by hired 4WD vehicle, allowing you to leave the tarmac road and head off down bush tracks. Don't leave the tracks, however; vehicles carving up the beaches or tearing through virgin bush are beginning to damage the environment and disturb wildlife, such as breeding turtles, crabs and nesting birds.

Some exploration of the southern coastal area is built into standard **group excursions**, notably the all-day adventures called "Bush and Beach" or "4WD Adventure", which combine village visits, bush-driving, and lunch on one of the beaches. These can be great fun, as well as a great introduction to the region. You can also join half-day group excursions to Tanji to go camel riding, with a beach barbecue thrown in.

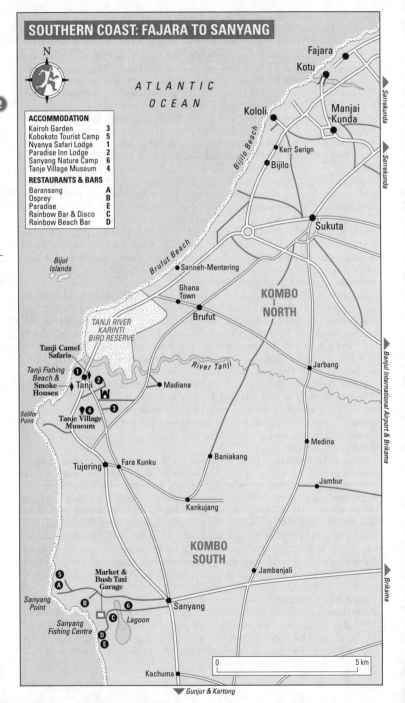

SOUTHERN COAST: FAJARA TO SANYANG

N

ATLANTIC
OCEAN

ACCOMMODATION
Kairoh Garden   3
Kobokoto Tourist Camp 5
Nyanya Safari Lodge   1
Paradise Inn Lodge   2
Sanyang Nature Camp   6
Tanje Village Museum   4

RESTAURANTS & BARS
Baransang   A
Osprey   B
Paradise   E
Rainbow Bar & Disco C
Rainbow Beach Bar   D

Fajara
Kotu
Kololi
Manjai
Kunda
Bijilo Beach
Kerr Serign
Bijilo
Sukuta

Bijol
Islands

Brufut Beach

Sanneh-Mentering
Ghana
Town
Brufut

KOMBO
NORTH

Jarbang

TANJI RIVER
KARINTI
BIRD RESERVE

Tanji Camel
Safaris

River Tanji

Tanji Fishing
Beach &
Smoke
Houses
Tanji
Madiana

Solifor
Point

Tanje Village
Museum

Fara Kunku
Tujering

Baniakang

Medina

Jambur

Kankujang

KOMBO
SOUTH

Jambanjali

Market &
Bush Taxi
Garage

Sanyang
Point

Sanyang

Brikama

Sanyang
Fishing Centre

Lagoon

Kachuma

0   5 km

Serrekunda
Serrekunda
Banjul International Airport & Brikama
Brikama

Gunjur & Kartong

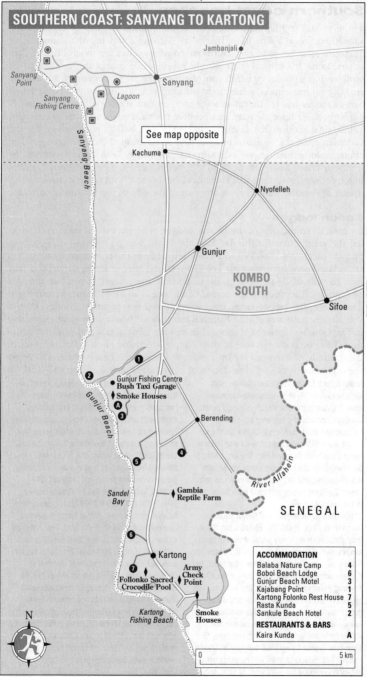

SOUTHERN COAST: SANYANG TO KARTONG

Jambanjali ●

Sanyang Point

▲

◎
▣
▣
◎
▣

Sanyang
Fishing Centre
▣
▣

Lagoon

● Sanyang

Sanyang Beach

See map opposite

Kachuma ●

Nyofelleh ●

● Gunjur

KOMBO
SOUTH

Sifoe ●

Gunjur Beach

❶
❷ Gunjur Fishing Centre
Bush Taxi Garage
◆ **Smoke Houses**
Ⓐ
❸

● Berending

❺
❹

Sandel
Bay

◆ **Gambia
Reptile Farm**

River Allahein

SENEGAL

❻

● Kartong
Army
Check
Point

❼
**Follonko Sacred
Crocodile Pool**

Kartong
Fishing Beach

Smoke
Houses

N

▸ Brikama

▸ Brikama

ACCOMMODATION
Balaba Nature Camp	4
Boboi Beach Lodge	6
Gunjur Beach Motel	3
Kajabang Point	1
Kartong Folonko Rest House	7
Rasta Kunda	5
Sankule Beach Hotel	2

RESTAURANTS & BARS
Kaira Kunda	A

0 _____ 5 km

Southern coast beaches

The Gambia's southern Atlantic coast is one continuous strip of shallow bays, altogether about 50km from Brufut to Kartong following the shoreline, or 35km by road. Some of the **southern coast beaches** are much broader than others; some are fringed with mature palms, while others are just backed by scrubby dunes bound by beach convolvulus; some are totally empty, while some are busy fishing centres; some rarely see tourists, while others have rustic beach bars or lodges where you can enjoy a meal or even stay for a few nights, enjoying barbecues under the stars, and, possibly, informal music sessions by campfire. While tidal erosion has claimed sand, trees and buildings elsewhere on the Gambian coast, the southern beaches have so far escaped the worst ravages. The contrasts sometimes come as a surprise to tourists who, before visiting the southern coast, have just stuck to the beach nearest their northern Kombos hotel, perhaps imagining that there can't be too much variation in such a short stretch of Atlantic shoreline – a tiny bite in the side of the African continent.

Beach lodges

It's possible to use one of the **beach lodges** as a base, even if you're just visiting the south coast for the day. Like the beach bars (see pp.144–145), all can provide meals, cold drinks and a shady retreat from the blazing sun. Life moves at a relaxed pace here, even for The Gambia, and after ordering a meal you may have to wait while the staff go off to find the ingredients. If you like the idea of drifting off to sleep to the sound of the ocean and maybe beachcombing at dawn along the empty sands, treat yourself to a few nights at a lodge, even if you already have a northern Kombos resort hotel booked for your entire stay in The Gambia – prices are reasonable, and the sense of tranquility worth a fortune. You could stay in one of their simple rooms, or pitch your own tent in the grounds, or even just rig up a mosquito net over a beach mattress to enjoy the night sky to the full. For details of bush lodges inland, see pp.147–150.

Boboi Beach Lodge Two kilometres north of Kartong ☏776736, ⓦwww.gambia-adventure .com. Right on a glorious stretch of empty beach, the lodge consists of a few very basic thatched roundhouses (each sleeping 2–3) in a small compound shaded by palm trees; there's also room to camp if you have your own tent. The lodge aims to be ecologically sound – there's only one shared washing block, and no mains electricity, just solar power. Transport can be arranged from the airport or the resort area. ❷

Gunjur Beach Motel South of Gunjur fishing beach ☏486065, ⓕ486066. Pleasant but slightly tatty guesthouse on a very pretty stretch of clean sandy beach. Unfortunately, none of the rooms has a sea view – they're separated from the beach by the restaurant, the kitchens and the garden. ❸

Kartong Folonko Rest House Near Kartong, high up on a breezy hill overlooking the sand dunes, this green-roofed house has a shared sitting/dining room and a couple of guest bedrooms; it also serves serious spaghetti and good espresso. ❷

Kobokoto Tourist Camp Near Sanyang ☏799478, mobile ☏922554. On a stark and isolated stretch of beach just round the point north of Sanyang's fishing beach, reached by a track signposted off the main coastal highway, this friendly beach bar has basic guest accommodation in a couple of rooms with private shower (more are planned) and there's solar power and a solar water pump. The restaurant does good breakfasts, fish dishes and tourist standards at reasonable prices. The thatched beach seating area is good for lounging; people come here to fish and hang out. ❷

Nyanya Safari Lodge Kombo Coastal Highway, Tanji ☏394759, mobile ☏797251. A beautifully located, homely place, with a breezy restaurant overlooking the mouth of the River Tanji and guest roundhouses scattered over sand dunes planted with trees, right on the beach. The rooms are very basic but newly decorated. Huge platefuls of Gambian stews with rice are served all day. ❷

Rasta Kunda Near Gunjur, ⓦwww.rastakunda .com. On the wonderful beach between Gunjur fishing beach and Kartong, signposted off the coastal highway. Newly refurbished, this camp is a laid-back place, its large beachside bar playing nonstop reggae. There are twelve simple twin rooms in huts. Come well prepared for mosquitoes. ❷

The beaches

At low tide, tackling the journey in manageable chunks, it's possible to cover the entire length of The Gambia's southern coastline **on foot** or **by bicycle** without leaving the water's edge. If you do take the time to trek along the sand, long-distance, you should make sure you're well protected against the sun and have plenty of water with you, as some of the beaches are more than five kilometres from the coastal highway, with long gaps between eating and drinking places.

Heading southwest from the tourist resorts of the northern Kombos, the beach first begins to change character south of Bijilo, near **Ghana Town**, where you're likely to see fishing *pirogues* bobbing just off shore, strung with flags and painted white with bold geometric designs in dazzling primary colours. Here and at the neighbouring **Brufut beach** you may also see boats waiting on the sand for the tide to turn, the fishermen mending nets and the women sorting out the latest catch. The fishing areas are very localized – away from these, the beaches are normally practically empty, bar a few kids larking about, young men jogging or working out, or villagers walking from one fishing centre to the next. It's a spot that's been earmarked by Sheraton for an ambitious five-star hotel and conference centre. On the cliffs above, accessible by a steep path, or from the coastal highway, is the holy site of **Senneh-Mentering**, a marvellously meditative spot around a craggy old baobab tree, the air wafting with incense burned by the incumbent marabout. Local people come here for cures, consultations and peace, and it's a good place to visit at sundown.

Tanji beach, about 3km southwest of Senneh-Mentering, is one of the biggest fishing centres. Tourists arrive here on organized excursions which give an overview of the whole region, to watch the flurry of birds, boats and people as the fishing boats come in, and sample the eye-wateringly pungent smokey aromas inside the large shed-like smokehouses where blackening bonga fish, neatly laid out in rows, are preserved for local consumption or export. South of here is **Tujering beach**, a long empty stretch, where, with supplies, you could pitch a tent under the stars in almost complete isolation – apart from the cattle often seen strolling freely; the herders take them down to the beach to lick salt from the rocks.

Sanyang beach, just round the point at the southern limit of Tujering beach, is called "Paradise Beach" by the tour companies – it's one of The Gambia's most appealing strands, a broad arc of pale sand backed by coconut palms, that seems to have escaped the recent tidal erosion vitually unscathed. There are a few good beach bars here, and a busy fishing centre, all of which make for a lively scene, but there's plenty of space if you're after isolation and tranquility – especially if you wander round the point, either north or south, to the next bays. Just behind the beach is a fish market where you can see the latest ocean haul laid out on slabs of ice; there's also a lagoon much frequented by wading birds.

More empty sand and a pretty track passing wonderful baobabs connects Sanyang beach with **Gunjur beach**, 10km further south, where the fishing centre is the biggest focus of Kombo South District – a messy, active seafront where fish are more important than tourists and you'll probably be ignored. Here, parked on the shore, you'll see smart, brightly painted Senegalese fishing *pirogues* and rather shabbier Gambian ones.

South of Gunjur fishing beach are some of The Gambia's wildest, emptiest and most beautiful bays, where the sand seems softer than anywhere else and the water is shallow and clean. The last working beach before the Senegalese

Southern coast fishing centres

Southern coast **fishing centres** always buzz with activity, and are absorbing places to spend an hour or so. The Gambian Atlantic is fished by communities of Gambians, Ghanaians and Senegalese, all of whom use heavy wooden *pirogues* with outboard engines and pointed prows, brightly painted in traditional designs. The boats sail out with the tide and back with the tide, hauled in and out of the water on logs, or (in the case of the largest ones) left a few metres out to sea at anchor. The biggest boats take a crew of a dozen, the smaller ones just three or four. Whatever the size of boat, fishing trips can be perilous and lives are lost in storms from time to time.

The **local catch** includes ladyfish, catfish, small sharks and seasnails; *bonga* fish are caught by night. Once the fish have been distributed among the crew and to waiting traders, the nets are spread out to dry beside the beached boats. Just behind the fishing beaches are small fish markets; practically all the fish served in the resort restaurants originates here. Meanwhile, jobbing fish salesmen make a living by pedalling round the remotest villages with the latest catch in handwoven baskets lashed to their bicycle handlebars.

Bonga, span-length, yellowish-white fish that are one of the commonest catches, are either sold fresh, or preserved by smoking over smouldering wood, typically by Ghanaians, Guineans or Malians resident in The Gambia. The **smokehouses** are long, low huts where racks of fish cure for two to five days in clouds of pungent smoke, the light slanting dramatically through gaps in the roof. The finished product, like kippers, and bony but good, can be seen all over The Gambia, packed in crates or baskets for export, or for sale to locals in the up-country markets. Unfortunately, the practice has contributed to rampant deforestation in the Kombos, although it may in time be superseded by freezing. Ice plant development is well underway at Sanyang and Gunjur's fishing centres, but the modernization process has been slowed by a serious slump in the local fishing market, caused by illegal trawler fishing.

border is **Kartong beach**, a long, lonely spit of sand where fishermen from Gunjur, Ghana and Senegal haul in squid, *bonga*, "lobsters" and small sharks for sale in the small shack that constitutes the fish market in this isolated spot.

Beach bars and restaurants

As you'd expect, the beach bars specialize in **fish** and **seafood** – this is probably the best area in the whole country to try local fish at its freshest, hauled out of the ocean only a matter of hours before, and prices are way below the northern Kombos restaurants. Most places have lobster on the menu, which are in fact large crayfish; they're relatively expensive, and not always available. Once caught, the fishermen corral them, alive, in buoy-marked baskets just off the beach, then bring them in to order. Other standards include giant prawns in garlic and grilled barracuda, ladyfish or butterfish, plus African stews and sauces. Some places stay open in the evening, lighting a campfire on the beach for a mellow session of drumming and dancing under the stars.

Baransang Beach Bar & Restaurant Near Sanyang, on the bay north of Sanyang fishing beach. Barely a shack, this modest little beach bar serves fish, curry, omelettes or salad at low prices. **Kaira Kunda Bar and Restaurant** Just south of Gunjur fishing beach ☏ 985819. Cool, relaxed, friendly shack-type beach bar, a place to play drums or just hang out over cheap drinks, cous-

cous or barbecued fish.
Osprey Beach Bar On the beach north of Sanyang fishing beach. The most popular beach bar on "Paradise Beach" – tour groups are sometimes brought here en masse, so you may find bumsters too. The pale powdery sand in front of the big thatched shack-type eating area is beautifully kept, as if groomed daily, a very pleasant

change after the scruffier beaches in the busiest resort areas. It serves big portions of the usual selection of grills at slightly above-average prices for Sanyang.

Paradise Beach Bar South of Sanyang fishing beach. More remote than Sanyang's other beach bars, this place serves the usual fish standards and cool drinks, at very reasonable prices.

Rainbow Bar & Disco Sanyang fishing village, just inland from the bush taxi garage and fish market ☎907796. Connected to the *Rainbow Beach Bar*, this nightspot gets lively on Friday and Saturday nights with a mostly local clientele. There's only one room plus a backyard, but people travel from the northern Kombos to hang out here and move to international dance music.

Rainbow Beach Bar Just south of Sanyang fishing beach ☎907796. Bright new enterprise, serving well-prepared food under a thatched shelter like a beach marquee. It's a little too close to the fishing beach to make swimming here comfortable, but there's open beach a couple of minutes' stroll south, and a freshwater shower here. There are regular sunset buffets and campfire nights, and you can camp out here. Competition between the Sanyang beach bars is stiff, so the food and drinks here are keenly priced. Groups should book in advance.

Sankule Beach Hotel Near Gunjur ☎486098. In a gorgeous, remote setting on the point north of Gunjur fishing beach, reached by an unmarked bush track from the highway or via the beach. Beautifully designed, this remote place functions as a restaurant (if you give them notice of your arrival) and a relaxing bar, all whitewash and clean lines; the beachside garden is pleasantly shaded with trees. The British owner is a drumming aficionado – Sankule Beach is often the scene of impromptu jamming sessions.

Kombo South villages

The **Kombo South villages** are small, traditional rural communities, typically home to half a dozen or so families representing The Gambia's four largest ethnic groups –Mandinka, Fula, Wolof and Jola. There are also small communities of animist Manjagos on the village fringes, making a living from palm-tapping and oil-making. In contrast, rural villages further up-country tend to be dominated by members of a single tribe. The Kombo South villages are built around their mosque and the marketplace, where women trade fruit and vegetables grown in the village vegetable plots, and fish, fresh and smoked, from the nearby fishing centres. With the exception of **Tanji**, which is close to The Gambia's only bird reserve and a unique museum of traditional culture, these villages have little in the way of conventional tourist attractions, but they're relaxed and enjoyable places to experience traditional village life. You'll nearly always find simple local places serving rice and sauce near the market or bush taxi garage.

The rich green forested and palm-planted countryside in this area is a great wilderness to explore on foot, mountain bike or by 4WD vehicle, where birds are easy to spot, particularly in the rainy season and the early dry season, and you may see several species of monkey – keeping them away from crops is a nightmare for farmers.

Brufut and Ghana Town

BRUFUT and **GHANA TOWN** are adjacent coastal villages lying between the ocean and the forest about 7km south of Kololi. Both are farming and fishing communities that don't see many visitors at present – although a new music school is soon to be established on the edge of Brufut, and the area will change completely if plans to build a vast new international hotel and conference centre on the nearby beach go ahead.

Brufut is a long-established village of old-fashioned brick compounds with corrugated iron roofs, home to Mandinka farmers and vegetable gardeners, while Ghana Town is a community of Ghanaian fish-driers and smokers. There's an unusually strong Christian community in Ghana Town, as well as Muslims. The village is also well known for its natural healer, Dr Alhaji Al-

Birdwatching in the Tanji River (Karinti) Bird Reserve

The Tanji River Karinti Bird Reserve is particularly good for sightings of both coastal and woodland species. Many gulls, terns and waders feed and roost around the lagoons near the mouth of the River Tanji, including Caspian, royal and lesser crested terns, and white-fronted plover. Inland you're likely to find four-banded sandgrouse, whistling cisticola, Bruce's green pigeon, yellow-fronted tinkerbird, yellow-crowned gonolek, northern crombec and western palearctic migrants such as melodious, olivaceous and subalpine warblers, and rufous nightingale. The area supports plenty of fish, small mammals and amphibians which make tempting prey for over thirty species of raptor, including African hobby. From March to September, royal terns, Caspian terns, western reef herons, kelp gulls and grey-headed gulls all nest and breed on the Bijol Islands – there are no other known breeding sites for these species in the country – and access to the islands is prohibited at this time. At other times, it's an excellent location to watch seabirds.

Hassan. Compared to Brufut, Ghana Town is a down-at-heel-looking place, with half-built cement block walls and unkempt compounds.

Apart from the beach, the main reason to visit the Brufut area is to go birdwatching in **Brufut woods**, a large area of community forest on Brufut's eastern edge, accessed via bumpy backroads. Species you may see here include Senegal batis, Verreaux's eagle owl and various sunbirds.

Tanji River (Karinti) Bird Reserve and Bijol Islands

The **Tanji River (Karinti) Bird Reserve** (daily 8am–dusk; D31.50), established in 1993, was the first bird reserve to be gazetted in the Gambia, due largely to the efforts of a group of passionately committed British bird enthusiasts. A narrow strip of land on the north side of Tanji village, encompassing the River Tanji, its estuary and the Bijol Islands, it contains in just over six square kilometres a wide variety of bird habitats, including mangrove, salt flats, lily pools, dry woodland, coastal dune scrub woodland and lagoons. Small though it is, over 300 species of bird have been recorded here. Unfortunately, little has been done to make the reserve visitor-friendly – there are no trails officially mapped or hides built, so to get the best out of a visit you should go with an experienced bird guide.

The **Bijol Islands**, or Kajonyi Islands, are the only offshore islands in The Gambia, situated in the Atlantic 1.5km from Brufut and Tanji. They form part of the Tanji River (Karinti) Bird Reserve, and they have important breeding populations of sea birds and green turtles, and visiting populations of sea turtles, the very rare Mediterranean monk seals, minke whales, Atlantic humpback dolphins and bottle-nose dolphins. Access to the islands is normally prohibited to protect the wildlife, but it's possible to join one of the boat trips to the islands organized by the Department of Parks and Wildlife Management, which run a few times a month between October and March, taking up to five visitors at D200 each. You leave from the beach at Brufut or Tanji, and may glimpse turtles and dolphins during the crossing. For further information, contact the Department HQ at Abuko (☎375888) or the TRKBR warden (☎919219).

Tanji

Around 12km southwest of Kololi, straight down the coastal highway and within easy cycling or driving distance of the resorts, is the coastal village of **TANJI**, (also spelt Tanje). One of the few South Kombo villages very close to the beach, it's the most-visited village in this area, featuring on "Bush and Beach" tours (see p.56). Unfortunately, its popularity with tourists means you often get "*toubabed*" mercilessly by local kids; even so, it's a friendly and accessible place, and a good opportunity to see the hectic, noisy, colourful scene of a Gambian fishing community at work. The beach here is not the best for swimming – it's a working beach, strewn with fishing nets and, inevitably, fish – but there are bathing places a short stroll or bike ride away. Tanji's main street leads inland from the coastal highway, which itself passes close to the ocean just south of the Tanji River. The village is regularly served by direct *gelleh-gelleh* van bush taxis from Serrekunda.

The most comfortable **accommodation** in Kombo South, and very popular with birdwatchers, is the *Paradise Inn Lodge* in Tanji village (☎922444, mobile ☎912559, ⓦwww.tanji.nl.paradise; ❸). This lodge, signposted from the main street through the village, is 3km by road from the coastal highway and the fishing beach; you can also be collected by boat from the bridge over the River Tanji. The twenty rooms are in Fula-style roundhouses set in woodland ringing with birdsong, right on the banks of the river. They're attractive, though some are a little small; all have mosquito nets and fans, and there's power from a generator twelve hours a day. In peak season the Sunday evening buffets include freshly barbecued fish, served under the lodge's huge spreading mango tree.

Even deeper in the backstreets of Tanji village is the *Kairoh Garden Guest House* (☎903526, ⓔkairohgarden@hotmail.com; ❷), a peaceful retreat on the far side of Tanji village, about 5km from the beach. Although the compound, planted with fruit trees and flowering shrubs, is huge, the twelve simple rooms (some self-contained) are all squashed together in thin-walled blocks, but they're clean, with African-style beds. There's also plenty of room to camp, and a sleepy bar/restaurant prepares Gambian- and European-style meals to order. You can phone for directions or arrange to be picked up from Tanji village.

Just south of the bridge over the River Tanji, near *Nyanya Safari Lodge* (see p.142), Tanji Camel Safaris offer's half-hour camel ride along the beach for around £3.50/$5 per person.

Tanje Village Museum

Right on the main coastal highway on the southern edge of Tanji village is the **Tanje Village Museum** (daily 9am–5pm; D40), a small but well-thought-out private museum of nature and traditional culture. It's an education centre that's all about participation – there are musical instruments to play, craftsmen and *kora* players to chat to, a traditional compound to nose around, and a nature trail to follow. Tour companies often build a stop here into their tours of the area.

Inside the gate is a small exhibition hall with information about Gambian **wildlife** and a roomful of **musical instruments** – visitors are free to find out what sounds they all make – the instruments, though traditional, are not irreplaceable. Much of the museum's interest is outside in the large garden, where the craftsmen, compound and nature trail are found. Part of the museum's policy is to promote traditional **crafts**, and you can usually watch weavers creating strips of cotton cloth on hand-looms, and blacksmiths making jewellery using hand-pumped bellows. Weaving is a traditional craft passed from father to son, and senior weavers present traditional ebony shuttles to their students in recognition of good progress. Weaving by hand is a painstaking process –

rethreading a loom can take a whole day. Blacksmithing, too, is a traditional occupation in Gambian society; smiths also make tools and knives, and have a further role in the village, circumcising boys at initiation rites.

A major part of the museum garden consists of a **family compound** arranged and furnished in traditional Mandinka style, with explanations of which family members would sleep in which huts and how their roles fit together. Much of the rest of the garden is taken up by a **nature trail**, planted with numerous indigenous trees, herbs and shrubs – a leaflet identifies and describes them all, explaining their uses, whether as food, medicine or building materials. Look out for the wild coffee plant – its roasted beans can be used as a coffee substitute, but when raw they're used as rat poison. You'll also see the locust bean tree, whose seeds cure all sorts of ailments and are known as the "Gambian Viagra". The trail is best appreciated at the very beginning of the dry season when it's lush; in winter, it's rather bare and forlorn-looking.

At the back of the plot is a new conference centre and some visitor **accommodation** in a few traditional huts (❷). In keeping with the museum's mission to demonstrate traditional village life, they're sparse, with straw and sacking mattresses and no electricity or running water. Guests have the run of the museum, so you can learn about traditional weaving or metalwork from the resident craftsmen during your stay. The museum also has a *bantaba* bar where there's often a *kora* player ready to entertain visitors, and a gift shop with some interesting goods not often seen elsewhere, such as *warri* boards (see p.249), hand-woven textiles made by the weavers, stools made from tree-stumps, and dried herbs such as *kinkiliba* and *wonjo,* used to make infusions.

Tujering, Sanyang and Gunjur

About 7km south of Tanji on the Kombo coastal highway, and 4km inland from the beach, is **Tujering**, a pleasant old South Kombo village that owes nothing of its character to tourism or colonialism. Here, you'll find instead whitewashed mudstone houses and a central crossroads with meeting place, mosque and market. South of here, the highway bends inland to **Sanyang**, 8km from Tujering, and, another 10km on, **Gunjur**, both mango-shaded settlements of sandy streets and cement-block compounds, little-visited by tourists. Both are around 6km inland, and each has an associated fishing community on its attractive beach (for details of beach bars and lodges here, see pp.144–145).

Signposted off the coastal highway, on the road that leads from Sanyang village centre towards its fishing beach, in bushland about 2km from the sea, is *Sanyang Nature Camp* (☎945730; ❷). This quiet, friendly lodge has small but attractive rooms in thatched roundhouses in a huge dusty garden compound. There's electricity from a generator – when there's enough diesel to run it. On the road leading from the highway from central Gunjur to Gunjur fishing beach, again about 2km from the ocean, is *Kajabang Point* (no phone, ❷), a bush lodge in a small garden compound. The facilities here are very basic, with wellwater for washing, but its four rooms in huts are pretty and well kept, and there's food on request.

All three village centres are served by *gelleh-gelleh* **bush taxis** from Serrekunda and Brikama, and are good places to find simple Gambian food in local eateries.

Kartong

One of the oldest villages in The Gambia, **KARTONG** (also spelt Kartung) lies close to the coast, near the mouth of the saltwater **River Allahein** (San

△ Makasutu culture forest (drumming and dancing)

Pedro), where The Gambia finishes and French-speaking Senegal takes over. The new coastal highway ends here, so it's a bit of a cul-de-sac, with an atmosphere distinctly different from the other villages of the southern Kombos. It's a remote and utterly relaxing place to enjoy the coastal landscape and its wildlife, and there's also a sacred crocodile pool and a reptile farm. It's surrounded by beach, bush, sand dunes and the eerily empty salt flats and mangrove swamps bordering the river.

Kartong has a population of around 3500, mostly Mandinka plus some Jola and other minority ethnic groups, and the sense of community here is extremely strong. There's an old-fashioned atmosphere of courtesy, order and calm about the village which makes it an appealing place. The sealed road is still something of a novelty here, and children watch wide-eyed when vehicles drive into the village. The sand mining that scarred the dunes between the village and the sea has now been outlawed; the new pools created where sand was removed now attract a stunning variety of **birds**, including migrants from northern Europe. Species commonly found here include African jacana, African crake, purple swamphen, green sandpiper, wood sandpiper and various plovers.

North of Kartong there's a **bush lodge** 2km from the beach, *Balaba Nature Camp* (T919012, ❷), reached by turning east off the main highway roughly halfway between Gunjur and Kartong. It's rustic in the extreme, with twelve round huts thatched with palm fronds in a garden compound that's right in the leafy wilderness. Village visits and music sessions are offered, but the place is a bit lifeless. A beach lodge, *Kartong Folonko Rest House* (see p.142) lies just outside the village, and a luxury ecotourism camp is due to open on the bay nearest the Reptile Farm. A few **bush taxis** run to Kartong from Serrekunda and Brikama.

Gambian Reptile Farm

Signposted off the main south coast highway north of Kartong, the **Gambian Reptile Farm** (W www.gambianreptiles.bizhosting.com; D35) is home to a fine collection of snakes, lizards, geckos, chameleons and turtles. The place is set up not as a zoo, but as a research and education centre. There has recently been a high-profile campaign in The Gambia attempting to raise awareness of the need to protect the wild snake population, since snakes have a crucial role to play in the natural ecosystem and can be very beneficial to humans – for example, they eat rodents that would otherwise damage grain stores). The Reptile Farm encourages people to get rather closer to snakes than they might normally choose. Among the healthy-looking collection here are slender, green common bush snakes and African beauty snakes. There are a couple of puff adders, a species which kill more people than any other African snake – their sluggish natures makes them easy to step on, and an adult specimen carries enough venom to kill eight elephants. The puff adders are kept at a safe distance, but you can have a more friendly two-metre-long royal python draped around your shoulders.

Follonko crocodile pool

On the seaward edge of Kartong near the dunes is the **Follonko crocodile pool**, a murky green, lily-choked swamp in a deep, shady grove; local kids will guide you there. Home to a fair number of crocs, it's an atmospheric and sacred place, similar to the Katchikali pool at Bakau, but far less visited by tourists and more regularly used as a place of pilgrimage and prayer. Female elders from two of Kartong's communities, Muslim Mandinka and Christian Karoninka

(Karoninka is a Mandinka dialect), visit to pray and ask favours on Monday and Friday mornings. They also preside over the pilgrims, who come here bringing money, salt, kola nuts, candles or other offerings. For more on crocodile pools, see the box on p.112.

The River Allahein

If you have your own transport, you'll be able to leave the centre of Kartong and drive south, through open countryside planted with gingerbread plums, big banana plants and palms, to the last extremity of Gambian territory, a military checkpoint near the mouth of the River Allahein. A short drive from here, you can turn right towards the ocean fishing centre (see pp.143–144). Alternatively, you can turn left towards the **river fishing base** on the River Allahein, where sharkfin and shark steaks are salted and laid out on tables to dry in the sun. Most of the shark caught here is sold to exporters with customers in Ghana and Asia (sharkfin destined for Hong Kong fetches well over £30/$48 a kilo). Some fishermen specialize in only hunting shark for this market, in small *pirogues* which you can see moored in the river. There are also *bonga* smokehouses on the shore.

From here it's possible to cross the river by *pirogue* and continue to **Abéné** in Casamance, Senegal. However, this is not the best place to cross the border, unless you're planning on coming straight back by the same route – the military officials at the Gambian post may check your stuff, but they won't necessarily stamp your passport with an exit stamp, resulting in questions and hassle in Senegal.

Brikama and around

Heading inland from Serrekunda and the resorts, the first substantial town you reach is **Brikama**, a regional capital and a gateway to the up-country provinces. It's famous for its rich musical heritage – many Gambian traditional musicians come from here – and its woodcarvers' market, a routine stop on tourist excursions to the area. It also has an increasingly vibrant club scene: a new sister club to *Jokor*, the legendary Serrekunda club, is pulling in crowds from all over the Kombos.

Nearby are two high-profile ecotourism projects. The first is **Makasutu Culture Forest**, a beautifully preserved area of woodland and mangrove – guided tours from the coastal resorts are extremely popular. The owners and managers of Makasutu have just opened a new luxury bush lodge on the site, **Mandina Lodge**, the Gambia's most exclusive and attractive accommodation by far. The other eco-venture in this area is a village camp, at the Jola hamlet of **Tumani Tenda**. South of Brikama, around the villages of **Marakissa** and **Darsilami**, is a little-visited area of woodland and savanna particularly good for birdwatching.

Brikama

If you're heading up-country, you have to make a deliberate diversion off the main highway to visit **BRIKAMA**, which lies right in the middle of the Kombo peninsula, about 35km southwest of Banjul. Its population has overtaken than that of Banjul, making it the Gambia's third largest town after Serrekunda and Bakau. It's not really geared up to tourism, with very little in the way of visitor accommodation, and until recently only one well-known

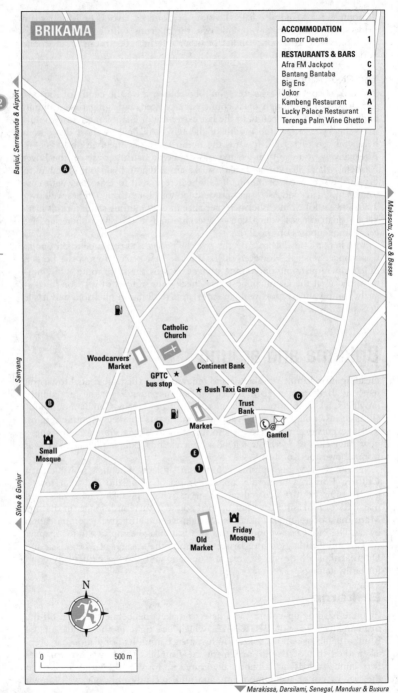

BRIKAMA

Banjul, Serrekunda & Airport

Makasutu, Soma & Basse

Sanyang

Sifoe & Gunjur

Catholic
Church

Woodcarvers'
Market

Continent Bank

GPTC
bus stop

★ Bush Taxi Garage

Trust
Bank

Market

Gamtel

Small
Mosque

Old
Market

Friday
Mosque

N

0   500 m

Marakissa, Darsilami, Senegal, Manduar & Busura

conventional attraction, the woodcarvers' market. In the past, few tourists have stayed overnight, but this is beginning to change. Brikama has always been famous for music, with a great many traditional musicians hailing from here, and the town now has a very cool new nightclub, *Jokor*. Similar in ambience to its sister club in Serrekunda, but much bigger, it hosts live music events featuring major Senegambian singers and bands.

The **people** of Brikama are generally very warm and welcoming. The social scene for most local families is quiet and provincial (though the opening of the new *Jokor* nightclub has begun to change that), and consequently naming ceremonies and other celebrations turn into big public events, going on late into the night; visitors are often invited along. Brikama is a good place to experience life in a Gambian compound; this is especially true if you're interested in **traditional music** and get invited to stay with one of the town's eminent families of musicians, some of whom can offer first-rate tuition in traditional drum, *balafon* and dance (see p.52). The town is home, or has been home, to much of The Gambia's musical "royalty", including Dembo Konte, Foday Musa Suso, Malamini Jobarteh and Tata Dindin. With such an abundance of home-grown talent, you'd expect Brikama's live music scene to be astounding. In reality, however, *Jokor* has filled a gap – even now, when the local *jalis* play in Brikama, it's normally at a low-profile private occasion in somebody's compound.

Although Brikama is a substantial town, it offers a much more easy-going urban experience than Serrekunda or even Bakau, with its busy but relaxed market and quiet sandy streets shaded by spreading mango trees. The community is known for being traditional, conservative and deeply religious, and the imams here are particularly powerful; they strongly opposed the opening of *Jokor*, concerned that this would attract sex workers and drug dealers and hasten the town's moral decline. It's a town with plenty of character and a good degree of apparent prosperity. Unlike most Gambian towns, the main road is lit by streetlights, all the major access roads are newly surfaced, and there's new housing being built on the western outskirts. Not far out of Brikama, at Nyamberi, on the road to Serrekunda, The Gambia's first large shopping mall is under construction. However, despite this relative affluence, the town suffers from acute **water shortages**. If you decide to spend some time in Brikama and are invited to stay in a family compound you may end up helping carry water from a shared tap, a few streets away.

Brikama is a busy transport hub. Minibus bush taxis arrive at the **taxi garage** in the middle of town. GPTC **buses** stop at the bus park a little north of the taxi garage. Approaching from Serrekunda along the main south bank highway, you turn right into Brikama, passing *Jokor* and the woodcarvers' market on the right before you reach the bush taxi garage, market and shops, all on your left, in the centre of town. Approaching from the east, you turn left off the highway onto the road taking you into the east side of town; once you're in the centre, the market will be on your right. Continuing along this road takes you out towards the Kombo South villages of Sifoe and Gunjur, or to Sanyang.

The town is small enough to explore on foot, but should you wish to venture further afield, there are always plenty of **yellow local taxis** waiting near the market and post office.

The Town

Brikama's famous **woodcarvers' market** (daily 8am–dusk) on the main road leading southeast from the south bank highway towards the town centre is much bigger than its rather tatty street entrance suggests. There's a large area of gift stalls inside the entrance, and behind this, the "factory" where craftsmen cut up newly arrived timber into rough forms for the carvers manning the stalls to finish with adze, sandpaper and wax polish. As you wander about you'll hear a constant background noise of tapping and rubbing over the usual racket of radios and cassette players. The market vendors can be very persistent, but they have to abide by a code of conduct which means you shouldn't be chased from stall to stall by touts. You'll need to hone your bargaining skills, and it's wise to visit at a quiet time, rather than with a big mob of tourists.

Most of the **carvings** here are formulaic – you'll see plenty of lions, hippos, giraffes, elongated Africans and abstract forms, plus ashtrays, dolls and masks, just like the ones for sale at tourist-trap craft stalls all over the Gambian coastal resort area – but, with careful sifting, you might come across something original with real style and character. The wood most commonly used is teak; mahogany is rarer and ebony extremely rare. Some "ebony" carvings are in fact teak rubbed with black shoe polish, and some carvings have been distressed to make them look antique. You won't find genuine fetish objects here, whatever the vendors claim, but some stalls sell beautiful masks and statues made to traditional ritual designs.

Brikama's **main market** is also worth a visit. The produce on sale is like that found at any other large Gambian market – there's still the same amazing jumble of ripe and over-ripe fruit and vegetables, malodorous fish, garish plastic household goods, richly coloured bolts of fabric and cheap imported clothing – but the atmosphere is comfortable, without the cramped areas of covered stalls that can be oppressive in markets elsewhere.

The southwest edge of town is a Manjago area, easily identified by the presence of hairy pigs scuttling around under the palms and mango trees. There are two palm wine "ghettoes" here where you can sample the local brew. On the outskirts of Brikama is the **Santangba** at Kotokali, a sacred grove of trees that's frequented by small animals and numerous birds, and which marks the site of the first settlement in this area of the thirteenth-century Mandinka migrants who travelled from Mali in the time of Sundiata Keita. The grove is said to be occupied by ancestral spirits, so the locals are forbidden from hunting and fruit-gathering here, and prior to circumcision ceremonies it becomes "bush school", where initiates are brought for their instruction in tribal lore. To visit the site, first ask for directions to the compound of the *alkalo* of Brikama, and then ask there for a guide.

Practicalities

The **post office** is open Mon–Sat, 8am–4pm. The Gamtel office next door is open daily, 8am–10pm for phone and Internet services. There are two **banks**, Trust Bank and Continent Bank, neither of which has an ATM. The main **fuel station** is opposite the bush taxi garage.

Currently, the only **accommodation** option in Brikama, unless you're invited to stay in a family compound, is is the *Domorr Deema Mini Hotel* on Mosque Rd (☏903302; ❷). This simple place with a very local feel is clean, but can be noisy. It has four very small rooms with fans and shared shower. There's also a small restaurant – you can sit at the streetside table and eat omelettes, chicken, steak, or rice and sauce at low prices – but you're usually better off heading for the *Kambeng Restaurant* (see opposite).

Eating, drinking and nightlife

The arrival of *Jokor* and its excellent restaurant has transformed Brikama's entertainment scene, drawing visitors from the northern urban areas and all over the Kombos, particularly for gala music events. Tour groups sometimes visit the *Bantang Bantaba* for a drink; all the other options in town are low-key, with a very local atmosphere.

Afra FM Jackpot Music Café ☎497141. On the main road east of the town centre, this club has an open-air stage and dance floor, and a small indoor bar area. There aren't many places to sit, and it can feel cramped when busy, but the atmosphere is good. Ladies' night is Wednesday, there's a live *sabar* band on Fridays and a rap DJ on Saturdays. Daily 5pm–5am.

Bantang Bantaba Methodist Mission, Sanyang Rd. The Brikama Methodists serve low-priced drinks including *wonjo*, sandwiches and snacks from their small kitchen adjoining an open-sided café area, but the place doesn't have much atmosphere. In the grounds there's a short forest walk and an orchard where fruit is grown for the mission's jam-making enterprise. Tour groups sometimes stop here, so local kids hassle visitors. Daily 10am–dusk.

Big Ens Bar and Restaurant Gunjur Rd. An echoey, garage-like space with a shiny corrugated iron ceiling and a youth-club atmosphere, serving drinks from the bar 24 hours a day, plus simple meals like chicken and chips. There's CNN on TV in the daytime, and on Friday and Saturday nights there's a club DJ playing ragga and rap, attracting a young crowd.

Jokor On the main road into town from Serrekunda. Brikama's newest club is cool, comfortable and upmarket, with a mellow atmosphere aimed at the slick young Gambian middle class. DJs play international and West African dance tracks, and there are three bars. Big name Senegambian artists sometimes play here – listen out for radio ads, or ask taxi drivers and guides. The main space is a pretty, crazy-tiled garden dominated by trees wound with coloured rope lights, hung with local contemporary art. Not many tourists come here as yet, partly due to Brikama's shortage of accommodation, but a hotel and swimming pool are planned. Leaving the club in the small hours, you may find a minibus heading for Serrekunda, but otherwise you'll have to pay a premium for a local taxi; better to come with your own cab and pay him to wait. Over-21s only, no trainers; daily till 4am; free Mon–Thurs, entry fee Fri–Sun (D25–100).

Kambeng Restaurant At *Jokor* 8am–1am. By far Brikama's best restaurant, and extremely good value; worth visiting even if you're not hanging out at the club. Excellent grilled barracuda and chicken *yassa*, plus other grills and prawn dishes at low prices. At lunchtime there's a daily African special with rice.

Lucky Palace Restaurant Mosque Rd. Guinean-run local restaurant, serving omelettes, chicken and rice with very fresh *tapalapa* bread and excellent coffee, Gambian-style. It looks shabby, but everything is fresh and tasty.

Makasutu Culture Forest

Makasutu Culture Forest (daily 8am–dusk; D400/350 per day/half-day) was The Gambia's first high-profile ecotourism project, and has been open to the public since 1999. It has since become one of the most popular day-trip destinations from the coastal resorts. It lies about 5km east of Brikama, situated on a lovely bend in the Mandina Bolon, a glassy-smooth mangrove creek. The forest here is inspiring and varied, with clearings and areas of dense foliage, termite mounds and some truly beautiful glades, mature trees and saplings – young trees are still growing to replace those lost to loggers. Visitors to the park are introduced to the natural environment on a guided walk through the forest and a cruise, by hand-paddled dugout, along the creek. There's also a chance to enjoy some high-energy local drumming and join in the dancing. For those who would like to spend more than a day in the area, there is new **luxury accommodation** at Makasutu's *Mandina Lodge*, a stunning creekside bush lodge that sets new standards of quality and service for hotels in The Gambia, and is colossally expensive in local terms – but worth it.

Most tourists visit Makasutu by organized one-day excursion, including return transport from the resorts and the park entry fee, for about £29/$46. The park entry fee covers the standard full-day **guided tour**, including lunch and entertainment. This is highly enjoyable, but not really recommended for ardent wildlife watchers, as you'll be touring in a group of up to 25 people,

The story of Makasutu Culture Forest

Makasutu is a testament to the remarkable vision of two unstoppably energetic British business partners, engineer **James English** and architect **Lawrence Williams**. The pair came across the forest in 1992, during a lengthy search for a site for a new travellers' lodge. At the time, Makasutu (meaning "ancient and sacred deep forest" in Mandinka) was uninhabited – local legend maintained it was haunted by djinns and giants plus a *ninkinanka*, or dragon-devil, and the area was therefore used mainly for tribal rituals. Undaunted, the Brits secured four acres of land here and left the country to earn enough capital to start construction. Unfortunately, in their absence, with the myth of the forest blown, locals set about cutting down trees, and hundreds of mature specimens were lost before English and Williams were able to buy the remaining four square kilometres of the forest and fence it, creating a woodland habitat conservation project.

English and Williams have succeeded in making the forest environment accessible to visitors, partly through building sympathetic and imaginative structures to a standard never before seen in The Gambia, using local craftsmen – only their design is non-Gambian. In the process, they have guaranteed the survival of this beautiful habitat and opened the eyes of many visitors not only to The Gambia's natural biodiversity, but also to elements of village culture and tradition. They have also shown great commitment to the local community, and have provided employment for over a hundred villagers.

and you won't be there at the best times of day to see birds or mammals. It's possible to visit independently, too. If you're staying at *Mandina Lodge* (see p.155) you can wander round the forest whenever you choose; if you're just visiting the park, you have to pay either the half-day or full-day entry fee when you arrive and join a guided tour, making it expensive compared to Abuko Nature Reserve. However, Makasutu offers more than Abuko – the site is larger and includes more habitats, and the guided walk, creek cruise, lunch and entertainment are all excellent. Visitor numbers are normally limited to a total of around fifty per day to minimize the daily impact on the forest environment. You find the site by heading east beyond Brikama along the main south bank highway, looking out for the roadside sign for Kinderdorf Bottrop, then turning north along an unmade track marked by a totem pole.

Guided tours of Makasutu

On arrival at Makasutu, you make your way towards the tour meeting place through a woodland area distinguished by an enormous **termite mound** (See box on p.158) and dotted with **treestump sculptures**, the work of a local artist. Representing highly kinetic running, leaping and flying creatures, they're like frozen animal spirits, breathing new life into the remains of trees cut down before the forest could be protected. There is then a welcoming talk at the *Baobab Bar and Restaurant*, a rather spectacular space like an open-sided cathedral of timber and cane, hung with carvings, with a soaring thatched canopy where bats sometimes sleep.

The order of the day's programme of guided walk and creek cruise depends on the tides. Along the route through the forest, which is an easy walk along shady paths, you're likely to pass the hideout of a **tradititional herbalist**, who makes remedies and infusions from plants found in the forest, and sells animist amulets made from knotted rhun palm fronds. There'll also be a stop to admire the athleticism of a local Manjago **palm-tapper**, who shins up a palm tree in typical style, with the help of a loop sling encircling his body and the tree trunk.

Your guide should point out some of the different species, such as the camel foot tree, whose bark is used to make *kankurang* costumes (see p.255); young mahogany trees, one of The Gambia's protected species; ironwood trees, named because their timber is so solid; and strangler figs, common in this area, wound around host trees. You probably won't see many birds or animals on the way, though, because of the size of your group and the time of day. The Makasutu monkeys are much more elusive than those in the woods at Abuko or Bijilo, but your guide may well spot one in the distance for you; the rainy season, when fruit is ripening on the trees, is the most likely time of year to see one.

The tour of the *bolon* in a traditional **dugout**, hollowed from a single mahogany log, is one of the highlights of the day. The water is glossy and utterly peaceful, with no noise but people's voices, the dip of the paddle, and occasional bird calls. You may see thick-knees and herons watching from the mud-banks under the shade of the mangroves. Lunch is an excellent **buffet** of Gambian food served in the Baobab area. It's here that you might notice that Makasutu is right beneath the flight path into Banjul International Airport – aircraft occasionally shatter the peace.

There's more noise of a much more melodious sort after lunch when a troupe of Jola **drummers** and **dancers** from the neighbouring village of Kembujeh, many of whom work at the forest full-time in other roles, start performing on the natural platform under the big baobab tree. Everybody is encouraged to join in – the women pass around strings of beads as an invitation to dance – and it's a lot of fun.

Mandina Lodge

The opening of *Mandina Lodge* (Ⓦ www.makasutu.com; book through The Gambia Experience, Ⓦ www.gambia.co.uk; ◑) was a new departure in Gambian tourism. It's the country's first truly luxurious bush lodge, and the first upmarket accommodation to be designed with ecologically sound principles in mind. The food and service are, as you'd expect, very good.

At the time of writing, only part of the accommodation is complete, attractively situated in the wilderness on the northern edge of Makasutu Forest, beside a peaceful stretch of the Mandina Bolon. When finished, there will be two lodges on stilts, and two floating like anchored houseboats in the *bolon*, housing a maximum of eight guests in total. The houses on stilts are reached by way of a timber walkway crossing a mangrove thicket, with water and mud

Makasutu Wildlife Trust

Makasutu Wildlife Trust (Ⓣ 782633, Ⓔ drumohq@qanet.gm) is a registered wildlife conservation charity based at Makasutu, operating a membership scheme, open to all. It aims to involve local communities in active preservation of wildlife and habitats threatened by urbanization, hunting, and farming, and to encourage greater awareness of The Gambia's biodiversity. Its activities include educational programmes for schools and community groups; training sessions in wildlife-guiding, biodiversity and conservation for various organizations; publishing conservation information; and running an animal clinic for injured and orphaned wild animals. The trust organizes guided walks and talks for tourists and locals; recent events have included an evening walk through Abuko Nature Reserve, a slideshow and talk on Gambian wildlife, and a morning walk in Bijilo, priced at D50–100 for trust members and D100–150 for non-members, with all proceeds going to the trust. Membership is open to individuals, families and groups.

Termite mounds

Termite mounds, found all over The Gambian countryside, are commonly well over two metres tall, and look rather like fairy-tale castles, with turrets and towers. Colonies of termites build these mini-kingdoms by binding the soil with half-digested cellulose, the by-product of their diet of wood and straw, fetched by the worker termites. Inside the mound, the queen termite spends her life breeding. When the queen dies the colony migrates elsewhere, and squirrels, snakes and lizards move in to the abandoned mound.

Active termite mounds are used by female **monitor lizards** as incubators for their eggs. The lizard digs into a mound and, depending on the species, lays between eight and sixty eggs inside. The termites then industriously repair the damage, effectively sealing the eggs inside in a protected and tempurature-controlled environment. It can take many months for the eggs to hatch, normally in the rainy season when the mound is soft enough for the young monitors to dig their way out.

Termites are generally seen as a **pest**, wreaking havoc anywhere wood and thatch are used as building materials. However, they do have a use in **water divining**: the presence of termites indicates a high water table, so villagers planning to dig a new well start by looking for a termite mound. In addition, the fine clay from mounds makes extremely good water jars, as it's a good insulator.

below and tangled roots to left and right. Inside, everything is exquisitely detailed, with a four-poster bed decorated with *bogolan* mudcloth, under a lofty thatched roof, and huge windows overlooking the *bolon*. There's also a private deck with hammocks, and above this is a timber tower with another bed, for sleeping or catnapping in the open air.

The shared areas of the lodge have stunning vistas and more lovely detailing – cowries, carvings, old drums and pounding pestles are all worked into the design, and the swimming pool must be the most beautiful in The Gambia, its curves inspired by the positions of the trees bounding the natural clearing chosen for the site. The lodge's ecofriendly credentials aren't impeccable – the pool uses a lot of water, there's a diesel generator and mahogany features heavily in the construction – but there are, at least, solar-powered lights and water-heaters, and composting toilets in rooms, designed to avoid polluting the *bolon*.

A little further downstream, *Joyea Lodge*, a low cost alternative to *Mandina*, is currently being renovated. This creekside lodge has timber cabin rooms, plenty of space to camp and a large garden; it will have a huge new à la carte restaurant with the same kind of swagger as the gorgeous timber constructions at Makasutu, and also a swimming pool.

Tumani Tenda

TUMANI TENDA is a hamlet in a picturesque location deep in the Gambian countryside, on the banks of the Kafuta Bolon, about 3km north of the main south bank highway, around 25km east of Brikama. It's home to a Jola community of seven extended families, and in many ways it's a typical rural village – but unlike many similar small communities it has the special distinctions of being economically self-sufficient, and of being the site of a community-run ecotourism project. Visitors are able to spend a day or longer at Tumani Tenda, learning about traditional rural culture and enjoying the peaceful environment.

In 1997, the villagers were awarded a £2000 prize for outstanding community forest husbandry, with the proviso that the money be spent on a community project. The result was *Kachokorr Camp* (☎462057, mobile ☎903662,

Ⓔtumanitenda@hotmail.com, ❷), established as a base for visitors, 500m from the village itself, in thin woodland right on the edge of the creek.

To **get to Tumani Tenda**, you can either travel all the way by private taxi, or take a bush taxi from Serrekunda or Brikama heading for Bulok or Bwiam, and get off at the signposted track between Sotokoi and Bulok. You have to walk the final stretch into the village and to the camp beyond, as the villagers don't own a vehicle. The camp has accommodation for 26 people in very simple rooms in thatched huts with little more than a bed, window and mosquito net. There's a separate washing block, and everything is spotless. It's rarely busy, as the villagers have made it a policy not to invite tour groups, in order to minimize the impact of visitors on community life. Near the creekside is an attractive *bantaba* with a bar, a kitchen, hammocks and a huge dining table.

Some visitors come here just to enjoy the complete peace – the camp has no electricity or phone and vehicles seldom come anywhere near here. Others come to experience something of village life, and there are plenty of activities to choose from, including guided tours of the village, the school, plantations and vegetable gardens, on foot or by cart; walking in the rice fields and community forest, where medicinal plants are gathered; exploring the mangrove creeks by dugout canoe; fishing for tilapia and ladyfish; salt-making, oyster-gathering, batik-making and tie-dying. There's a flat fee of D200 per group for each activity. In the evening, the villagers can arrange a night of traditional Jola drumming and dancing, including the re-enactment of tribal ceremonies (D500). Meals are provided using local ingredients including fish from the *bolon* and fruit and vegetables from the orchards and gardens.

All the money raised from visitors goes to community projects such as running the nursery school, fencing the vegetable gardens, planting trees in the forest, and buying new dugout canoes for the fishermen and oyster-collectors. The camp is entirely owned and managed by the villagers themselves, and is very much a shared enterprise. Village children are taught to view visitors neither as aliens nor as patrons – you won't hear any yells of "*toubab!*" here.

The *Kachokorr Camp* **guides** speak good English and are friendly without being pushy. The only slight disappointment is that the camp is distinctly separate from the village, so if you'd like a true sense of integration as a guest you have to make sure your guide knows this: there's nothing to stop you spending a day with the villagers as they work in the rice fields or clear land to plant new cassava, or you could just hang out under one of the village *bantabas* with some of the kids. The best way to get the most out of a stay at Tumani Tenda is to come with a clear objective in mind – the guides are not very proactive in "entertaining" guests, but respond well to suggestions and requests for particular activities.

Marakissa

South of Brikama are the villages of Marakissa and Darsilami, reached by way of attractive stretches of savanna, palm stands and woodland. It's a quiet rural area that's popular with birdwatchers and other wildlife enthusiasts. The road from Brikama is unmade, and the red dust becomes boggy and impassable during the rainy season, but in the dry season bush taxis ply the route several times a day.

MARAKISSA is a quiet rural village of around 5000 inhabitants, 6km south of Brikama. A little under 3km south of the village, on the road to Darsilami, is the recommended *Marakissa River Camp* ☎905852 6–7pm only, Netherlands ☎31-653/371901, Ⓔmarakissa@planet.nl; ❷. This guesthouse is run by a

Birdwatching around Marakissa

The area around Marakissa is particularly good for kingfishers (including the African pygmy kingfisher), raptors, rollers, and parties of migrating waders and other birds. Black crake are seen regularly around the pond by the bridge over the River Allahein, between the village and *Marakissa River Camp*, and African green pigeons are sometimes seen in the village. The grassland around the camp is also good birdwatching territory, with Verreaux's eagle owl, various species of snipe, yellow-throated leaf-love, white-breasted cuckoo shrikes and hammerkops all seen in the vicinity.

Dutch-Gambian partnership, and is beautifully situated in a palm grove on a lovely meander in the river Allahein, on the Senegalese border. There are five rooms in small huts, which are cool even in the heat of the day, with nets and screened windows, and fresh, northern European-style decor. Solar panels power the water pump and a few lights; apart from that, you have to rely on candles and lanterns. In the garden is a tiny swimming pool. The reasonably priced restaurant is open to non-residents (groups should call ahead); above it is a sun trap of a roof terrace, with a great vantage point overlooking the river. It's a quiet spot and keen birdwatchers will typically clock up sightings of more than one hundred species in a morning here, including hornbills, plantain eaters and kingfishers. It's also a good place just to relax and watch the sun dip behind the palms in the late afternoon. There have been no recent sightings of crocodiles in the river, so people do swim there, but you should be very cautious and never swim alone.

The Senegalese border post, 4km south of Marakissa, at the unremarkable village of **Darsilami** is lax enough to be used by smugglers from time to time. This makes it an awkward border crossing for tourists, as you may get a Gambian exit stamp but no Senegalese entry stamp, creating problems later on. If you're going to Kafountine on the Casamance coast from Serrekunda or Brikama, it's much easier to take the main road south towards Ziguinchor and go through the border formalities at Séléti.

Travel details

Buses

Brikama to: Bansang (6–7hrs); Basse (7–8hrs); Sankulay Kunda for Janjanbureh (5–6hrs); Serrekunda (40min–1hr); Soma (3–4hrs).

Bush taxis

Abuko to: Serrekunda (20min).
Brikama to: Bansang (5–6hrs); Basse (6–7hrs); Sankulay Kunda for Janjanbureh (4–5hrs); Serrekunda (40min); Soma (2.5–3hrs); plus to Séléti, Senegal, for other towns and villages in Casamance.
Denton Bridge to: Bakau (10mins); Banjul (5mins); Serrekunda (10mins).
Lamin to: Serrekunda (25min).

The north bank:
Niumi district

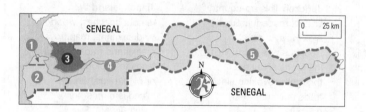

CHAPTER 3　Highlights

＊ **Dolphin-spotting**
Between November and January, bottlenose dolphins are regularly seen cruising in schools along the Atlantic coast or leaping in the bow waves of boats in the river mouth. See box on p.166

＊ **Juffureh** This up-country village, made famous by Alex Haley's novel *Roots*, is well worth visiting for its small but thought-provoking slave trade museum. See pp.170–177

＊ **James Island**
Squabbled over for decades by the Portuguese, British and French, this tiny midriver island's fort is now a crumbling ruin, but remains a tangible reminder of slave trading days. See pp.175–176

＊ **Jinack Island** With remote beaches, woodland savanna, mangrove creeks and traditional villages to explore on foot or by *pirogue*, Jinack Island is a must for nature-lovers. See pp.176–180

3

The north bank:
Niumi district

S eparated from the Kombo peninsula by the wide brown mouth of the River Gambia, **NIUMI DISTRICT** is worlds apart in pace and style from the tourist and residential development mushrooming to the south. It's a district that's rich in historical sites and areas of natural interest, but the shortage of hotels, lodges or camps this side of the river means that, for now, few visitors end up staying here overnight. Most choose instead to dip in and out for a day on a "Roots" tour to **Juffureh**, **Albreda** and **James Island**, or a road-and-river trip to **Jinack Island**, part of **Niumi National Park** on the Atlantic coast. Others only see Niumi fleetingly, through a car window: long-distance travellers heading from Banjul to Dakar and elsewhere in northern Senegal tend to rush straight across the district via the overlanders' corridor that connects Niumi's small district capital of **Barra** with the border post at **Amdallai**. For some visitors, however, the limitations of Niumi's tourist infrastructure are a positive attribute: Niumi is largely unspoilt, and can be a supremely relaxing region to spend a few days.

Much of Niumi District is very accessible by public or private transport. The ferry from Banjul can churn across the estuary to Barra in under thirty minutes on a good day and, while few visitors would choose to spend long in Barra itself, both Juffureh and Jinack Island are less than an hour away overland by private transport (a little longer with bush taxis). The newly surfaced road from Barra to Kerewan, 52km to the east in Baddibu district, is one of the best in the country, and opens up much of inland Niumi, including the village of **Berending**, famous for its sacred crocodile pool.

Meanwhile, for those keen to spend time off the beaten track, there are rural backroads ideal for exploring on two wheels or four. The region is scattered with traditional **Fula and Mandinka villages**, mostly clutches of thatch-roofed huts surrounded by mango trees, rhun palms and baobabs, and you may find places to stay in family compounds. The backroads are no more than rough tracks, and the best time to explore them is the first few months of the dry season, when the going is firm but the vegetation is still spectacularly lush.

The area is an essential stop for anyone interested in the history of the West African slave trade. Niumi's best-known destination by far is **Juffureh**, receiving as many as 200 visitors on peak days in the tourist season, most of them arriving on a **Gambia river cruise** upstream from Banjul. The most famous

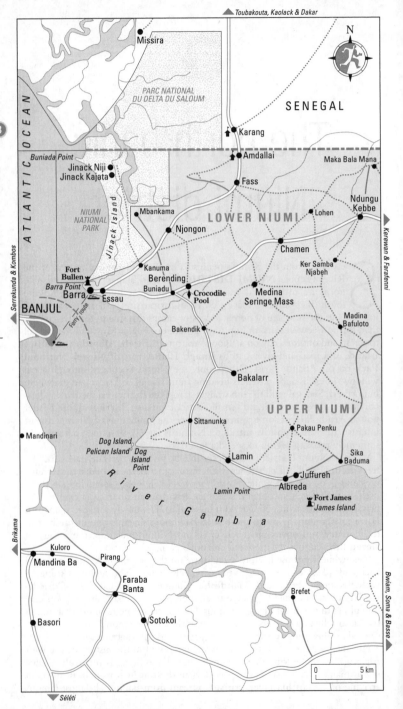

village in up-country Gambia was once just another rural backwater close to the river in Upper Niumi – until African–American author Alex Haley's genealogical researches led him here, catapulting Juffureh, its inhabitants and The Gambia itself into the international spotlight.

While Juffureh's claim to fame as a historical site is rather arbitrary, there are less questionable remnants of The Gambia's precolonial past nearby. The badly ruined period buildings in the village of **Albreda**, the bush-covered architectural remains of **San Domingo** and the crumbling fort on **James Island** were all once European trading stations. Slaves were among the most valuable commodities bought and sold here between the seventeenth and nineteenth centuries, and Juffureh's **Exhibition of the Slave Trade** pulls no punches in documenting the grisly details. Together, Juffureh, Albreda, San Domingo and James Island comprise one of The Gambia's most cherished cultural heritage sites, and the area figures prominently in the country's biennial **International Roots Festival** (see p.50).

Another attraction of Niumi district is its unusually rich **biodiversity**, mostly overlooked by the "Roots" pilgrims and Dakar-bound travellers who pass through at speed. Bounded by the Atlantic coast to the west and the last lazy sweep of the River Gambia to the south, and watered by snaking creeks and streams, the district is little affected by the encroaching aridity of the Sahel, and during the rains the bush is gorgeously green. **Birdwatchers** visit in search of species rarely seen south of the river, and there are plenty of reptiles and mammals here, including the rare, extremely shy West African manatee and a leopard or two. The northwest coastal region forms part of **Niumi National Park**, a little-known protected area that neighbours Senegal's Saloum Delta. Glimpses of this wilderness of beaches, wetlands and woodland savanna feature on a few tour operators' itineraries. To do the park justice, however, it's worth staying for a few days on **Jinack Island**, a remote and peaceful corner of The Gambia that's becoming a favourite stopover for nature-lovers, its unspoilt coastal, wetland and savanna habitats harbouring a varied wildlife population.

Barra

The small town of **BARRA** is the kind of place you pass through rather than choose to visit for its own sake. Barra's defining feature is its **ferry**, which connects the north bank of the River Gambia with Banjul, around 5km away. For traffic and travellers heading north from Banjul and the Kombos, the terminal is the gateway to Niumi and Jokadu districts in northwest Gambia, and a pivotal point on the route to Kaolack and Dakar in Senegal. Heading south, those travelling from northwest Gambia or Senegal and aiming for southwest Gambia or Casamance converge on Barra, since the next point on the river with a regular public ferry service is over 60km up-country, just south of Farafenni, at Bambatenda. All this traffic gives the otherwise impoverished Barra a distinctive bustle; it's rare for the town not to be crowded with people either actively on the move or kicking their heels waiting for a ferry or vehicle to materialize.

If you find yourself with time to spare between transport connections, you could do worse than nose around the daily **market** which runs from the main market hall in the town centre right down to the pedestrian exit from the ferry terminal, selling seasonal produce and a jumble of shoes, clothing and household items. Those with an interest in military history should investigate the squat hulk of **Fort Bullen**, built by the British in the early nineteenth century. The fort is visible from the river crossing, on the grassy shore at Barra Point on the northwestern edge of town. The town's only other landmark is its groundnut-loading plant, looming over the wharf near the ferry and disused for most of the year, with Serer boatbuilders working on the shore close by.

Some history

In the nineteenth century, Barra had a significant role in Britain's armed crusade to stamp out the slave trade in this part of West Africa. Britain outlawed slave trading in all its territories in 1808; however, the French and Portuguese slavers based on the River Gambia defied the ban so, in 1816, the British leased Banjul Island and set up the **Bathurst Six Gun Battery** on the shore to police the river mouth.

Since the Bathurst cannons lacked sufficient range to cover the whole breadth of the river, **Barra Point** was chosen as the site of a second battery. However, acquiring the land on which to establish this defensive position proved problematic. In the early nineteenth century, Barra Point was the southwestern limit of the Mandinka kingdom of **Niumi**, which had several capitals, one of which was at Essau, the village on the eastern edge of what is now Barra. The British traders at the new settlement of Bathurst had for some time been harassed and intimidated by the natives of Niumi, the Niuminka; the fortification of Barra Point was intended not only to restrict the movement of slave ships, but also to guard against the possibility of land-based attack. It was only in 1826, after a period of lengthy negotiations and, finally, naval pressure, that Mansa (king) Burungai Sonko of Niumi agreed to hand over the mile-wide strip of his people's shoreland where Barra now stands.

Over the next ten years, **Fort Bullen** (named after regional naval commander Commodore Charles Bullen) was built. Straightforward defence, however, was not the fort's sole purpose; as long as they could be said to be upholding the law, British naval vessels had free rein to harass their enemies the French under suspicion of illicit slave trading, and the fort provided artillery backup for this. The cannons proved a successful deterrent, and the fort was to see little active conflict. It was abandoned in 1870, but adapted for service by the British once again at the beginning World War II, when Senegal, having sided with the Vichy government in France, posed a potential threat.

Practicalities

The Banjul to Barra vehicle and passenger **ferry service** and the less sluggish but more precarious passenger **pirogues** operate daily (see box on pp.86–87).

Dolphin-watching

The sight of **dolphins** plunging in the bow wave adds an unexpected touch of magic to the otherwise prosaic experience of crossing the mouth of the River Gambia by the Banjul–Barra ferry. Small schools of bottlenose dolphins are regular visitors to the area around Barra, especially between November and January, and sometimes venture upstream: very occasionally, they're seen as far east as James Island. The Gambia's Atlantic coast north of Barra is sometimes patrolled by Atlantic humpbacked dolphins, endemic to this part of West Africa. Several tour operators (see pp.54–55 & 137) offer dolphin-watching trips that take you out by boat to the most likely parts of the Gambia estuary. Sightings are far from guaranteed, but the cruise is enjoyable for its own sake.

Moving on from Barra

Bush taxis from Barra run to Kerewan (D20 by van; 1hr) and Farafenni (D45 by van or D60 by car; 5hr) via Berending (15min) and Kuntair (45min); to Albreda and Juffureh (D15 by van; 1hr); to Jinack Kajata in the Niumi National Park (D15 by Land Rover; 40min); and to Amdallai (D15 by van or D18 by car; 1hr), where travellers to Kaolack and Dakar will need to change vehicles. GPTC runs two **buses** a day from Barra to Dakar (see box on p.88); all other bus services from Barra are presently suspended.

Most of the **road** traffic into Barra is heading from either the Senegal border to the northeast, or from Kerewan and Farafenni in up-country Gambia. The road from Senegal via Fass is pockmarked with potholes all the way from the border at Amdallai. The 55km from Farafenni to Kerewan is a bumpy four-hour drive along a laterite and dust road that's barely passable in the rainy season, and deeply rutted for weeks afterwards; by contrast, the road from the new bridge crossing the Jowara Bolong at Kerewan, to Essau just outside Barra, is a ribbon of perfect new tarmac.

If you arrive in Barra as a foot passenger on the ferry from Banjul, you'll find it difficult to avoid the **bush taxi garage**, close to the ferry terminal – the crowds and hustlers will all jostle you in that direction, and you'll be greeted by taxi touts as soon as you enter.

Barra has a couple of petrol stations, a Gamtel office, some telecentres and plenty of moneychangers, particularly around the areas of the market and bush taxi garage. There's only one **hotel**, the *Barra Hotel* (☎795134; ●), close to the ferry dock – follow the road towards Fort Bullen after leaving the terminal. Probably only worth considering if you're broke or stranded on the way to or from Banjul, the self-contained rooms here are a decent size, but grubby and uncomfortable, with unreliable water and power, and questionable security. The large downstairs bar sells cold drinks at low prices, and there's a short menu of local fare. A second accommodation option is the *Fort Bullen Rest House* (●), just beyond the fort. Though not really set up as a tourist stopover, the caretaker of the fort sometimes allows visitors to stay here in simple rooms for a day or two at a time.

Eating and drinking possibilities are as you'd expect in a town that is essentially a transport stop – you'll find simple bars, eateries and street vendors around the market, ferry terminal and bush taxi garage, all within easy walking distance of each other; a good choice is *Awa Jarra Jensuma*, a local restaurant near the terminal.

Fort Bullen

Proclaimed a national monument in the 1970s, **Fort Bullen** (daily 9am–5pm; D25) was built over the course of a decade or so from 1826, and stands as a lasting reminder of the British campaign to eradicate slavery in West Africa. While earlier European-built forts like Fort James on James Island (see p.175) had been set up for the express purpose of exploiting West Africa's natural resources, slaves included, for profit, Fort Bullen is different: it postdates the British abolition of the slave trade, and the presence of its cannons helped enforce the ban. Today, its primary function is to house the navigation light that marks Barra Point. The Gambia's National Council for Arts and Culture had hoped a **restoration programme** would give Fort Bullen a new lease of life as a performance space. In reality, however, the fort is seldom visited, and for now the old officers' quarters within the courtyard, earmarked for a tiny museum, remain empty.

While the history of Fort Bullen is interesting, the building itself has little to detain you for long. The fort is essentially an open courtyard enclosed by a rectangle of low, sturdy walls of russet-coloured laterite stone, cemented with oystershell lime and patched up with concrete. There's a commanding view of the estuary and the northern shoreline from the circular bastions, one in each corner – with binoculars, you can pick out the massive perimeter wall of the State House in Banjul, behind which the Six Gun Battery, counterpart to Fort Bullen's cannons, is hidden. The southeast bastion still contains a World War II anti-aircraft gun emplacement – disarmed, stuck fast and overgrown by a tree. In the opposite corner of the courtyard is a magazine uncovered during restoration work, but quickly refilled with rubble when a stash of live ammunition was discovered inside. Lying in the grass outside the fortifications are three cannons including one, trained across the river, which is said still to be loaded.

The elegant but decrepit timber house on stilts at Barra Point, near the fort, was once a government rest house, but is now defunct. At low tide it's possible to cross the Niji Bolon near the point onto Jinack Island (see pp.176–180) and walk along the beach; it's an isolated stretch, with gulls and terns overhead and wading birds picking along the shoreline.

Around Barra

Barra's hinterland is dominated by its busy transport route – a high volume of Senegambian traffic thunders in and out of town and tears along the **road to Senegal**. As well as bush taxis and haulage vehicles, this region also sees tourist trucks pretty regularly: some group day-trips to Jinack Island which take in the *bolons* of Niumi National Park (see pp.176–180) drive northeast through **Fass**, Amdallai and Karang in order to approach the park's remarkable wetlands from the Senegalese side of the border.

Away from the road to Senegal, the countryside around Barra is peaceful, thinly scattered with villages where chickens scuttle across compounds fenced with palm fronds and women work in well-watered vegetable plots. The bush here is luxuriant in the rainy season and the first months of the dry season, with mango and cashew trees shading the villages and mature palm stands fringing the horizon.

South of Barra, the lower River Gambia curves gracefully into a bay, thickly bordered with mangroves, and fed by the Buniadu Bolon that flows down from **Berending**, a village easily accessible from Barra. Berending's sacred crocodile pool is lusher, quieter and more rural in feel than the much-visited Katchikali pool in Bakau, though the chances of actually seeing any crocodiles are slim.

The route to Senegal

Travelling along the main road from Barra towards Dakar or the Parc National du Delta du Saloum in Senegal, the last Gambian town vehicles pass through before the border is the small but busy commercial settlement of **Fass**. Here, opportunistic traders pitch their stalls along the highway – even butchers, whose stock can't be improved by exposure to the fumes and dust stirred up by passing traffic. The only reason to stop is to pick up basic provisions if you're travelling long-distance independently. The shell-and-tar road that leads between

Barra and the border is in desperate need of repair, the potholes deepened by the lorries that ply this route.

Travellers heading into Senegal are required to stop at the tiny border town of **Amdallai** to clear customs and have passports stamped by immigration. On passing through Amdallai, you are immediately in Senegal; at **Karang**, 2km north, there are Senegalese border formalities to complete. The change of atmosphere is immediate, not least because of the French signage everywhere, and the sudden improvement in the road surface. Both Amdallai and Karang have clutches of market stalls, itinerant hawkers and moneychangers. If you're travelling between Gambia and Senegal by bush taxi, it's normally necessary to change vehicles a couple of times (see box on p.88). From Karang, it's a drive of around four hours to Dakar, or less than an hour to the attractive, though pricey, tourist lodges in Toubacouta and Missirah, both good jumping-off points for excursions into the rich wetland environment of the Saloum Delta.

Berending

The small Mandinka village of **BERENDING** lies 8km east of Barra, on the smooth new Kerewan road that forks off the road to Senegal a couple of kilometres beyond Barra. The village is unremarkable except for its **crocodile pool** nearby. Like its more famous counterpart at Katchikali in Bakau (see p.111), the pool is a sacred place, and pilgrims come here to offer prayers to the ancestral spirits represented by the Nile crocodiles lurking, rarely seen, in its weed-clogged waters. Typically, the supplicants are women desperate to conceive, or farmers wishing for a bumper harvest. Visitors will be lucky to see any crocodiles, but it's a picturesque spot.

The crocodile pool is one of a series of small pools linked by stands of reeds and surrounded by rhun palms and luxuriant shrub foliage. Villagers bathe and wash their clothes in the water, apparently unperturbed by any potential threat, but if you ask them where the crocodiles are, they'll all point together in the same direction to one particular pool. Its custodians are the Sonko family, descendants of Burungai, the incalcitrant Mandinka king who caused so much trouble to the British settlers in Niumi in the early nineteenth century. If you have time, and an interpreter, you can learn the entire family history from the elder who is currently the senior guardian. If you'd like to visit the pool you should, in any case, make a polite visit to the *alkalo* of the village, and ask for a local guide.

Berending is easy to reach by public transport: **bush taxis** from Barra or Kerewan will stop here on request. The village is marked by a vast silk-cotton tree close to the main road. To find the *alkalo's* compound, take the sandy road that leads off the main road northwards opposite this tree into the main part of the village, and ask somebody to point it out. The pool itself is then reached by returning to the main road and taking the track that leads off southwards, just before the silk-cotton tree if approaching from Barra.

Birdwatching around Barra

The Atlantic shoreline and the mouth of the Niji Bolon north of Barra, and the tidal mudflats near Essau to the east, are home to a unique combination of bird species, including some rarely seen on the south bank of the river. Among the species recorded here recently are African darter, lesser crested tern, black-headed heron, crested lark, white-billed buffalo weaver, African goshawk, blue-cheeked bee-eater, black-eared wheatear, village indigobird and white-rumped seedeater.

Juffureh, Albreda and James Island

The area around **JUFFUREH** would have had its place on the tourist circuit even if Alex Haley's "roots" had never made the village internationally famous. This corner of the north bank includes San Domingo and James Island, two of the few sites in The Gambia in which ruins of buildings dating from the slave trading era still exist. The Mandinka villages of Juffureh and Albreda, which rub shoulders on the north bank of the River Gambia in southern Upper Niumi, plus nearby San Domingo and James Island with its ruined fort, a couple of kilometres offshore, together comprise The Gambia's longest-established destination for heritage tourists. Most of its visitors are escorted around briefly on one-day **Roots tours** – an enjoyable excursion, though seriously over-rated as a meaningful experience.

The district is rich in history and deserves greater attention than a high-speed visit can afford. Juffureh itself is a good place to take the opportunity to stay in a simple village lodge. When there's a tour group around, the villages have a hectic, slightly artificial "showtime" atmosphere, and the hassle from locals can be persistent. However, after the tourist boats and vehicles have departed for the day, the villages become serene once more, with women chatting good-humouredly to their neighbours, men lounging under the *bantabas*, and children chasing home-made toys through the sandy streets.

To the many visitors to Juffureh who have never visited an up-country village before, it's the simplicity of the place that makes the biggest impression. Like any other unremarkable Mandinka village, Juffureh has its corrugate-roofed, mudbrick cottages, its shady *bantabas*, goat pens, dusty lanes, gigantic trees and gaggles of scruffy kids squawking "*toubab!*" when any white visitor comes in range. What *is* remarkable is that this simplicity has endured through well over two decades of world attention.

Juffureh lies just inland from its neighbouring village, **ALBREDA**, also known as Albadarr, which is situated on the north bank of the river, around 30km upstream from Barra; the two villages have merged into one community. If you're visiting Juffureh and Albreda by boat, you moor at Albreda's lengthy jetty and make your way to the village's main riverside "square", an open space dominated by towering silk-cotton trees. Down on the shore a hundred metres or so upstream is the shell of an old trading house, the **CFAO building**, sometimes fancifully described by would-be guides as a slave-house. In reality, the building may never have been used by slave traders, as it was probably built in the early nineteenth century, a few years after the British started enforcing abolition of the trade.

Albreda also has a cannon, pointing fiercely out across the river from the "square". Nearby is the stump of what might have been the original **Freedom Flagpole** – legend has it that any slave who managed to break loose, make a dash for the flagpole, and touch it, would be granted their freedom. Albreda's other monument is a roofless structure which is billed as the "oldest chapel in West Africa" but the iron cross that marks it is clearly not original and the building was probably just a store.

Heading north from Albreda to Juffureh, the **Exhibition of the Slave Trade** hosted by Juffureh's National Museum (see pp.174–175) is about 500m from the "square" on the right-hand side. Beyond this is the **Roots Heritage Trail**, intended as a place of reflection: it's a gentle thirty minute walk along paths through the kind of creekside landscape that Kunta Kinte, and thousands of captured Africans like him, might have longed for bitterly on the harrowing Atlantic crossing.

For ruins which have a definite, documented connection with the slave trade (as opposed to more recent commercial dealings in other commodities), the only site in the on-shore area around Juffureh is **San Domingo**, just off the road that leaves Juffureh in the direction of Kerewan, about 500m from the museum or 1km from Albreda's village "square". All that remains of this slave traders' substation is a crumbling chunk of a laterite stone building, under a much-carved baobab tree.

Some history

From the fifteenth century onwards, the region that is now The Gambia was a crucial base for European traders. **San Domingo** was settled by the Portuguese in the early fifteenth century and, later, by the British as a retreat and a source of fresh water for troops from the mid-river trading station of Fort James, on James Island. It was at San Domingo that African middlemen of the **Luso** tribe acted as host brokers in trading slaves for commodities such as cloth and guns.

Albreda, too, was once a trading station, where not only slaves but also gold and vast quantitites of ivory changed hands. The station was controlled by the French from 1681 to 1857, and was one of Senegambia's four principal slave "factories". Two of the others, St Louis and Gorée Island, both in what is now Senegal, were also in French hands; the fact that the fourth, Fort James, not far offshore from Albreda, was more often than not occupied by the rival British, caused a near-permanent state of high tension in the region. It was largely thanks to their good relationship with the local Mandinka population that the British managed to cling on to another, smaller, trading base at **Juffureh**, which remained active until the early nineteenth century when the traders diverted their energies into developing the new commercial settlement of Bathurst (now Banjul).

When, in the late 1960s, **Alex Haley** embarked on a passionate quest for the place of origin of one of his African ancestors, he found an end of the line of sorts in Juffureh, and the inspiration to write his bestselling novel. Haley, and the myth-making machine that his novel engendered, turned this corner of the north bank into a legend. The Gambia's tourist industry was quick to grasp the potential of the *Roots* connection presented, but slow to develop it in a sustainable fashion. For years, visitors to Juffureh, black or white, brought here aroused by curiosity as to whether or not their own ancestors had played a part in the story of the transatlantic slave trade, found themselves in a hot, dusty village, besieged by irritating children, and with little to see but villagers carrying out traditional roles to order – pounding millet and tinkering with carvings. It was only in 1996 that Juffureh seemed to realize it was time to rethink what it was actually offering visitors. The creation of the small but well-thought-out **Exhibition of the Slave Trade** (see p.174), now a national museum, gave the village something new of genuine interest to tourists, and the exhibition remains one of the area's best features. Further improvements within the village were made prior to the 2002 **International Roots Festival**. The festival programme includes a one-day pilgrimage to Juffureh, and a walk along a new path named the Roots Heritage Trail, ending at a living reconstruction of a traditional village compound as it might have looked in Haley's supposed ancestor's time.

Practicalities

While most visitors to Juffureh, Albreda and James Island arrive in a **tour** group (see pp.56–57), it's perfectly possible (and sometimes speedier) to cross to

There's no doubt that The Gambia owes the African–American author **Alex Haley** a debt of gratitude. Before 1977, the year that Haley's bestseller **Roots** won the Pulitzer Prize and the television mini-series based on the novel broke all previous popularity records (over 130 million viewers tuned in to the first run in the US), few Americans, black or white, had heard of The Gambia, and even fewer could point to it on the map. Wittingly or otherwise, Haley blazed the trail for a new brand of West African tourism that's still thriving – the ancestral homecoming tour.

Roots is a rambling family saga that spans two centuries, describing the Juffureh boyhood of a young Mandinka named **Kunta Kinte**, his capture by white slavers in the 1760s, and the horrors of his lengthy Atlantic voyage, then following his fortunes and those of his family, generation by generation, as they struggle through life on the plantations in America's Deep South. Haley claimed that his celebrated novel was inspired by the experience of meeting the people of Juffureh, and sensing a deep spiritual connection with them that, he felt, confirmed a shared ancestry centuries old.

Haley first set foot in Juffureh in 1967. During his visit, his escorts assured him that Juffureh *griot* **Kebba Kanji Fofana** had a detailed knowledge of the history of the Kinte clan that stretched back many generations; Haley hoped that Fofana's histories might include reference to Kinte, from whom he was directly descended, and whose name had been preserved in the oral history of his American family. Sure enough, Fofana's tales included one about Kunta Kinte, which seemed to match the story that Haley had learned on his grandmother's front porch.

From the way that Haley describes his encounter with Fofana in the epilogue of *Roots*, it's evident that the *griot* had been primed prior to Haley's visit, and cynics have suggested that Fofana simply recited a story he knew Haley wanted to hear, passing it off as genuine history (possibly under pressure from Haley's escorts, who were anxious to satisfy their client, possibly with an eye on the potential rewards). What's certain is that Haley was profoundly moved by his encounter with the Juffureh villagers. He describes the bewildered shame he felt on comparing his own brown skin to the dark colour of the Mandinkas as if he were "impure among the pure", and the paradox of feeling intimately connected to these people, yet isolated by his inability to understand their language. It was this encounter that led him to spend the next nine years of his life working on *Roots*.

Haley, already well known as a Black Power activist and as the author of *The Autobiography of Malcolm X*, which sold over six million copies, now found an eager audience in a generation of African–Americans who had allowed themselves to be persuaded that they were not so much American, as victims of Americanization, and that they and their ancestors were a lost African people. Inspired by Haley's search, both academic and literal, for a corner of West Africa that he could claim as his ancestral home, others wanted to do the same. Those that had no way of pinpointing the geographical origin of any of their forbears chose to make a symbolic journey instead, by following in Haley's footsteps to Juffureh.

Inevitably, tour operators caught on to the **commercial potential** of excursions to Juffureh. When the *Roots* industry was at its peak, thousands of African–Americans made the pilgrimage to see the village they believed Haley had been describing in the opening chapters of his book. So convincing was the hype that the author himself embraced it completely – pictures of Haley with Binta Kinte, widow of *griot* Fofana, became part of the myth of modern Gambia, used to boost the small coun-

the north bank by ferry from Banjul to Barra (see box on pp.86–87) and then take either a **bush taxi** for D15 or a **private taxi** (price negotiable) from the Barra taxi garage (see p.167). To reach Albreda and Juffureh with your own vehicle from Barra, take the road to Kerewan and right turn off the tarmac at try's respectability on the world stage. But then the rumour came out that Haley had already written his Africa passages when he first came here, which explains why his account of Juffureh doesn't fit with the location of today's village. In the book, Kunta Kinte is surprised by a slave-raiding party, yet present-day Juffureh is only a few hundred metres from the River Gambia and close by the sites of the trading stations of Albreda and Fort James, which would have been there throughout Kunta's childhood. It's also unlikely that the slave-raiders (as opposed to the buyers) would have been white. The likelihood that Juffureh used to be 1km from its present site does little to iron out the inconsistencies.

Haley made a crucial mistake in presenting his novel as "fictionalized fact", taking creative reconstruction to an extreme. Research by investigative reporter Philip Nobile and others has shown that many of the key characters described in the book never existed. Even if we forgive Haley's feeling a stronger familial identification with Kunta Kinte than with any of his 63 other sixth-generation forbears, it's hard to understand why he seemed so determined to persuade his audience that the Kintes of present-day Juffureh were definitely his own people: Kinte is a common enough family name, and the story Fofana told, taken by Haley as proof of the connection, was a simple and familiar history. Doubts about Haley's motives exploded into a near-total debunking of the *Roots* story when, in 1979, writer Harold Courlander successfully sued for **plagiarism** – significant chunks of *Roots* were proved to have been lifted almost verbatim from Courlander's 1967 novel *The African*. Haley's publishers coughed up the bulk of Courlander's $650,000 settlement, and all interested parties rallied to protect Haley from f urther discreditation.

Even after Haley's death from a heart attack in 1992, powerful forces continued to work to preserve the *Roots* myth and when, in 1997, the BBC produced a documentary based on Nobile's damning investigations, US television networks refused to show it. Their argument was that any critical examination of what was by now a sacrosanct work of African-American literature could spark a race-related incident. In 2002, Haley's younger brother George, who served as US Ambassador to The Gambia from 1998 to 2000, unveiled a Kunta Kinte–Alex Haley memorial in Annapolis, Maryland, as if to cast the myth in stone. Today, the future of the *Roots* message is in the hands of a Florida investor, who bought all the literary rights and royalties for $10,000 after Myran Haley, the author's widow, filed for bankruptcy. While *Roots* earned Haley several million dollars, there's little evidence that much of it ever found its way to Juffureh: Haley put up the cash for a new village mosque, and the Kinte compound seems more affluent than some, but most villagers still live very simply. Tourists on organized trips pay a tour operator to take them there; few spend much time, or money, in the village.

Haley himself claimed that his intention had always been to "give his people some myths to live by". In this he has been extremely successful, despite the controversy since his novel was published. Historical inaccuracies aside, *Roots* tells a story that's still well worth reading. The several millions of copies sold since 1976 have played a significant part in raising awareness about the transatlantic slave trade and its legacy, as well as stimulating debate about origin and identity within black communities of the diaspora. And the villagers of Juffureh are still proud of the fame that Haley's saga bestowed upon them: "Yes, it is a lie," they'll tell you, "but it is a good lie."

Buniadu, then follow the laterite and sand road south. The going can be rough, and you'll need 4WD after recent rain. Approaching from Kerewan, turn left off the tarmac at the village of Kuntair and again head south along dirt tracks. The road sometimes forks with no indication of which way to follow, so it's best to keep checking with passers-by. If you'd like to travel from the Kombos by river, but not by large tour boat, check out the operators based at Denton Bridge (see box on p.137) outside Banjul, who can organize day-trips by small boat, or Gambia Watersports Centre (see p.127), who can get you from Banjul to Albreda in 40 minutes by powerboat.

If you're interested in sifting through the *Roots* hype in search of Juffureh's genuine character, then your best chance of a satisfying experience is to stay here overnight, rather than limiting yourself to a standard day-trip (see box on pp.176–177). However, **accommodation** options are limited. By 2004, Juffureh may have a new riverside eco-lodge, set up with the support of George Haley, the former American Ambassador to The Gambia and brother of the late Alex Haley. At the time of writing, however, the best bet is the *Juffureh Rest House*, a little beyond the museum, on the main dirt road that leads west towards Barra and northeast towards Kuntair and Kerewan (℡710276, c/o Juffureh Museum; ❶). Founded as a community project by the French-run Kounta Kinte Association, it's used as a regular venue for residential music classes and workshops. The *Rest House* has very simple small rooms, open to participants and non-participants – some in a block, some in iron-roofed round huts – and shared washing facilities that are just about acceptable. There's a generator here, but if only a few people are staying you'll have to rely on candlelight. Simple meals can be prepared if ordered in advance.

The most obvious place to **eat and drink** is the *Rising Sun Restaurant*, on Albreda's main "square" by the jetty. Although unashamedly touristy, it's a welcoming place, with a canopy roof smothered in bougainvillea and a short menu of fried standards including omelettes and garlic shrimps (D55–80). It's also the most likely spot to meet Albreda and Juffureh's one badged Official Tourist Guide.

Exhibition of the Slave Trade

If doubts about Alex Haley's integrity (see box on pp172–173) leave you in need of some solid facts about what really happened in slave trading days, it's worth visiting Juffureh's tiny **National Museum of the North Bank** (Mon–Thurs & Sat 10am–5pm, Fri 10am–1pm; D35). The museum is roughly on the border between the neighbouring villages of Juffureh and Albreda, a short stroll inland from Albreda's jetty, just off the laterite road which connects Juffureh with Barra and Kuntair.

The permanent **Exhibition of the Slave Trade** here has plenty of well-written display boards, and you'll come away with a good insight into the origins, mechanics and eventual abolition of slavery in this part of the world. Quotes from period sources throw the brutality of capture and transportation into vivid relief. One describes how the process of branding with a hot iron "caused little pain, the mark being usually well in four to five days, appearing very plain and white thereafter" and, in another, a ship's captain claims with satisfaction that out of a consignment of 700 slaves he "delivered 372 to the company's factors in Barbados, alive". There are a few artefacts, too: shackles, beads and small iron bars which the Europeans used as currency to buy slaves. A coffle – an iron neck brace with a huge lock and a heavy chain – is displayed graphically on a life-size cutout of an African slave, suggesting just how painfully it must have dug into the wearer's neck.

Inevitably, there are some nods towards the **Kunta Kinte legend**, such as a copy of the cutting from the *Maryland Gazette* unearthed by Haley in his researches. The snippet, dated October 1, 1767, is an announcement, in which "a cargo of choice healthy slaves" is advertised for sale. This particular batch of slaves had left The Gambia on July 5, 1767, aboard a British ship named the *Lord Ligonier*, and it's certainly possible that Kunta Kinte was among them.

The Manuel Freres Building in which the exhibition is housed was British-built in the 1840s, and has the feel of a Victorian village hall transplanted from England. Outside, you'll find a *bantaba* and a booth selling drinks.

James Island

A visit to **James Island** by cruiser or *pirogue* is highly recommended to anyone interested in the history of the transatlantic slave trade. It was on this bleak, rock-strewn outcrop – barely 200m in length, and vulnerable to erosion by the relentless drag of the River Gambia's tidal waters – that many slaves spent their last days on African soil, a fact that leaves few visitors unaffected.

Situated at a pivotal defensive position mid-river, 30km upstream from the Atlantic coast, James Island was one of the first European settlements in West Africa and an obvious location for a trade fort. Discovered by Portuguese explorers in the mid-fifteenth century, the island was bought two centuries later by agents of the Duke of Courland (now Latvia and Lithuania), who in 1651 set about fortifying it in order to develop trade between Courland and the West Africans living near the River Gambia. Over the century to follow, the fort was subjected to occupations, routings, sackings, desertions and rebuildings – whoever controlled the fort had almost total control over of the shipment of trade goods into and out of the area. In 1661 it was seized by the British, who bundled out the Baltic occupants and set themselves up under the Royal Patent of Charles II, buying gold, ivory, peppers, hides and slaves for the American colonies – Britain's first imperial exploit in Africa.

In one mercantile guise or another, the British and the French fought over the fort for more than a century. In the late eighteenth century, friction between the two rival powers reached a peak, as France continued to run their slave trading "factory" at Albreda on the nearby shore long after the British had opted for a new role as anti-slavers. In 1779, French troops, under orders to stamp out all potential threats to their nation's trading interests, kicked the "meddlesome" abolitionist British off the island for good, and destroyed the fort. By 1829 James Island had been completely abandoned, by which time British efforts to police the river had shifted downstream to Bathurst and Barra.

The remains of **Fort James**, founded in 1651, still haunt the island. The outcrop provided only just enough space for a simple fortified arrangement of apartments, courtyards and strategy rooms, which must have been almost as claustrophobic for the occupying troops as for the slaves housed in shed-like buildings outside the walls. Since the mid-seventeenth century, the island has shrunk considerably, and preserving the fort against further decay has become a serious concern. Today, what little remains of the fort – some crumbling bastion walls, fragments of the central administrative quarters and a few strewn cannon – is dominated by a grove of large baobabs, skeletal and streaked with guano in the dry season. There's next to nothing left of the outbuildings where slaves were held, at the southern tip of the island, furthest from the landing stage.

Practicalities

A visit to James Island is automatically included in the "Roots" day-trips which cruise up-river from the coastal resorts (see box on pp.176–177). The cruisers moor

Roots tours

One-day **Roots tours** from the resorts are among The Gambia's most popular organized excursions, although rather overrated. If you're interested in learning more about the machinations of slave trade, examining tangible relics of the trading stations and trying to imagine what went through the minds of the African captives as they were bundled aboard ship, never to return, you may feel frustrated. Being herded around on a "Roots" trip is not conducive to quiet contemplation, and you're likely to miss out on much of your guide's (limited) explanations, and many of the exhibits in the museum, just because there are too many heads in the way. What you can expect, if nothing else, is a relaxing river cruise (if you choose the river route), followed by a brief glimpse of north bank village life with enough of a taste of the place to enable you to decide whether you'd like to arrange to stay longer, or to return another time under your own steam.

The tour groups either travel to Juffureh from Banjul by boat (generally a cruiser with two decks, offering both sun and shade, and a bar) or, much less typically, by road from Barra, having crossed on the Banjul–Barra ferry. If you're familiar with Alex Haley's *Roots* then you're likely to find the road route more interesting, as it takes you through the open country that Haley describes so vividly in the opening chapters of his book. Coming by road, you'll miss out on James Island, however, unless, once at Albreda, you make your own arrangements to get there by "unofficial" (and uninsured) *pirogue*.

The **boat trip** from Banjul typically takes a couple of hours, and begins with great views of whatever action there might be that day at the port: containers being loaded or unloaded; ships hovering midstream as they await a vacant berth; the Barra ferry churning across the estuary; passenger *pirogues* coursing through the waves. While you might be lucky enough to see dolphins at the river mouth near Banjul, the rest of the journey is a lazy cruise with little to see. The river here is salty and broad – over 12km at its broadest – and the scenery pretty monotonous, with near-featureless water banked by dense mangroves. The boats don't usually take a central course, but shallow muddy water generally prevents them from sailing close enough to the north bank for you to spot much in the way of wildlife in the foliage. Meanwhile the opposite bank is an indistinct strip of greenish-grey sandwiched between the glare of the river and the glare of the sky.

at a safe distance from the island and passengers are ferried to the rickety jetty in groups by *pirogue* or launch. If you're travelling independently, you should be able to hire a **pirogue** in Albreda to take you to James Island and back (ask around near Albreda's jetty or at the *Rising Sun*; the round trip should cost no more than D300 in total for a boat taking six passengers).

Niumi National Park and Jinack Island

North of the River Gambia, all but half a kilometre or so of the Gambian coastline lies within one of the country's most intriguing wilderness regions, **Niumi National Park** (D31.50, included in the price of organized visits, or payable at the park office near Kanuma). This protected area was gazetted in 1987 and is as yet relatively unexplored; it's possible to visit as part of an organized excursion, or independently, but either way you'll encounter few other travellers during your visit. The park's 49 square kilometres contain a remarkable range of habitats – not just the Atlantic coast with its dunes, lagoons and

While Albreda's concrete jetty and massive silk-cotton trees are still dots in the distance, and James Island, mid-river, a vague shape beyond, a welcome party may motor up to the boat in *pirogues*: locals waving Gambian flags and shouting "Welcome back!" Thus begins the part of the trip which black visitors making the trip as a pilgrimage may find most moving. The sense of completing a river journey that might have been made centuries ago by a distant ancestor, but in reverse, is a powerful one, and the shouts of welcome as the boat approaches the jetty, increased as the visitors set foot on dry land, are likely to heighten a bittersweet feeling of homecoming in anyone psyched up about the history and mystique of the place.

Once ashore, your visit will probably include a quick skirt round the colonial buildings and the museum. You should, for the sake of politeness, be invited to pay your respects to the **alkalo** who, at the time of writing, is one of The Gambia's small minority of female village chiefs, and you may be asked to sign a battered visitors' book, just as Alex Haley did on his visits. You will definitely be escorted to the **compound of the Kinte family**, or rather to the ugly corrugate-roofed and concrete-floored meeting area attached, in which you will meet some representatives of the Kinte clan, including Binta Kinte, the ancient widow of Kebba Kanji Fofana, the *griot* who impressed Alex Haley so much. Proudly displayed are framed **photos** of Fofana, of Binta with Haley, and of one of the actors who played Kunta Kinte in *Roots*; cash donations are expected for any photos you take yourself. Somewhere along the line there will be some **traditional musicians** playing (and stopping abruptly once the group has moved on). There will also be an obligatory stop at the **tourist craft market**. Few groups make the extra walk to the Roots Heritage Trail and the San Domingo ruins.

Whistlestop tour over, it's back to the boat for lunch (generally good) and the short cruise to **James Island**, if the boat didn't take you there earlier. At some point in the proceedings you may be given a photocopied "**certificate of visitation**" stating that you've visited Kunta Kinte's ancestral home, and the "popular slave prison, James Island" – so now you know it's official. (For details of operators running "Roots" tours see pp.54–55.

shallow waters, but also dry woodland savanna, grassland, cultivated land and saltwater wetlands. Niumi adjoins the Parc National du Delta du Saloum in Senegal, and together the parks protect one of the last remaining untouched stands of mangroves in West Africa.

At the heart of the park is the **Massarinko Bolon**, a broad mangrove-flanked creek overlooked by laterite escarpments which provide commanding lookout points. Massarinko Bolon connects with a narrower creek, the **Niji Bolon**, which runs roughly north–south, and in places is so shallow at low tide that local fishermen leave their boats midstream and continue on foot, as if walking on water. The long curving kilometre-wide strip of land west of here, between the Niji Bolon and the sea, is known as **Jinack Island** (sometimes spelt Ginak or Ginack). Like many of the beaches further south, the 10km stretch of sand along Jinack's Atlantic coast is gradually narrowing, due to tidal erosion; at high tide, the waves lap against the beach convolvulus, but at low tide the sand is broad and firm. Inland, the savanna landscape, flat and thinly wooded with baobabs, tamarisk and twisted acacia trees, is rewarding to explore on foot, especially for birdwatchers.

Niumi National Park is rich in **bird species**, including an abundance of

Birdwatching in Niumi National Park

The bird population on Jinack Island has been studied in detail by a group of British ornithologists who have recorded a few rarities including European Scops owl, bar-breasted firefinch and red-footed falcon, and a nesting population of white-fronted plover. Inland, the birdwatching opportunites are outstanding, with an abundance of woodland and grassland species and seventeen species of warbler, distinguished by subtle variations in plumage. Offshore, Jinack's shallow waters provide excellent feeding for gulls and other fish-eating birds, and pelicans are often seen in and around the lagoon near Buniadu Point, where a sandspit reaches far out into the Atlantic. Here, and in Niumi National Park's beautiful mangrove creeks, hunting ospreys soar overhead with eyes trained on the water, and terns zoom downwards like darts. Equally conspicuous on mangrove perches are numerous herons and kingfishers.

palearctic migrants who stop here during the European winter to build up their fat reserves before continuing south. Other wildlife includes the elusive West African manatee, once hunted for meat and now few in number and very rarely seen; the endangered clawless otter; and green turtles, which lay their eggs on the beach by night. Monitor lizards, snakes and mammals such as bushbuck, spotted hyena and even leopard are also around, but keep a low profile; the sharp-eyed will spot plenty of tracks. More conspicuous are the large schools of bottlenose and Atlantic hump-backed dolphins that sometimes play offshore, but their visits are only occasional – December and January are the months you're most likely to see them.

Most of Jinack Island is Gambian, but the northernmost chunk is in Senegal. The ruler-straight border that has divided the countries since colonial times slices through the island just north of Buniadu Point, but it's unmarked, and is of no great conseqence to the small population, who pass freely between the Gambian villages of **Jinack Niji** and **Jinack Kajata**, and **Djinack Diakoto** on the Senegalese side. Conveniently enough for them, the island is wreathed in mystique and taboos powerful enough to keep officials well away – local legend holds that any government law-enforcer who tries to set foot on the island will be attacked by ancient spirits. Thus the islanders pursue whatever variety of cultivation and trade they choose, notably marijuana, while the law turns a blind eye. Despite the potential for mild anarchy, visitors have no need to feel vulnerable.

Some of the tour companies that bring groups to Jinack Island on **day-trips** (see p.56) market the place as "Treasure Island" or "Paradise Island", names which conjure images of a palm-fringed coral atoll lapped by a turquoise sea, setting their clients up for disappointment. In fact, Jinack doesn't really have an island feel, as it's basically a long narrow chunk of mainland that happens to be cut off by a creek, and the beach landscape is stark rather than exotic, with baobabs, not palms, punctuating the skyline, and scrub tangling over low dunes. However, Jinack does have an attractive feeling of remoteness so complete that when, after dark, the line of lights across the bay confirms how close Banjul is, it's something of a surprise. The Atlantic beach may not conform to the tropical ideal, but at low tide the broad grey-blond sands are perfect for long, lonely walks, and heaven for inquisitive children, with animal and bird tracks to follow, crabs to chase into their holes, and shallow water that's safe for swimming – although watch out for sea urchins.

Visiting Niumi National Park on a standard organized day-trip from the Kombos will give you a feel for the geography and atmosphere of the place. You're likely to cruise the Massarinko Bolon and the top of the Niji Bolon by rustic *pirogue*, pass through the village of Jinack Kajata, cross Jinack Island on foot or by local cart, and have lunch under a thatched shelter on the empty beach. For wildlife enthusiasts, however, these trips are pretty much a non-starter, as you'll be cruising the wetlands and crossing the bush in the middle of the day when birds are hard to spot, the presence of the group will make mammals and reptiles even shyer than usual, and your guide may not be as clued up about the local ecology as you might like – some tourists come away from "Treasure Island" excursions without even realizing they've spent most of the day in a national park.

Practicalities

Most visitors arrive on organized excursions from the resorts. To reach Niumi National Park by public transport, however, you can take one of the infrequent Jinack-bound **bush taxis** from Barra (D15), which set off up the road towards Fass and Senegal and turn left into the park at Kanuma, and can drop you just across the Niji Bolon from Jinack Kajata, the second of the two Gambian villages. This road through the park, bumpy but passable without 4WD in the dry season, runs roughly north–south, parallel to the Niji Bolon. A small **pirogue** will ferry you across to the island for D5 – although the *bolon* may look very shallow, the presence of crocodiles makes it inadvisable to wade across. The pirogue owners have mobile phones, and can call a taxi for your return journey to Barra. If you'd rather not wait for a bush taxi to get you into the park, it's easy enough to hire a **private taxi** at Barra to take you to whichever part you'd like to explore independently – but be aware that taxi drivers here have a reputation for trying to overcharge, as do the *pirogue* owners at Niji Bolon and some of the would-be guides from the villages. If you make an early start and are content with the briefest of visits, it's possible to get to the park and back from the Kombos in a day.

The best way to get to the ocean side of the island and *Madiyana Safari Camp* (see below) is to make arrangements with the owners to take you, usually by motorized *pirogue* from Banjul: the run across the estuary and up the Atlantic coast of Jinack Island takes around an hour, and you may be lucky enough to spot dolphins on the way. Alternatively, from Jinack Kajata, follow the path west across the island towards the sea. It's hard to get lost – even if you miss the back gate and end up on the beach, you should be able to spot the lodge's jetty – but the village has no shortage of youngsters willing to show visitors the way. If you'd rather not walk, ask around in the village for a horse and cart (it's twenty minutes or so along sandy paths, sometimes spiky with burrs, or water-logged, depending on the season, so tough going if you're heavily laden).

Jinack Island has a few **accommodation** and **eating** options which fit the island's best-kept-secret atmosphere perfectly: they have a beguiling, castaway feel. *Madiyana Safari Camp* (book through Paradise Tours, ☎494088 or mobile ☎920201, ✉trawallyfoday@hotmail.com; ❹), right on the beach on the seaward side of the island, not far from the Senegalese border, is a beautiful and relaxing hideaway. The lodge's very attractive mudbrick and thatch *bantaba* restaurant, all muted shades of terracotta, ochre and ginger, is perched above the sands, and visitors who stop by for lunch often decide on the spot to stay overnight, won over by the peaceful character of the place and the excellent cooking. The sleeping arrangements are romantic – a few reed-walled huts with brick floors and slatted windows that dapple the mudcloth bedspreads with sunlight. The washing arrangements, however, are shared bucket showers using slightly brackish water, and there's no electricity. To enjoy the lodge to the full, you need to be ready to enjoy simple pleasures like pottering on the beach, stargazing (the owner has a telescope), drifting off to sleep to the sound of the ocean and waking to the dawn chorus.

There are also a couple of budget options near Jinack Kajata village. *Dalaba Lodge* (mobile ☎925052; ❷), inland on the western edge of the village, is a laid-back place with a few rooms in thatched huts in an open sandy compound. The shared shower block is well kept, there's light from a solar generator, and simple food can be provided. There's rather more energy at *Coconut Lodge* (mobile ☎954814; ❷), on the south side of the village. The rooms here are bright, clean and colourful, with solar electricity, and there are hammocks slung under the gingerbread plum trees. Generously sized meals are available to order. The resident English co-owner runs an alternative therapy clinic for the village and has plans to set up a community craft centre and even build a swimming pool.

Travel details

Buses

Barra to: Dakar (2 daily; 4–7hrs).

Ferry

Barra to: Banjul (daily, hourly on the hour; 30min–2hrs).

Bush taxis

Barra to: Albreda & Juffureh (1hr); Amdallai (1hr); Farafenni (5hrs); Jinack Kajata (40min); Kerewan (1hr); Kuntair (45min).

Central Gambia

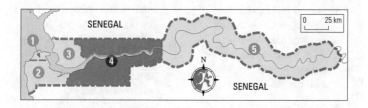

CHAPTER 4 # Highlights

✴ **Kanilai** This remote up-country village comes comes alive during festivals and wrestling tournaments; it's also the location of one of The Gambia's most relaxing bush lodges. See pp.188–191

✴ **Tendaba Camp** A perennially popular riverside lodge which makes an ideal base for short wildlife excursions and longer journeys up-river. See pp.191–193

✴ **Kiang West National Park** A large, little-explored expanse of upcountry woodland and bush, harbouring more

of The Gambia's wildlife species than any other protected area in the country. See pp.193–195

✴ **Farafenni** Up-country town famous for its Sunday *lumo,* a real Gambian country market, bustling with activity and bright with colourful produce and textiles. See pp.199–201

✴ **Bao Bolon Wetland Reserve** One of The Gambia's most fascinating protected areas, excellent for birdwatching, with a maze of mangrove creeks to explore by boat. See pp.201–202

Central Gambia

W ith the country's tourist industry firmly anchored in the coastal resorts, and its transport infrastructure in desperate need of improvement, even the briefest journey into **central Gambia** can feel like an adventure. Up-country road travel can be exhausting, so it's best not to rush your explorations. However, if you have time to spare there is much to discover a few bumpy hours outside the coastal and urban areas, including accessible traditional villages, country markets and national parks.

The Gambia's two principal highways, running between its western and eastern limits, one along the south bank and one on the north, mimic the River Gambia's meanderings. The contrast between north and south is apparent as soon as you travel beyond the Kombos. On the **south bank**, the roads are dusty, potholed and tiring to travel; even so, long-distance drivers tackle the highway at top speed, leaving dust-covered villages (and their inhabitants) choking in their wake, and accelerating even more when they hit a rare stretch that's recently been resurfaced. Fringing the road are lofty palms, well-watered fields, and mango trees that are laden with fruit from May to September. Meanwhile, on the arid, impoverished, but scenically dramatic **north bank**, speed is not an option – all the roads here are unpaved – and life, too, moves at an unhurried pace. The central Gambian stretch of the north bank highway is one of the worst roads in the country, but it passes some outstanding areas of unspoilt wilderness, scattered with remote mudblock and thatch villages, where subsistence farmers sustain traditions that have barely changed for centuries.

Travelling east along the south bank highway from the Kombos, you first pass through **Foni district**, its creeks and palm groves once the haunt of European slavers who set up trading stations here, strategically located a short river crossing away from the larger outposts of Albreda and James Island. Today, by contrast, the shortage of river transport means that north–south commercial interaction of any sort is relatively rare. A highlight of Foni district, deep in the Jola heartlands, is the village of **Kanilai**, President Jammeh's birthplace and home; there's an irrepressible new energy here, showing itself most plainly whenever a major festival is held.

Throughout central Gambia, there are side tracks off the main road which quickly get you within sight of the river, broad and slow-moving even before its final yawning arc towards the Atlantic. Well-worn tracks lead to **Tendaba**, a small village with a large, well-established riverside lodge. This is a favourite stopover on up-country safaris – it's adjacent to **Kiang West National Park**, home to an unequalled population of Gambian mammals and birds, and just across the river from Bao Bolon Wetland Reserve.

Senegal, never more than 25km away wherever you are in the region, has a noticeable commercial influence, creating a growing sense of cultural osmosis, despite resistance from the most staunchly nationalistic Gambians. This is most strongly felt in the east of the region, where the river is barely one kilometre wide, and an international route, the **Trans-Gambian highway**, cuts right across The Gambia to connect Dakar with Casamance. **Soma** and **Farafenni**, the highway's Gambian towns, both benefit from the interchange. While Soma, on the south bank, is up-country Gambia's transport hub and a noisy small town, Farafenni, a relaxed rural centre, is the north bank's focal point, and a good starting place for overland travels into the beautiful and unspoilt **Bao Bolon Wetland Reserve**.

Foni District

Bounded to the north by the River Gambia and Bintang Bolon, the river's longest and most majestic tributary, and to the south by the northern reaches

Bignona & Ziguinchor

of Senegal's richly fertile Casamance region, **Foni district** is a well-watered slice of woods and farmland. If you're heading east into the interior of The Gambia from the Banjul area, Foni is the first up-country district you'll reach after leaving the Kombos.

Like Casamance, Foni district has a distinctively **tropical** flavour, punctuated by pockets of green where winding creeks descend to the river, creasing the otherwise flat terrain into a series of shallow valleys. Graced by tall palms, these little oases are a blaze of emerald in the rice-growing season between August and early December. As in Casamance, much of the population of Foni is **Jola**, and the district is the birthplace and home of the Jola people's most celebrated son, President Jammeh.

European traders operated from bases here in the seventeenth to nineteenth centuries, notably at what are now the small creekside villages of **Brefet** and **Bintang**. The river and its creeks were once the area's main thoroughfares, and a considerable amount of traffic, friendly and hostile, used to make the crossing over to the once-pivotal trading centres of Albreda and Fort James, a short paddle away by dugout *pirogue*. While there's practically nothing left to see of the traders' warehouses and slave "factories", the area is sometimes visited by travellers tracing West African slave trade routes. Now that the usual means of travel around the country is by road, this sense of proximity between north and south bank settlements has been almost completely lost.

The district's largest village is **Bwiam**, where a brand new hospital stands as a visible sign of the present government's commitment to rural regeneration – and its predeliction for showy architectural projects. President Jammeh's partiality, and popularity, is conspicuous elsewhere in Foni, with dark green APRC flags fluttering outside family compounds and over village shops. The six-kilometre side road that leads south off the main Banjul to Basse highway to the village of **Kanilai**, his birthplace and habitual residence, is currently the only relatively good, well-surfaced road in the district.

The main **highway**, which passes almost due east through this section of the south bank from the Kombos to the bridge across Bintang Bolon at **Kalagi**, is generally narrow and in an appalling state of repair. In the places where the road has been graded prior to resurfacing, everything by the roadside – animal, vegetable or mineral – is coated with a thick, sticky layer of russet dust, stirred into smog by passing vehicles. It can also be a dangerous route, especially at dusk, when all it takes is one speeding 4WD to overtake your vehicle for visibility to be near zero. Where the roadworks have yet to start, it's a matter of swerving to avoid the potholes, or driving with two wheels on the road and two on the verge. Bush taxi drivers know the road extremely well and fly over the bumps; as a passenger, all you need to do is hang on and try not to inhale too much dust (or get stressed about the state of your clothing). With your own vehicle, it's best to pace yourself – if you're heading on towards Soma, the worst is yet to come.

Brefet and Bintang

The creekside hamlet of **BREFET**, 6km north of the main south bank highway and very close both to the Kombos and to the River Gambia, was once the site of a European trading station, active from the mid-seventeenth to the early nineteenth centuries; today it's a quiet and unremarkable settlement. The very badly ruined colonial buildings, lying 1km west of the village, are all but obscured by vegetation much of the year – there's practically nothing to see – but the remoteness and wildness of the Foni bush can give you a good idea of the conditions under which slaves were captured. A succession of British and French trading parties ran ruthless operations here, and violent incidents flared up regularly, both between Europeans and Africans, and between rival traders.

There's another former colonial trading post at the small, traditional village of **BINTANG**, 5km north of the south coast highway and about 73km east of Serrekunda, but it's no more visible today than the ruins at Brefet. The village is a relaxed place with a tiny commercial district and an impressive mosque. Rather than hunting for evidence of this area's trading past, a better reason to visit is simply to spend time in the quiet creekside environment; it lies right on the bank of **Bintang Bolon**, The Gambia's longest tributary, and one of its most beautiful. The *bolon* snakes its way from its source in Senegal, around 25km south west of Soma, to meet the River Gambia at Bintang Point, 50km upstream from Banjul. This is Foni District's northern limit, densely forested with mangroves. Like all the River Gambia's mangrove creeks, the bolon is tidal and, at Bintang, 10km inland from Bintang Point, stretches of gunmetal-grey mud are exposed at low tide, inspected by crabs and wading birds. At other times fishermen glide by in dugout canoes and women search for oysters, and at high tide the scene is gorgeous, the water generally broad, calm and shimmering.

Practicalities

Brefet is reached by turning north off the main south bank highway at the village of **Bessi**, 53km from Serrekunda and 30km from Brikama (**bush taxis** running along the Brikama to Bwiam, Kalagi and Soma route will stop at Bessi on request), then following the five-kilometre sandy track on foot or asking around in Bessi for a lift by local cart.

It's possible to get all the way to Bintang, further east, direct from Brikama – two bush taxis leave Bintang in the early morning to take the day's fish and oysters to market, and return from Brikama (D30) in the afternoon. Ask at Brikama which taxi is going all the way to Bintang rather than just passing its junction, at Killy, which is 45km from Brikama, between Somita and Sibanor. If you end up getting dropped at Killy, it's a hot but pleasant six-kilometre walk along the track to Bintang through riverine woodland that's leafy all year round. Heading from the direction of Soma by bush taxi, you may have to change vehicles at Sibanor, which has the nearest petrol and Gamtel office to Bintang. Leaving Bintang, it's best to take one of the early morning village taxis – if you walk to Killy, you may be in for a long wait at the junction as taxis zoom past full.

There are no tourist facilities in Brefet, and most visitors to Bintang don't stay overnight, as there's only one **accommodation** option, *Bintang Bolon Lodge* (☏929362; ❷). This used to be an enchanting place, but now looks ready to collapse into the creek – some of its huts already have. Perched over the mangroves on stilts, the reed and thatch huts each have a veranda overlooking the grey-green water and mud of the *bolon*; three of these are still habitable, but have very basic washing facilities, with drainage straight down into the *bolon* below. The main attraction is the large *bantaba* restaurant, a peaceful, breezy spot, also built out over the water. Given a little notice, the staff will prepare a meal from whatever's available locally – fish is abundant, of course. They can also make arrangements for you to explore Bintang Bolon by canoe.

Bwiam

The small town of **BWIAM** is a progressive rural settlement, further east along the main south bank highway, about 18km from Bintang and 88km from Serrekunda. Conspicuous on the north side of the south bank highway as you pass through town, the new **Sulayman Junkung Hospital** is the town's most prominent landmark. This government-funded hospital has a crucial role to play in improving the quality of basic healthcare available to up-country Gambians south of the river, and it has received much-needed equipment, supplies and training from Europe and the US.

St Joseph's Family Farm, signposted off the main road close to the hospital, is a community development project where women who have been engaged in subsistence farming all their lives are being trained in sustainable agricultural practices, with a view to increasing their productivity while raising environmental awareness. Typical projects include helping women set up a cooperative to run an orchard, or just giving a young girl a bucket, a spade and a banana plant – one plant can generate enough income to pay for the owner's schooling. It's possible to visit the farm and watch whatever practical work is going on that day.

Plans are underway to develop the expanse of waterfront land near Santamba, northwest of Bwiam, as a **safari park**. This area of woodland, enclosed on three sides by the natural boundaries of Bintang and Jurungkumani *bolons* and, to the south, by the supremely unnatural boundary of a massive electric fence, will be the permanent home of the animals presently residing at the Kanilai Game Park (see below).

Bwiam also has a peculiar totem, the **karelo**, or iron pot, a knee-high lump of metal sunk into the ground in such a way that locals claim it's impossible to dig up. In spite of its apparent immobility, legend has it that the *karelo* would spin round in times of conflict, indicating the direction of oncoming attackers. In reality, it's just an old gun emplacement, set in concrete, and not worth a special visit except for curiosity's sake.

Bwiam is easily accessible by **bush taxi**. There are direct services from Serrekunda (2–3hrs; D45), Brikama (1.5–2hrs; D35) and Soma (1.5–2hrs; D35), and any vehicle travelling between Soma and the Kombos will stop there on request.

Kanilai

The Jola village of **KANILAI**, close to the Senegalese border, about 9km southeast of Bwiam and 6km from the south bank highway, is the birthplace of President Jammeh. It's mysteriously hard to find on most pre-1994 maps of The Gambia but, since Jammeh took control of the country in that year, Kanilai's fortunes have changed radically. This once-obscure up-country village now has a good access road, a luxury lodge, a large wrestling arena, a game park stocked with imported wildlife, good healthcare facilities, an electricity supply – and a vast presidential palace.

President Jammeh seems to spend as much time in Kanilai as possible, leading critics to accuse him even of trying to shift the seat of government out of Banjul. Jammeh's presence makes the atmosphere in Kanilai unlike that of anywhere else in The Gambia, even when he's at home in the palace, out of sight to outsiders, not least because the palace generators run the village streetlights – a luxury that even the Senegambia area of Kololi still lacks. Thanks to the entourage of highly armed military vehicles accompanying him everywhere, Jammeh's movements are hard to miss. He has bestowed many gifts upon his home community, which, in return, is fiercely loyal to him. As a visitor, you can experience this if you're in the village for a major event such as a wrestling championship or circumcision ceremony, when Jammeh's drummers, dancers, praise-singers and various camp-followers are out in exuberant force. The President himself likes to party, and will often be seen living it up with the best of them until the early hours.

The village is made up of a clutch of simple scattered compounds – simple apart from the unusual number of television aerials bristling from the roofs. Its natural focal point is the particularly impressive central *bantaba* area, a rough circle of immense silk-cotton trees with deeply pleated trunks, where special events are sometimes held. In recent years, Kanilai has been the venue for what are arguably the most exciting and extraordinary two days of the **International Roots Festival** (see pp.49–51), when visitors can undergo a ceremonial version of the *futampaf* (traditional Jola initiation rites); part of the ceremony takes place under the silk-cotton trees amidst a riot of colour and noise.

Very near the presidential palace is **Kanilai Game Park and Zoo** (daily 7–10am & 5–7pm; D25), a holding area for animals eventually to be moved the new Safari Park at Santamba near Bwiam (see above), one of President

Jola festivities

The Jola people have a special relish for loud, spectacular **cultural celebrations**, and Kanilai is a good place to witness them at their best. Occasions such as national holidays, wrestling matches and community rites of passage are times of communal celebration, and strangers may well be invited to watch the proceedings, or even join in.

Jolas are distinguished from many other Senegambian cultures by not having a caste of *griots* (traditional musicians and praise-singers whose role is hereditary, and who are the custodians of ancestral history); instead, Jolas are free to choose to be musicians, whatever their parentage. This might in some way explain their particular passion and enthusiasm as performers.

As all over West Africa, the **percussionists** set the tone of the occasion and get pulses racing. The Jola are famous for the warm-toned *boucarabou*, a threesome or foursome of drums of different pitches played simultaneously by one drummer, but they also play *soruba* and *sabar* drums, single goblet-shaped drums played with hand and stick. Women, with long loops of beads crossed over their body from each shoulder to the opposite hip, bang on iron or palm-stalk percussion blocks and sing strident choruses, then take it in turns to dance at high speed with stamping steps and flapping or whirring arm movements to a crescendo of drumming and whistle-blowing. Unnerving but compulsive to watch are the baggy-trousered knife-dancers, who strut about fiercely, displaying elaborate *jujus*. Every few steps they knock back potions prepared by their *marabouts* to make them invincible; they then set about mutilating themselves (or, at least making a big show of attempting to do so) with cutlasses and razor blades – none of which leave as much a scratch, no matter how energetically they hack at their chests, limbs and, particularly horribly, eyes and tongues. Even the sanest of Jolas believe implicitly that there's nothing fake about the blades these dancers use.

Then there are the genuinely daring stunts performed by fire-eaters, blowing plumes of flame out over the crowd, and the *kumpo* dancers, who bounce around like animated haystacks under shaggy palm-frond costumes, suddenly upending themselves onto a wooden spike and spinning round in a blur. Meanwhile, a gang of cannon-firers may be playing sweet, gentle flute music somewhere in the crowd, but don't be fooled by their apparent sensitivity – when it's time for them to spring into action, they drive iron tubes stuffed with gunpowder into the ground, light the fuses, and run like hell as the charges explode with ear-splitting force. Every drum beaten, chime struck, whistle blown, chant chanted and cannon fired rings out simultaneously at top volume, and the sheer noise can be overwhelming.

Jammeh's pet projects. Keen to reintroduce some of the African savanna species hunted out of existence in The Gambia long ago, he has organized the acquisition of a number of wild animals from South Africa. Lurking in the park are zebra, impala and wildebeest, plus a couple of rhinos, but the grass is so tall that sightings can be infrequent, unless you stake out one of the water holes. There are also some lions, hyenas, jackals and ostriches in enclosures. Entry is by vehicle only, and there's a trail to follow. To arrange your visit, you should first call at *Sindola Safari Lodge* (see p.191); if you don't have your own wheels, the lodge can provide a car and driver (D150 per person for 2hrs).

The area around Kanilai, close to the Senegalese border, is generally quiet and well wooded, and the traditional occupations here are cereal farming, hunting and livestock rearing – Jammeh's parents tended cattle and sheep. *Sindola* can arrange **excursions** in this area with a vehicle, driver and guide, including birdwatching trips (D300 per person for 2hrs) and village visits, offering an insight into traditional Jola lifestyles and music (D250 per person for 2hrs), as

Senegambian wrestling

Watching traditional **Senegambian wrestling**, which has its origins in the thirteenth century, is a favourite pastime of President Jammeh, and of Jolas in general. Wrestling teams comprise members of a single tribe, and the Jola are renowned for winning most of the time (for some years, the Gambian champion was a native of Kanilai) and for losing with good grace, a sure sign of a true sportsman in Gambian society. Officially, wrestling is The Gambia's national sport, but it's been gradually fading over the last decade or so with the universal onset of football fever. Jammeh is keen to keep the sport alive, and the large arena at Kanilai is one of the few places where major are still held, albeit irregularly. Events at The Gambia's other main arena, in Serrekunda (see p.120), are far more occasional, a result of the sport getting over-commercialized, with wrestlers spending more time touting for tips than actually wrestling, and popular interest drying up.

Visitors are welcome at wrestling matches, and there's a small entrance fee. The Kanilai arena is basically a square of sand surrounded by long, thatched, shaded areas for the audience to sit, between the *bantaba* area and the palace. Drumming and whistling teams (from various ethnic groups, each with their own distinctive drums and tunes) keep up steady competitive rhythms as the action builds slowly, the first few wrestlers pacing or dancing around the court, flexing their muscles and psyching themselves up, daring the others to challenge them to a bout. Stripped to the waist, they wear special trunks known as *dala*, made for them by female followers and decorated with coloured cloth strips and tassels. All but the most supremely self-confident wear an abundance of *jujus* or amulets. Superstition plays a large part in the wrestlers' preparation, and they may be required by their *marabouts* to blow dust at their opponents, or recite an incantation, or go through a special sequence of body movements in order to activate the most powerful charms.

The referee starts whistling the men into order and gradually the opponents pair off to start their bouts. Contestants are evenly matched, it being unusual for small wrestlers to take on bigger men, however much the crowd roars its approval. The object is to land your opponent on his back as quickly and cleanly as possible; with dust flying, bodies slicked with sweat and charmed potions to weaken the opponent's grip, this usually takes a few seconds. However, some bouts can last for several minutes, as contestants bluff and threaten, facing each other with backs bent and hands trailing in the dust to make a good grip. Dozens of bouts take place during a session, and judges keep track of results. The winner of each bout takes a triumphal turn around the edge of the arena, accompanied by his drum team, and collects a few dalasis in appreciation as he goes – you should take a pocketful of small notes.

Taking **photos** is quite accepted, but you'll need a telephoto lens and fast film to capture the excitement as the contest develops and the sun goes down. Events at are sometimes organized and cancelled at short notice; for the latest information, listen for announcements on Radio Gambia (see p.48) or ask the staff at *Sindola Safari Lodge* (see opposite).

---

well as visits to Bintang Bolon, near Bwiam, for fishing trips (D300 per person for 2–3 hrs) and cruises by pirogue (D250 per person for 2–3hrs).

Practicalities

The turning for Kanilai leads southwards off the main south bank highway around 106km east of Serrekunda, at a junction marked by a rigorous police checkpoint and a sign for *Sindola Safari Lodge*. Most people visiting Kanilai do so as an **excursion** to *Sindola* arranged with the *Kairaba Hotel*, travelling from Kololi or direct from the airport in a pre-booked hotel vehicle, or by other private means. It's not easy to reach the village by public transport, but if you're dropped at the highway junction you may find a lift with a private vehicle for the last 6km.

Kanilai's only tourist **accommodation**, the up-market *Sindola Safari Lodge* (☎483415, ✉sindola@gamtel.gm, or c/o *Kairaba Hotel*, Kololi ☎462940, ⓦwww.kairabahotel.com; ❺, suite ❻) lies on the edge of the village, not far from the presidential palace, and is one of the best up-country lodges in The Gambia. More of a hotel than a bush camp, it's a sister lodge to the *Kairaba*, and an ideal place for peaceful relaxation or to use as a base for trips. The accommodation is in forty decent-sized rooms, in picturesque thatched roundhouses. The decor is unimaginative, but the rooms are comfortable and well kept, with air-conditioning, fan and fridge. The beautifully landscaped gardens include an excellent swimming pool, an organic vegetable plot that supplies both the *Sindola* and the *Kairaba*, a children's playground and and a lily pond that resonates with frog calls by night. The attractive **restaurant** (open to non-residents) opens onto the gardens, with a menu that includes good sandwiches (such as chicken and mozzarella, or sauteed prawns) and a very international mixture of main meals including *nasi goreng*, grilled sirloin steak and local specialities.

Kalagi

Situated on the main south bank highway at Foni district's eastern tip, immediately south of Kiang West district, **KALAGI**, 120km east of Serrekunda, is the kind of village that travellers on the way to *Tendaba Camp* and Kiang West National Park would pass straight through if it weren't for the police checkpoint. However, just off the highway outside the village on the northeastern side, is the *Kalagi River Site*, an attractively situated **bar/restaurant** that serves basic drinks and snacks and makes an ideal stopover in a longhaul journey over the potholes. It's a quiet, peaceful, wide open space, on the bank of Bintang Bolon, where the creek runs through a broad floodplain bristling in places with the eerie but beautiful skeletons of lofty mangrove trees, the victims of a shift in the salinity of the water here. Next to the bar is the bridge across the *bolon*, over which the main road continues in the direction of Dumbuto (for the Kiang West park HQ), Kwinella (for Tendaba) and Soma.

Tendaba and Kiang West district

One of The Gambia's longest-established up-country tourist destinations is **Tendaba Camp**, in the village of Tendaba. It lies on the River Gambia, 5km north of the south bank highway, just over 140km from Serrekunda by road and 100km upstream from Banjul. This large riverside bush lodge is a good base for river trips and off-road explorations by 4WD or on foot – it's only a short boat trip away from **Bao Bolon Wetland Reserve** (see pp.201–202), and lies right on the edge of **Kiang West district**. This expanse of forest, farmland and mangrove, sandwiched between the River Gambia to the north, and Bintang Bolon to the south, includes **Kiang West National Park**, a wild and little-explored protected area sometimes visited by tourists from Tendaba on dusty bush-drives.

Since *Tendaba Camp's* early days in the 1970s, a couple of alternative accommodation options in Kiang district have opened, but *Tendaba Camp* remains the most accessible and most-visited: the four bumpy hours it takes to get there by road from the coastal resorts are about as much as many tourists can take when they're only visiting for a day or two. The nearest sizeable village, 5km south of Tendaba and 138km from Serrekunda on the main highway, is **Kwinella**, which is at its liveliest on market day (Thurdays). If you have to hang around in Kwinella for a while on the way to or from the lodge, it's worth seeking out the group of silk-cotton trees in the village, the habitual roost and nesting site of hundreds of cacophonous pelicans – an extraordinary sight close up.

Only 40km east of Banjul as the crow flies, but cut off from the coast by the twin barriers of the river and the bolon, Kiang West district is thinly populated, and is a haven for birds and other wildlife. Few tourists visit the interior of the district except to visit Kiang West National Park, and off the potholed highway all roads are unmade and very rough. However, if you'd like to experience an isolated waterfront lodge it's worth making the effort to get to the riverside hamlet of **Kemoto**. The river itself, close to 2km broad in the Kiang area and majestic rather than beautiful, is a major draw.

Tendaba

The village of **TENDABA**, huddled around the grounds of *Tendaba Camp*, has a down-at-heel, shanty-town atmosphere and is little visited by tourists staying at the lodge. Hassle from begging local children can make some new arrivals at *Tendaba Camp* slightly uncomfortable, although it's no worse here than in any other area of The Gambia frequented by tourists.

Even though Tendaba ("Big Wharf" in Mandinka) is a considerable distance from the Atlantic, the River Gambia here is still very broad, salty and tidal, exposing swathes of mud twice a day. Hazy in the distance is the grey-green fringe of tall mangroves that mark the opposite bank; the sense of space here makes for romantic sunsets and stunning nights lit by a dome of stars.

Practicalities

Most visitors arrive on organized two-day standard excursions (see p.58) from the coastal resorts, or as part of a tailor-made itinerary with a specialist tour company or a privately hired driver and guide. It's also possible to travel independently by public transport. Both the village and lodge are reached by taking one of the two signposted north-bound turnings off the main south bank road at the village of Kwinella. **Bush taxis** running between Serrekunda or Brikama and Soma will drop you at Kwinella, and there's a telecentre here from which to call the lodge to pick you up. Otherwise, you could walk the five kilometres to the river from Kwinella, or ask around to arrange for a local donkey cart to take you.

Tendaba Camp (☎541024, mobile ☎911088; ❸), by far the best-known **accommodation** option in Kiang West District, lies in a prime location on the riverbank side of the village of Tendaba. The "VIP rooms", self-contained and complete with TV, all have views over the water, as does the restaurant, with its huge cone-shaped thatched roof, and the *Bambo Bar* by the jetty. The remaining accommodation (the lodge has 150 beds) is in thatched and white-washed roundhouses, crammed together in a grove of *neem* trees as tightly as caravans in a holiday resort, and out of sight of the river. These rooms are very plain, with African-style cement and foam beds and shared washing facilities, but they have more a genuinely Gambian character than the pricier riverside rooms. All the rooms have mosquito nets and are sprayed every evening, with good reason: as the staff's T-shirts declare, "One million mosquitoes cannot be wrong – *Tendaba Camp* is fabulous!" Although *Tendaba* is rarely fully booked, a place on this scale could never be described as intimate, and it has more of a mass-tourism feel than any of the other up-country bush lodges.

One of the lodge's greatest assets is its small but clean **swimming pool**, with decent showers, available to anyone visiting for the night or just for a meal – reason enough to make a diversion here if you're travelling on the highway. *Tendaba* started up as a hunting lodge, but tends to downplay this these days, since birdwatchers far outnumber hunters among the guests. There's a reminder of old times in its trademark: a strutting bushpig (and bushpig is still a regular feature of the **restaurant** menu, along with more standard fare, generally well prepared and reasonably priced). After dinner, bands of villagers drum and dance round a campfire.

Standard **excursions** organized by the lodge include a three-hour trip by road to Kiang West National Park (see below) – these trips are fun but dusty, bumpy and not much good for wildlife-watching – and a recommended boat trip either to Toubabkollon Point or across the river to a couple of the creeks within Bao Bolon Wetland Reserve (see pp.201–202). All excursions cost around £4/$6.50 per person, subject to a minimum cost of £24/$39 per jeep or £16/$26 per *pirogue*. If you'd rather explore independently, Kiang West is within walking distance of the lodge. The jetty near the lodge is also the starting or finishing point for three-day river trips between Tendaba and Janjanbureh with Gambia River Excursions (see pp.55&56).

Kiang West National Park

Kiang West National Park (daily 8am–6.30pm; D31.50) is among the country's wildest, least-explored regions, a chunk of southern riverbank land west of Kwinella and north of Bintang Bolon, 145km from Banjul. The 115 square kilometres – mainly dry deciduous woodland and Guinea savannah, but also mangrove creeks and tidal flats – was designated a national park in 1987, and is one of the most important wildlife reserves in The Gambia. Most of the wildlife will elude the casual visitor but, with patience, it's possible to see primates, antelopes and plenty of birds.

Bounded to the north by the River Gambia and dissected into three areas by the Jarin, Jali and Nganingkoi *bolons*, the park contains habitats rich in animal species. Every single wild mammal ever recorded in The Gambia has been found here at some time, and Kiang West presently harbours most of the

Birdwatching around Tendaba

Tendaba is a standard stop on Gambian bird-watching itineraries, since there's an abundance of species in the countryside lying within easy walking distance of *Tendaba Camp*. These include river eagle, African darter, sacred ibis, marabou and white-necked storks, wood ibis, plus herons, parrots and the lumbering ground hornbill. At night you may hear Scops owls, milky eagle owls and standard-winged nightjars, which have the perilous habit of resting on the warm road after dark; carry a torch if you want to see some. The rarely used airfield southeast of the lodge is visited by various raptors, and sandgrouse may fly up from under your feet in the adjoining savannah woodlands, behind the camp to the south. Other species to look out for include blue-breasted kingfisher and white-shouldered black tit. Keen birders generally find enough to keep them interested in the Tendaba area for at least a couple of days.

remaining mammal species permanently resident in the country, including sitatunga (an unusual semi-aquatic antelope that thrives in salt marshes), bushbuck and duiker, clawless otter, warthog (bushpig) and spotted hyena. Humpbacked dolphins and West African manatees, which are very rare, are occasionally seen in Jarin Bolon. The area also possesses an impressive tally of over three hundred bird species, more than half the total recorded in the country (see box below).

A good place for wildlife watching is **Tubabkollon Point**, close to a sandy beach on the river in the extreme northeast of the park, and reachable either by boat or on foot from *Tendaba Camp*, 7km along the river. There was once a Portuguese trading station here, hence "*toubab kollon*" ("white man's well").

There's a hide, with elevated views over a waterhole visited by warthogs, bushbucks and sitatunga; the surrounding area is patrolled by troops of guinea baboons and western red colobus monkeys. Also seen here are the world's fastest monkeys, the patas (see p.260). Night-time explorations may reveal nightjars, more often heard than seen, and Senegal bushbabies. A leopard, also nocturnal, was seen here recently, but they are generally extremely elusive. Just west of Tubabkollon Point is a 25-metre **escarpment** which runs parallel to the river, giving an extra dimension to this otherwise flat region; there are good views of the riverbank from the top.

Practicalities

Most visitors approach Kiang West from *Tendaba Camp* (see p.191), driving around by group 4WD excursion or privately hired vehicle. You can also **drive** straight into the park from the south bank highway via the Kiang West National Park headquarters near Dumbuto, which is on the highway, 12km north of Kalagi and 6km south of Kwinella. The park HQ is reached by a rough, overgrown one-kilometre track leading off the highway from the village towards the river. Alternatively you could travel to Dumbuto by public transport – **bush taxis** running along the highway from Serrekunda, Brikama and the up-country south bank towns pass the village – and hire a vehicle having walked to the park HQ (at around £14/$22 per day or £7.50/$12 per half-day for the whole vehicle, this is generally cheaper than at *Tendaba Camp* if you're in a small group). Staff at *Tendaba Camp* and the park HQ can recommend guides. Driving in the park is, of course, noisy and usually dusty, and you will see more wildlife by boat from *Tendaba* or the *Kemoto Hotel* (see opposite), or on foot.

> ## Birdwatching in Kiang West National Park
>
> Kiang West National Park is becoming well known as a birdwatching destination, and a high proportion of The Gambia's native species can be found feeding and breeding here. The official symbol of the park is the bateleur, named for its aerial acrobatics (*bateleur* means "juggler" or "tumbler" in French). This striking short-tailed eagle is frequently seen here, hunting for pigeons and sandgrouse, especially between July and September. It's possible to see the booming ground hornbill in Kiang West, and all ten Gambian species of kingfisher. Rarer species include the endangered brown-necked parrot, a chattering bird which breeds among the mangroves here. During the dry season, the concentration and variety of raptors – 21 species, including vultures, harriers, eagles, hawks and falcons – is particularly high in the park.

The park HQ offers guest **accommodation** for up to 24 people in plain but comfortable self-contained bungalows (no phone on site; for enquiries and to arrange to be picked up by vehicle, if there's one available, contact the Department of Parks and Wildlife office at Abuko, ☎472888, ❶). The bungalows were originally intended for visiting natural history students and researchers, but in practice they're open to all with prior arrangement. It's an isolated spot, with minimal facilities and intermittent electricity, but a reasonable option for intrepid wildlife enthusiasts interested in exploring Kiang West on foot by night. There's a plan underway to open a community-managed Kiang West lodge for ecotourists at **Batelling**, north of Dumbuto, signposted from Wurokang.

If you're interested in flora, the best season to visit is the end of the rainy season (Aug–Oct), when the trees are greenest and shrubs are in flower. August to January is the best time to see the widest variety of bird species, including winter migrants. By March – or May at the latest – much of the tall grass and other vegetation that can block views and clog paths has shrivelled and died or been burnt off by bush fires, making this a good time to look for mammals. In the dry season (Nov–June), as in many parts of The Gambia, particularly near the river, you can occasionally be pestered by biting flies, so it's best to use plenty of insect repellent.

Kemoto

The riverside hamlet of **KEMOTO**, 20km downstream from Kiang West National Park by river, is a long bumpy drive from the nearest sealed road. As the crow flies, it's less than 40km from Sankandi or Dumbuto on the south bank highway, but the journey along winding country tracks can take over two hours – Sankandi is in turn over three hours from Serrekunda. It's worth the effort if you'd like to experience the peaceful countryside en route to this remote stretch of river, from which you can visit Kiang West by boat. On the riverbank at Mootah Point is the *Kemoto Hotel* (☎990031 or 460606; ⓕ460252; ❺), a pleasantly laid-back hotel that's close to some of the river's most interesting creeks, and has panoramic views. The recently refurbished rooms are clean and comfortable, and there's a swimming pool. An alternative route to Kemoto is to start from Banjul, take the ferry to Barra, follow the road to Kerewan, and then, from the disused Jowara Bolon ferry wharf on the Kerewan side of the road bridge, take a *pirogue* across the river. You may be able to arrange this crossing with the hotel staff in advance, but if you just turn up at Kerewan and are in no rush, you could ask around until you find someone willing to take you across.

Soma and Farafenni

The area around **Soma** and **Farafenni** is The Gambia's off-centre fulcrum, a crossroads between Dakar and Ziguinchor in Senegal and between eastern Gambia and the Atlantic coast. The grand-sounding **Trans-Gambian highway**, heading from northern to southern Senegal, cuts through Farafenni to the Bambatenda–Yelitenda ferry across the River Gambia, then picks up again to continue through Soma and on to the Casamance district.

Travelling between western and eastern Gambia, you'll pass through Soma on the up-country south bank road route from the Kombos to Janjanbureh or Basse. Farafenni, 18km north of Soma by road and ferry, is Soma's couterpart, an essential staging post in explorations of The Gambia's north bank. While neither town has any tourist attractions in the conventional sense, as junction towns, they do have places to stay, and they offer visitors the chance to gain a real insight into what makes an up-country Gambian town tick.

Nowhere is The Gambia's north–south divide more evident than in the difference in atmosphere and affluence between the two. Soma's population is barely a third of Farafenni's, but Soma has a much grittier, faster-paced, urban atmosphere, and it's more affluent, with better roads. It's an efficient place to make transport connections, but a less immediately appealing town to spend time. Farafenni is The Gambia's fifth largest town, and is expanding fast, as north bank farms struggle to survive poor groundnut harvests and people migrate to the town seeking work. It feels like an overgrown village, animated but traditional and easy-going; Farafenni's roads are mostly unpaved, and the town has begun to benefit from rural development programmes such as the building of an impressive new hospital. Its weekly country market, selling colourful produce from all over the region, is its greatest attraction for visitors. Farafenni is also a jumping-off point for explorations of unspoilt countryside – **Bao Bolon Wetland Reserve**, The Gambia's largest protected area, lies to the west of the town.

In theory, this part of the country should benefit from excellent connections, but in fact its main **highways** are in desperate need of repair. Some residents of Banjul and the Kombos avoid travelling this far up-country from one year to the next simply because of the inevitable wear and tear on vehicles and drivers' nerves. A resurfacing plan is underway, but progress is slow. The Trans-Gambian highway is in a particularly deplorable state, with Gambians pinning the blame on the overloaded Senegalese and Guinean haulage vehicles that grind along the route to and from Dakar. In truth, Gambians in the region benefit nicely from their role as hosts to traffic from other West African states – both Farafenni and Soma are small but bustling commercial centres, where the mechanics and street food vendors are kept constantly busy serving the passing trade.

Soma

The thinly spread town of **SOMA**, about 183km from Serrekunda, sits at the junction of the Banjul to Basse south bank highway and the Dakar to Ziguinchor Trans-Gambian highway. As such, it's effectively a gateway to eastern Gambia, up-country northern Senegal and the Casamance district. There are other routes to southern Senegal further upriver, but this is the easternmost point in The Gambia at which you can easily turn north towards Kaolack if you're heading towards Dakar overland.

Soma is little more than a bustling truck stop, an innocuous but ultimately charmless string of fuel stations, cheap restaurants, bars and shops where you can get all sorts of Senegalese imports, including Gazelle beer and the latest cotton fabrics. There's a Gamtel office but, at the time of writing, no banks or public Internet access. Buses stop here, at the bus park on the Basse road, and bush taxis whirl up the dust, collecting passengers for the short ride to the ferry crossing for the north bank and Farafenni.

A couple of kilometres outside Soma to the northeast is Mansa Konko ("King's Hill"), prominently marked on maps of The Gambia because it's a regional capital. However, all there is to see here is a collection of local government offices and schools that's quiet and uncommercial in inverse proportion to Soma's racket. If you're in the Soma area, but looking for somewhere

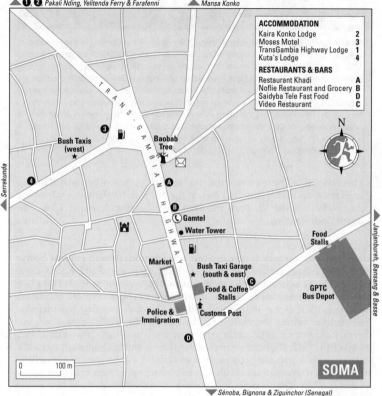

▼ Sénoba, Bignona & Ziguinchor (Senegal)

quiet to stay, it's best to head for the little haven of calm that is **Pakali Nding**, a satellite village 3km north up the Trans-Gambian highway, on the way to the Yelitenda river ferry. It's basically a clutch of compounds with a telecentre, but it has a couple of accommodation options, including the best – and cheapest – lodge in the area.

Practicalities

Soma sees a great deal of through-traffic, and there's a variety of places to stay and eat in the town centre and in the nearby village of Pakali Nding. None of these are specifically geared towards tourists – they're more often used by travelling Africans or foreign volunteers.

Soma is the hub for **bush taxis** from all points on the south bank highway, and for points immediately north and south on the route from Senegal. Bush taxis from Serrekunda stop on the Serrekunda road, near the junction with the Trans-Gambia highway; most other bush taxis stop at Soma's main garage in the middle of town. From eastern Gambia, there are services from Sankulay Kunda near Janjanbureh (D35), Bansang (D35) and Basse (D40). Local vehicles arrive here from Pakali Nding and the Yelitenda ferry (D4) north of town, and from the Gambia–Casamance border (D4). Long-distance Senegalese bush taxis from Dakar via Kaolack and Farafenni and from Ziguinchor via Bignona also pass through.

Yelitenda–Bambatenda ferry

The Yelitenda–Bambatenda vehicle **ferry** that carries Trans-Gambia highway traffic across the River Gambia operates from 7am to 6.30pm (cars D65, foot passengers D3). The Yelitenda ramp is on the south bank, 10km north of Soma, and Bambatenda is on the north bank, 6km south of Farafenni. Travelling with a vehicle, you first need to buy a ticket from the Ports Authority; on each side of the river there's an office just off the highway, a few hundred metres before you reach the ferry dock. The river is less than 1km wide here, and the crossing takes only ten minutes; however, vehicles, particularly trucks, can get stuck in a queue for some time – even days – with plenty of hawkers working the captive clientele. Bush taxis and private vehicles can normally queue-jump the trucks.

The two GPTC **buses** a day that run in each direction between Kanifing (Serrekunda) and Basse stop for lunch at the bus park on the south side of the Basse road at around 12.30pm and 2pm from Basse, and around 12pm and 1.30pm from Kanifing.

Accommodation

Unlikely though it may sound, the best **accommodation** in **central Soma** is at the headquarters of the Soma Scout Group: the *Kaira Konko Lodge* (℡531453, ❶), adjacent to the scout hut on the Serrekunda road. This place has five cool, breezy rooms, secure and spotlessly kept, and an old-fashioned, institutional feel – the lino-floored hall is hung with scouting memorabilia. Intended for visiting scouts, anyone can stay, and food can be provided, but there's no generator. The other option in town is *Moses Motel* (℡531462, mobile ℡919542; ❶), on the Serrekunda/Trans-Gambian highway junction, a Rasta-run place attracting at a mixture of Gambians and shoestring travellers. It has a dozen scruffy rooms with fans but no mosquito nets crammed round a courtyard, and a bar/restaurant; live music events are occasionally held in the large yard.

At **Pakali Nding**, 3km north towards the river, is the highly recommended *TransGambia Highway Lodge* (℡531402; ❶). Although it's right beside the highway, past the centre of the village on the left if you're heading north, it's quiet, and a favourite of locally based NGOs. The large compound provides secure parking and accommodation for individuals and groups. The best rooms (self-contained, with fans) are in neatly painted thatched roundhouses, and simple but good food can be provided on request. There's a generator, and after dark everyone gathers round the TV outside the lodge's *bantaba* – there's little else going on in Pakali Nding. Another good option is *Kuta's Lodge* (℡531572 or 531558; ❷), signposted off the Trans-Gambia highway in the centre of Pakali Nding, off the road to Mansa Konko. Its brand new self-catering accommodation is aimed at passing businessmen; the rooms in the house are well furnished, with air-conditioning, and the use of a kitchen and a living room area with a TV; there's also a generator.

Eating and drinking

Central Soma has an abundance of informal **eating** options, including good street food in the open-air canteen-like area of small benches, tables, coffee stands and braziers around the bush taxi garage. Here slabs of meat are chopped up in front of you, seasoned, sizzled over charcoal and served in *tapalapa* bread while you wait. Street-food vendors also set up stalls outside the GPTC bus garage, springing into action when the buses drop in at lunchtime.

Competition is stiff as few buses ply the route, and you may have several vendors begging you to try free samples of grilled beef or fish balls. The **restaurants** in town are all simple local places where you can get omelettes, hot drinks and bread in the mornings, and chicken, fish or rice and sauce from lunchtime onwards. *Noflie Restaurant and Grocery*, on the main road near the Gamtel office, has good views of whatever's going on in the street, but there's better-quality food to be had in the smaller places. A good choice is the *Video Restaurant* on the Basse road, which has a shaded roadside terrace, and benches inside permanently set up for video nights. There are more local restaurants in the quiet spot just south of the police and immigration post.

Farafenni

Less than 3km from the Senegalese border at Keur Ayip, **FARAFENNI** is, like Soma, a cosmopolitan junction town, but more isolated, situated as it is on the north bank of the River Gambia. Consequently there's a more rural feel to the town, despite the high level of commercial activity that gives the town centre some buzz.

The highlight of every week is its energetic **lumo**, or country market (Sun 7am–6pm), held on the northern edge of town, beyond the stadium. Market day is by far the best day of the week to be in Farafenni, when the place is busy

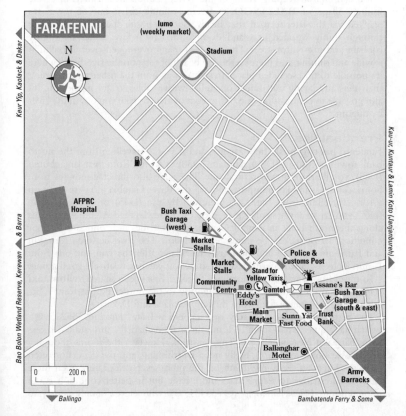

with horse and donkey carts, carrying buyers, sellers, and huge bundles of merchandise. If you don't have your own transport, the best way to get here is to join the locals in travelling by cart, which operate like bush taxis from the centre of town (D2). Visitors generally find the *lumo* much more relaxed than the crowded urban markets like those at Serrekunda and Banjul: the air here is fresher, and you have more room to wander and browse. The merchants are a mixture of Gambians, Senegalese, Guineans and Mauritanians, and you'll hear plenty of Wolof and French spoken as well as Mandinka. From rickety stalls laid out in a sandy area shaded with tarpaulins and thatch, you'll see vendors selling vermillion palm oil, locust beans by the canful, and kola nuts from large sacks. Despite the fact that this is an impoverished area, the sheer volume of produce on sale after the harvest can be staggering – lorry-loads of pumpkins in October and November, and great heaps of tomatoes in January. There are oddities like fetish items, and plenty of household goods on sale too; it's a good place to shop for fabric from Senegal and Guinea, including Fula indigo cloth and wax cotton designs that have yet to make it to the Kombos.

Incongruous for its sheer size is Farafenni's new **hospital**, functioning since 1999, but only officially opened by President Jammeh in 2003; it has already made significant progress in reducing infant mortality in the poorly connected up-country villages in this region. Visitors requiring medical attention are able to attend the outpatients department.

You can enjoy sweeping views of the River Gambia near Farafenni at the fishing village of **BALLINGO**, a twenty-minute drive out of town. It's reached via the laterite road that heads south opposite the hospital, passing through thinly wooded grassland distinguished by a few circles of mighty baobabs and silk-cotton trees. The curve of mangrove-edged river at Ballingo is wide and shining, and there's a muddy beach of sorts on the riverbank, where it's possible to find secluded places to swim, away from the fishermen mending their nets and laying out mullet on millet-weave tables to dry in the sun. It's also possible to commission one of the boat owners to take you out in the river by dugout.

Practicalities

Farafenni has two **bush taxi** garages, and if you're travelling from the north bank towns of Kau-ur (D20), Kuntaur (D30) or Lamin Koto near Janjanbureh (D45), you'll arrive at the central one. There are also direct minibuses from Soma, central Gambia's transport hub, via the River Gambia ferry (see box on p.198). Travelling from Barra via Kerewan by van (D45) or Peugeot estate (D60) you arrive at the smaller garage, on the Kerewan road. All the main roads along the north bank in central Gambia are unmade, and some are in poor condition; transport can be infrequent and slow. The road between Kerewan and Farafenni is rutted and arduous, particularly after the rain; the one from Lamin Koto is graded laterite and, bar some soft patches, relatively good going.

To travel from Farafenni to northern Senegal, first take a shared **yellow taxi** (D4) north up the Trans-Gambian Highway to the border post at Keur Ayip, where you can change for Nioro du Rip, Kaolack and Dakar.

The best-known **place to stay** in Farafenni is *Eddy's Hotel* (☎735225; ❷), which has a quiet, small-town feel, and the mango-shaded courtyard (with resident bats) is a pleasant place to enjoy a drink. However the rooms, though a decent size (some with a/c), badly need refurbishing, and the generator often plays up. There's a seedy nightclub on the premises, but it's rarely open these days. An alternative to *Eddy's* that's more basic but in better condition is the unpretentious *Ballanghar Motel* (☎735431; ❶), with eleven simple courtyard rooms in a quiet residential neighbourhood. There's no generator, so you're reliant on the vagaries of Farafenni's intermittent power supply.

While **food** is available at *Eddy's*, the wait can be so long it's better to head for one of the simple local restaurants on the main road. *Sunn Yai*, centrally located on the east side of the road, doesn't look much but serves excellent chicken and chips, and allows you to bring along your own drinks; there are a few other small places nearby which offer standards like *domodah* and *benechin*. The best **bar** is in town is an unmarked place called *Assane's*, not far from the post office, which serves Gambian Guinness and cold Gazelle beer from Senegal. Bands sometimes play at the Community Centre next door to *Eddy's*.

You can get fuel in Farafenni, and there's a branch of Trust Bank (Mon–Thu 8am–1.30pm, Fri 8am–11.30pm), but, for now, no public Internet access.

Bao Bolon Wetland Reserve

Across the River Gambia from Kiang West is **Bao Bolon Wetland Reserve**, a vast complex designated a site of international importance by the Ramsar International Wetlands Convention. At 220 square kilometres it's The Gambia's largest protected area, distinguished by outstanding marshland flora, and home to West African manatees, African clawless otters, sitatungas, crocodiles, breeding fish and the occasional hippo.

Bao Bolon itself is a tributary of the River Gambia, trickling south from northern Senegal to meet the river in a broad shallow valley on the north bank, across the river from Tendaba (which lies 8km downstream). Five other tributaries also feed in to the river in the area between the villages of **Salikene** and **Katchang**. The result is a riverside region that's a maze of pristine, briny creeks, fringed by unusually tall mangroves, some reaching over 20m. The creeks are as enjoyable as any in the country, but what makes this region unique is the fact that two other ecosystems, salt marsh and savanna woodland, are found in close proximity to the mangroves. Behind the mangroves is a large area of dazzlingly green waterweed; beyond this, the terrain is higher, rising to a dramatic citadel-like escarpment that's home to the tiny fishing community of **Duntumallang**, surrounded by beautiful, ancient baobabs. Beyond this are occasional patches of delicate woodland amid broad, empty mud flats, which give a powerful sense of open space. The mud flats are driveable in the dry season from November to June, when the earth is baked to a salty crisp; after the rains, however, they become softgoing, with some parts impassable, and the terrain is green with reeds and grasses stretching as far as the horizon.

Birdwatching in Bao Bolon Wetland Reserve

Bao Bolon Wetland Reserve is one of The Gambia's most rewarding areas for birdwatchers. The call of the African fish eagle is the reserve's most distinctive sound; other species to be found in the maze of creeks across the river from *Tendaba Camp* include the woolly-necked stork, striated heron, mouse-brown sunbird, goliath heron, the endangered brown-necked parrot and the whimsically named fairy-blue flycatcher. African darters with strangely mobile necks sit on low branches and Senegal thick-knees watch passers-by from the mud banks. The rare white-backed night heron, Pel's fishing owl and African finfoot are also seen occasionally.

You get the best impression of the variety of remote habitats enclosed by the reserve by visiting by vehicle from the north bank of the river: there are **access tracks** from the Kerewan–Farafenni road at Konti Kunda Niji, Njaba Kunda, Katchang and Salikene. The reserve has nothing in the way of formal infrastructure for visitors, so you'll have to make the trip under your own steam in a hired 4WD, or arrange a bespoke tour with a tour operator (see pp.54–55). Exploring this way, you'll have the opportunity to visit some of the 21 villages in the vicinity of the reserve, which receive few foreign visitors. There are at present no vehicles available for hire at the park headquarters near the village of **No Kunda** but, assuming you arrive with your own wheels, the staff there may be able to help with guiding and with negotiating a trip through the creeks by dugout *pirogue* with one of the fishermen from Duntumallang (this should cost no more than D500 per party).

A more usual way to visit, though one that shows you only a fraction of the reserve, is to take one of the highly enjoyable **pirogue excursions** organized by *Tendaba Camp*, likely to be advertized as a "creek trip" rather than a visit to Bao Bolon. Your *pirogue* takes you across the River Gambia first, then to the Kissi and Tunku creeks, where you can often see birds at very close range. The trip will have to be timed carefully to make the best of the tides. The closest hotel **accommodation** to the reserve is at Farafenni, on the north bank to the east, or Tendaba, over the river to the south.

Travel details

Buses

Soma to: Bansang (3–4hrs); Basse (4–5hrs); Brikama (3.5–4.5hrs); Sankulay Kunda for Janjanbureh (2–2.5hrs); Serrekunda (4–5hrs).

Bush taxis

Bintang to: Brikama (1.5hrs).
Bwiam to: Brikama (1.5–2hrs), Serrekunda (2–2.5hrs), Soma (2.5–3hrs).

Farafenni to: Kau-ur (1–1.5hrs); Kerewan (4hrs); Kuntaur (3–4hrs); Lamin Koto for Janjanbureh (3.5–4.5hrs).
Kwinella to: Brikama (2.5–3hrs); Serrekunda (3–3.5hrs); Soma (1.5–2hrs).
Soma to: Bansang (2.5–3.5hrs); Basse (3.5–4.5hrs); Brikama (3–4hrs); Sankulay Kunda for Janjanbureh (1.5–2hrs); Serrekunda (3.5–4.5hrs).

Eastern Gambia

CHAPTER 5

Highlights

✱ **Traditional villages** A visit to some of The Gambia's most remote up-river settlements is a great way to learn about tribal ritual and rural life in a harsh environment. See p.205

✱ **Wassu stone circles** Mysterious relics of ancient Senegambian culture, the Wassu stone circles are the most impresssive of The Gambia's prehistoric sites. See pp.210–212

✱ **River Gambia National Park** These lush, jungle-covered islands are a high point of trips up-river by *pirogue*, offering a chance to spot chimpanzees and hippos. See pp.213–214

✱ **Janjanbureh** Once a crucial river-trading centre, this island is now one of The Gambia's emerging ecotourism destinations, excellent for birdwatching, fishing and river excursions. See pp.214–220

✱ **Basse** Experience small-town, up-country life in Basse, a busy commercial crossroads beautifully located on a fine stretch of river. See pp.223–228

Eastern Gambia

Visually, **eastern Gambia** conforms to a stereotypical European view of
Africa – a thin scattering of picturesque villages with grass-thatched
huts, fenced with woven millet stalks or pickets of twisted branches, isolated in open countryside where sheep and cattle roam in search of pas-
ture. Outside the villages, women bend over vegetable plots, pound grain under
shade trees, or collect immense loads of firewood to carry home on their heads;
under the *bantabas*, men discuss village politics or just lounge about. The massive, statuesque baobabs that dominate the landscape wherever there's a settlement – or wherever one used to be – bear witness to the ancient roots of these
communities.

Up-country villagers eke out an existence with minimal resources, particularly on the **north bank** of the river, where communications are slowed by the
complete lack of paved roads and the fact that few households have electricity. The living environment, and the climate, can be harsh: while the land adjacent to the River Gambia is thickly wooded and green all the year round, just
a short walk away from the river the ground is blackened by bush fires or dessi-
cated by the heat by the middle of the dry season, and only the hardiest trees
and shrubs survive.

Culturally, there is much to discover about rural Gambia in this region, particularly if you know at least a few basic phrases in Mandinka, or have a good
guide to translate – preferably both. **Tribal traditions** are in many ways more
intact here than anywhere else in the country, and villagers are generally proud
to share and explain elements of their culture, such as music and dance, with
interested visitors.

Road travel along the south bank is far more comfortable in eastern than in
central Gambia, partly because the tarmac sees very few heavy vehicles – as
soon as you enter the region via the districts of **Jarra** and **Niamina**, the highway is almost empty of traffic of any sort, you'll often see neatly turned-out
children walking long distances to and from school, right in the middle of the
road.

One of the region's main attractions is the **River Gambia** itself, which at
most times of year is still fresh water as far west as the rice-growing town of
Kau-ur and some way beyond. As it flows through eastern Gambia, the river
is not yet fringed by the mangrove forests that characterize its lower reaches;
instead, the banks are wooded with palms and tropical evergreen trees, sometimes overshadowed by dramatic laterite escarpments.

On the north bank, close to the north bank town of **Kuntaur**, are the **Wassu
stone circles**, an atmospheric remnant of Senegambian prehistory whose
original purpose continues to puzzle archaeologists. Mid-river, east of Kuntaur,

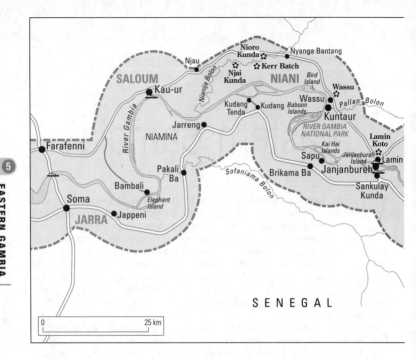

lies a series of islands, each covered with tropical forest, the closest The Gambia gets to jungle. One group of these, **Baboon Islands**, comprises the **River Gambia National Park**, part of which is set up as a chimpanzee rehabilitation centre. It's not possible for visitors to set foot on the islands that make up the park, but you can still get good views of the primates by boat, and this is also the most likely stretch of river for spotting hippos.

The usual starting point for boat trips in the region, and for short excursions to the stone circles, is **Janjanbureh Island** (also called MacCarthy Island). The island is becoming one of The Gambia's foremost ecotourism destinations, with the best choice of accommodation up-river; it's also home to the small, sleepy town of **Janjanbureh**, an old British colonial settlement.

The arc of land east of Janjanbureh is the tail end of the country, where the river makes its first winding inroads into The Gambia. On its south bank is the town of **Bansang**, impoverished and with a world-weariness that doesn't recommend itself to most visitors, but legendary among birdwatchers for its large population of bee-eaters. **Basse**, a riverside trading town further upstream, is a more appealing place, which, though small, has a distinctive energy. Well connected, it's convenient as an endpoint for a long-distance trip up-river by *pirogue*, or as a stopover en route to Senegal's famous Parc National de Niokola-Koba. The area east of Basse is scattered with villages which are some of the remotest in this far-flung region, including **Fatoto**, just 10km from The Gambia's eastern tip, a quiet, unassuming village huddled around the country's easternmost river trading post.

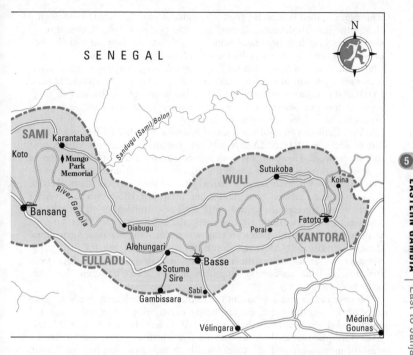

East to Janjanbureh: the south bank

Travelling up-country from central Gambia towards Janjanbureh and Basse along the south bank highway, the first districts you'll pass through after Soma are Jarra and Niamina. After the appalling state of the highway west of Soma, the conditions further east come as a great relief if you're travelling this way: as you leave Soma and continue through **Jarra district**, the potholed oyster-shell mix gives way to hot, black tarmac, with less frequent cracks and holes. On the way towards the village of **Jappeni** by road, you pass through a fairly wild stretch of bush where you're likely to see baboons and other monkeys. Jappeni itself is a good place to look out for marabou storks and wood ibis, which nest in trees in the village. The next sizeable village along the highway is **Kudang**, 18km to the northeast, set back from the river. Its wharf, Kudang Tenda, lies four kilometres north of the village along a bumpy track. Kudang Tenda is the endpoint of some of the river cruises that head downstream from Janjanbureh Island, passing Baboon Islands and some of the River Gambia's most outstanding stretches of riverine forest.

Heading up-river into **Niamina District**, the highway bears north to follow the river's meanderings. The first sizeable village you pass is **PAKALI BA**, 50km from Soma, a village by the Sofaniama *bolon*. It's an attractive village of traditional huts and compounds, marked by a ridge of small rocky hills – an unusual feature in this region of otherwise gently undulating savannah.

Pakali Ba is not the kind of place where tourists usually stop, but it has a vibrant local **story-telling tradition**. *Griots* here tell a tale about a local crocodile hunter called Bambo Bojang ("Crocodile Bojang"), related to the Bojang clan of the Katchikali crocodile pool in Bakau (see pp.111–112), whose magical powers gave him immunity from crocodile attacks. Not surprisingly, he's now the patron saint of crocodiles; his descendants live in the area.

Niamina district is mostly flat, with open grasslands giving way to palm stands nearer the river, and palm beds, chairs and other furniture are hand-made here. **JARRENG**, 12km north west of Pakali Ba, is one of the handful of small towns in this area where you'll see an impressive – and very cheap – range of furniture laid out for sale beside the highway.

A few kilometres beyond the limit of Niamina in Fulladu West, and 110km east of Soma, is **BRIKAMA BA**, which is just another roadside village most days of the week. However, it springs into colourful life on Saturday, the day of its *lumo* (market), with stalls lining the highway and crammed into the backstreets, piled with fresh local produce, plus brightly striped plastic kettles, flower-patterned enamel bowls and other cheap household goods. Travelling traders weave through the crowds with trays of commodities on their heads, and livestock buyers size up bleating sheep and bellowing goats. There's a convenient and comfortable **place to stay** in this area – the National Agricultural Research Institute (NARI) rest house (☎ & ℻678073, ask for the Station Manager; ❷) at **Sapu**, on the riverbank some 3km down the slope from Brikama Ba. With air-conditioning, fans and a kitchen, its seven rooms are often booked up.

The river in this area is broad and smooth, ringing with birdsong, with palm trees arcing over the water, and jungly vegetation behind. Across the river and connected to the south bank by a speedy GPTC ferry is the village of **BARA-JALI**, birthplace of ex-President Jawara, for which reason it was declared a national monument in 1985. Occasional bush taxis run from here to **Wassu**, the site of The Gambia's most famous stone circles (see pp.210–212).

East to Janjanbureh: the north bank

The north bank of the River Gambia between **Elephant Island** and **Baboon Islands** (42km apart as the crow flies, but over double that by dusty road or winding river) is one of The Gambia's most fascinating areas – particularly for those with an interest in African prehistory and spirituality, as the country's greatest concentration of megalithic sites is found here. Most of these are in open bush between the rice-growing towns of **Kau-ur**, a small town at the point of one of the river's sharper bends, and **Kuntaur**, about 50km upstream. Just inland from Kuntaur, and very close to the main north bank highway, are the Gambia's most notable prehistoric remains, the **Wassu stone circles**. These famous, atmospheric stones are easily visitable within a day from Janjanbureh, 20km southeast of Wassu, and are a highlight of any broader exploration of archaeological sites in the region.

Kuntaur is the only sizeable north bank town east of Farafenni; most of the area's population are subsistence farmers living in traditional, isolated villages. There's a sense of the area being scarcely affected by the passage of time – village women still fetch water by hand from the river and its tributaries to tend their vegetable plots, and private vehicles are practically unknown. A few pockets of the area are home to ethnic groups little found elsewhere in The Gambia, such as the Fana Fana, a Wolof-speaking group distinct from the Wolofs of coastal Gambia and Senegal.

The main road from Farafenni that skirts the river's extravagant loops to Kau-ur and on to Kuntaur is broad graded laterite. Apart from a few dips full of powder-fine dust, it makes for reasonable, though slow, driving conditions. Away from the river, the terrain is extremely dry for most of the year, with immense baobab and silk-cotton trees looming over an otherwise almost featureless scrubby landscape. Around the villages in the growing season are swaying stalks of millet and grass-like couscous; after the harvest, however, the fields are bare except for golden stubble.

The bends of the river upstream of Elephant Island are particularly beautiful, the banks lined with gallery forest, resonating with bird calls all year round. Travelling long-distance by boat allows you to enjoy the scene to the full, and sharp-eyed visitors will spot families of **monkeys** staring from the treetops, and maybe even submerged **hippos**, their ears and nostrils just visible. Large well-wooded islands lie mid-river, and the richest in foliage are **Baboon Islands**. These five islands make up the **River Gambia National Park**, part of which is home to an isolated population of West African **chimpanzees**, reintroduced to The Gambia under a rehabilitation programme – you can sometimes spot them from the river.

Elephant Island and Bambali

If you're travelling up-river by boat, the first stretches of water in which you might see hippos are a few kilometres east of the Bambatenda–Yelitenda ferry, where the estuarine part of the river ceases and the mangroves peter out. The no-longer appropriately named **Elephant Island** mid-stream appears to be the lowest grazing ground of The Gambia's small, threatened population of hippos, and there's a chance of catching a glimpse of them – or at least hearing them – anywhere between here and Janjanbureh.

On a north bank peninsula enclosed by a tight curve of the river between Farafenni and Kau-ur, the village of **BAMBALI**, 20km from the main road and right opposite Elephant Island, is sufficiently isolated to feel like an island community. Boat-trips between Tendaba and Janjanbureh (see p.56) sometimes stop at the jetty here. Visiting with a group, and walking up the broad red path to the village, you may, after shaking a few hands, be treated to a semi-impromptu drumming and dancing session from some of the village women – a display more full of joy and spontaneous energy than many of those given by professional troupes found elsewhere in the country. By opening their village to visitors, the community at Bambali has raised the money to buy a grain milling machine.

Kau-ur

KAU-UR, only 40km from Farafenni but well over an hour's drive away, is a small, conservative Wolof town, where the biggest activity is rice cultivation. The extensive irrigated ricefields between the river wharf and the town are lush in the growing season, and are worked almost exclusively by women, while the men concern themselves with the cash crops – groundnuts, couscous, millet and maize. Despite the fertility of the region, the town doesn't manage to grow enough rice to feed itself all year round – nine months is the best they can hope for, sometimes only six if the rains fail – and the peanut works on the river wharf is long abandoned. While the rice fields are fresh and beautiful before the harvest, at other times of year, there's little in Kau-ur to detain visitors. The town itself, though not large, is spread out well away from the river, but the bush taxi garage, post office, telecentres and market, plus a few very basic shops are all very near the small central square. There's a petrol station on the Farafenni to Kuntaur highway.

Kuntaur

KUNTAUR, 56km east of Kau-ur, is also a **rice-growing** town, on a beautiful bend in the river. The town centre, set back from the river, is sleepy, torpid even, except on the day of its weekly market. It's an impoverished place, with the highest fertility rates in the country – women on average having seven children each. The main reason to pass through is to find transport from here to the Wassu stone circles, if you're on your way through the region by river. With some hunting around, it's possible to hire a pick-up bush taxi, or a horse and cart, for the two-kilometre journey – the easiest day for this is Monday, the day of Wassu's *lumo*.

The area upstream of Kuntaur is one of the most likely places on the River Gambia to spot **hippos** – good news for wildlife enthusiasts, but bad news for local farmers, whose crops are often destroyed by these hungry creatures. It's bad news, too, for locals travelling to and from their fields by river: in January 2001, seven people lost their lives when a hippo capsized their canoe. Survivors reported that the hippo attacked the boat after one of the seven threw an orange at it in an attempt to scare it away.

The Wassu stone circles

The **Wassu stone circles** (daily 8am–sunset; D25), a national monument, are vestiges of a prehistoric society about which virtually nothing is known. Located on the edge of Wassu village, a little over 2km inland from Kuntaur and 20km northwest of Janjanbureh, the site is The Gambia's second most-visited tourist attraction on the north bank, after Juffureh. Most visitors arrive here with some idea of what the circles look like, as part of the site features on the back of the 50-dalasi note. It's no Stonehenge, so adjust your expectations accordingly, yet it's an atmospheric place, even for visitors with no particular interest in prehistory.

The hardened laterite pillars, clustered in eleven loose rings around burial places, vary from mere stumps to veritable menhirs weighing several tonnes and standing three metres high. Carbon dating has pinpointed some of them to 750 AD, predating the migration of the Mandinkas to this area; local oral history therefore contains no clues about the stones' precise cultural origins. It's considered good form to leave rocks on top of the pillars – again, no one knows why.

The compound enclosing the standing stones contains a small **museum**, with detailed illustrations and explanations showing how the stones were quarried and rolled into place, and models of the burial sites beneath the circles. As this is a much-visited site in a relatively isolated area, visitors are hassled incessantly by local kids; the museum's watchman tackles this by running at them with a large stick.

The Wassu stone circles are worth visiting at different times of year, if you have the opportunity, as the landscape changes radically with the seasons. After recent rainfall the stones are surrounded by billowing swathes of long green grass. By the end of the dry season, however, they stand in near-desert – apart from a few fruit trees, the only remaining vegetation nearby is the areas of grass outside the compound that have escaped both the bushfires and the grass-harvesters.

Wassu itself is a small village that sees tourists regularly, but it's only really busy on a Monday, the day of its *lumo*, when the village's main thoroughfare (which is also the north bank highway) and the street behind it are clogged up with a jumble of stalls selling fabric, household goods and foodstuffs.

Stone circles are subtle, mysterious and a puzzle to archaeologists; nowhere else in the world is there such a concentration of these as in the large area between eastern Gambia and the River Saloum in Senegal. The Gambia has around a hundred stone circles, mostly well over a thousand years old and very well preserved, in over thirty sites north of the river between Farafenni and Basse.

It's logical to assume a connection between The Gambia's swathe of megalithic sites (not just stone circles, but also isolated standing stones, tumuli or burial mounds, and cairns known as *tombelles*) and those of places as far-flung as Guinea-Bissau, Brittany and the Orkney Islands, the similarities are so apparent. However, their original purpose remains uncertain. Possibly, the circles were used as clocks or astrological calendars of some sort, or were merely there to mark and decorate **graves**. Some researchers have also suggested the stones might represent points of the compass, celestial bodies or phases of the human life cycle, and might have been used as places of healing, insight and prayer.

The consistent appearance and construction of The Gambia's stone circles seem to suggest the work of a single, localized culture, its identity now completely lost. All are rings of between 10 and 24 **cylindrical pillars**, and all the pillars in any one ring are the same height, typically around shoulder height (elsewhere in the region, most stones are 60–310cm high and 30–115cm in diameter). Carbon dating has shown they were created over a period of around 1500 years between the third century BC and the thirteenth century AD, and they enclose a **burial area** which in some cases predates the circles by a significant period, suggesting the sites themselves were sacred. The **grave goods** found by excavation offer few solid clues: tombs have yielded iron arrows and spear heads, pottery vessels, and gold and bronze ornaments, all badly damaged by time. Such **skeletons** as have been discovered near the circles (notably at Sine Ngayebe in Senegal) appear to have been buried hastily, rather than neatly laid out in the manner of kings or chiefs, suggesting they may have been the victims of sacrifice or disease. Their appearance would have been similar to present-day Senegambians, and some have decorative notches between their two upper front teeth, a practice that persists today among some Jola tribes.

All the stones in the Senegambian stone circles are hewn from **laterite**, the deep russet-brown iron-rich sandstone that colours escarpments and outcrops all over the region, and is used as a road surface in lieu of tarmac. Laterite has a rough, spongy-looking surface texture that makes the stones seem even older than they are, as if bitten by rust over centuries. It's relatively easy to quarry and carve, gradually hardening after exposure to air, and it's a source of iron ore – the stones would have been cut using iron tools made from this raw material. Once carved into pillars, they were moved laboriously into position using wooden rollers, and held in place by a trench and retaining wall of small stones just below the ground. While most are still upright, centuries on, some have sagged backwards or fallen flat where the ground supporting them has softened.

Today, plenty of local **superstition** and spiritual belief still surrounds the stone circles, and their custodians will sometimes come to the circles to pray, bringing offerings of vegetables, candles or money. Some say that certain stones are luminous by night; others say that harm will befall anyone who tampers with the circles – which might partly explain why few exhaustive excavations have taken place.

Practicalities

Wassu is a standard stop on **group tours** of the area, by road or by boat, from or via Janjanbureh. Long-distance riverboat cruises run by Gambia River Excursions (see p.55 & p.56) from Tendaba, Janjanbureh or Basse, stop at Kuntaur to visit Wassu. To get there independently, your most likely starting point is

Janjanbureh, a bumpy, dusty 45-minute ride away by **bush taxi**. *Gelleh-gelleh* bush taxis leave from the Lamin Koto ferry ramp on the north bank of the river opposite Janjanbureh town; those heading to the village of Wassu or on to Kaur or Farafenni will drop you a few hundred metres from the stones. The best chance of transport there and back in a day is to go on a Monday, the day of Wassu's *lumo*. Approaching along the north bank from the west, Wassu is served by bush taxis from Farafenni and Kau-ur; however, if you'd like to explore any other stone circles in the area adjoining this route, you'll need a hired vehicle or private taxi.

Wassu has one **place to stay**, the *Berreto Village Camp* (no phone; ❶), signposted just off the highway, but it's not really recommended. This very basic local drinking hole has a guest room in a roundhouse, with straw mattresses and no guarantee of security. The only advantages are its proximity to the stones and its rock-bottom prices; Janjanbureh's accommodation options are a much better bet (see pp.218–219). For simple **meals** in Wassu, a few places serve rice and sauce or *afra* along the highway in the village.

Kerr Batch and other stone circles

While Wassu is the most visited and arguably the most impressive of the stone circle sites in this region, there are other circles to discover on the north bank, and even more if you pursue the quest into the Sine-Saloum region of Senegal. Many of these are hardly worth a second glance, but some are very striking. All but a couple stand in open bush, rather than fenced and groomed as at Wassu, giving them a wilder, more spiritual atmosphere. While these circles are sometimes still used as places of prayer and reflection, and even as burial sites, villagers are not precious about outsiders visiting them, and active interest from outsiders has led to organizations such as UNESCO supporting efforts to preserve the stones. In The Gambia, the sites are thinly scattered over a large area, more than 4000 square kilometres in extent. For visitors with limited time, the best area to investigate is the valley of the **Nianija Bolon**, between Wassu and the village of Njau, about 40km west of Wassu via the main north bank road.

The best-known site after Wassu, and the only other one for which there's an entrance fee (D15), is **Kerr Batch**, famous for its **lyre stone** near the centre of the site, a bizarre V-shaped megalith about 2m high. Legend suggests lyre stones indicate the co-burial of two people who died on the same day, and there are only a few examples in The Gambia; when this one toppled and broke a couple of decades ago, locals ham-fistedly patched it together with cement, leaving it looking rather forlorn. Kerr Batch, enclosed in a small compound, lacks the atmosphere of the unfenced circles and, unlike Wassu, has no museum; the couple of dilapidated huts that look as if they might contain some displays are, for now, empty, but a programme of renovations is planned, assisted by UNESCO funds. Kerr Batch is well signposted along the dust track from the main road at the village of **Nyanga Bantang**, 16km north east of Wassu via the north bank highway. If you approach from another direction, it's useful to know that the local name for the place is Sinchu Demba.

Other standing stones in the Nianija valley include those on each side of the road at **Niani Maru**, 11km northwest of Kuntaur (a total of eight circles), and three more, including two concentric ones, 7km north west of Nyanga Bantang at **Nioro Kunda**. The largest stones in the region (over 3m high and possibly weighing as much as 10 tonnes) are found in the two circles at **Njai Kunda**, near the village of Charmen, on the south side of the bolon, about 17km southwest of Nyanga Bantang.

To find the circles, you'll need an independent means of travel, and preferably a **guide** who can ask for directions and information in Mandinka, Serahule and Wolof. If you're not already travelling with a hired vehicle and guide from the Kombos (a journey best broken over at least two days), you could make enquiries at Janjanbureh's lodges. Without a guide, your best chance of information about the stones is to seek out a bright youngster in the nearest village to each site, as few adults in the off-road areas speak fluent English.

The villages in the vicinity of the stone circles are quiet, appealing places to visit in their own right. The landscape along the Nianija Bolon is lush with tall rhun palms and reed beds, and the villages are small fenced settlements of mud-brick huts. Those along the track from the main road at Nyanga to Kerr Batch see a fair number of visitors passing through; beyond this, the villages see very few travellers.

The closest circles to the ones at Wassu are at **Pallan Mandinka** and **Jakaba**, near the Pallan Bolon. There's also a small circle at **Lamin Koto**, within easy walking distance of Janjanbureh, nine short, dumpy stones right beside the main road in the shade of a *kuling* tree, around 1km north of the ferry ramp.

Baboon Islands

The collection of five small forested islands immediately southwest of Kuntaur, **Baboon Islands** (so called even though baboons are now less common here

Baboon Islands Chimpanzee Rehabilitation Project

The Gambia's **Chimpanzee Rehabilitation Project** (UK contact: ☏01242/675720, ⓦwww.chimprehab.com) is the longest-running project of its kind in Africa. It currently protects and monitors a population of 63 chimpanzees. These include animals that prior to their adoption were struggling to survive, let alone breed; now, however, their offspring, born on the islands, have in some cases produced young of their own. Once reasonably common, chimps had been hunted out of existence in The Gambia by the 1900s, and the islands are now the only part of the country where they're found in the wild.

Set up in 1969 by Stella Marsden, daughter of Eddie Brewer, the founder of Abuko Nature Reserve, the project's original purpose was to provide long-term care for a group of chimpanzees confiscated from hunters and traders by the Gambian wildlife authorities. The success of this endeavour led Stella to rescue and rehabilitate more West African chimpanzees that had been orphaned by poachers, or maltreated in captivity.

Animals discovered in distress in locations as far apart as Senegal and Germany are now brought to the Gambia to be nurtured back to physical and psychological health. After an initial period of assessment and care, they're integrated into the independent communities of chimps living on three islands within the River Gambia National Park. Here, in forest uninhabited by humans, they can rediscover their natural environment.

The project is registered as a UK charity under the name of the **Chimpanzee Rehabilitation Trust**. You can contribute by joining the chimp adoption scheme for £30 a year. Sponsors receive updates on the progress of their chosen chimp, with photos, twice a year, as well as a newsletter covering the community and its day-to-day life. While the project receives many enquiries from individuals wishing to visit or to volunteer as assistants or researchers, the nature of the rehabilitation programme requires the chimpanzees to have **minimal contact** with people, so few requests can be accommodated – the closest views you can get are from a boat passing by on the river.

than elsewhere along the river), constitutes the **River Gambia National Park**. While it's not possible for visitors to land on the islands, you can get good views of the forest fringes from a couple of hundred metres away, mid-river, on **river tours** by boat to or from Janjanbureh (see below and p.220). The islands, which cover an area totalling a little under six square kilometres, include areas of swamp and savannah as well as forest. When tourist boats enter the waters of the park, patrol boats collect a D100 per person entry fee (normally included in the cost of your tour). They also ensure that visitors don't anchor close to the islands, and it's essential that their directions are followed, both for the welfare of the island wildlife and for visitors' own safety. Three of the islands are populated by chimpanzees introduced here by the **Baboon Islands Chimpanzee Rehabilitation Project** (see box on p.213), some of which behave aggressively when there are humans in sight. As your boat passes, you may be able to see families of chimps moving through the foliage or, with territorial screeching, shaking the branches.

Janjanbureh Island

Three hundred kilometres upstream from Banjul, and twenty square kilometres in area, **Janjanbureh Island** (also still known by its colonial name, MacCarthy Island) is the only one of the River Gambia's wonderful, bird-rich islands easily accessible to tourists. A leafy retreat for visitors wanting to escape the tourist traps on the coast, the island is fast becoming one of the country's foremost ecotourism destinations, with excellent opportunities for exploring the river and viewing wildlife, and it offers the best range of accommodation in eastern Gambia. For most visitors, their stay is focused around one of Janjanbureh's bush lodges. The most-visited lodges are situated in beautiful riverside woodland, and make good bases for river swimming, boat trips and wilderness walks.

If you're staying in the bush, you'd be forgiven for giving **Janjanbureh town** a miss. Also known as Georgetown, it's a characterful place, but backwaters don't come much further back than this – even the local bumsters are chronically lethargic. It lies at a crossroads of sorts, halfway between Kau-ur and Basse and with river access to both the north and south banks. Once a crucial river trading post and administrative centre for the British, the town's present-day layout, and many of its buildings, date from the colonial period.

It's possible to visit Janjanbureh by two or three day group **excursion** by road from the coastal resorts, travelling by small coach, stopping at places of interest along the way, and staying at one of the lodges, usually *Bird Safari Camp* or *Janjang Bureh Camp*; a half-day river trip may be included (see p.56). It's also possible, and highly recommended, to visit by double-decker *pirogue* with Gambia River Excursions (see p.55 & p.56), cruising upstream from *Tendaba Camp* and spending two nights on board on the way, or downstream from Fatoto or Basse.

Some history

Over the centuries, Janjanbureh's mid-river location and its mild, fertile terrain have provided a **safe haven** for runaway slaves, *marabouts* fleeing religious persecution, and traders looking for somewhere secure and well connected to buy and sell groundnuts and other commodities. In 1823, when the **British** were ceded the island of Janjanbureh by the King of Niani for five cases of coins and a case of wine, it included no permanent settlements. Oral history suggests there were people already here, but little is known about them. The British began to use the island as a base for trading, farming and missionary work, and as a suitable point from which to defend the river against illegal slave traders. The first settlers included a group of Wesleyan missionaries, who established what is now West Africa's oldest remaining Methodist church (still visitable in the town centre), a number of traders from the embryonic Crown Colony of Bathurst (now Banjul), and an attachment of the West Indian Regiment, who, on the north side of the island, built a small mudbrick fort and named it **Fort George** after King George IV. These pioneers went on to construct Georgetown's wharves and warehouses, and trading in cloth, guns, iron and local produce such as beeswax, ivory and skins began in earnest.

Akus, the African slaves liberated by the British, arrived in the 1830s. Many of them were skilled artisans and labourers, and they helped develop the island's agricultural potential. They also benefited from Georgetown's unusually good **mission schools**: by the mid-nineteenth century, the town was firmly established as the best centre of education in up-country Gambia and the prestigious Armitage High School, founded in 1927 as a school for the sons of the Gambian aristocracy, and now the country's only government-funded coeducational senior secondary boarding school, is still highly respected.

When the trading and transport of **groundnuts** between the interior and the coast gathered pace in the 1930s, Georgetown was the hub of the business, its economy booming. By this time it was The Gambia's second town and an administrative centre for the Protectorate. In the 1960s, with the assistance of experts from China, **rice cultivation** by irrigation was introduced, although the momentum of development didn't last. After Independence in 1965, Georgetown's fortunes changed. Much of the island's significance was lost in the 1970s after the completion of the south bank highway, and its fate was sealed by the closure of the riverboat service, leaving mainland towns like Bansang in a far better position for commerce. Georgetown's residents began to drift away to the Kombos now that the new road had made the distance much more manageable. Economic depopulation is still a problem in Janjanbureh: the island's youth are, on the whole, disillusioned about local career prospects, and the 1990s saw a series of closures of shops, restaurants and other businesses.

With the growth of **ecotourism**, however, the community appears to be turning a corner. Although rice and groundnut cultivation are not wholly compatible with woodland conservation, the farmers here are beginning to appreciate the long-term merit of limiting the area of land farmed on the island in order to safeguard the natural environment and its sizeable population of birds and mammals.

Arrival and orientation

Janjanbureh Island is connected to the mainland by two small vehicle **ferries** (8am–8pm; vehicles D50, foot passengers D4), one on the south side and one on the north. These take one truck or a couple of cars at a time, and the crossings normally only take a few minutes.

The ferry from the south bank of the River Gambia at **Sankulay Kunda** is pulled by a cable – whenever the engine is out of order everybody on board is expected to help heave. The south side of the island is connected to Janjanbureh town, 2.5km away by a tarmac road. This leads through rice fields and pleasant countryside and eventually becomes the town's high street; it effectively connects the two ferry ramps. The cheapest route into town from Sankulay Kunda is to cross the river by ferry as a foot passenger, then

Janjanbureh Island is accessible from both banks of the river. Most visitors approach by road from the Kombos along the main **south bank** highway, a 300km drive from Serrekunda, but it's also possible to approach via the less-travelled **north bank** highway, which is shorter in distance and more scenic, but takes longer. Either route takes you along rough roads for a significant part of the journey.

The south bank route

Travelling from the Kombos to Janjanbureh by the **south bank route**, you follow the main south bank highway via Soma to the well-marked turning for the hamlet of **Sankulay Kunda** (this turning is west of Yori Beri Kunda and east of Sulolor Mandinka). After 3km, you reach the Sankulay Kunda ferry ramp; the ferry (see p.215) takes vehicles and passengers across the river channel to the island. Travelling nonstop from Serrekunda to Janjanbureh town takes a minimum of six hours; you have to suffer the dusty and badly potholed stretches between Sotokoi and Soma on the way.

To travel up-country to Sankulay Kunda by **bush taxi**, you can take a *gelleh gelleh* minivan bound for Sankulay Kunda, Bansang or Basse from the garage at Bundung on the south side of Serrekunda – the Bansang and Basse vehicles will make the diversion to the Sankulay Kunda ferry for any passenger that requires this – or take a vehicle to Soma and then change. Alternatively, the GPTC **buses** from Kanifing bus terminal (daily, 8.30am and 10am; D75) call at the stop 50m from the Sankulay Kunda ferry before continuing to Basse (for running information from Kanifing, call ☎394776). Similarly, travelling down-country, buses leave Basse daily at 8.30am and 10am, calling at Sankulay Kunda about 75 minutes later, then heading on towards the Kombos (for running information from Basse, call ☎668868).

The north bank route

Starting from the Kombos, you can join the **north bank route** by first taking the ferry from Banjul to Barra, and then continuing along the north bank highway from there, travelling via Kerewan, Farafenni, Kau-ur and Wassu, to the Lamin Koto ferry ramp (see below), close to *Janjang Bureh Camp* and right across the channel from Janjanbureh town. The advantage of the north bank route is that you pass through some particularly interesting parts of the country, including the region east of Farafenni, where most of The Gambia's stone circles are concentrated. The road from Barra to Lamin Koto is about 60km shorter than the south bank road from Serrekunda to Sankulay Kunda but, on the north bank, you have the rutted and bumpy Kerewan–Farafenni road to tackle. If travelling nonstop, you should count on at least eight hours (not including the Barra ferry crossing).

Bush taxis cover the north bank highway from Barra to Farafenni, where you can change for Lamin Koto. There are presently no buses along this route.

---

either walk along the road or catch one of the island's few **bush taxis**. Alternatively, if you're staying at *Janjang Bureh Camp* or *Dreambird Camp*, you can call their office (☎676182) from the telecentre near the Sankulay Kunda ferry ramp and ask them to send a boat round the island to collect you (from D380 per group).

The ferry from the north bank of the River Gambia at **Lamin Koto**, a short walk away from *Janjang Bureh Camp*, brings you straight across the northern channel to Janjanbureh town. As an alternative, hand-paddled iron tubs carry foot passengers across to the *badala* (shore area) which doubles as the town's bush taxi garage, when there's demand. The *Janjang Bureh Camp* boats shuttle their guests for free across the channel to the jetty near *Dreambird Camp*. If you

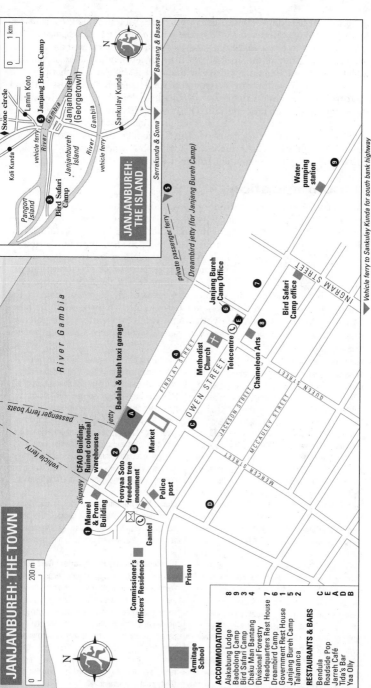

JANJANBUREH: THE TOWN

River Gambia

Lamin Koto for Wassu & Kuntaur ▶
Lamin Koto for Wassu & Kuntaur ▶

vehicle ferry

passenger ferry boats

slipway

CFAO Building; Ruined colonial warehouses

Maurel & Prom Building **1**

jetty

Badala & bush taxi garage

A

2

Foroyaa Soto freedom tree monument

B

Market

Police post

Commissioner's Officers' Residence

Gamtel

D

FINDLAY STREET

OWEN STREET

4

C

JACKSON STREET

Methodist Church

Telecentre

E

6 Janjang Bureh Camp Office

7

8

Chameleon Arts

Bird Safari Camp office

QUEEN STREET

MCCAULEY STREET

MERCER STREET

INGRAM STREET

Water pumping station

9

Prison

Armitage School

private passenger ferry

Dreambird jetty (for Janjang Bureh Camp)

Serrekunda & Soma ▶ **5**

Vehicle ferry to Sankulay Kunda for south bank highway ▶

0 200 m

JANJANBUREH: THE ISLAND

Kuntaur & Wassu ▶
◆ Stone circle
Lamin Koto

Koli Kunda

Pangoi Island

Bird Safari Camp **3**

Janjanbureh Island

River Gambia

vehicle ferry

Janjang Bureh Camp **9**

Janjanbureh (Georgetown)

River Gambia

vehicle ferry

Sankulay Kunda

Bansang & Basse ▶

0   1 km

N

ACCOMMODATION

Alakabung Lodge	8
Baobolong Camp	9
Bird Safari Camp	3
Chaku Man Bantang	4
Divisional Forestry	
Headquarters Rest House	7
Dreambird Camp	6
Government Rest House	1
Janjang Bureh Camp	5
Talamanca	2

RESTAURANTS & BARS

Bendula	C
Roadside Pop	E
Jarreh Café	A
Tida's Bar	D
Yaa Olly	B

EASTERN GAMBIA | Janjanbureh Island

5

217

have to wait for connections to the island, there's a pleasant new riverside bar near the Sankulay Kunda ferry ramp, the *Independent Bar and Restaurant*.

Once you're in town, *Bird Safari Camp* is a boat ride away down the island to the west, using one of the small boats that normally wait at the *badala* (around D200 per group), or a bumpy drive by bush taxi (D75). All the other places to stay are in town, within easy walking distance. The town has a **post office**, a **Gamtel** office and a hardware shop that doubles as a **telecentre**. Communications are unsophisticated here: neither *Bird Safari Camp* nor *Janjang Bureh Camp* has a phone on site (both use the landlines at their offices in town) and there's little or no mobile phone signal – mobile-owners here have been known to climb trees to make a call, hoping this would improve reception. *Alakabung Lodge* has intermittent **Internet access**.

Accommodation

Janjanbureh's **accommodation** options, mostly European–Gambian partnerships, are either bush lodges (well geared-up for tourists interested in exploring the natural environment, and comfortable but not luxurious) or simple guesthouses. Most are on the island itself; one is opposite the island on the River Gambia's north bank. Most of the places on the island are in Janjanbureh town, on the island's north shore. They're all are either right on, or very near, the riverbank, and close to unspoilt woodland. Some have generators, but a few rely on candles and lanterns by night, adding to the romance; none has hot running water, but you can ask for some to be heated for you. If you're travelling with a tent, you'll find some scenic potential pitches at *Baobolong Camp*, *Bird Safari Camp*, *Janjang Bureh Camp* or *Bendula Bar and Restaurant*.

Alakabung Lodge ☎676123, @alakabung@qanet.gm. On the main street, a decent budget option with ten basic rooms with shower and fan in small thatched roundhouses. Gambian meals are available to order; this can take some time, but the compound, with jaunty murals, is a pleasant enough place to wait. ❶

Baobolong Camp ☎676133. Gambian-run lodge, a ten minute walk east of the centre of town, a little off the beaten track, in a quarter with a village atmosphere. Spotlessly kept, its 37 brightly furnished rooms are in small houses around a compound. Meals can be provided when there's a group staying. ❷

Bird Safari Camp ☎676108 (Georgetown office), @bsc@gamtel.gm, ⓦbsc.gm. Bush lodge near the island's westernmost point, well away from the town, secluded in woodland that's excellent for short bird-walks. To get there, you take the dust track that leads westward from town, past the Armitage School and the colonial cemetery, through a grove of neem trees and some rice fields, and out into the bush. The eleven safari tents by the river are a little spartan, but with good private showers; there's also accommodation in spacious and comfortable self-contained thatched roundhouses, with West African-style beds. The rooms and tents all have electric light and fans,

and there's also a river-water swimming pool (chlorinated but murky). The food is decent but nothing special, and the overall atmosphere of the place can vary – it's an isolated spot, and everything goes into hibernation when it's not busy. Catch the place at its liveliest, though, and it's a great place to be, with exuberant after-dinner fireside drumming and dancing. Activities include drumming lessons, canoe hire, Gambian cooking sessions, village visits and an excellent boat-trip to Kudang which passes through the River Gambia National Park. ❹

Chaku Man Bantang (no phone). In town, close to the river, this batik artist's compound is shady and quiet, with a hut for guests; facilities are very basic, with shared latrine and bucket shower. ❶

Divisional Forestry Headquarters Rest House ☎676198. Self-catering accommodation in the Forestry HQ compound in town, intended for visiting researchers, but others may stay if there's room. This is a gem of a place, set in a lush, wild garden by the river, with plenty of trees and a jetty perfect for diving off. The accommodation is in an attractive bungalow, with three bedrooms with fans and mosquito nets (room for six), a living room, a good kitchen and shower-room, and electricity from a generator. ❶

Dreambird Camp ☎676182, or book through Gambia River Excursions, Bakau, ☎497603, ⓕ495526, ⓔgamriv@gamtel.gm, ⓦwww.gre.gm. Under the same management as *Janjang Bureh Camp*, but even more reasonable in price. There are only four small self-contained rooms and no restaurant, but the place has character, with hammocks slung outside the rooms. ❶

Government Rest House (no phone). The building, in a fine location in the town centre, beneath large shady trees, may look a little abandoned, but you can still stay here, although it's run down and the electricity is intermittent. ❶

Janjang Bureh Camp ☎676182 c/o Dreambird Camp, or book through Gambia River Excursions, Bakau, ☎497603, ⓔgamriv@gamtel.gm, ⓦwww.gre.gm. Right opposite the island, in a beautiful grove of trees near Lamin Koto on the north bank of the river, this is Janjanbureh's most charming and friendly lodge. It's simple (no hot water or electricity) but comfortable, and very

good value. The 27 thatched, whitewashed huts, rather like hobbit-houses, are all individually designed, curvy on the inside with interesting nooks and mini lofts. Meals here are good, but don't vary much. The lodge is often visited by monkeys, and its environs are excellent for bird-watching. You can hire a small motorboat or large *pirogue* by the hour or the day; possible trips include Sankulay Kunda (from D380 per group), right round the island (D450) and to Baboon Islands (D1000). Local drummers and dancers perform round a campfire when groups are staying. Phone from the Sankulay Kunda tele-centre to be collected by boat; you can also be ferried for free to and from the *Dreambird Camp* jetty. ❸

Talamanca (no phone). Primarily a bar, the rooms in this small compound in town are cheap but extremely basic, and not a good choice if you're looking for peace and quiet. ❶

The Town

Janjanbureh town is laid out in a **grid system**, a reminder of its past as a British colonial administrative outpost. Much of the **architecture** in the old town dates from the late nineteenth and early twentieth century and there's a strong sense of buildings having been left to decay, whether in use or not, ever since Independence. Look carefully and you'll find the town's last-remaining **colonial lamppost** (on the corner of Jackson and Mercer Streets), once one of a network of functioning gas lamps, now sadly beheaded. There's also, on Owen Street, a single **timber-clad house**, similar to those found in Banjul, and very typical of the houses built in the 1830s by the Aku settlers.

The northeast quarter of the town resembles an open museum of the old trading days, with the tiled floors and ornate plasterwork of derelict warehouses disintegrating behind an onslaught of tropical vegetation. The **Maurel and Prom building** just west of the vehicle ferry ramp and the big roofless barn-like **CFAO building** are sometimes labelled "slave houses", but in fact both were built in the 1890s, and were probably stores for perishable goods. Just inland from the vehicle ferry ramp, in front of the police post, is the **Foroyaa Sooto Freedom Tree Monument**, a small triangular park with walls emblazoned with the Gambian colours. In the middle is a young, struggling *bantang* tree, planted to commemorate the Freedom Tree that used to stand in Fort George, near this spot. After the British ban on slave-trading in the early nineteenth century, MacCarthy Island became a refuge for runaway slaves from the surrounding area; the story goes that those that touched or hugged this tree had their names recorded by the British soldiers at Fort George, and were granted their freedom. These days, Janjanbureh is better known as a place of incarceration of another sort – it's the site of the country's main **prison**, a place so grim that a number of prisoners died of malnutrition in the early 1990s.

For local **crafts**, try *Chameleon Arts*, next to *Alakabung Lodge*, a colourful shop and artists' studio selling professional *koras* and *djembés*, jewellery and tie-dyed or painted handmade clothing. Down by the river is *Chaku Man Bantang*, a compound that's the home of a batik artist, who willingly brings out trunkfuls of his work for you to see. He offers tuition to anyone interested in learning batik techniques, and also very basic accommodation (see p.218).

By far the town's most appealing asset is the **river** itself. Locals will assure you that it's safe to swim here, since the level of human activity keeps crocodiles well away. Fishing enthusiasts will find plenty of good specimens in the water, and a trip by boat may well yield large catfish and even fierce-toothed, acrobatic tigerfish. You need the right bait, of course – apparently fly fishing is a non-starter, but live bait or balls of monkey dung work well. When deciding where to cast your line, remember that the River Gambia is tidal throughout the country. To arrange a fishing trip, or any other boat-trip, enquire at *Bird Safari Camp*, *Janjang Bureh Camp* or *Baobolong Lodge*. Janjanbureh is in reach of stunning stretches of river, and Sapu, the Kai Hai Islands, the River Gambia National Park, Kudang and Bansang all make good excursions. It's also a jumping-off point for long-distance **river-trips** to Tendaba and Basse (see p.56); this is a highly recommended way to experience the peaceful and scenically varied river environment.

Eating and drinking

Guests at *Janjang Bureh Camp* and *Bird Safari Camp* invariably make their lodgings their base for **eating** and **drinking**, and non-residents may visit these camps for breakfast, lunch or the evening buffet (laid on whenever there's a group visiting), but there are also a few local-style options in town. *Bendula Bar and Restaurant* (daily 7am–late) has recently been revamped, with a jazzy tropical island mural brightening up an otherwise stark interior; they serve cold JulBrew, soft drinks, some spirits and Gambian food. Also open late for decent Gambian meals and drinks is *Roadside Pop*, near *Alakabung Lodge* and *Dreambird Camp*. *Tida's Bar*, a very local drinking place in the residential part of town, is run informally by Janjanbureh's methodist headmistress, in her compound. There's also a clutch of simple eating and drinking places around the *badala* (wharf area) where the passenger ferries land and the bush taxis wait: *Jarreh Café*, a shack which serves tea, coffee, sandwiches and eggs in the mornings, *Yaa Olly* (daily 8am–5pm) providing basic meals like *benechin* or rice with *domodah*, and *Talamanca*, a small, noisy compound doubling as a drinking hole, with basic accommodation (see p.219).

East from Janjanbureh

Although eastern Gambia is, geographically at least, a gateway to the rest of West Africa, there's an increasing sense of remoteness the further east you go. The few travellers who take the time to explore the backroads of the districts beyond Janjanbureh will find a scattering of isolated Mandinka, Fula, Serer and Serahule villages, in a landscape which, on the **south bank**, is relatively lush with palms and towering mahogany trees; the **north bank**, by contrast, is austere, arid and breathtakingly hot.

The usual mode of transport for villagers in this region is by simple horse-drawn cart, or on foot. You'll see people covering considerable distances in the heat of the day, shading their heads with golf umbrellas. Only schoolchildren go bare-headed when the sun is at its highest, and women wear brightly patterned shawls over their turban-like *tikos*.

The first town east of Janjanbureh is **Bansang**, a small place on the south bank. The oldest hospital is up-country Gambia is located here, but it's otherwise insignificant, except to birdwatchers. Further east but on the north side of the river, and best approached direct from Lamin Koto, is a memorial to the great explorer **Mungo Park**, in a quiet riverside spot just outside the village of **Karantaba**.

The hub of the region is **Basse**, the eastern Gambian town with the strongest connections to nearby Senegal and the countries beyond. It's a long-established trading centre, located at a crossroads of road and river routes. Despite being right at the heart of an impoverished region, Basse is an energetic and characterful place that's very welcoming to travellers; after the vegetable harvest in the dry season, its produce market becomes one of the country's best.

With your own transport, or with time and patience, there's a rewarding **overland loop** to be traced from Janjanbureh, starting from Lamin Koto. You then follow the newly graded laterite road east past ancient baobab trees and mud-built villages of the north bank, all the way to the river ferry which connects the north shore to **Fatoto**, The Gambia's easternmost sizeable settlement; finally, you return via Basse along the south bank route. A shorter circuit takes you from Lamin Koto straight to Basse via the turning at Yarobawal, which leads to the Basse ferry, skirting The Gambia's easternmost reaches. Also highly recommended is a **river trip** from Janjanbureh via Karantaba to Basse, and possibly on to Fatoto. Throughout this region, the river is outstandingly peaceful, and empty apart from monkeys, birds and a few fishermen flinging out their nets from their dugout *pirogues*.

Bansang

If you're covering The Gambia by road from west to east along the southern highway, you pass the small town of **BANSANG**, 138km east of Soma and 16km southeast of Janjanbureh, on the way into the tail end of the country. Few travellers stop in this small town, but it's famous with birdwatchers, since on its outskirts is a quarry that's one of the best places in The Gambia to see bee-eaters.

The highway bypasses the town, but an older road leads down through Bansang's town centre, hugging a magnificent bend in the River Gambia. Between the buildings are rare, urban glimpses of the river which manages to elude highway travellers all the way from Banjul to Basse. The opposite bank is a thick green ribbon of bushes, their branches hanging over the water, interspersed with mango trees. There's a hand-pulled vehicle ferry here, with room for two cars, and rudder-paddled boats for foot passengers. For elevated river views, the low hills behind the town, bristling with communications masts, are easily accessible. The town itself is a rather listless place, a ramshackle collection of oblong cement-block houses, with corrugated iron roofs held down with old tyres and bricks.

To Gambians, Bansang is best known for its **hospital** (☏674222), which was the only one up-river before the opening of the new sites at Farafenni and Bwiam. It's on the main highway, just east of a prominent sign saying "Say No To Bribery", a telling indication of Bansang's defiance in the face of adversity: the hospital has only 120 beds and yet has a malaria-ridden catchment area of over 600,000 people.

If you're **staying the night** in Bansang, your best bet is *Carew's Bar* (☏674290; ❶) near the bus stop in the middle of town; this friendly place has basic accommodation in a few thatched huts. The bar, a favourite hangout for foreign volunteers posted at the hospital, serves cold drinks and simple food like chicken or omelette and chips all day, and hosts occasional music sessions; there's also Internet access. Alternative lodgings are *Kuteh Jumbulu* (☏674479; ❷), a very run-down place down by the jetty, or as a last resort the *Bunyadu Hotel* (❷) at the Basse end of town.

The GPTC **buses** that run daily between Kanifing and Basse stop in Bansang on the way (two a day in either direction: westbound at around 9.30am and 11am, eastbound at around 3.30pm and 6pm). Bansang is also served by **bush taxis** from Serrekunda, Soma, Sankulay Kunda and Basse.

Karantaba and the Mungo Park Memorial

Ten kilometres northeast of Bansang, the River Gambia sweeps north into a luxuriant loop, its westward course blocked by fortress-like laterite cliffs. Glassy green, it turns west again at the small north bank village of **KARANTABA**, 16km northeast of Bansang and 25km by road from Lamin Koto, before flowing on south through a sparsely populated landscape, far from the main roads on either bank. The riverbanks near Karantaba are a tangle of rhun palms and leafy shrubs; if you're travelling this stretch by boat, you have a good chance of seeing little bands of red colobus and callithrix monkeys in the foliage, or larger troops of baboons.

Karantaba features on tourist excursions cruising the river between Janjanbureh and Basse, or following the north bank along the road from Lamin Koto. Visitors come here to pay their respects to the memory of the great West African explorer, Scottish doctor **Mungo Park**. The point from which Park set out in search of the source of the Niger, in two separate expeditions in 1795 and 1805, is marked by a very plain twelve-metre obelisk on a concrete plinth close to the riverbank, a couple of kilometres upstream from Karantaba's wharf.

It's helpful to ask local children to guide you there; it's a thirty minute walk along a sandy path through thinly wooded bush.

Karantaba village is a collection of hamlets, each with a different ethnic make-up, and marked by huge, gnarled baobabs, testament to the great age of the settlement. On Wednesdays, the whole district, seemingly, congregates at Karantaba Wolof, the hamlet nearest the highway and 2km from the wharf, for the *lumo*, which is the oldest weekly market in this area. The action kicks off around 9am, when the first bush taxis lurch in, dangerously overloaded with buyers, sellers and produce, and the place is packed by noon. While it's not really a market for souvenir hunters, you can watch everyday scenes of up-country village commerce acted out, and it's possible to pick up good, cheap, freshly made food from the women serving spoonfuls of sauce out of enamel bowls.

Wednesday is the best day to visit Karantaba independently by bush taxi; these run infrequently along the newly graded laterite road from Lamin Koto, a forty-minute drive away to the west. The only Gambian north bank settlement larger than a small village in the 90km between Karantaba and the eastern border with Senegal is **Diabugu**, 25km southeast. This a busy, purposeful little place set back from the the river, with a telecentre, some shops and an impressive mosque in the midst of tightly packed cement-brick compounds and thatched huts.

Basse

BASSE (Basse Santa Su, in full) is The Gambia's easternmost town, a surprisingly animated centre that gets its energy from its proximity to Senegal. It's 375km from Banjul, on the south side of the country, right on the riverbank, connected to the north by a small vehicle ferry, and it's been a busy trading centre since well before colonial times. This is a town that sees plenty of travellers from West Africa and elsewhere, so visitors blend easily with the cosmopolitan crowd. It's a polyglot place, with English, French, Wolof, Mandinka, Serer and Arabic in the mix; the traders here include well-established Senegalese, Guineans, Mauritanians and Lebanese. As a consequence, many travellers find it one of the Gambia's most relaxing towns. You need to be prepared, however, for shortages: of power, running water and, at certain times of year, even food.

Basse is the destination of long-distance **river cruises** from Tendaba via Janjanbureh with Gambia River Excursions (see p.55 & p.56). The town is situated on a graceful, tree-lined bend in the river, which, even this far upstream, is affected by the tides, so you'll see it flowing east and west at different times of day.

One reason to stay in Basse is to break your journey if you're heading into Senegal to visit the Parc National de Niokolo-Koba. Even if you're not travelling that far, the riverine countryside around Basse lends itself well to off-the-beaten track exploring, and the riverbank in the town itself is one of the best places in the world to get a good view of a bird species much sought-after by birdwatchers: the **Egyptian plover**.

Arrival and orientation

Most of Basse's activity is centred round the area just south of the river wharf: this is the commercial hub where the market, bush taxi garage, banks, telecentres and post office are all located. Buildings stretch out along the route to the west, and there's a small suburban quarter beyond the fields to the south, Mansajang.

Basse has only one **bush taxi** garage, roughly between the market and the river, and all bush taxis, including *gelleh-gellehs* from Serrekunda (D90), Soma

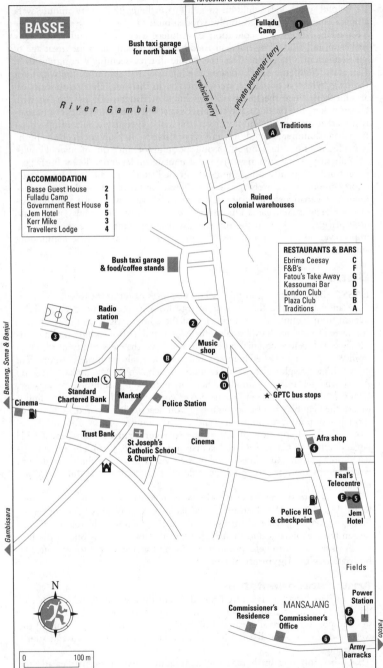

Yarobawal & Sutukoba

BASSE

Fulladu Camp ❶

Bush taxi garage for north bank

vehicle ferry

private passenger ferry

River Gambia

Ⓐ Traditions

ACCOMMODATION

Basse Guest House	2
Fulladu Camp	1
Government Rest House	6
Jem Hotel	5
Kerr Mike	3
Travellers Lodge	4

Ruined colonial warehouses

RESTAURANTS & BARS

Ebrima Ceesay	C
F&B's	F
Fatou's Take Away	G
Kassoumai Bar	D
London Club	E
Plaza Club	B
Traditions	A

Bush taxi garage & food/coffee stands

Radio station

❸

❷

Ⓑ

Music shop

Ⓒ

Ⓓ

★ ★ GPTC bus stops

Gamtel ☎

Standard Chartered Bank

Market

Cinema

Police Station

Trust Bank

St Joseph's Catholic School & Church

Cinema

Afra shop

❹

Faal's Telecentre

Ⓔ ➤ ❺

Jem Hotel

Police HQ & checkpoint

Fields

MANSAJANG

Power Station

Commissioner's Residence

Commissioner's Office

❻

Ⓕ
Ⓖ

Army barracks

N

0   100 m

Sabi, Vélingara (Senegal)

Bansang, Soma & Banjul

Gambissara

Fatoto

Basse marks the end of the tarmac road; east of here, the roads are laterite or dust. **Bush taxis** from Basse serve all points west along the main south bank highway, including Bansang, Soma, Serrekunda, plus the nearby pottery-making villages of Sotuma Sere and Alohungari. Transport to and from the villages lying on minor roads off the highway is most readily available on *lumo* days (Sunday in Fatoto and Sabi). If you're travelling from Basse to Vélingara in Senegal (20km from Basse), it's best to find a bush taxi going the whole distance: connections from the Gambian border post of Sabi are infrequent. If you're aiming for Senegal's Parc National de Niokola-Koba, you'll need your own transport.

The GPTC **bus** service to the Kombos has been greatly reduced over recent years. Now there are only two buses daily, from the bus stop in the town centre, leaving at 8.30am and 10am, the earlier one covering the distance in eight or nine hours, stopping at Bansang, Sankulay Kunda, Soma, Brikama and Kanifing (Serrekunda); the later one is a slower service. For information and reservations, call ☎668868.

(D40), Sankulay Kunda (D20), Bansang (D15) and all other points on the south bank highway, arrive here. The two daily GPTC buses from Kanifing (Serrekunda) via Brikama, Soma, Sankulay Kunda and Bansang arrive in the late afternoon or early evening at the bus stop in the centre of town.

The vehicle **ferry** from the north bank (daily 7.00am–6.30pm; vehicles D40, foot passengers D1) takes four cars or one truck at a time across the 100m wide river, and the screech of the ferry's ramp is one of the town's most familiar noises. The slipway on either side is steep, and the ferry loads on one side only, spinning around midstream, so if you have your own vehicle, prepare yourself to reverse sharply uphill to disembark. There are also small hand-paddled boat taxis for foot passengers (D1).

Basse has two **banks**: a branch of Trust Bank (Mon–Thurs 8am–1.30pm, Fri 8am–11.30am) and, opposite, a Standard Chartered Bank (Mon–Thurs 8am–1.30pm, Fri 8–11am); neither has an ATM. The **post office** (Mon–Fri 8.30am–12.15pm & 2–4pm, Sat 2.30am–noon) is close by. The Gamtel office has no **Internet access**, but you can get online at Faal's Telecentre (10.30am–7.30pm), just off the road towards Mansajang, on the way to *Jem Hotel*.

Accommodation

You're far enough up-country in Basse to appreciate a significant difference in climate between here and the coast; temperatures are more extreme, so it's wise to choose a room with either a good fan or blankets, depending on the time of year.

Basse Guest House ☎668283. The best of the cheap options, which isn't saying much. Its advantages are its central location, and its large communal living room area and balcony overlooking the busy street below. The rooms are basic, with fans but no mosquito nets, and grubby shared washing facilities. ❶

Fulladu Camp ☎917007. In theory, this is Basse's upmarket bush lodge, in a great position by the river on the opposite side to the town (a small boat shuttles its guests across free of charge). In practice, it's rather haphazardly run,

with an inconstant water supply (the pump only operates in the evenings and early mornings). There are 48 rooms in thatched roundhouses that look pretty from the outside but are not over-large. When tour groups visit, there are lively drumming and dancing sessions in the evening; at other times, the place can be chronically quiet, and the staff hang out in the huge, empty open-sided bar/restaurant watching television; the cooking is simple but good. Trips can be arranged to the Niokola-Koba National Park in Senegal, or up or down the river. ❸

△ River Gambia near Janjanbureh

Government Rest House ☎668262. Pleasant and roomy, with an old-fashioned atmosphere, but quite a walk out of town in Mansajang. ❷

Jem Hotel ☎668356. Something of an institution in Basse, and notorious for the eccentricity of its owner, this place receives few guests, but the rooms are pleasant enough, off a pretty courtyard that would be quiet if not for the generator. Surprisingly good meals are served from a spotless kitchen in the large restaurant area. Attached is the *London Club*, a semi-dormant nightclub (see p.228). ❷

Kerr Mike ☎931848. A bit out of the way on the western side of town near the football field, this is a typical urban compound with a block of concrete floored, corrugate roofed rooms, shared latrines and bucket showers, and a small bar. It's slightly dilapidated, but worth considering if you're on a strict budget. ❶

The Town

Basse's wharfside area has a slight ghost-town feel, with neglected colonial-era warehouses crumbling away under the elements but, just inland from here, the commercial district is lively, colourful and noisy. Trade with Senegal from here is thriving, so the **shops** selling fabrics and household goods tend to be well stocked; you'll find an abundance of pots and pans, bootleg cassettes, and excellent wax printed cotton and other textiles (cheaper here than in Banjul or Serrekunda, and very good value if your taste matches that of the locals). There are also groceries, pharmacies and places where you can buy essentials such as batteries. The **produce market** is best well into the dry season (Jan–June), when local women sell the vegetables grown in the town's community gardens: shiny aubergines, fluted bitter tomatoes, juicy looking lettuce, pyramids of fat red chillies, bundles of mint and a great abundance of other foodstuffs. To one side you'll see shelled groundnuts and brilliant green cassava leaves being minced to a paste.

Highly recommended is a visit to the **craft shop** *Traditions* (☎668533, ⊛www.traditionsgambia.com, daily except Tue, 9am–6pm), housed in a 1906 trading post on the river near to the ferry, with a gloriously situated first-floor veranda overlooking the river. It sells West African art, crafts and traditional textiles, some using rich-coloured indigo and kola nut dyes; there's also a café here (see p.228), one of the best places in Basse to meet people and watch the incessant activity on the water.

The Basse area has a tradition of **dyeing and weaving**, and *Traditions* can arrange tuition with local artisans; you will also often find weavers working their strip-cloth looms in an open space not far from the post office. The local clay produces particularly good **pottery** of the rustic terracotta sort, called *dar* in Mandinka; there's a compound in Mansajang, more or less opposite the Commissioner's Residence, with a small *dardula* (pottery works), where you can watch pots being made if you're here from around March to the end of the dry season. The Mandinka family here make *jibidas* (water cooler jars), colander-like rice steamers, storage pots and incense burners.

Birdwatching around Basse

The Egyptian plover, or crocodile bird, is a "holy grail" species for many birdwatchers visiting The Gambia. Basse is the best place in the country, and probably the world, to get a good view of this smartly plumaged, honey-beige and black-coloured bird, which regularly patrols the muddy riverbank near *Traditions* in small groups between August and February (particularly Nov–Jan); good vantage points are the wharf and the *Traditions* balcony. Vultures and carmine bee-eaters are also regularly seen in the area.

Pottery-makers also work in compounds and community studios in the Serer and Serahule villages just west of Basse, including **Alohungari** and **Sotuma Sere** – their work is set out for sale beside the highway.

Eating, drinking and nightlife

All the **eating** and **entertainment** options in town have a definite local, rather than tourist, atmosphere, but Basse is very welcoming towards visitors. As well as the places mentioned below, there are a couple of unmarked *afra* grills in town, good places to stock up on protein if you're out late. There are also a great many women stationed along the main street, selling fruit, pasta sauce, or rice and fish from enamel bowls to passing travellers. By night, Basse feels like one big lorry stop, with long-distance drivers overnighting here and making the most of the abundance of good street food.

Ebrima Ceesay, International Coffee Maker A flyblown indoor local coffee and sandwich place, where the coffee is first class (if you like it local style) and you can grab an egg or meat sandwich for next to nothing – great for breakfast.

F&B's Bar and Restaurant Quite a trek out of town beyond the fields but before Mansajang, this place has a loyal following among foreign volunteers, but the service gets mixed reports. On offer are cheap, basic meals (rice, chicken, cow foot) and cold drinks. Daily 2pm–4am.

Fatou's Take Away Situated between *F&B's* and Mansajang's power station, this cheerful little place serves decent rice and sauce at lunchtime, and brochettes, chicken and burgers at night, at low prices.

Kassoumai Bar An unmarked palm wine "ghetto" in the centre of town that sells soft drinks, beer and, of course, palm wine, in an unadorned concrete box of a space.

London Club At *Jem's Hotel*. A cavernous space with bizarre murals, this rarely functions as a nightclub now, except when hired for a naming ceremony or similar event – there's a permanent layer of dust on the bottles and fairy lights behind the bar – but you can still drink here, and there's good food to order.

Plaza Club Once the town centre's buzziest nightspot, great for reggae and West African music, this now opens on Saturdays only, with occasional special events on Fridays.

Traditions The upstairs balcony here is by far Basse's most relaxing hangout; there's a short menu including sandwiches, spaghetti and soup, plus treats like crisps and Mars bars. Daily except Tues, 9am–6pm.

From Basse to Fatoto

Whether travelling through The Gambia by road or by river, there's a certain sense of completion to be achieved by travelling all the way to **Fatoto**, on the south bank, the easternmost sizeable village in the country, and the place where The Gambia stops, to all intents and purposes. It's an hour's drive from Basse along a bone-shaking, forty-kilometre laterite road, but it's also reachable by the little-travelled, but scenically impressive, north bank road, passing some of The Gambia's remotest villages on the way.

Travelling east from Basse along the south bank, the greenest spot in the landscape is at **Charmoi**, where the road crosses a *bolon*. On either side of the small bridge are mango trees, lily ponds and vegetable gardens, where some of the produce that fills Basse market with colour is grown.

The north bank route, from the Basse ferry to **Yarobawal** then heading east, takes you close to **traditional Mandinka villages**, widely spaced and remote, where cereal crops sway in the rainy season and, in the dry season, women pound millet under the shade trees, or draw water from wells to sprinkle on vegetable plots. These fenced-off pockets of green are oases in a landscape that is arid in the extreme for eight months of the year. Life here is simple, and most settlements are small, attractive collections of mud-walled huts with a cone of thatch for a roof. Eventually you dip down through the grove of trees opposite Fatoto to the river, green and inviting with a sandy shore, a welcome vision of coolness after the heat of the interior. There's a hand-hauled chain ferry here, which can take two vehicles (vehicle D145, foot passenger D2) and runs on demand.

If you're travelling to Fatoto by river from Basse, you'll find more and more wildlife the further upstream you are. The north bank, in particular, is very rich in birds, taking advantage both of the quiet, fresh water and of the abundance of vegetable gardens near the bank, occasionally seen through the acacias and shrubs that border the river.

FATOTO itself, spread out over an area of low, scrubby hills, has a forgotten-by-time atmosphere, its commercial area only just livelier than the derelict trading station by the river. There are no hotels here, but you'll find a couple of places where you can buy rice and sauce, a few workshops and *bitikos*, and the *Konkodouma*, a place that calls itself a nightclub, but is really a bar that sometimes shows videos. Bush taxis between Fatoto and Basse are infrequent, but Sunday market days are busiest.

Birdwatching around Fatoto

The banks of the River Gambia between Basse and Fatoto offer excellent birdwatching opportunities, especially if you're on the water, with various species of roller, glossy starling, plantain-eater and bee-eater conspicuous on perches high in the trees, or flying at speed over the foliage. Plovers are easy to spot on the banks and are impressive in flight, their backs and wings strikingly marked. You'll also see raptors soaring overhead or surveying the scene from the higher branches.

Travel details

Buses
Bansang to to: Basse (1hr); Brikama (6–8hrs); Sankulay Kunda for Janjanbureh (1hr); Serrekunda (7–9hrs); Soma (3–4hrs).
Basse to: Bansang (1hr); Brikama (7–9hrs); Sankulay Kunda for Janjanbureh (2–2.5hrs); Serrekunda (8–10hrs); Soma (4–5hrs).
Sankulay Kunda to: Bansang (1hr); Basse (2–2.5hrs); Brikama (5–7hrs); Serrekunda (6–8hrs); Soma (2–3hrs).

Bush taxis
Basse to: Bansang (45min); Brikama (6–7hrs); Fatoto (1hr); Sankulay Kunda for Janjanbureh (1.5–2hrs); Serrekunda (7–8hrs); Soma (3.5–4hrs).
Bansang to: Basse (45min); Brikama (5–6hrs); Sankulay Kunda for Janjanbureh (1–1.5hrs); Serrekunda (6–7hrs); Soma (2.5–3hrs).
Lamin Koto to: Farafenni (3.5–4.5hrs); Kau-ur (3–3.5hrs); Wassu & Kuntaur (45min–1hr).
Kau-ur to: Farafenni (1–1.5hrs); Lamin Koto (3–3.5hrs); Wassu & Kuntaur (2–2.5hrs).
Kuntaur to: Farafenni (3–4hrs); Kau-ur (2–2.5hrs); Lamin Koto (45min–1hr).
Sankulay Kunda to: Bansang (1–1.5hrs); Basse (1.5–2hrs); Brikama (4–5hrs); Serrekunda (5–7hrs); Soma (1.5–2hrs).
Wassu to: Farafenni (3–4hrs); Kau-ur (2–2.5hrs); Lamin Koto (45min–1hr).

Contexts

Contexts

History

The first known inhabitants of what is now The Gambia were a succession of ethnic groups who migrated to the fertile basin of the River Gambia from elsewhere in West Africa. European traders began to settle near the river from the mid-fifteenth century; the present-day borders of The Gambia were first drawn in 1889, in Paris, by British negotiators, with ruler and compass. Legend has it that the country's optimum dimensions were determined by measuring the extent of territory that could be defended by cannon-fire from a gunboat sailing up the river – hence The Gambia's long, thin and crooked shape.

Gambian prehistory

The **earliest people** of the Gambia valley may have been the Jola, who by tradition have a very limited oral history. The hundred or so Gambian **stone circles**, including the famous ones at Wassu, are compelling evidence of a civilization that lived near the river between 800BC and 1000AD, but hard facts about their ethnic origin have so far eluded archaeologists and ethnologists. The first known written record referring to The Gambia appeared in the Carthaginian **Hanno**'s account of his voyage down the west coast of Africa around 470BC. His mission was to establish colonies on the Atlantic coast for the purpose of trade in ivory and gold, and it's thought that he made it all the way down to Cameroon and back; his account, though geographically sketchy, was still being used as a reference by seafarers in the age of exploration two thousand years later.

Our knowledge of the intervening centuries is very incomplete. The introduction of camels to Africa in the second century AD, facilitating long-distance desert travel, opened up West Africa to Arab traders in **slaves** and **gold**, who gave the indigenous Africans an appetite for commerce. Between the fifth and eighth centuries, the area that is now The Gambia was part of the ancient **kingdom of Ghana**, ruled by members of the Serahule tribe. Seven centuries on, control had transferred to **Mandingo** and **Susu** overlords from the Fouta Djalon plateau in Guinea, part of the Songhai empire. By the fifteenth century, most of the valley was under the control of small **Mandinka kingdoms** founded by Manding immigrants from the Mali empire.

The dawn of the colonial era

The European settlers of the fifteenth and sixteenth centuries were mostly **Portuguese** who set themselves up as trading partners with local headmen. Their larger game plan was to trace a route to the spice islands of the Far East, and in the process track down the fabled riches of the West African kingdoms and possibly find the source of the Nile. The River Gambia was assumed to be an open door to the interior of Africa. The first Portuguese adventurer to explore the mouth of the river was **Nuno Tristão**, sent to West Africa in 1447 by Prince Henry the Navigator. Ten years later, other Portuguese explorers started to establish trading stations along the river, to purchase slaves and other

commodities in exchange for cloth, guns and manufactured goods. They land-
ed on an island twenty miles up-river and named it St Andrew's Island after a
sailor who died and was buried there; this was later renamed James Island.
Some made Africa their home, marrying the daughters of chiefs; the descendants of these mixed unions often grew up to became local leaders and mediators.

In the late sixteenth century, when the Mali empire was in decline, the
British arrived in the area and started trading along the River Gambia. Other
nationalities soon followed suit. From the mid-seventeenth century, English,
Dutch, French and Baltic merchant-adventurers shared and fought over trad-
ing rights from the small (but strategically invaluable) neighbouring bases of
Fort James on James Island, mid-river, and **Albreda** on the north bank. In
1765, the British gained the upper hand in the area, instituting their first West
African colony, the province of **Senegambia**, with its headquarters in St Louis
on the banks of the River Senegal and its River Gambia base at Fort James.
The colony was dissolved less than twenty years later, under the terms of the

The Transatlantic slave trade

There are no exact records of how many West African **slaves** were captured and
shipped to the Americas between the seventeenth and nineteenth centuries. The figures are hazy partly because so many died in the process of capture, imprisonment
and transportation, but estimates of the total range from several hundred thousand
to fifteen million: around twenty thousand per year in the sixteenth century, rising to
one hundred thousand per year in the eighteenth century, when the trade was at its
peak. Of these, approximately one-sixth were shipped out of the Senegambia area.
West Africans had been enslaving fellow Africans long before the arrival of the
European traders, but the basis of these slaves' bondage sometimes included a get-
out clause: if they had offered themselves as slaves through destitution, rather than
being captured in war, they had a chance to earn back their freedom. For the slaves
displaced by the Europeans, there was, prior to the abolition of the trade, absolutely no chance of return.

In The Gambia, the first European slave traders were **Portuguese**. Later, from the
seventeenth century on, it was the **British** who held the greatest influence over the
trade – though the French, Portuguese and Dutch were also heavily involved – and
it was the British who banned the involvement of their own ships in the trade (but
not the ownership of slaves) in 1808; total **abolition** came in 1833.

The shipping of slaves from West Africa to the New World was just one leg of a **tri-
angle of trade** that began with slave ships sailing from Europe carrying cloth, iron
bars, guns and other manufactured goods to be exchanged for human cargo which
was shipped to Brazil, the Caribbean and the southern United States to be sold to
the plantation owners. The demand was a long-term one, as plantation owners
found it a better investment to keep supplementing their labour force with fresh
slaves rather than to treat those they already owned well enough for them to provide
more than a few years' useful service, or to wait for these slaves' children to reach
working age. The shippers were paid in cash, sugar, cotton or tobacco, which was
then transported to Europe, where the cycle began again. In Britain, the economies
of the major ports of Bristol and Liverpool prospered as a result. The River Gambia
was a highly prized trading ground, since conditions were favourable for the mer-
chant seamen, with ample opportunites to anchor safely. Pickings from the trade
were rich enough to justify the substantial risks posed by malaria, yellow fever and
other diseases; many Europeans lasted less than two years in the tropics.

The Europeans tended to avoid the risky process of capturing slaves, relying
instead on African intermediaries using whatever means necessary. Some slaves
were undoubtedly taken by extreme force, and villages were ransacked and burned

Treaty of Versailles; most of the territory was handed over to France, but the River Gambia section remained under British control.

British interests in West Africa began to alter radically towards the end of the eighteenth century, as **slave trading** began to be not only less and less profitable, but also a positive hindrance to other trading enterprises. Even after the 1808 ban, the Gambian slave trade continued, illegally, for many decades, partly because the ban was a unilateral one that some French and Portuguese traders chose to ignore, and partly because the Gambians themselves profited so handsomely from the trade.

The British won lasting influence in the River Gambia area after the Napoleonic wars, and Captain Alexander Grant founded the city of **Bathurst** (now Banjul) in 1816. This defensive post was named after Henry, 3rd Earl of Bathurst, who governed the region from Freetown (Sierra Leone) as British colonial secretary at the time. In the 1820s, Britain declared a **Protectorate**, the "Settlement on the River Gambia" and Alexander Grant acquired a small up-river island, which he named **MacCarthy Island** (later Janjanbureh), and

to the ground by raiding parties. Once on board the slave ships, the captured Africans, already humiliated and traumatized, suffered such brutal treatment that mere survival was a challenge. Eighteenth-century ship-captains' logs suggest that if only a third of the lives on board were lost between Africa and the New World, that constituted a satisfactory result.

While first-hand reports from disinterested parties such as the explorer **Mungo Park** and humanitarian movements led by visionary campaigners like **Thomas Clarkson** and **William Wilberforce** played a significant part, ultimately it was economic factors that brought about abolition. By the early nineteenth century, the trade was barely profitable and, in 1805, when the US Congress imposed a new import duty of $10 per slave, the margins became almost unworkable.

West African tribal leaders held a significant position of power in the chain of transactions that led from Europe, to Africa, to the American colonies and back to Europe again. They profited handsomely by exchanging hostages captured in inter-tribal disputes for commodities that would otherwise be completely beyond their grasp, particularly guns. Enough was at stake for a delegation of chiefs from The Gambia and other territories to visit London and Paris around the time of abolition in order to argue fiercely against banning the trade. It was not until 1895 that the Gambian chiefs and rulers finally agreed with the British to abolish inter-tribal slave trading and the keeping of house slaves.

Today, there's a vocal movement calling for financial **reparations** to Africans for the slave trade. In the United States, this takes the form of African-American civil rights activists suing major corporations for damages on behalf of their ancestors, claiming that such corporations' financial strength was built at the expense of the slaves that laboured on the plantations. In West Africa, campaigners demand that the United States government pay reparations to every African state whose population was stripped by the transatlantic trade. So close to the heart of some Gambians is this issue that British High Commissioner Eric Jenkinson was questioned on the subject in a Gambian press interview shortly after his arrival in late 2002. His reply was that the concept of redress was "more of an intellectual concern than a real issue", a neat dodge of an extremely sensitive issue.

More positively, **educational programmes**, monuments, commemorative days and ceremonies are now bringing together communities which, at this remove, feel a complex mixture of abhorrence, bewilderment and guilt at the events of the past. In The Gambia, the preservation of Juffureh, Albreda and James Island as a **heritage site** has a crucial part to play in the healing of old wounds.

built Fort George to defend it. In the following decade, **groundnuts** (peanuts) were introduced to the area for the first time and become the Settlement's most important cash commodity after beeswax, ivory and skins, soon accounting for one-third of its total export income. Around the same time, the protectorate gained a new, willing labour force in the parties of **freed slaves** who were moved from the slave ships and plantations via Freetown to Gambia and settled in Bathurst and Georgetown. Gambia's first **Legislative Council** was introduced in 1843, and the protectorate was given its own colonial administration, based in Bathurst, rather than being governed from Freetown.

In the second half of the nineteenth century, while the British hesitated and focused their attentions elsewhere, the French were battling their way deep into the *Soudan* (present-day eastern Senegal, Mali, Burkina Faso, Niger and Cote d'Ivoire), actively engaged in a mission to conquer in Africa. From 1850 to 1901 the whole of the Gambia region was in a state of social chaos as the **Soninke-Marabout Wars** repeatedly flared up between renegade Muslim leaders and Mandinka kings, and the British were forced to consolidate the region or else lose it to France.

Britain's establishment of "The Crown Colony and Protectorate of the Gambia" was formally agreed at the Paris conference of 1889. The **Colony** comprised St Mary's Island and the capital Bathurst, the district of Kombo St Mary, and MacCarthy Island, where Wolofs predominated; the **Protectorate** was the rest of present-day Gambia, at the time ruled by headmen and chiefs and populated by Mandinkas. Britain's decision to claim this territory stemmed less from commercial ambitions than from **imperial strategy**. The intention was to pawn off the country in exchange for some better French territory. Gabon was one chunk favoured by the British – they'd already turned down the offer of the Ivory Coast sea forts. But the temporary expedient of holding the river became permanent when, having failed to agree on an exchange, the British succeeded merely in delimiting a narrow strip of land on each side of the River Gambia, burrowing into the heart of French territory: France acquired most of Senegal at the Paris conference, and Casamance was later transferred to France from Portugal. Yet Britain wasn't fully reconciled to its responsibilities along the Gambia River until after World War I – thus, in practical terms, The Gambia's era of effective colonialism lasted only from the 1920s to the 1960s.

Colony and Protectorate

The imposition of **British hegemony** lacked both cohesion and commitment. Beyond the limits of the Colony, in the up-country Protectorate, the country's headmen and chiefs, some of whom were appointed by the Crown, were allowed to rule their people little disturbed by the two "travelling commissioners" to whom they were answerable. Two or three African representatives from Bathurst were nominated to the Legislative Council after 1915, but there was no representation of the 85 percent of the population who lived in the Protectorate.

The main relationship between the people and the government soured over the issue of **taxes**. Gambia's first **currency**, the penny and the tenth-of-a-penny, was introduced in 1907, followed by pounds and shillings ten years later. Two-thirds of Gambia's revenue was accounted for in the salaries of the colonial administration. The remainder was insufficient to develop the country's infrastructure, education or health systems. "Benign neglect" is about the best that can be said of the administration's performance – only the most rudimentary infrastructure was set up during this time. One of the few positive developments was the establishment of the **Medical Research Council** in Fajara in 1913, for the study of tropical diseases. When the **Armitage High School** in Georgetown, a boarding school for the sons of village chiefs, was founded in 1927, it was one of The Gambia's few educational institutions. Until the 1930s, only one public passenger and cargo river boat service, the MV *Lady Denham*, operated on the River Gambia.

Things started to improve only after World War II, though the government was gravely embarrassed by the **Yundum egg scheme**, a plan to mass-produce poultry and eggs, which ended in fiasco when fowl pest resulted in a loss of £500,000. **Groundnuts** had been a successful export crop since the middle of the nineteenth century, and the country was self-sufficient in food (remaining so until the 1970s). There were minor advances in transport, education and medical services, and traffic and trade increased on the river. By 1961, the country had five doctors and 37 up-country primary schools.

Financial pressures on the Colonial Office in the 1950s and mounting international demands for decolonization were as much instrumental in the **push to independence** as Gambian nationalism. Britain was at least as anxious to rid itself of the financial liability as the country's own senior figures (they were barely yet leaders) were to take power. From Britain's point of view, there was no reason to delay the country's return to independence – except, perhaps, a measure of concern over the fate of such a small and unprotected nation. Colonial civil servants were in broad agreement that The Gambia would be forced to merge with Senegal, but chose to defer the move.

The road to independence

In a manner similar to that of many other countries in West Africa, The Gambia's progression to independence was not a heroic one – the men who led the country into the neocolonial era were not so much nationalists as ambitious politicians.

The **Bathurst Trade Union**, founded in 1928, mounted successful campaigns for workers' rights, but the first **political party** wasn't formed until shortly before the Legislative Council elections of 1951. Through most of the 1950s, the Gambian parties were reactive, personality-led interest groups rather than campaigning, policy-making, issue-led organizations. All the early 1950s parties – the Democratic Party, the Muslim Congress Party and the United Party – were Wolof, and Colony-based (that is, based in Bathurst, rather than up-country) and highly sectional. Gambia had to wait until 1960 before a party with a genuinely grass-roots programme emerged. This was the Protectorate People's Party, quickly relabelled **People's Progressive Party** (**PPP**), led by an ex-veterinary officer from MacCarthy Island Division, **David Jawara**. The PPP looked to the people of the Protectorate for support, but was distinctly anti-chief. Instead it spoke for rural Mandinkas and others in their resentment against corrupt chiefdoms, and for disenfranchised and younger Wolofs of the Colony.

The administration had overhauled the constitution in 1951 and finally, after consultation with senior Gambian figures, produced a complicated new constitution in 1954. This gave real representation to the up-country Protectorate peoples for the first time, but precipitated sharpened demands for greater responsibility for Gambian ministers in the government. It also put extraordinary power in the hands of the chiefs, who were, for the most part, supporters of the colonial status quo. To avoid a crisis, another constitution was formulated in 1959 which abolished the Legislative Council and provided for a parliament – the **House of Representatives**.

In the run-up to the 1960 elections, the Democratic and Muslim Congress parties merged as the **Democratic Congress Alliance** (DCA), but couldn't shake off the popular impression that their nominees were all puppets of the British administration. As a result, the DCA took only three seats, while the United Party of P.S. N'Jie (with whom the governor had recently fallen out) and David Jawara's PPP took eight seats each. The British governor, in a move to placate the Protectorate chiefs, offered the post of prime minister to P.S. N'Jie, to the consternation of Jawara, who became education minister. But the 1959 constitution gave rise to further indecisive election results. More talks in 1962 resulted in yet another constitution, providing for a 36-seat House of Representatives with 32 elected seats and just four chiefs nominated by the Chiefs' Assembly, and granting universal suffrage to all citizens of 21 years and above.

The balance of power now shifted against the United Party. Jawara and the Democratic Congress Alliance found room for cooperation and, in the **1962 elections** – which were to determine the political configuration for full self-government – the two parties contested seats in concert to squeeze out the UP. The results of this electoral alliance were highly successful for the PPP, who won seventeen out of the 25 Protectorate seats and one of the seven Colony seats. The DCA, however, managed to gain only one seat in the Colony, and couldn't shift the UP from its urban power base. As a result, with the support of the DCA's two elected members, Jawara had an absolute majority in parliament. Jawara and his party were to remain in power for the next 32 years, until the 1994 coup.

After the 1962 elections, Jawara entered into a coalition with the experienced P.S. N'Jie of the United Party to form the first fully **independent government**. Independence Day came on February 18, 1965, when Gambia was admitted to the **Commonwealth** as an independent constitutional monarchy and began five years as a parliamentary democracy, with Queen Elizabeth II as titular Head of State and Jawara as Prime Minister.

Independent Gambia

In 1966, Jawara was knighted by the Queen in London, and P.S. N'Jie backed his United Party out of the coalition government to lead the opposition. Four years later, on April 24, 1970, following a referendum, The Gambia became a **republic** with prime minister Dawda Kairaba Jawara (now using his Muslim name) its president. In contrast to the many other African countries operating as single-party states, The Gambia opted for a multiparty democracy with a five-year parliamentary term. However, at every election, the PPP continued to win the vast majority of seats, and at every election N'Jie claimed that the vote was rigged. Despite the corruption allegations, the PPP, with its roots in the Mandinka villages, managed to establish credible support across the country.

The first fifteen years of independence were peaceful, and the groundnut economy fared better than expected due to high prices on the world markets.

In 1971 the Central Bank of The Gambia was established and launched the new **dalasi currency**. In 1973, with the Gambian population exceeding 500,000 for the first time, Bathurst was renamed Banjul with much patriotic pride, and in the same year a record groundnut harvest earned a balance of trade surplus of D25.2 million, increasing the per capita income of the population by half.

However, by 1976 prospects for the government were less favourable. Two new opposition parties had formed: the somewhat Mandinka-chauvinist **National Convention Party** (NCP), led by dismissed vice-president Sherif Mustapha Dibba, and the more left-wing **National Liberation Party**. Groundnut prices fell in the late-1970s, and The Gambia experienced a string of disastrous harvests. This economic recession and political opposition to the government – perceived increasingly as incompetent and corrupt – partly account for the conditions that led to the formation of two new **Marxist groupings** in 1980 and an **attempted coup** in October of that year. Senegalese troops were flown in under a defence agreement and the leaders of the **Gambia Socialist Revolutionary Party** and the transnational **Movement for Justice in Africa-Gambia** (MOJA-G) were arrested and their organizations banned.

The Senegambia Confederation

A far more serious coup attempt on July 30, 1981 (while Jawara was at the wedding of Prince Charles and Diana in London), resulted in a force of 3000 Senegalese troops arriving with a group of SAS soldiers from Britain, to put down sporadic, bloody fighting around Banjul. The trouble lasted a week and may have cost as many as a thousand lives.

The insurrection shook the government and immediate steps were taken to maintain Senegal's support. The subsequent **Senegambia Confederation**, ratified on December 29, 1981, assured The Gambia of Senegal's military protection while ostensibly assuring Senegal of The Gambia's commitment to political union. **Treason trials** in the wake of the attempted coup led to long jail terms, but the increasing importance of tourism and international opinion meant there were no executions.

In 1982 the constitution was amended once again to make the president electable by the people rather than by members of parliament, and Jawara scored another conclusive victory in the subsequent **presidential election**, receiving a personal vote of 137,000, with Sherif Mustapha Dibba, who was in detention at the time, receiving 52,000. A 1984 cabinet reshuffle brought in some popular reformist MPs, and in the following year public opinion led to the dismissal of several ministers after allegations of corruption. The government also launched an **Economic Recovery Programme** designed to attract foreign aid.

After Dibba's release, the NCP mounted a serious challenge at the 1987 general and presidential elections. However, it was a new opposition grouping, the **Gambia People's Party** (GPP), led by the respected former vice-president **Hassan Musa Camara**, that made the most impact on the government. President Jawara's own vote was reduced from 72 to 59 percent but, though his party's share of the vote was also reduced, the PPP still managed to win 31 of the 36 elected seats in the House, with the NCP holding the remaining five. Supporters of the GPP, particularly in its Fula- and Serahule-speaking strongholds upriver, were left frustrated, as were supporters of the new socialist party, the People's **Democratic Organization for Independence and Socialism**, a party with close ties to the banned MOJA-G. Meanwhile, government and services were known to be plagued by corruption and mismanagement, the education system was in desperate need of improvement, and malnutrition was widespread up-country, as a direct result of a public expenditure squeeze and cutbacks in subsidies to farmers. At the Independence Day celebrations in Banjul on February 18, 1986, a teenager named Baboucar Langley staged a solitary protest before the presidential platform on behalf of the Gambian farmers forced into poverty by government policy, declaring that "the people are dying of starvation". He was arrested and sentenced to eighteen months' imprisonment.

A new **coup plot** – really a long-running, conspiratorial rumble – was uncovered in February 1988. The conspiracy involved both Gambian leftists and Casamance separatists from Senegal. It was suggested at the trials that the Senegalese opposition leader, **Abdoulaye Wade**, had been involved in planning it.

Throughout the end of the 1980s and the first years of the 1990s, with the Economic Recovery Programme still grinding through its measures, the country began to face up to the causes of its hardships. Senior ministers, bankers, customs officials and heads of the Produce Marketing Board (GPMB) and the Utilities Corporation responsible for the intermittent electricity supply were all investigated for corruption, and President Jawara routinely "cleaned out" public offices. However, accountability was not enforced with tough sanctions, and a prevailing sense of stagnation and recycled rhetoric hung over Banjul.

On the broad economic front, the **liberalization of groundnut sales** removed the GPMB's monopoly and allowed farmers to sell their harvest to the highest bidding private trader. Although this risked forcing down the price in remote areas, the net effect was to keep more of the crop from being smuggled to high-paying Senegal. Tourism, too, benefited from the sale of the state's hotel interests and an increased profile abroad, with more than 100,000 tourists visiting every year.

But the wider future was marred by the **breakdown of the Senegambia Confederation** (officially dissolved on September 30, 1989), as a result of Senegal's frustration at the slow pace of moves towards union. Senegal, in its latent conflict with Mauritania, withdrew the troops which provided The Gambia's security (and indeed President Jawara's personal security), saying they were needed at home.

The end of the Senegambia Confederation left a huge question mark over The Gambia. It had been the national controversy for the best part of a decade, supported by the mostly urban Wolof but generally mistrusted by the Mandinka, whose dominant position in the country was always threatened by a powerful Senegal. For The Gambia's opposition parties and ethnic minorities, the breakdown of the confederation represented an opportunity lost.

Attention was focused in 1990 on **Liberia**, with numbers of Liberian refugees making their way to safe haven in The Gambia and Jawara sending a small detachment of Gambian troops to support the West African ECOMOG forces trying to maintain the peace in Liberia – The Gambia's first overseas military expedition. Administrative failures resulted in the soldiers not being paid, and a dangerous confrontation was narrowly averted when they returned to Banjul. The chief of the armed forces resigned, admitting he'd lost the confidence of his men, and was replaced by a Nigerian officer. It was a warning of changes to come.

President Jawara was **re-elected** for a sixth term in April 1992, a month before his 68th birthday, after being persuaded to stand, despite his professed wish to retire. He polled 58 percent of the vote; his nearest rival, Mustapha Dibba, polled 22 percent. Jawara softened his stance against MOJA-G and the Gambian Socialist Revolutionary Party, announcing an amnesty for all members of the previously proscribed organizations. He also began again to make noises about corruption in public life. In 1993 The Gambia's population passed the one million mark, and in the same year the country became the first African state to abolish the death penalty.

Military rule

The **corruption** issue boiled up quickly through the end of the 1994 dry season. In April there were demonstrations in Brikama – the country's third largest town, close to the coast but not benefiting from tourism – over the unaffordable cost of public utilities. Then, on July 22, after returning ECO-MOG soldiers complained of abusive treatment by Nigerian commanding officers at Banjul airport, their widespread anger and demands for unpaid salaries coalesced through the day into a successful **coup** led by **Lt Yahya Jammeh** with the support of a hastily assembled **Armed Forces Provisional Ruling Council** (AFPRC). Jawara and some of his cabinet fled to the sanctuary of an American ship docked at Banjul, and received asylum in Senegal, but others were arrested.

Jammeh, only 29 years old and an uncharismatic figure in regulation dark glasses, made a poor impression on the international community. Casual observers had long harboured the illusion that Jawara's Gambia was one of the few admirable political cultures in West Africa. Indeed, it appeared hard at first to find an altruistic justification for a coup in The Gambia. Though the country's human rights record was not unblemished, the fundamental fairness of its multiparty system had not seemed open to question. Opposition parties were consistently frustrated at elections, but the evidence for vote-rigging was limited: Jawara won because he commanded a popular following, albeit also a largely Mandinka one.

However, the AFPRC managed to convince sceptics that, fair or not, the political system was shoring up a Gambian state riddled with **corruption** from bottom to top; President Jawara himself was said to have spent the equivalent of the annual health care budget in a six-day shopping trip to Switzerland just weeks before the coup. Jammeh insisted his administration, which included some civilian members, would seek the return of stolen state property.

His announcement, however, that the AFPRC would not step down to an elected civilian government for four years, was greeted with disbelief. After an unsuccessful counter-coup, in which several soldiers were killed, and a reported threat by Jammeh to the safety of citizens of any countries that might be planning the forcible reinstatement of Jawara, the British Foreign Office warned tourists that The Gambia was unsafe to visit. Nearly all the tour operators and charter airlines pulled out, and **tourism** plummeted to twenty percent of normal levels, precipitating a genuine crisis. The response was pragmatic: Jammeh brought the date of transition forward by two years, which led to the withdrawal of the Foreign Office's advisory notice and the tour operators' resumption of holiday bookings.

The Second Republic

Jammeh's first few months in office convinced him he had considerable grass-roots support; most Gambians noticed no downswing in their fortunes since his coup, and the country at large anticipated some results from the AFPRC's efforts to return looted Gambian funds. They were to be disappointed: rumours circulated that the AFPRC itself was not squeaky-clean; ministers previously sacked by Jawara for corruption were given posts by Jammeh, and the story quickly spread that Jammeh had engineered the counter-revolt himself in order to eliminate potential rivals. Throughout 1995, a number of high-ranking officers fled the country, and there was a rash of accusations and counter-accusations of corruption and theft from the public purse on a grand scale. The finance minister died in suspicious circumstances; a new secret police service, the National Intelligence Agency, was created, with sweeping powers of arrest and interrogation; and the death penalty was reinstated. Meanwhile, Jammeh sponsored several showy architectural projects designed to mark his regime out as a force to be reckoned with; Senegalese architect Pierre Goudiaby was commissioned to design a triumphal arch for Banjul, and to build a striking new international airport.

Jammeh's first real test came in 1996, as the country prepared for the return of an elected government and the electorate began to realize that it would almost certainly be headed by Jammeh himself, in civilian clothing. A **constitutional review commission** was established to hear the views of Gambians and to usher in a new republic. But it was manipulated by the AFPRC to give Jammeh and his coterie every advantage over all opposition elements: the age for presidential candidates was set at 30–65, thus making the youthful Jammeh eligible and ruling out many senior politicians of the Jawara era; political parties which had been active in the Jawara era were all banned from competing; and the timing of the presidential and parliamentary elections was set such that Jammeh's opponents had virtually no opportunity to campaign, while the AFPRC had effectively been on the campaign trail throughout the country since soon after coming to power.

The **presidential election**, which eventually took place on September 26, 1996, was flawed in every respect. Jammeh retired from the military and his 22 July Movement, which was to be dissolved, was replaced by a new party, the aptly acronymic **Alliance for Patriotic Reorientation and Constuction** (APRC) – the AFPRC out of uniform. They managed to hog the media spotlight, with The Gambia's new TV station almost entirely neglecting the opposition; meanwhile the military intimidated the minor parties. Jammeh took 55 percent of the vote, while lawyer and human rights advocate **Ousainou Darboe** of the **United Democratic Party** received 35 percent. In the legislative elections, which took place in January 1997, the severely limited resources of most of the opposition meant they could only field candidates in a proportion of the country's 45 constituencies. The vote itself, however, was observed to be fairer than the presidential poll, with less intimidation of rival candidates. Jammeh's party took 33 seats, five of them unopposed, while the opposition was lucky to secure twelve seats spread among three parties and two independent MPs.

Early parliamentary sesssions in the **Second Republic** were undignified affairs, with opposition members prevented from asking difficult questions by the Jammeh-appointed speaker of the house, and repeated complaints that the president seems unable to abide by the country's new constitution in his dealings with parliament. Jammeh, meanwhile, continued to consolidate his power base and in 1998 further reduced his cabinet.

Ripples of **violence and unrest** rose to the surface in 2000, when fourteen people in the Kombos were shot dead during student demonstrations in protest at the alleged torture and murder of a student by police the previous month. A few weeks later, opposition leader Ousainou Darboe and twenty of his supporters were charged with the murder of an APRC activist; they were released on bail. Shortly after this, nine people, including several soldiers, were charged with treason in connection with an alleged coup, just one of a series of conspiracies and attempted coups.

In October 2001, Jammeh won a second five-year presidential term, with a **landslide election victory** over Ousainou Darboe. Despite rising tension beforehand, foreign observers considered the polls the most democratically run elections Africa had seen for some time. However, in January 2002, the opposition boycotted the parliamentary elections, claiming that the October presidential poll had been fraudulent and marred by APRC harassment of UDP candidates. Amid widespread voter apathy, the APRC scooped a victory.

Ousainou Darboe and **Yankuba Touray** – Tourism Minister, APRC Mobilizer and one of Jammeh's right-hand men since the 1994 coup – continue to lock horns, and in November 2002 new amendments to the Criminal Procedure Code were drafted, denying bail to anyone on a murder charge, and allowing Darboe to be rearrested.

Jammeh's latest themes are **development, agricultural reform** and **investment** – preferably of foreign money; he has been at pains to cultivate the image of a model Muslim president in order to successfully attract donations from the Arab states, and in 2003 the **national debt** stands at £375 million. While rewarding his fellow Jolas with positions in the government and civil service, he has also been quick to connect with the Mandinka majority in the up-country provinces. In February 2003 Jammeh spent two weeks attending countrywide rallies on a "Meet the people" tour, during which his primary message was that Gambians should "get back to the land" and reinvest time and resources in farming. The fact that at many of his up-country stops he was greeted by rapturous crowds, in scenes relayed to the nation in colourful detail on national television, suggest that his up-country popularity power base is growing steadily, as is his carefully cultivated personality cult. He appears keen to promote the interests of Gambians over those of foreign residents, and a new **alien registration scheme** was introduced in 2003, whereby all foreign residents were required to pay D1000 (around £25/$40, a considerable amount in local terms) per family member per year – resulting in the exodus of a large section of the work force, leaving some Gambian industries, such as small-scale fishing, teetering on the brink of collapse.

The optimism and energy generated by **populist** but undeniably worthwhile development projects such as long-overdue road, school and hospital construction works disguises a growing sense of wariness throughout the country, particularly among journalists and non-APRC politicians. Clumsy **censorship** has included the closure and hypertaxation of radio stations and the arrest of newspaper staff. There has been **harassment of the opposition**, including detentions without charge; government disputes with the supreme court (whose independence is guaranteed by the constitution); and undisguised **corruption** and solicitation of bribes. These are only the most public displays of insecurity and incompetence in the Banjul government. With **inflation** spiralling out of control, The Gambia is now showing signs of a country in serious financial trouble, and there's little indication that Jammeh's youthful and inexperienced government has the ability to avert a crisis.

Society

The Gambia's population of around 1.5 million is a multiethnic, multilingual mosaic of peoples, originating from all over West Africa and beyond, and coexisting remarkably peacefully. In a continent where interracial rivalry and oppression have been the root cause of problems ranging from routine discrimination to full-blown genocide, Gambians are proud of their reputation for tolerant acceptance of all races and religions.

Closely contained in a tiny, densely populated landmass, Gambian society is very tightly knit. Gambians are born, married and laid to rest in **village communities**, where people live outdoor lives in extreme proximity to each other. **Islam**, practised by ninety percent of the population, is a significant unifying force, but, whatever their religion, all Gambians observe traditional **rites of passage** in virtually the same manner. The birth, initiation, marriage and death of every individual are marked and celebrated by family and community events, often involving music, dancing and the consumption of vast quantities of food.

Peoples of The Gambia

The Gambia's racial and cultural categories are unevenly spread, and overlap with neighbouring communities in Senegal and beyond. While it's common for families of the same ethnic origin to be concentrated in a particular home patch, the boundaries between these territories are fuzzy and bear no relation to political boundaries. West Africa's national borders and divisional boundaries were, after all, drawn up by Europeans, and ethnic distribution was barely acknowledged in the process.

The most enduring and meaningful ethnic indicator is **language** – a person's first language is still important as an index of social identity. Children adopt their father's tribal identity, in name at least, and his first language as their first language (although in practice, if their mother is from a different tribe, children grow up speaking two tribal languages equally fluently).

Distinctions between ethnic groups would be simple for outsiders to pinpoint if all those who speak the same language and share a common culture also had obvious similarities in physical appearance. The term "tribe", though commonly used by Gambians about themselves, tends to imply homogeneity. But tribes have never been closed units, and language, appearance and culture have always overlapped. While it's possible to make broad generalizations about each group's characteristic build and facial features, these distinctions are becoming more and more dilute as Gambians become increasingly mobile, with rural youngsters moving from their home villages to find work elsewhere and marrying outside their tribe. Intermarriage between Gambians of different tribes has always been reasonably common, and Gambians believe that this, and the unifying force of Islam, are the keys to their success as a peaceful multiethnic society. Over the last few generations, as the country has become more outward-looking, tribal identities have broken down and have been replaced to some degree by broader **class distinctions** based on wealth and influence rather than language and culture.

Even so, an individual's ethnic identity is still a matter of personal pride, and a significant means by which Gambians define and categorize their friends and acquaintances. Loyalty towards "brothers and sisters" of the same tribe is deeply felt, and there is much joking banter between members of rival tribes, even those who are great friends, whereby "tribe-ist" insults are traded and quickly retracted in good-natured style. This habit of categorizing people according to their ethnic group partly explains why Gambians will refer to and address white people by the blanket label "*toubab*", even after they've known the individual concerned for a long time.

The Mandinka

The **Mandinka** make up 42 percent of the population and are by far the most populous tribe in the up-country rural areas. They dominated the Gambian political scene from 1962 to 1994, when President Jawara, himself a Mandinka, rewarded extended family members with positions of power and influence. Post-coup, Mandinka influence has diminished in inverse proportion to the increased influence of the Jolas, Jammeh's own tribe.

Traditionally, Mandinkas are devout Muslims, who make a living as farmers (particularly groundnut-farmers) and fishermen. They tend to take real pride in displaying their material wealth, and prefer houses built of cement blocks to traditional constructions of mud bricks and thatch; Mandinka villages therefore generally appear more established than those of the rural Fula or Jola. Men, if they're dressing up (that is, every Friday, or for traditional celebrations and occasions), wear formal West African Muslim attire: an embroidered brimless cap, and a *haftan*, like a long shirt, often in pastel-coloured damask with intricate embroidery round the neck, over damask trousers and pointed-toed, backless white shoes. Women wear a *tiko* or head-tie with hand-tailored dresses and ruffled sleeves and bodices, nipped waists and plunging backs: the classic West African styles that were originally inspired by the fashions of eighteenth-century France, as worn by colonialists' wives.

Mandinkas have a strong musical tradition that culturally they share with their Malian cousins, the Bambara and Mandé; they're particularly famous for virtuoso *kora* playing. Mandinkas celebrate Muslim festivals and family celebrations with great gusto, when the music also includes danceable drumming and *balafon*. Many ceremonies are marked by the appearance of the *kankurang*, or devil-dancers (see p.xiv & p.255).

The Fula

The Gambia's second largest ethnic group, the **Fula** people, are widespread within West Africa, particularly in Senegal and Mali, and within this broad range they have various names including Fulani, Fulbe, Peulh and Peul. Their cultural homeland is in northern Senegal, and their traditional occupation of cattle-herding, always searching for good grazing, explains their broad dispersal. They are well adapted to life in the Sahelian semi-desert and are skilled at keeping cattle healthy in relatively harsh environments, sometimes tending cattle for other tribes on commission.

The Fula's nomadic lifestyle means that they tend to avoid cement-block buildings, preferring instead simple, round, mud-brick houses, roofed with thatch. Most Fula are Muslim, and they tend to have lighter skin and straighter hair than most other tribes. Traditional dress for Fula women includes huge gold earrings, and they sometimes tattoo their gums and faces (especially round the mouth) with dark dye. Herders are always men and boys, and traditionally wear tunics made of rough-weave undyed cotton and conical hats. Fula music is desert music, with mournful tunes played on herders' flutes (made from wood, bamboo or millet stalks) and the rasping, violin-like *riti*. As well as work songs, love songs and lullabies, they compose songs in praise of cattle, sung to them as they graze.

The Wolof

The **Wolof** are descended from the aristocratic founders of the Jolof Empire. Today, theirs is the language most often heard in the Kombos; they also dominate Dakar and coastal Senegal. The up-country villages on the north bank of the river east of Farafenni are populated by Wolofs with long family lineages known as *Fana Fana*. Almost all Wolofs are Muslim, and earn their living in the Kombos as traders and businesspeople, or up-country as farmers. Many Wolof-speakers in the urban area are not ethnically Wolof, but people from other tribes who have adopted Wolof as their first language. In fact, while the Wolof are in many ways a highly respected group, other ethnic groups have begun to object to the "wolofization" of Gambian culture – the Wolof are a minority, but their influence has become extremely pervasive.

Traditionally, Wolof society was rigidly hierarchical, although today status is defined far more by wealth or education than by caste. Wolofs are typically fine-featured, with high cheekbones and very dark skin. They tend to have expensive tastes and are snappy dressers, the men in flowing robes and the women in gorgeous flowing *mbubas* (traditional gowns, often a voluminous tunic-like dress with an embroidered or embellished neck, worn over a *wrapper* or wraparound skirt) with elaborate hairstyles, towering head-ties and killer heels.

The Wolof are superb drummers and dancers, and the lion-like *simba* or *zimba* dancers (see p.viii & p.50) are a favourite feature of Wolof festivals. Wolof music such as *mbalax, ndagga* and *sabar* drumming dominates the Senegalese music scene and is hugely popular in The Gambia, with Youssou N'Dour one of its most celebrated exponents.

The Jola and the Manjago

Related to the Diola of Senegal and Guinea-Bissau, the **Jola** are mostly concentrated in southern Gambia, near the border with the Casamance district of Senegal. The origins of the tribe are obscure, but the Jolas seem to be the earliest known settlers in The Gambia. The tribe is currently in meteoric ascent, in profile, confidence and influence, since President Jammeh is a Jola and he has favoured many of his kin with prestigious positions in public life.

Unlike the Wolof social hierarchy, Jola **society** is segmented and flexible, with no lower castes. Even those Jola who are Muslim tend to be heavily influenced by traditional animist beliefs and practices. Jola wrestlers, for example, famous for their strength and skill, would not consider entering a tournament without first visiting a sacred crocodile pool and seeking *jujus* and magical potions from a *marabout*.

Traditional dress for Jola men is shirts or waistcoats with huge baggy trousers, while women wear long strings of beads crossed from each shoulder to the opposite hip. Unusually for a West African tribe, the Jola do not have a strong oral tradition; they have plenty of traditional music, but no *griots* to act as praise-singers and historians. They are a bellicose tribe, and their celebrations (see box on p.189) include a great deal of noise and eccentric bravado.

Traditionally, the Jola are farmers, hunters, fishermen and palm wine tappers. Most palm wine tappers are **Manjago**, a subsection of the Jola tribe originally from Guinea-Bissau, who are usually animist or Christian rather than Muslim. As well as running palm wine "ghettoes", the Manjago gather palm nuts for oil, and keep pigs. Because their practices run so contrary to Muslim tradition, their compounds are often semi-isolated on the fringes of villages.

The Serahule, Serer and Aku

The **Serahule**, **Aku** and **Serer** are the least numerous of The Gambia's West African ethnic groups, together accounting for less than fifteen percent of the total population.

Resident up-country in eastern Gambia, the **Serahule** are related to the Soninke of Mali and Burkina Faso, and are thought to be one of the oldest ethnic groups in West Africa. Traditionally they are Muslim farmers and potters. Many are also gold- and silver-traders, and Serahule women often wear gold hoop earrings wound with red thread.

The **Serer** are best known as fishermen, and are originally from the valley and delta regions of the River Senegal. They, along with the Jolas, were among the first ethnic groups to settle in The Gambia, and there are Serer boatbuilders and fishing communities around the mouth of the river, particularly in and around Barra on the north bank. Some communities are nomadic, following the migration of fish up and down the river.

The **Aku** are the descendants of freed African slaves, repatriated to Africa in the nineteenth century. Some Aku are descended from Europeans, who had children with African women. There was once a large population of Aku in Georgetown (now Janjanbureh), but they have since migrated to the Kombos; the sizeable and long-established community in Banjul is still active. Most Aku families have very English names, like Roberts and Jones, passed down the generations from the days when slaves were given the surname of their owner and master. While most are Christian, some are Muslim, and have Muslim first names and English surnames. The Aku language is a mixture of English and creole.

During the colonial era, the Akus' good English, relatively high standard of education, and experience of European customs all stood them in good stead to take up positions in local government, and they became part of the local elite. Aku were dominating the political scene at the time that Jawara took over the reins of government; subsequently their influence faded as Jawara favoured Mandinkas for positions of power. While Jola have taken over from many Mandinka under Jammeh's regime, there remains a strong Aku presence in the Gambian civil service.

The Mauritanians and the Lebanese

Concentrated in Banjul but also found running businesses in up-country towns are the **Mauritanian** shopkeepers, traders, teachers, tailors and jewellery-makers, conspicuous in their ankle-length robes (usually sky-blue) and cotton turbans. They are Muslim, and to outsiders look more Middle-Eastern than African; they're known for being enterprising in business, and usually speak French, Hassaniya Arabic and Wolof.

The **Lebanese** are a prominent feature of the commercial and social scene, running import–export businesses, foreign exchange bureaux, hotels, restaurants and retail enterprises. Most are Muslim, including some Shi'ites; some are Christian. Lebanese migrants first moved to West Africa in the late nineteenth and early twentieth centuries, settling and often intermarrying with Africans, and a second wave arrived during the Lebanese civil war of the 1970s and 1980s. They tend to have a love–hate relationship with Gambians, who admire their business acumen, but object, jealously, to their chanelling their Gambian-earned profits out of the country to relatives in Lebanon.

The Gambian village

The Gambia is a nation of villagers. Even the larger towns – Serrekunda, Bakau, Brikama, Banjul – are essentially overgrown **villages**, or collections of villages that have merged into one. While colonial Banjul, Janjanbureh and parts of Bakau were planned to a degree, with streets laid out on a grid pattern of sorts, all other Gambian settlements have evolved organically, growing out from a central meeting place, market and mosque.

There's little room for privacy in this country, where Western-style family houses are rare, except in the expat enclaves – instead, most people live in a compound with their extended family, which may number thirty individuals or more, sharing rooms with curtains for doors, where every sound can be heard. While some might see such a way of life as claustrophobic, Gambians choose to appreciate it as a support mechanism. The Gambia has no social security system – no unemployment benefit, or care homes for the elderly – so it is the responsibility of every working Gambian to house and give financial support to every member of the family who is not earning. In areas where agriculture is foundering and there are few employment opportunities, one wage-earner may be supporting as many as fifty others, including babies, children and elderly relations. Non-earners are, in turn, expected to pull their weight in the daily routines of domestic maintenance, which are highly labour-intensive and time-consuming, as few Gambians are able to afford private transport or domestic machinery, many are without mains electicity, and many have to leave their compound every day to fetch water from a shared well or pump.

Every Gambian village has at least one notable **natural feature** to define its location – a creek, an escarpment, a ring of huge and ancient baobabs or silk-cotton trees, a sandy bay, or a stretch of the River Gambia that's good for fishing. Often the village will be named after this feature, after the founder of the village, or after the primary occupation of the villagers. It's not unusual up-country for a whole village or even a whole area, to be populated by just one ethnic group. In the Kombos, however, it's more usual for villages to be mixed, but known, say, as a Fula village, if Fula are in the majority or if it was a prominent Fula who founded the village.

A Gambian **village** is a microcosm of rural life: a self-contained unit where people eat, sleep, care for their families, farm, trade, worship, share information and make political decisions. Gambian **villages** have not one central focus, but several: the **bantaba**, a meeting place for the men of the village; the **water supply**, in isolated areas a well or wells, where women go to draw water but also to catch up on local gossip; the **market**, the commercial heart of any village; and the **mosque**, the village's spiritual focal point. Each extended family lives in a compound, a collection of huts or a brick-built block enclosed by a fence or wall. Compounds often contain fruit trees, and there may be larger orchards, plus fields and vegetable gardens, on the outskirts of the village. Some villages are enclosed by a wall or a fence of wooden stakes or woven millet stalks.

In The Gambia, where illiteracy is high and many people don't have regular access to television, radio and the Internet, leisure-time social interaction often revolves around music, storytelling and games, particularly board games and cards.

Gambian children grow up without manufactured toys, so instead play chasing games, **noughts-and-crosses-type games** using sticks or counters, or make do with whatever they find, bending models out of wire or pushing old bicycle tyres around with sticks. On street corners in urban areas you may see men playing **backgammon** or **checkers** under shady trees, with a social gathering of onlookers monitoring the game. Outside bars, young Gambians battle it out in table football games, while the bar game of choice is pool.

Warri, the game of holes and seeds, is an ancient game for two that's played all over Africa. The game has a handful of seeds, cowries or pebbles as playing pieces, and a board, but since this just consists of two opposing rows of six small hollows, a "board" can easily be hollowed out on the beach. It's a game that's simple to grasp but, at the same time, mathematically highly complex in its endless chain of cause and effect – financial analysts love it.

Crazy eight is the classic Gambian card game, though, again, it's not unique to The Gambia. Like *warri*, it's deceptively simple, but highly strategic. If you're new to the game it might all seem childishly simple – but after a few rounds of being beaten hollow by a Gambian six-year-old, you may think again.

Larger villages may have several *bantabas,* which are always shaded, often by a huge, centuries-old baobab or silk-cotton tree. Baobabs and silk-cotton trees are spiritually significant to Gambians and it's rare to come across a village without at least one spectacular specimen; a ring of baobab trees out in the bush generally marks the place where a village once stood. They act as village notice boards as well as meeting places. The *bantaba* is usually a platform of planks or logs, though some are made from scrap metal. Male villagers of all ages while away hours in conversation sitting here in the shade, playing cards, checkers or warri (see box above) and drinking *attaya*, while their wives and sisters are working in the compound or in the fields. They justify this division by arguing that men are the decision-makers, so need to discuss; and that men's work – such as clearing fields before planting, rethatching huts and building new ones – is just as laborious as women's – pounding grain, cooking, child-care, planting, weeding and watering – but more seasonal.

Until recently, many up-country villages lacked a reliable source of clean water, and had to make do with open wells which are vulnerable to contamination. Few villages are built close to the banks of the River Gambia, because of the malaria risk, and only those settlements closest to urban centres had mains water. A major advance occurred during the 1980s and 1990s when a series of foreign-funded aid programmes brought potable water to practically every village, in the form of **hand-pumped tripod wells** or **solar-powered boreholes**. Women who previously had to face a long walk to the nearest clean water supply, followed by an even harder walk back with buckets or basins of water balanced on their heads, have had their lives transformed. However, some Gambian women say that they preferred the old days, when they had a good excuse to spend time away from the compound, chatting with friends.

Gambians typically practice subsistence farming, so village **markets** tend to offer a limited quantity and variety of produce: fruit, vegetables, spices, fish and meat. It's the women who grow the vegetables for market, sell them (often through a third party) and do the shopping, and markets are therefore a social focal point for Gambian women. They are also eating places: women sell rice and sauce or bread and fish balls or fritters from enamel bowls. The market may be an open-sided brick and cement building in which each trader has a rented pitch, or it might just be a gathering of women sitting under a shade tree with their produce laid out on pieces of fabric. Some villages also have a once-weekly *lumo*, a larger market held in a separate marketplace, often on the edge of the village, at which goods from all over the region and further afield are sold – including fabric, clothes, furniture, livestock and household goods. If the village has a **shop**, it won't have windows, but is more likely to be a storeroom with a counter, possibly caged off with chicken wire. All but the smallest villages have a general grocery store (*bitiko* in Mandinka) with a very rudimentary stock of household commodities.

The stature and style of the village **mosque** is a key indicator of the age and affluence of the village. The humblest mosques are mud-brick huts with a Muslim crescent symbol on the roof, but some mosques are large cement-block buildings painted white and green, decorated with patterned airbricks, and with one or more minarets from which the *imam's* call to prayer blasts out five times a day. The buildings may also be decorated with verses from the Koran, but all other decorations are abstract, since representations of living things are forbidden in Islamic art.

Mosques are normally found near the village centre; if a village mosque is small but the population is wealthy, the villagers will upgrade by building a new mosque large enough to house the entire congregation for Friday prayers. It's considered a great honour to take part in the building of a new mosque and every devout villager will make a point of wielding a shovel at some time during the construction process. Women must be dressed appropriately in the vicinity of a mosque, with covered head, arms and legs; they don't normally join the men inside the mosque for Friday prayers, but pray outside, or at home in their own compounds.

The Gambian compound

Domestic **compounds** are shared living spaces consisting of a collection of huts or a block of rooms within a yard. They may be enclosed by beautifully woven palm-frond or millet-stalk fences, rows of bound-together rhun palm stalks, or barricades of wooden stakes, often just gnarled, twisted and unfinished branches planted upright in the earth as a ready-made feast for termites. Hedges are rarer, while sturdy walls of cement blocks are regarded as a status symbol. The purpose of the compound boundary is just to mark out a space, not to keep anybody in or out: children are free to play wherever they choose, and generally roam about in gangs in the vicinity of their compound and beyond; it's normal for villagers to drop in on their neighbours uninvited, and small domestic animals – chickens, sheep and goats – are free-ranging. Many Gambian compounds are built around mango or orange trees, which give the compound colour and shade, as well as an abundance of fruit in season; paw-paws and bananas are also commonly grown.

Inside the compound fence is the courtyard, usually of vigorously swept bare earth, where domestic life is lived out. The day starts just after dawn, between 6.30 and 7am for most of the year. The first meal of the day is often a type of porridge made with millet and sometimes served with rich, creamy sour milk, like crème fraîche. Either within the compound, or outside under shade trees, women stand for several hours a day pounding grain (millet, sorghum or couscous), using long, heavy wooden mortars in large, bucket-sized wooden pestles. Some compounds have a roofed-over kitchen that also acts as a store and smokehouse (for preserving fish and corncobs), and others just have an outdoor cooking area. Women tend pots over open fires for a considerable part of the day, most Gambian specialities being slow-cooked stews, and everybody eats together outside, sitting or squatting round communal bowls laid on mats, one for the men and another for the women. In the evening, if the family owns a TV, they may bring the set outside for everyone, neighbours included, to gather round.

Mud-brick huts with roofs thatched with grass or palm fronds are very common in rural villages, and are practical, as they are cool by day and warm on cold nights. However, many villagers opt for cement-block rooms with corrugated iron roofs if they can afford them, as they require less maintenance, even though they make buildings roastingly hot in the sun and deafeningly noisy in the rain. Hanging just over the doorframe inside each hut or room is a collection of domestic *jujus*, which may be verses from the Koran bundled up in pieces of cloth, shells or other fetish objects blessed by a *marabout* to bring good fortune upon the house.

It's not unusual for the huts or rooms in a compound to be used only for sleeping and storage; but, if a visitor arrives, they may be ushered into a room to take a seat in the best chair in the compound and, at meal-times to eat there alone. Women often share their huts or bedrooms with their children; if a man has several wives, they take it in turns to spend the night with him, on a strict rota. The men's houses are generally at the front of the compound, so there's no chance of anybody visiting the women unnoticed. If the compound is home to craft-workers, such as potters or batik-makers, then one area will be set aside for their work.

Plumbed-in sanitation is very rare in rural villages; instead, there's a fenced-off area at the rear of the compound with a long-drop latrine and a "shower" area for washing with bucket and soap.

Village social structure

Gambian society is patrilineal and stratified, with clearly defined roles for members of each generation, and a structured system of meetings and consultations for dealing with problems and challenges. Traditionally, the **village elders** were the decision-makers, although central government, the police, the armed forces and the judiciary also have an official role to play which affects Gambians at village level.

The **chief** of the village, or *alkalo*, is typically a male (one current exception is the *alkalo* of Juffureh), and is usually the eldest descendant of the founder of the village, but may be appointed by election. Once appointed he holds the post for life unless unusual circumstances preclude this. Anybody visiting a village for the first time should start by introducing themselves to the *alkalo* and offering him a gift, such as some kola nuts or a token amount of money. He may be able to offer assistance in the form of local information or a place to stay: *alkalos* are duty-bound to find accommodation for stranded travellers who request their help. The *alkalo*, who takes care of disputes but has no judiciary power and is answerable to the *seyfo* or district chief, is also responsible for the distribution of land within the village.

Equal in stature to the *alkalo* is the *imam*, the resident **Muslim leader** who leads prayers at the mosque and presides at religious rituals. It is his voice, either live or recorded, that calls out from the minarets of the mosque at prayer times, five times a day. The *imam* is also sometimes a *marabout*, a charismatic Koranic teacher who can offer votive prayers and make *jujus* for people with specific requests. The *imam* sits on the village council of elders in an advisory capacity.

Each village has a **village development committee** which coordinates village development projects and mobilizes young people to act as a labour force. In villages where the majority are illiterate, news of committee decisions is passed around the village by traditional announcers, like town criers, who go around beating drums and singing out messages.

The **head of the compound** is legally responsible for everyone living in his compound, and is required to mediate in any family disputes. Groups of extended families who are part of the same clan live in neighbouring compounds, and are overseen by the **head of the clan**, who is usually the most senior of the compound heads.

Religion

Islam has a very tangible influence over many facets of Gambian society – in people's names, their manner of dress, eating, drinking and washing habits, marital practices, their adherence to special observances such as Ramadan and the Hajj, and even the manner in which they greet each other. Despite this, Islam has not extinguished traditional beliefs; even the most devout Gambian Muslims practise a brand of Islam that blends the teachings of the Koran with **animist beliefs** that long predate the arrival of Islam in West Africa. Today, most Gambian Muslims are **Sunni**, and the *imams* are their spiritual guides and leaders.

Far out-numbered by Muslims, but nonetheless conspicuous in the urban areas, are the **Christians** of various denominations.

Islam

Islam was introduced to West Africa via North Africa, and existed in pockets in the region since the time of the great Empire of Ghana in the eleventh century, but it was not until the nineteenth-century *jihads*, or holy wars, that Islam became the majority religion and a unifying force within the region. One important reason why Islam was so readily accepted was that the Muslim scholars provided services that were compatible with traditional animist beliefs, such as offering prayers for people, and making amulets and charms. Islam also brought writing to The Gambia: children were taught the Arabic alphabet by Koranic teachers, and basic literacy among Muslims was generally much higher than among non-Muslims.

The presence of Islam in The Gambia has countless manifestations in everyday life. The **mosque** is one of the focal points of every town and village, and the **call to prayer**, which in some districts can be an ear-shattering chant broadcast through crackly speakers, and in others the most beautiful, ethereal music, is heard in every neighbourhood. The prescribed routines of the faithful punctuate the days, with five prayer times daily; the weeks, with everyone dressed in their finest for Friday prayers at the mosque; and the years, with the observance of **festivals** and the holy month of **Ramadan**.

Many Gambians have traditional **Muslim names**, or Gambianized versions of them, such as Modou for Mohammed, or Fatou for Fatima. **Islamic phrases** colour everyday speech: the universal greeting that all Gambians use is an Islamic one, "Salaam aleikum/Maleikum salaam", meaning "Peace be upon you/And upon you", and common interjections include "Insh'Allah", meaning "If Allah wills it", the equivalent of "God willing", and "Alhamdoulila", meaning "thanks be to Allah". It's common for young children to receive an Islamic **education** by studying under a *marabout* – before secular state schools became widespread in the up-country areas, this was the only education available to many families.

Gambians are very proud of the sense of morality, discipline and cleanliness engendered by their faith, and some (though not all) view the Islamic sanctioning of **polygamy** as a great privilege – many Gambian men aspire to having more than one wife. Like Muslims everywhere, their holy book is the Koran, believed to be the words of God as revealed to the prophet Mohammed, and containing the religious laws and doctrines of Islam. Muslims are required to follow the tenets known as the **Five Pillars of Islam**: recognition of Allah and the prophet Mohammed, daily prayer, fasting during Ramadan, alms-giving and making the Hajj (pilgrimage to Mecca). Other Muslim practices include abstention from **alcohol**, commonly but not always strictly followed in The Gambia. The Gambian brand of Islam is not fundamentalist or fanatical, and Gambian Muslims are tolerant of non-believers.

Animism

West African **animism** is based around the conviction that natural phenomena, such as trees and animals, plus specially created objects, such as idols and fetishes, have spiritual power. Every ethnic group has their own distinctive version of similar beliefs. Most Gambians, though professing to be Muslim or Christian, also believe in the existence of non-abstract supernatural forces,

---

Gambian superstitions and taboos

Animist beliefs are bound up in a complex web of **superstitions and taboos** that are often taken very seriously, even by devout Muslims and Christians. Some are so secret they're never discussed. The following are a few that are commonly held:

A **water jar** should never be left empty in one's compound, as the dead may wish to drink when they pay a visit.

Pouring cold water on the ground first thing in the morning brings good luck for the day.

Seeing a **snake** in a dream is a sign of pregnancy.

Seeing a **horse** in a dream means a new wife is on the way.

If you are **laughing** in a dream, you will soon be crying.

If you sit in a **doorway**, evil spirits may strike you.

Somewhere in the River Gambia lives the *ninki-nanka*, a **dragon-devil**.

Every family has a **totem animal** they should never harm: for the Jobartehs, it's the chameleon, for the Mbyes, the monitor lizard, for the Ndeys, the rabbit, and for the Jammehs, the goat.

It's bad luck to buy or sell **soap** at night.

Don't answer a **call at night** for it may be a devil.

It's bad luck to **whistle** after dark.

Owls are the carriers of messages from evil spirits.

Throw **newly cut hair** away because if a bird finds it and makes it into a nest, you will have a constant headache.

Anything that happens on a **Saturday** will soon happen again, so avoid visiting the sick on this day.

It's bad luck to do anything on a **Wednesday**.

If a **pig** crosses your path and you don't mention it to anyone, you'll have good luck.

some harmful and some beneficial, and that witch doctors, herbalists, diviners and *marabouts* have powers over these forces. These spiritual guides can also act as mediators between the living and the dead, enabling people to communicate with their ancestors, revered in all African societies.

Practically every Gambian wears at least one *juju*, or sacred amulet, a piece of leather into which is stitched a fetish object, such as a sliver of bone, feather or wood, or a piece of paper inscribed with specific verses from the Koran prescribed by a *marabout* for their spiritual potency. Thus *jujus* may be either semi-Islamic or non-Islamic. They may be decorated with beads or cowries and worn on arms, legs, neck or waist, and are thought to enable the wearer to to control the supernatural. Their effect may simply be to protect against evil spirits, but particular *jujus* may be made for more specific purposes. For example, stitching somebody's hair into a *juju* may cause them to fall in love with the wearer, and making a *juju* with the fur of a black cat is thought to make the wearer invisible. *Jujus* may also secure a promotion or a bank loan, cure mental illness or impotence, or make rivals get ill, die or disappear. Certain prayers or requests require the sacrifice of an animal. Others require the supplicant to bathe in sacred water, notably water drawn from a sacred crocodile pool (see box on p.112).

Christianity

The European settlers and their missionaries first brought **Christianity** to The Gambia, and there are now over 100,000 Christians of various denominations in the country. The spread of Christianity increased a little when freed slaves, many of whom had converted to Christianity, migrated to The Gambia and settled there in the early nineteenth century.

Most Gambian Christians live in the Kombos, and can be seen piling into churches in their best clothes on Sunday mornings. **Missionary movements** are as active as ever, but their missions are now less about conversion and more about exchange of skills and ideas. Gambian Muslims tend to show devout Christians a great deal of respect, and there is a long-standing relationship between The Gambia and the evangelical Christian-run Mercy Ship organization which provides crucial medical care and services to various nations, by rota, from a floating hospital.

Rites of passage

In The Gambia, an individual's passage through life is marked by a series of cornerstone rituals that bestow blessings and confirm the individual's position and role in their family, their clan or extended family, and in society at large. These rites of passage, and the social structures that underpin them, are mutating as Gambian society becomes more outward-looking, but Gambians are generally extremely proud of their cultural heritage and are reluctant to give up the ways of the past.

Naming ceremonies

Whereas in the Western world **pregnancy** is usually a time of great excitement, anticipation and exhaustive discussion with friends and relatives, Gambians treat the matter with shyness and discretion and do not talk about the baby before the birth, from a deep-seated superstition that to do so could endanger the baby's life.

Once the baby has been born, invariably at home, the mother remains indoors for a week, throughout which a fire is kept burning in her compound. When the baby is exactly a week old, a **naming ceremony** is held (*kulliyo* in Mandinka, *ngente* in Wolof). In preparation for this, the mother dresses in new clothes, has her hair elaborately plaited, is showered with gifts and is generally treated like a princess. The women of the compound spend the whole day, from the early hours, preparing food for the guests. The ritual part of the naming ceremony takes place in the morning, when a *marabout* or an elder cuts a lock of the baby's hair, says a silent prayer and whispers into the baby's ear the name that has been chosen by the parents, while a chicken, goat or sheep is slaughtered. A *jali* or *griot* then proclaims the name to everyone in the compound. The Mandinka nearly always name their first born sons Lamin; otherwise names tend to honour relatives and friends on the father's side of the family. Kola nuts and specially prepared food are distributed among the guests, and the lock of hair is buried while everone present wishes the child health and long life.

At the end of the day the celebration turns into a major party. All Gambian family celebrations of this type involve music, dancing and plenty to eat and drink (though rarely any alcohol unless the family are non-Muslim). This sometimes lasts for several days, particularly if the guests have travelled some distance for the occasion. The type of music played depends on the tastes of the family but traditional bands of singers accompanied by *balafon* and drums, paid for by the family and their guests, are very popular.

Births are such regular occurences in The Gambia that anyone staying in a village for a few weeks will almost certainly experience at least one naming ceremony, and whenever you hear drumming in the distance in the crowded urban areas, there's a good chance that the neighbourhood is welcoming another baby into the world.

Initiation ceremonies

The **circumcision of boys**, shortly before reaching puberty, marks an important step in the transition from childhood to adulthood. These days it's no longer common for boys to go through the lengthy process of "bush school" and they may instead be circumcised by a medical practitioner at a clinic, but in rural areas ancient tribal practices persist.

Traditionally, the ceremony itself (*sunnaro* in Mandinka, *jonga* in Wolof, *futampaf* in Jola) is accompanied by a lengthy period of elaborate ritual, much of which is secret – the initiates are forbidden from telling anyone the details of what happens and what they are taught. The process begins when the initiates are rounded up to be taken away for their period of preparation. Among the Mandinka it is the *kankurang* (see p.xiv) that does the rounding up, a devil dancer who comes in various guises but is usually dressed in a costume made of leaves and the red bark of the camel-foot tree, a piece of which he clamps between his teeth. He also waves a cutlass, intended to scare off any malign spirits that may attempt to prey on the initiates while they are most vulnerable.

The boys are circumcised in the bush by the village blacksmith, and while they are healing they undergo a period of private instruction at "bush school" at the hands of a *marabout* or a tribal elder. Over the course of a few days or weeks they learn all about sex, tribal lore and the essentials of good conduct such as respect for one's elders. Gambians are increasingly fearful that with urbanization, secular education and the popularity of foreign media, the current generation of teenagers is exposed to influences that could subvert the tradition of showing unquestioning respect for age and experience – and that irrevocable moral decline is just around the corner.

The villagers make elaborate preparations for the return of the initiates from the bush, and the occasion may be marked by more ritual elements, including the planting and watering of trees and the slaughtering of sacrificial animals, plus more socializing and masquerade dancing from the *kankurang* (in Mandinka communities) or *kumpo* (Jola). The newly initiated, dressed in white hoods, are the guests of honour.

Female circumcision, though much more controversial, is still widespread in The Gambia, and is legal, although it has been outlawed elsewhere in sub-Saharan Africa. Referred to by its detractors as female genital mutilation, female circumcision is an act prescribed by African, not Muslim, culture, and it is currently performed on around eighty percent of Gambian girls, either in babyhood or aged 10–12 years. The operation takes different forms, and can involve clitoral or labial removal. The operation, which in remote rural areas is carried out by a female elder, is extremely painful (unless carried out under anaesthetic, which is rare). Complications that may arise include excessive bleeding, septicaemia, sexual dysfunction, difficulty giving birth and severe psychological scarring. The practice persists because there are strong cultural associations between circumcision and feminine virtue in traditional Gambian society and, in a social structure in which being a single woman is a difficult option, mothers do not like to contemplate the possibility of their daughters becoming unmarriageable outcasts just because they neglect to perform the operation. Girls, too, often too young to fully understand the situation, feel that they don't want to be left out of a celebration in which they would receive special attention and be treated as women for the first time. Men, meanwhile, are not usually the ones to put pressure on for the operation to be performed: many, when questioned, do not express any particular preference either way.

Marriage

In traditional Gambian society, all marriages are **arranged** by the couple's parents, although the marriage cannot take place against the will of either party. In the urban areas it's now becoming much more more common for couples to marry by personal choice, and they may or may not stick to other elements of marriage ritual; even so, parental wishes hold sway over many young people's choice of partner.

Traditionally, the first overture leading to marriage negotiations is the sending of a gift of kola nuts from the man's family to the woman's parents. The father of the bride-to-be discusses the matter with his wife and their daughter, and if everyone agrees then consent is signalled by sharing the kola nuts among their relatives, friends and neighbours. Expensive gifts pass from the man to his in-laws-to-be before the marriage takes place, including luxuries such as more kola nuts, cash, new beds, jewellery and new clothes, to a total value that is a matter of negotiation. If the bride's parents don't think the gifts offered are up to scratch, they may start considering offers from other suitors. Gifts given to the woman remain hers even if the couple later split up. Her parents, in turn, provide her with a dowry, consisting of all the utensils and equipment she needs to set up home.

Typically, a woman is much younger than her husband: in up-country villages, men in their 30s marry girls in their teens, because it can take years for a man to be able to afford the price of a wedding and, as in so many other cultures, virgins are thought to make the best brides.

A legal **ceremony** may take place at the mayor's office, but is not necessary. If this does happen (usually in the urban areas) it's followed by a procession of cars all driving from the office to the woman's compound with horns blaring at top volume. In villages the marriage is made official either in her compound or at the mosque, in a ceremony that the husband and wife don't actually attend. The *imam* blesses the union with prayers in the presence of both families, and after this formal ceremony everyone joins in a great celebration with music, dancing and feasting. Guests all contribute to the cost of the food and fees for the musicians but, if the groom is particularly short of cash, the celebration may take place some months after the ceremony.

The woman does not always go to live with her husband straight away, particularly if she is young; she may sometimes stay with her parents until after the birth of her first child. The time of her transfer to her husband's compound is another cause for festivity, when her hair is specially braided, she is formally received by her new family, and there's more celebratory music and feasting.

Islamic tradition allows a man up to four wives, if he can afford to support them all, and there's a certain kudos attained by having more than one wife in The Gambia, so **polygamy** is not uncommon. The rise of the women's movement has given women more freedom to express their feelings on polygamy but not all of them, by any means, are negative. In an unmechanized society where daily household chores such as fetching water, cooking, washing and cleaning can be extremely laborious and time-consuming, a co-wife with whom to share the graft may be a boon. Nevertheless, there's no escaping the feelings of rivalry and betrayal that polygamy can stir up, and women generally have absolutely no say in the matter of their husband marrying again. It's not unusual for husbands and wives to live apart after a few years of marriage, with the children living in the husband's compound, cared for by a second wife. Divorce, however, is almost unheard of, and would cast great shame upon the woman involved, and leave her at a serious financial disadvantage.

Funerals

Gambian **funerals** are cathartic occasions marked by much loud vocalization of grief, particularly from the female relatives of the deceased. The person who discovers a death immediately emits a loud wail. Elders then start to make funeral arrangements without delay, and send word to relatives and friends.

Funerals are not normally private occasions, and the bitter reality of short life expectancy in The Gambia means that death is too familiar an occurrence to be surrounded by taboo. The body is washed, wrapped in a white shroud, and then either rolled in a mat or placed in a coffin. It is then taken by the men of the family to the mosque for prayers, while the women remain in the compound. After prayers, the burial takes place, and charity is given to the family of the deceased, customarily money or food. The family observe a forty-day period of mourning, marked by their neighbours and the village elders offering them charitable gifts on the third, seventh and fortieth days after the burial.

According to traditional Muslim practice, a widow must remain in **mourning** for four and a half months, during which time she is supposed to wear mourning dress (basically anything plain and modest) and not leave the compound. The idea behind this is to determine whether any child she later gives birth to was the child of her late husband. Widowers do not have to observe any such practice.

Wildlife and nature

The Gambian landscape includes an impressive variety of habitats for such a small territory. The landscape is dominated by Sahelian scrub and Guinea woodland savanna, with extensive mangrove wetlands concentrated near the mouth of the river and along its lower reaches, and narrow strips of tropical forest along the riverbanks further east.

Habitats

The Gambia's defining feature is the **River Gambia**, which winds gently across the country from east to west, through a shallow valley punctuated by occasional low cliffs of deep red laterite. The valley is so shallow, and the tides so pronounced, that its waters are salty from the Atlantic for over 200km upstream in the dry season (slightly less in the rainy season), and there is noticeable tidal movement throughout the country. Riverbank habitats change dramatically from east to west, from the **jungle** of palms and tropical evergreen trees in the freshwater reaches to the thick low forests of **mangroves** closer to the estuary. Around the estuary, muddy mazes of creeks and salt flats are the dominant features. Increasing salination upstream causes problems for Gambian farmers, who are trying to introduce salt-adapted strains of rice in order to exploit the areas of transition between salt and fresh water.

The classic up-country Gambian landscape is flat **grassland savanna** thinly scattered with acacias, thorn trees and baobabs – lush and green in the rainy season and straw-blond, or blackened by bush fires, in the dry season. In rural areas many Gambians view trees as a waste of good groundnut-farming space: deforestation is rife and soil erosion a major problem, particularly in the mid-to-late dry season when the rice, millet, couscous and sorghum crops are all cleared and hot winds skim off the topsoil as dust. Fortunately, small pockets of forest survive here and there, where community forest husbandry schemes are in operation.

The Gambia's **beaches** are sandy, with shallow waters, backed either by dunes or by soft laterite cliffs. Once firmly bound by forests of palm trees, deforestation now endangers the coastal environment, and sand-mining has had the disastrous effect of exacerbating natural tidal erosion. Erosion stripped the coastal reaches of sand in the 1990s, and it's likely to take many years for them to recover.

One of the most striking silhouettes on the Gambian horizon is that of the **baobab tree**, sometimes nicknamed the "upside-down tree" because it looks as though it's been uprooted and replanted the wrong way up. Baobabs live for centuries and have a timelessly majestic presence in The Gambia; massive when mature, they are rarely cut down because they have spiritual significance – some tribes used to bury deceased *jalis* in hollows inside their stubby trunks. Baobabs are leafy only during the rainy season; by November they are hung with velvety pods like large oval Christmas tree baubles. The seeds ripen in January and contain a sherbet-like substance that's a source of tartaric acid, and can be chewed to stave off thirst or made into cordial or sorbet. The trunk contains water which can be tapped in the dry season, and the bark is sometimes stripped to make rope. There are particularly wonderful baobab specimens in up-country villages on the north bank of the river.

Equally huge and impressive features of up-country villages are the mature **silk-cotton trees** which produce kapok inside long, pointed, pod-like fruit. Silk-cotton trees, with their elaborately pleated exposed roots and shade-giving foliage, have similar spiritual significance to baobabs, and village *bantabas* are often built beneath them.

On the coast, in the Kombos and in well-watered areas everywhere are various varieties of palm tree of which the **rhun palm** is the most distinctive, for its oddly top-heavy-looking trunk and fan-like leaves. **Oil palms** and **coconut palms** have more feathery leaves. Palm oil is made by boiling away the husks of the palm fruit that grow in clusters at the top of the trunk; the palm-nut kernels, meanwhile, make palm nut oil. The trees are tapped for palm wine, the tapper shinning up each tree using a brace that loops round his waist and the tree trunk, making an incision at the top of the trunk and inserting a funnel to allow the sap to run into a bottle over the course of a day or so. Palm trees everywhere are used for timber, and the fronds for roofing and fencing.

The **mangrove** is a useful, saltwater-adapted tree, and mangrove forests are as crucial to wetland ecosystems as rainforests are to inland ecosystems. Mangrove creeks act as nurseries for breeding fish, crabs, shrimps, oysters and other aquatic creatures and, as a consequence, constitute rich feeding grounds for many birds and animals. With their complex aerial salt-filtering roots and salt-excreting leaves, they are natural processors of nitrates and water pollutants.

Other distinctive Gambian trees include the **flame tree**, stunningly florid in the rainy season; the small, flat-topped thorny **acacias**; and the **African locust bean trees**, whose pods are, like many seeds and leaves, used in natural remedies. Mature **kola nut trees** are found in the older villages: kola nuts have ritual significance in many West African societies as a traditional gift (see box on p.64). Village **orchards** are planted with grapefruit, orange, banana and cashew trees, and mango trees are encountered everywhere.

Wildlife

The Gambia's **birdlife** is astonishingly diverse, and the 560-plus bird species have relatively few predators. Characteristic sights are pied crows, urbanite magpie-like birds that are common throughout the Sahelian region; electric blue Abyssinian rollers perched conspicuously on telephone wires and on bare branches; the marvellous, lurching flight of hornbills swooping across the road in forest areas; and unmistakable gaggles of noisy, glamorous long-tailed glossy starlings just about everywhere. For more details on bird species found in The Gambia, see pp.xv–xxiv.

Because the country has such a rich and varied bird population, a number of ornithological studies have taken place here. By monitoring the behaviour of selected bird species, ecologists are able to keep up to date on changes to the Gambian ecosystem, and formulate environmental policy recommendations. For example, if a bird that usually frequents up-river areas is seen near the coast, this can indicate a change in the sea level and in the salinity of the River Gambia.

The large mammals most often seen out on the road or in the bush are **monkeys** and **baboons**. The country has three species of monkey – callithrix, patas and western red colobus – and an up-country population of Guinea baboons. **Callithrix**, the most numerous, have grizzled golden-green fur, a dark grey face and paler grey hands and feet, and are unique to West Africa, though very similar to the green vervet monkeys found elsewhere in Africa. Male **patas** are sandy coloured with russet crowns and tails, white limbs and shaggy grey shoulders; the females are plainer in colour. The **western red colobus** is an extremely attractive monkey with rich russet and grey fur, a dark tail, and a blue-black face. All three species are a similar size in adulthood, the males slightly larger than females, with a head and body 60–80cm in length, and long, slender limbs and tails. African monkeys don't have prehensile tails, nor do you see them brachiating (swinging from branches), but they're impressive leapers and swift runners. The patas, largely terrestrial, is the world's fastest monkey, capable of speeds of up to 55km/hr on the ground – which will come as no surprise to anyone who's had their lunch stolen by one. All three species live in troops of one or two dozen family members, the babies clinging to their mothers' fur. They are well adapted to woodland savanna habitats and range widely in search of food. They're most commonly found on forest fringes – they rarely stray too far from the safety of the trees – but they do sometimes raid crops, causing havoc for the farmers. It is the up-country Guinea baboons, though – larger than the other primates, with dog-like faces – that are the real rogues when it comes to crop-raiding.

Small **antelopes** are quite common in The Gambia, but they're shy and well camouflaged, so hard to spot. **Bushbuck** and **Maxwell's duiker** are occasionally seen grazing near the *bambo* pool at Abuko, and it's sometimes possible to spot the water-loving **sitatunga** on the banks of the river in the Kiang West area.

Elephants and most other big game were finally eradicated from the country some time ago (the last Gambian elephant was shot in 1913). Today, despite long-term conservation efforts such as ex-president Jawara's much-vaunted "Banjul Declaration", the faunal heritage continues to diminish while the human population expands, causing a chronic shrinkage in wildlife habitats. A very small population of **leopards** remains, nocturnal and rarely seen, though tracks are occasionally spotted in the Niumi National Park.

Nile crocodiles are seen in the river and its creeks from time to time, particularly in the coolest months (Dec and Jan) when they often bask on the banks. They are mercilessly hunted because they occasionally attack children and domestic animals. There are also a few **dwarf crocodiles** at Abuko, where they live in the forest and are active by night.

The Gambian **hippo** population is thought to have dwindled to well under a hundred animals; though strictly protected, like all wild animals in The Gambia, they're persecuted because of their danger to rice fields and threat to human life. The Gambian fear of hippos is well founded: despite their placid appearance, they are dangerous if threatened, causing more human deaths in Africa than any other creature apart from the mosquito, and they regularly devastate crops. Sightings are now rare, and the likeliest place to see one, or at least a pair of ears and nostrils, is by taking a boat through the River Gambia National Park (see pp.213–214). The mid-river islands here are also home to a population of rehabilitated **chimpanzees**. The Gambia no longer has a indigenous chimp population, apart from those born to animals reintroduced to the park, most of which are thought to have been born in other West African countries.

Fearsome-tusked **warthog** (known locally as **bushpig**) are common in Gambian woodlands, but overhunted – by farmers, sportsmen and for the tourist restaurant trade. Other woodland mammals include the curious, termite-eating **aardvark** and clans of **hyena,** which prowl by night; neither species is seen often.

Spiders, scorpions and various other invertebrates are less often encountered than you might expect. **Butterflies**, well over a hundred different species in total, are numerous and colourful, especially in the rainy season, when they flutter in clouds at the edge of forests and in sunny clearings.

Lizards are common everywhere, especially the brightly coloured **rock agamas**, typically seen performing vigorous push-ups on sunny rocks. Some places positively swarm with them, no doubt in proportion to the insect supply. Large lizards (all species are quite harmless) include two species of monitors, of which the grey and yellow **Nile monitor** grows to an impressive two metres. They live near water, and are often seen dashing across the road or through undergrowth. **Chameleons**, unmistakable for their prehensile tails, swivelling eyes and ability to change colour for camouflage, may be spotted in trees by the sharp-eyed. In most areas, at night, little house **geckos** come out like translucent aliens to scuttle usefully across the ceiling and walls in pursuit of moths and mosquitoes.

The Gambia has around forty species of **snake**, all of which are elusive and most of which are harmless. The nine that are dangerously venomous, including the **puff adder**, the **spitting cobra** and the **green mamba**, will only strike if threatened, and walking heavily will usually scare them away (they're highly sensitive to vibration). Impressive looking, but harmless to humans, is the black-and-tan, rodent-eating **rock python** and the smaller, stocky **royal python**, which shelter in burrows. The best place to see snakes at close range is to visit the reptile farm near Kartong (see p.150).

Two species of dolphin, the **Atlantic hump-backed dolphin** and the slightly larger **bottlenose dolphin**, patrol the Atlantic coast and the shallow waters of the Gambia estuary in schools of between half a dozen and five hundred animals. A rare mammalian inhabitant of the coastal mangrove creeks is the **West African manatee**, a whiskery vegetarian that is superbly adapted to life in shallow saltwater.

Gambian waters are rich in tropical **fish** including barracuda, tigerfish, tarpon and bonga, plus small sharks and rays. Particularly numerous in the mangrove creeks are **tilapia**, a species found all over Africa.

Books

West Africa has produced quite a few world-class authors, but The Gambia doesn't have a vibrant contemporary literature scene of its own and Gambian fiction is rarely available outside the country. The in-print choice of books about The Gambia is also pretty limited; books about Africa that include mention of The Gambia are not much easier to find. A few publications that may be useful to travellers visiting The Gambia, such as the various hand-stapled Mandinka and Wolof language manuals, are sold in hotel shops, at the airport and in *Timbooktoo*, the country's only well-stocked bookshop, in Fajara. Books marked with the ⊡ symbol are highly recommended.

Travel and literature

Jens Finke *Chasing the Lizard's Tail: By Bicycle across the Sahara* (UK). Entertaining and insightful travelogue, recounting Rough Guide author Finke's solo journey from Morocco to The Gambia, with vivid descriptions of pre-coup Banjul, where his travels came to an abrupt end.

⊡ **Mark Hudson** *Our Grandmothers' Drums* (UK). Rich, absorbing story of the author's stay in the village of "Dulaba" (Keneba) in the Kiang West area; Hudson immersed himself in traditional rural Gambia by befriending a group of village women, and become an honorary member of their *kafo*, or working cooperative. Occasionally shaky on anthropology, but frank and revealing on the intricacies of Gambian women's lives.

Elspeth Huxley *Four Guineas* (UK; o/p). This account of Huxley's trip through the four Anglophone colonies on the eve of independence is full of credible conversations – and the occasional lapse into racist angst.

⊡ **Rosemary Long** *Under the Baobab Tree*; *Together Under the Baobab Tree* (UK; o/p). Cheerful and chatty autobiographical accounts of a Scottish writer's new life married to a Gambian, running a tourist guesthouse on a shoestring in the Kombos in the early 1990s, with plenty of homespun wisdom about grass-roots Gambia as seen through expat eyes.

Mungo Park *Travels into the Interior of Africa* (various edns). A bestseller in its time, this is the Scottish explorer's account of his two journeys in search of the source of the Niger.

⊡ **Ann-Britt Sternfeldt** *The Good Tourist in The Gambia* (Sweden). Brief but refreshingly thoughtful and honest guide to responsible tourism in The Gambia, showing how to enjoy the best of the country's attractions while supporting local businesses and appreciating the natural environment.

Bamba Suso et al *Sunjata* (UK). The legend of the founder of the Mali empire, which once reached as far as present-day Gambia. This Penguin edition presents two strikingly different Gambian versions of the epic.

Michael Tomkinson *Gambia* (UK). Large-format book that's worth leafing through for its excellent photographs of real people, places and daily life – with a supplement reviewing all the country's accommodation options.

History and politics

A.E. Afigbo et al *The Making of Modern Africa* (UK). A detailed, illustrated guide in two volumes, putting West Africa in the wider African context up until the first big changes after independence.

Adu Boahen *Topics in West African History* (UK). An excellent introduction to basic themes in West African history by one of Ghana's most respected historians.

★ **George E. Brooks** *Landlords and Strangers* (US). The history of West Africa prior to the peak of the colonial era, drawing on oral records and written documentation to trace the significance of climate and intercultural communication in the region's development.

Basil Davidson *Africa in History* (UK). Lucidly argued and readable summary of Africa's dominant nineteenth- and twentieth-century events.

★ **Ada Dinkarala et al** *Historic Sites of The Gambia* (The Gambia). Solid background information on topics as diverse as slave-trading, forts, shell-mounds and stone circles.

Cheikh Anta Diop *Pre-Colonial Black Africa* (US). Diop asserts that the origins of Western civilization began in Africa. First published in the 1950s, this book encouraged a whole generation of students to reinterpret the past from an African perspective.

Arnold Hughes and David Perfect *A Political History of The Gambia, 1816–1994* (UK). The history of the country prior to the 1994 coup, focusing on The Gambia's coming of age as a multi-party democracy.

Arnold Hughes and Harry Gailey *Historical Dictionary of The Gambia* (US). Recently updated, this covers the country's history from pre-colonial times to the present, with short biographies of key figures and entries on events, institutions and cultural topics.

Patrick Marnham *Dispatches from Africa* (UK; o/p). Although published in 1980 and now inevitably dated, this journalism remains devastatingly sharp. Includes an essay on The Gambia.

Society and culture

Thomas D. Blakely et al *Religion in Africa: Experience and Expression* (US). Thorough examination of religion in Africa and the diaspora.

★ **Simon Broughton et al** *The Rough Guide to World Music, volume 1* (UK). This authoritative work discusses the Gambian *kora* masters in the context of West Africa's musical heritage, and includes features on Senegambian stars.

R.J. Harrison Church *West Africa*

(o/p). A traditional geography reference – excellent and unexpectedly absorbing.

Thomas A. Hale *Griots and Griottes: Masters of Words and Music* (US). A comprehensive look at *griots* – male and female – of Niger, Mali, Senegal and The Gambia and their roles as historians, genealogists, diplomats, musicians and advisors.

Patience Sonko-Godwin *Ethnic Groups of the Senegambia* (The

Gambia). A brief and graspable social history of the region.

Claudia Zaslavsky *Africa Counts: Number and Pattern in African Cultures* (US). Includes a chapter on *warri* games.

Natural history

Clive Barlow et al *Field Guide to the Birds of The Gambia and Senegal* (UK). Excellent, authoritative bird bible for the region, by a renowned British ornithologist resident in The Gambia.

Stella Brewer *The Forest Dwellers* (UK). The story of Brewer's chimpanzee rehabilitation project, now located in the River Gambia National Park.

W. Serle and G. Morel *A Field Guide to the Birds of West Africa* (UK). Comprehensive guide for the whole West African region, with specially commissioned illustrations.

Rod Ward *A Birdwatchers' Guide to The Gambia* (UK). Detailed information on some of the country's prime ornithological sites, accessibly presented.

Fiction

T. Coraghessan Boyle *Water Music* (UK). Lengthy, meticulous fictionalization of Mungo Park's explorations, at times outrageously funny.

William Conton *The African* (o/p) A rags-to-premiership story by a Gambian writer from the colonial era: still a classic, this was a bestseller in 1960s Gambia.

Ebou Dibba *Chaff in the Wind*; *Fafa* (both o/p). In *Chaff in the Wind*, this highly accomplished Gambian author, now living in Britain, describes life in 1930s Gambia. *Fafa* is the tale of a remote trading post on the River Gambia.

Alex Haley *Roots* (various edns). An entertaining American saga to read on the beach – only the first few chapters are set in Kunta Kinte's semi-mythical Gambian homeland, but village life is vividly described.

Lenrie Peters *The Second Round* (o/p). A readable, if downbeat semi-autobiographical account of an African doctor's experience of culture shock when he returns home after working abroad. This Gambian author has also published several collections of poetry.

Tijan Salleh *Kora Land* (o/p). Verse with an uncompromising take on West African politics and social manoeuvring, from a Gambian poet and essayist who tackles themes such as corruption, poverty and injustice.

C

CONTEXTS | Books

Music

Nowhere in the world has quite the same rhythm, melody and musical colour as West Africa. Throughout the region, every rite of passage is marked by a musical celebration of some sort, but music is also an integral part of everyday life, embroidering urban and village landscapes with a rich background texture of drumming and song.

Gambian music overlaps and interweaves that of Mali, Guinea and, above all, Senegal. Music is the Senegambians' main creative outlet, and is far more significant (and widespread) in traditional society and daily life than any of the visual arts. Improvization around familiar themes plays a big part in Gambian musicians' creative processes, since a great deal of Senegambian music is based on well-known ancient songs, tunes and rhythms passed down from generation to generation by the *jalis*, the hereditary caste of musicians and storytellers whose music accompanies traditional dances. Storytelling, music and dance are intricately connected all over West Africa.

The Gambia's musical heritage is as rich as its ethnic make-up, and each tribe has a distinctive set of traditional instruments: the flutes and rasping *riti* violins of the Fula, the pounding *boucarabou* and driving percussion of the Jola, the thunderous *sabar* and rippling *tama* drums of the Wolof and the Mandinkas' melodious **kora**. Arguably the country's most distinctive music is the traditional repertoire of the Mandinka *jalis*, sung solo to tunes on the *kora*, but the music you're most likely to hear on the radio or on cassette, blaring out of workshops, bars and bush taxis everywhere, is *ndagga* and *mbalax* **dance music** from Senegal.

Traditional music and dance

The Gambia's Mandinka *jalis* are, like the Manding *jelis* and *griots* elsewhere in West Africa, the custodians of folk history, which they convey through rhythm and song. Largely untouched by Western influences, their music is all sweet melodies, hypnotic rhythms and ancient stories, and has a lilting quality. The title of *jali* is possessed only by certain very old families, notably the Kontehs, Kuyatehs, Jobartehs and Susos. Traditionally, the **kora** and many other instruments are played exclusively by them.

A *jali's* reputation is built upon humility and correct behaviour as well as his knowledge of history and family genealogies. Originally, the job involved singing the praises of the noble and wealthy (no occasion – a wedding or naming ceremony for example – would be complete without a *jali*), but now they're just as likely to have business or civil service patrons. Some *jalis* are also philosophers or satiricists who deliver social comment in musical form.

Jalis call on a great **repertoire** of songs, but if you listen to several artists you'll start to recognize lyrical variations on common melodic themes. A *jali's* skill lies in the improvised flourishes and ornamentation (*birimintingo*) that he brings to the recurrent theme or core melody (*donkili*).

While *kora* music is generally quiet and contemplative, Gambian **percussion** – drums, xylophone-like *balafon*, and all manner of simple instruments to shake, chime or rattle – are played at top volume. Every ethnic group has its own brand of exuberant percussion. The **dances** associated with Gambian drum

Traditional instruments

Traditional Senegambian instruments are made from indigenous materials such as wood, calabash, animal skin, millet stalks and horn, and each one has **spiritual significance** as something alive, possessing its own language – this is why the skin of the goat (the most talkative of animals) is used for drums and lutes. Some instruments are used **seasonally**, for example at harvest time, and some instruments are gender- or generation-specific.

Drums

Drums are the most basic and familiar instruments played by all Gambian ethnic groups; they feature at most events, whether ceremonial, ritual or social, and have multiple functions including issuing announcements and warnings.

Boucarabou Three or four drums of different pitches played simultaneously by one Jola drummer.

Mandinka drums Three conical drums of differing height played together by three musicians.

Sabar Tall, freestanding cylindrical Wolof drums, played with hand and stick in drum bands of up to twelve players.

Tama Small, hourglass-shaped talking drum, which produces an amazing series of high-pitched tones.

Other percussion

As well as the main **percussion** instruments below, a wide range of simple instruments are used to beat out complex syncopated rhythms, including rattles, bells, whistles and, universally, clapping hands.

Balafon Rosewood and gourd xylophone with between 17 and 27 keys, known to have been around since the fourteenth century.

Kiring and **tombolong** Small or large hollow log with closed ends and a long slot from end to end, played with sticks for a hollow sound.

Sheikeire Calabash covered with beads or shells, shaken or struck.

Water drum Calabash in a basin of water, played with a stick, often by women.

Stringed instruments

Bolom (or *bolombato*) Percussive harp-lute with three or four strings, a skin-covered calabash base tensioned with cords and an arched neck that used to be played for warriors going into battle. It's now an instrument played by men who are not of a *jali* family.

Kontingo Small, oval lute with five strings.

Kora Mandinka, Manding and Mandé *jali* harp-lute made with a large decorated half-gourd covered with a skin. The 21–25 strings, usually made from fishing line, are attached with leather thongs to a rosewood pole put through the gourd. The player plucks and strums the strings to produce a melody, bass line and embellishments all at the same time. The top of the body has a large sound hole, doubling as a collection point for money from the audience. It's played at waist level, standing or seated.

Riti Fula violin with one to four strings, played with a bow.

Xalam A single-string *jali* lute with a half-gourd, skin-covered soundbox.

Wind instruments

Flute Made from terracotta, wood, millet stalks, bamboo, horn or calabash, and played by the Fula and Jola tribes.

music – high-stepping, arm-flapping, stomping solos that elicit shrieks and applause the faster they go – are an expression of individuality and, at the same time, of community solidarity. It's a tradition that The Gambia shares with other West African countries, and which resonates far beyond Africa's shores: the principles of West African music and dance inhabit the collective cultural memory of African descendants throughout the diaspora. Within Senegambian rhythms are the foundations of music and dance made famous by Western stars of funk, jazz, soul and hip-hop. See a Fula dance and you understand exactly where breakdancing comes from.

Modern music

Modern music in The Gambia is essentially Senegalese, largely because of Senegal's cultural domination of its tiny neighbour. Gambian musicians have always had great difficulties breaking into the international music scene. The country has poor infrastructures for professional musicians; The Gambia has yet to pass any copyright laws, so any profits from recordings are swiftly eaten away by pirating. Most Gambian musicians scrape a living from tips for live appearances, or from teaching. As a result, it's difficult to state categorically who are the greatest Gambian musicians. Few are well known outside their homeland – in fact, there are many master musicians whose music is never heard outside their own compound.

Heading for Senegal to expand their musical influence further takes cash and commitment. Those musicians who can afford it go to Dakar, the nerve centre of the Senegambian music scene, a city that swaggers to the rhythm of the music it gave birth to, **mbalax**. The city's soundtrack seeps out of the roadside stalls, bars and clubs: the call of the *tama* (talking drums) and *sabar* (tall drums), and the nasal keening of the *gewels* or *gawlis*, traditional Wolof singers and counterparts of the *jalis*. Everybody who is anybody in Senegambian music either hails from Dakar, or gravitates here, drawn by the magnetism of big audiences and serious money. In West African terms, the Dakarois recording industry is a sophisticated machine, which holds an overwhelming sway over Gambian musicians' livelihoods.

The *kora* is usually a solo instrument, accompanied by solo voice, but in the 1990s, young *jalis* breathed new life into traditional *kora*-playing by setting up semi-acoustic ensembles combining amplified *koras* with percussion and other instruments, and playing in an up-tempo, tumbling, danceable style. One of the *jalis* at the forefront of this movement was Jaliba Kuyateh, one of The Gambia's most popular live performers, who makes regular appearances at festivals and other important events.

Recently Gambians have been experimenting with new styles, mostly American influenced, and local **rap** or **hip-hop** acts to look out for include Dancehall Masters, Sing-Jay Rebellion, DJ Lamin "Champion" Cham and Freaky Joe. Meanwhile, a whole generation of Gambian youth sways along to **reggae** and **ragga**.

Discography

Much of the music you'll hear in The Gambia is by Senegalese stars, who regularly work with Gambians, and outnumber them in the list of artists below.

This selection of recordings, all available internationally, includes the best of *mbalax*, *kora*, and the region's irresistible take on Afro-Latin jazz.

Tata Dindin *Salam – New Kora Music* (Network Medien, Germany). While this talented *jali* is known for his innovative compostions and technique (he sometimes even plays his *kora* with his teeth, Hendrix-style), this recording finds him in traditional, meditative mode.

Ifang Bondi *Gis Gis* (Warner Basart, Netherlands). This band has been a pace-setter in the Gambian music scene since the 1960s (when they were known as the Super Eagles); here they combine Fula, Mandinka, Jola and Wolof influences in smoothly produced, modern-edged sound.

Pa Bobo Jobarteh & Kairo Trio *Kaira Naata* (Real World, UK). Evocative *kora* from this young Gambian *jali*, recorded live on the beach and in other low-key locations: plaintive melodies, with bird calls and ocean waves between tracks.

Cheikh Lô *Bambay Gueej* (World Circuit, UK). Youssou N'Dour's brilliant protegé stirs up a warm, potent mix of Cuban *guajira*, *soukous*, reggae, urban funk and makossa jazz, with addictive results.

Ismaël Lô *The Balladeer* (Wrasse, UK). Lô represents the gentler style of Senegalese music, with whimsical ballads woven around harmonica and acoustic guitar melodies.

Baaba Maal *Mi Yeewnii/Missing You* (Palm Pictures, UK). Known as The Nightingale for his clear, high-pitched voice, Senegal's second biggest star has an electrifying onstage energy. He also has a contemplative side, and this acoustic album, produced by John Leckie (producer of Radiohead's *The Bends*), finds him in sweet and soulful mode.

Youssou N'Dour *Set* (Virgin, UK); *The Guide (Wommat)* (Sony, UK). Two classic recordings from the region's greatest cultural ambassador. N'Dour's huge body of work is patchy, varied and fascinating, continually reworked to cater to the separate demands of his markets at home, in France and in the English-speaking world. You're likely to hear his voice at least once every day, anywhere where music is played in The Gambia. *Set* is the aficionado's favourite; *The Guide* includes *Seven Seconds*, the duet with Neneh Cherry that catapulted Youssou to international fame.

Orchestra Baobab *Specialist In All Styles* (World Circuit, UK). Genius producer Nick Gold gives the veteran band the *Buena Vista Social Club* treatment with this, their first album for fifteen years. The Casamance meets Cuba in a fresh, danceable, instant classic.

Yan Kuba Saho *Yan Kuba: Kora music from The Gambia* (Latitudes, USA). Spirited and atmospheric recording made in Serrekunda with vocals and *konkondiro* (percussive tapping on the body of the *kora*) from Saho's wife Bintu Suso.

Mansour Seck *Yelayo* (Stern's, UK). Seck, the childhood friend and mentor of Baaba Maal, is a supreme singer and guitarist; this is Fulani music at its best.

Jali Nyama Suso *Gambie: L'Art de la Kora* (Ocora, France). Classic 1970s recording from the late *kora* master who in his prime was one of the country's most influential artists.

Various *Kairo – Songs Of The Gambia* (Arch Records, UK and The Gambia). Showcase collection of established Gambian talent, including some of the nation's greatest virtuoso singers, drummers and *kora* players.

Various *The Rough Guide to the Music of Senegal & Gambia* (World Music Network, UK). Compelling introduction to the best of the region's music.

Language

Language

Language

West Africa is the most linguistically complex region in the world. The Gambia alone, though the second smallest country in the region, has dozens of languages and dialects, of which six – English, Mandinka, Wolof, Fula, Jola and Serer – are in common daily use.

Many Gambians speak several languages – their own tribal language, at least one other and English. English is the country's official language, and it dominates the media, but it's not the lingua franca; Gambians rarely use it between themselves, preferring **Wolof** in the Kombos and **Mandinka** up-country. English is, however, the only language permitted in schools, so as education standards rise it's likely to become more widely spoken and understood. At present, an individual's fluency in English usually corresponds directly to their level of education and their degree of interaction with foreigners. Naturally enough, English is much more commonly spoken in the tourist areas than anywhere else in the country, and some Kombos-dwellers, even those with little formal education, have also picked up German, Danish or Swedish. Most Gambian languages include a peppering of words and phrases adapted from English, French and Arabic, including the universal Arabic greeting *Salaam aleekum – maleikum salaam* used by all ethnic groups. Gambians that trade with or travel to Senegal generally speak good French.

None of the Gambian languages had a written form before the arrival of the Europeans, and it's only recently that linguists have made any attempt to standardize spellings – definitive rules do not yet exist.

Pronunciation and grammar

Most Gambians speak Mandinka or Wolof (often both) more fluently than English, even if neither is their mother tongue. A little of these therefore goes a long way in making yourself understood.

Mandinka is not difficult to get your tongue around, though grammatically it's likely to feel unfamiliar. A characteristic of spoken Mandinka is the omitted final vowel, lending a "clipped" quality to the language. Wolof grammar is different again; as a beginner you're best off learning a few phrases by ear. In both languages, a double consonant makes the sound harder, as in English, and a double vowel spelling lengthens the sound, as indicated below.

Vowel sounds

a short, as in "cat"

e short, as in "bet"

i short, as in "fit"

o short, as in "sock"

u short, as in "sugar"

aa long, like the vowel sound in "cart"

ee long, like the vowel sound in "bear"

ii long, like the vowel sound in "feat"

oo long, like the vowel sound in "sort"

uu long, like the vowel sound in "food"

Mandinka consonants

ny like the "ni" in "onion"

kh like the "ch" in "loch"

ng like the "ng" in "sing"

Wolof consonants

x like the "ch" in "loch", but throatier

Greetings

No interaction in The Gambia ever begins without at least the most basic of **greetings**, so learning a few simple ones will make your encounters with local people far more rewarding. Responses to greetings are normally ritualized, and effectively evasive rather than specific.

Universal greeting (exchanged by all Gambians)

Peace be upon you	Salaamaaleekum
... and peace be upon you (response)	Maaleekum salaam

Mandinka greetings

I wish you peace	Kayira be
How are you? (to one person)	I be kayira to?
How are you all?	Ali be kayira to?
– Peace only (in response to any of the above)	Kayira dorong
How are things? (lit: it is how?)	A be nyaadii?
How is everyone? (lit: where are the people of your compound)?	Suu moo lee?
– They're well (lit: they are there)	I be jee
No problem? (general, further greeting)	Kortanante?
– No problem	Tanante
Well done, good work (lit: you at work; said to one person if they're working, or even just chatting)	I nimbaara
Well done, good work (said to several people)	Ali nimbaara
– I'm working (response to either of the above)	I nimbaara, nimbaara
How is the work?	Dookuwo be nyaadii?
– It's coming along (lit: small, small)	Domanding, domanding
How is your wife? (lit: where is...?)	Ila musoo lee?
How is your husband? (lit: where is...?)	I keemaa lee?
How are your children? (lit: where are...?)	Dindingolu lee?
– They're well (lit: they are there, response to any of the above)	I be jee
– No problem with him/her	Tana taala
– No problem with them	Tana teela
Good morning (response identical)	I saama
How's the morning?	Somandaa be nyaadii?
– Fine (lit: the morning is here only)	Somandaa be jang dorong

Good afternoon (response identical)	I tiinyang
How's the afternoon? – Fine (lit: it is there)	Tilibuloo be dii? I be jee
Good evening (response identical)	I wulaara
How's the evening? – Fine (lit: it is there)	Wulaaroo be dii? I be jee
Goodbye	Fo waati koteng

Wolof greetings

Hello (how are things?) (colloquial)	Nakam?
How are you? – I'm fine (lit: I'm here only/I'm here)	Nanga def? Mangi fii rek **or**: mang fi
Do you have peace? (formal greeting) – Peace only – Thanks be to God/thank goodness	Jaama ngaam? Jaama rek Alxamdu lillaax
How are things in your compound? – Everybody's fine	Naka waa ker ga? Nyung chi jaama
How are the people in your compound? (lit: where are the people in your compound?) How are things in England? (lit: where are the people of England?) How is...? (lit: where is...?) – They're fine (lit: they're there, response to either of the above)	Ana waa ker ga? Ana waa England/Angleterre? Ana... ? Nyung fa
Did you spend the night peacefully? – Yes thank you (lit: peace only) How's the morning? – Fine (lit: the morning is there only)	Jaama nga fanaan? Jaama rek Naka suba si? Suba sangi fii rek
Are you having a peaceful afternoon? – Yes thank you (lit: peace only) How's the afternoon? – Fine (lit: the afternoon is there only)	Jaama nga endu? Jaama rek Naka becheg bi? Beche bangi fii rek
How's the evening? – Fine (lit: the evening is there only)	Naka ngoon si? Ngoon sangi fii rek
How's the night? – Fine (lit: the night is there only)	Naka guddi gi? Guddi gangi fii rek
Have a good day Have a good night – Yes thank you (lit: peace only)	Nyu endu chi jaama Nyu fanaan chi jaama Jaama rek
How's the work? – Fine (lit: the work is there only)	Naka ligey bi? Ligey bangi fii rek

Fula greetings

How are you?	Nambata?	I'm fine	Jamtan

Jola greetings

How are you?	Kassumai?	How is the family?	Kissindi?
I'm fine	Kassumai kep	They're fine	Cocobo

Serer greetings

How are you?	Nafio?	I'm fine	Memehen

ⓛ Further greetings in Mandinka and Wolof

Almost as important as asking someone how they are and how everything's going at home is, if they're a stranger, to ask their name, where they're from, where they're living or staying and where they're going. This is not nosiness, but common politeness. Again, the responses don't have to be too specific.

	Mandinka	Wolof
What's your name?	I tondii?	Naka nga tudda?
My name is Kebba	N too mu Kebba le ti	Kebba laa tudda or: Mangi tudda Kebba or: Sama tuur Kebba la
What's your surname?	I kontongo dung?	Naka nga santa?
My surname is Suso	N kontongo mu Suso le ti	Suso laa santa or: Mangi santa Suso or: Sama santa Suso la
Where do you come from?	I bota mintoo le?	Foo jogee?
I come from England	M bota England le	England laa jogee
Sit down (take a seat)	Sii	Toogal
Where are you going?	I ka taa mintoo le?	Fooy dem? or: Fan ngaay dem?
Are you going to the market?	I ka taa marisee le to bang?	Ndax marse ngaay dem?
I'm going to Basse	N ka taa Basse	Basse laay dem
Where are you staying/living?	I be sabatiring mintoo le?	Foo dekka?

Mandinka and Wolof words and phrases

Basic expressions

	Mandinka	Wolof
yes	haa	waaw
no	hani	deedeet
OK	awaa	baax na
perhaps	tumandoo	xej na
Thank you (thanks, blessing)	abaraka	jerejef
Thank you very much	abaraka baake	jerejef bu baax
You're welcome (lit: amen, response to a blessing)	Amiin	Amiin
You're welcome (lit: blessings, response to thanks)	Abaraka	Sa waala
Where is...? (used for people, and moveable things)	...lee?	Ana... ?
Yes, I'm here (when called)	Naam	Naam
I'm sorry	Hekatu	Baalal ma
I don't speak (lit: hear) much Mandinka/ Wolof	M mang mandinka moy baake	Man deeguma wolof
I don't understand	M mang a fahaam	Xamuma
Please repeat	A fo kotenke	Waxaat ko
Do you speak English?	I ye English moy le bang?	Deega nga English?
Don't you understand English?	I mang English moy bang?	Deeguloo English?
a little bit	domanding dorong	tuuti rek
please (for God's sake!)	dukare	ngir yaala
if you like	naa dyaateeye	su la neexee
I don't mind/care	Nna haaji te jee	Suma yoon neeku chi
no problem	tanante/problem taala	amul solo
I didn't invite you	M mang i kumandi jang	Ooyuma la fii
I don't like/want...	M mang lafi... la	Buguma ...
I don't know him	M mang a long/M maa long	Xamuma ko
I don't know you	M mang i long/M mee long	Xamuma la
I don't need your help	M mang lafi ila deemaaroo la	Buguma sa ndimbal
Leave me	M bula/Fata m ma	Baay ma, waay!
It's none of your business	A manke ila haajoo ti	Du sa soxla
Someone's waiting for me	Moo le ka m batu	Am na ku may xaar
You go/Clear off! (to children)	Ali taa/A cha!	Dem leen!
I like your car	Ila nying motoo ye n nyaabo	Buga naa sa woto
You have no equal	I mang nyong soto	Amuloo morom
Your dress is lovely	Ila nying parewo nyinaata	Sa mbuba rafet na
Till the next time	Fo waati doo	Be benen yoon
Goodbye (lit: I am going)	N ka taa le	Mangi dem
Pass on my regards (lit: you (all) greet them)	I si i kontong/Ali si i kontong	Nuyu leen
Say hello to them	Suumoolu kontong	Nuyul waa ker gi
– They will hear	I saa moy	Dinenyi ko deega
See you soon	Fo nyaato	Be si kanam
I'm coming back later	M be naa la nyaato	Dinaa nyow chi kanam

Getting around

	Mandinka	Wolof
Let's go	Ali nga taa	Nyu dem
Stop (here)	Loo (jang)	Taxawal (fii)
Come (here)	Naa (jang)	Kaay (fii)
Where is…? (used for places)	… be mintoo le?	… mungi fan?
Where is the road to Gunjur?	Gunjur siloo be mintoo le?	Yooni Gunjur fan la neeka?
Show me the way to the post office	Post-office siloo yitandi n na	Won ma yooni post-office bi
That way?	Jana?	Nale?
There?	Jee?	Fale?
Here?	Jang?	Fii?
How many kilometres?	Kilometre jelu?	Nyaata kilometre?
right	bulubaa	ndeyjoor
left	maraa	chaamong
near	sutiyaa	jegeng
far	jamfa	sori
When?	Muntuma	Kanyi?
fast/it's very fast	tariyaa/tariyaata baake	gaaw/gaaw torop
slowly	domang domang	ndanka ndanka

Shopping and ordering food

What would you like?	I lafita mune la?	Lan nga buga?
Do you have any bananas?	I ye banaanoo soto le bang?	Amuloo banana
Is… available?	… sotota le bang?	… am na?
I don't have any money	M mang kodoo soto	Amuma xaalis
I want some bananas	N lafita banaanoo la	Buga naa banana
Sell me some bananas	Banaanoo sang n nye	Jaay ma banana
How much (money) is it?	Jelu le mu?	Nyaata la?
Please give me some water	N so jiyo la	May ma ndox ngir yalla
I will give you …	M be…dii leela	Dinaa la jox…
five dalasis	dalasi luulu	juroomi dalasi
It's expensive! (lit: difficult)	A koleyaata!/A daa jawuyaata!	Dafa seer!
It's much too expensive!	A koleyaata baake!	Dafa seer torop!
Lower the price!	A daa talaa!	Wanyi ko tuuti!
Hey! you're killing me!	I be m faa la!	Hey! yangi may rey!
enough	a kaanyanta	doy na
full	faa	fees
more/again	lafaa	dolil
a little	domanding	tuuti
a lot (of sauce)	(soos) jamaa	(soos) bu bari
many (books)	(buk) jamaa	(buk) yu bari
OK/that's all	A beteyaata	Baax na
What do you have? (eg food)	I ye mune soto?	loo am?
Bring me…	…naati n nye	Indil ma …
It's (very) delicious/nice (for food/drink/places)	A diyaata (baake)	Neex na bu baax
It's (very) good (for anything: good taste/quality/quantity)	A beteyaata (baake)	Baax na torop
nice/beautiful	nyinyaata	rafet
good/best	beteyaata/beteyaata baake	baax/baax torop
cheap (it's price is easy)	(a daa) diyaata	yomba na

	Mandinka	Wolof
inexpensive	a daa mang koleyaa	seerut
funny	manee	doy waar
I'm very happy	N kontaanita baake	Kontaan naa
I'm very tired	M bataata baake	Soona naa torop

At a celebration or festival

	Mandinka	Wolof
You've done well (congratulations)	I ye a kata baake	Jeem nga bu baax
May you witness many more feasts (salutation at a religious festival)	Ala maang na sali siyaa la	Yal nenyi feekee dewen
May God let the baby live long (salutation at a naming ceremony)	Ala maa deenaanoo siimaayaa la	Yal na xale bi guda fan
You're welcome to come in (bisimila is also said before eating, like saying grace)	Bisimila	Bisimila
It's time to eat	Domori waatoo siita	Waxtu leeka jot na
What do you want to eat?	I lafita mune domo la?	Loo buga leeka?
gift marking a ceremony	jansoo	ndooli

Vocabulary

	Mandinka	Wolof
morning	somandaa	suba
afternoon	tilibuloo	becheg
evening	wularoo	ngoon
night	suutoo	guddi
white person (vocative)	tubaab	tubaab
white person (referring to one)	tubaaboo	tubaab
black person	moo fingo	nit ku nyuul
Arabic/Lebanese	Naaroo	naar
tip	buunyaa	mayee
bribe	dukoo	duku
present/gift	presentoo	mayee or: present
today	bii	tey
now	saaying	léegi
tomorrow	saama	eleg
next time	waati doo	benen yoon
food	domoroo	leka
drink	minfengo	naan
bread	taapalaapa, senfuur	mbuuru
rice	maanoo	maalo or: chep
meat	suboo	yaapa
fish	nyee	jen
millet	nyoo	dugub
groundnut (peanut)	tiyoo	jerte
palm oil	tulusee	diwtiir
water	jiyo	ndox
palm wine	tendoloo	senge

Numbers

	Mandinka	Wolof
1	kiling	beena
2	fula	nyaar
3	saba	nyet
4	naani	nyenent
5	luulu	juroom
6	wooro	juroom beena
7	worowula	juroom nyaar
8	sey	juroom nyet
9	kononto	juroom nyenent
10	tang	fuka
11	tang ning kiling	fuka ak beena
20	muwang	nyaari fuka
35	tang saba ning luulu	nyeti fuka ak juróom
100	keme	teemeer
1000	wuli (kiling)	(beena) juni

Glossary

Aku ethnic group, originally the descendants of freed slaves
Al-Haji name given to someone who has made a pilgrimage to Mecca
alkalo village chief
APRC Alliance for Patriotic Reorientation and Construction, the political party led by President Yahya Jammeh
ba big, as in *tenda-ba* (big wharf)
baa river
badala waterfront, beach
balafon traditional West African xylophone
bambo crocodile
banabana wandering street vendor
bantaba village meeting place and men's communal siesta platform, found in every village and in many compounds
banto faro river flood lands
bengdula craft market
bitiko small shop
bolon or **bolong** creek
boubou or **mbuba** voluminous Wolof dress
brother friendly term of address for any male
bumster beach boy, hustler or tourist tout
bush taxi shared public transport
butut one-hundredth of a dalasi
car minibus
chop local-style meal

chop-shop local restaurant
dalasi Gambian currency
dash bribe
djembé Guinean drum
duma lower
fanal paper and bamboo lanterns, usually in the shape of ships, traditionally paraded at Christmas and New Year
fodeh/foday teacher or *marabout*
Fula ethnic group, traditionally cattle herders
futampaf Jola tribal intiation ceremony
Gamtel Gambian telecommunications company
garage bush taxi park
gelleh-gelleh (Mandinka) or **tanka-tanka** (Wolof) bush taxi, a converted van with forward-facing seats
gewel (Wolof) traditional musician and oral historian
ghetto unofficial bar where palm wine is sold by Manjago palm tappers
griot traditional musician and oral historian
haftan man's traditional long shirt
Hajj Muslim pilgrimage to Mecca
harmattan cold dusty wind that sometimes blows across West Africa from the Sahara between December and March
imam Muslim religious leader

Food and drink terms

afra – barbecue, or grilled meat stall
attaya – chinese green tea, brewed in ritual style
benachin – literally "one pot", a spicy stew of rice with chicken, meat or vegetables
bonga – common Gambian fish
bui – baobab cordial
chakery – dessert made from yogurt, sour cream, couscous, nutmeg, vanilla and fruit
chawarma – Lebanese-style mutton or lamb kebab, usually served in pitta bread
daharr – tamarind juice
domodah – rich peanut sauce, sometimes including meat or fish
foofoo – pounded cassava
kinkiliba – dried leaves used to make an infusion
mbahal rice – rice with dried fish, groundnuts and spicy peppers
minties – black mints, a Gambian weakness, sold in *bitikos* everywhere
plasas – sauce made from cassava leaves and okra
senfour – Gambian bread, lighter than *tapalapa*
sisay yassa – chicken yassa, chicken with onion, garlic, chilli and lime
tapalapa – Gambian bread, like French bread but chewier (literally "thin stick")
wonjo – bright red cordial made from sorrel flower pods

jakalo bush taxi, a converted van with a truck back where passengers sit on benches

jali (Mandinka) traditional musician and oral historian

juju or **grisgris** magical amulet

JulBrew Gambian lager

Jola ethnic group (President Jammeh's tribe)

kafo traditional "youth club" or working association of men or women of one age group

kankurang Mandinka masquerade dancer, appearing at circumcision ceremonies and festivals

kerr place or compound

kola the nut of the kola tree, chewed as a stimulant and exchanged as a ritual gift

kora traditional harp-lute

Koriteh Muslim festival marking the end of Ramadan

koto old

kuliyo (Mandinka) or **ngente** (Wolof) naming ceremony

kumpo Jola masquerade dancer, who wears a costume that looks like a haystack with a pole sticking up from his head, and dances by whirling around upside down

kunda place or home

kuta new

Lamin first name given to most Mandinka first-born sons

lapa thin

lumo weekly (or regular) rural village market

Mandinka a West African ethnic group, The Gambia's largest tribe

Manjago a West African ethnic group, traditionally non-Muslim palm-tappers

Maolud Nabi the Prophet's birthday, an Islamic festival

marabout powerful Koranic teacher thought to have magical powers as a mystical healer and granter of wishes

mbalax dance music, from Senegal

nakko garden

ndagga dance music, from Senegal

nding small

nyamo spiritual strength, conferred by *jujus*

pagne (pronounced "pane") dress length of cloth

PPP People's Progressive Party (the banned party of ex-president Jawara)

pirogue traditional canoe, used for fishing or transport, sometimes a hand-paddled dugout, or sometimes a larger boat with an outboard engine

Ramadan lunar month of fasting prescribed by Islam

riti Fula violin

sabar traditional Gambian drum, played with a stick

santo upper

saliboo a gift given to celebrate a religious festival

sept-places Senegalese bush taxi, an estate car taking seven passengers

Serahule ethnic group, traditionally silver traders and potters

Serer ethnic group, traditionally boat builders and fishermen

seyfo district chief

simba or **zimba** Wolof lion dancer

sister friendly term of address for any female

soft fizzy drink

su home

sunnaro (Mandinka) or **jonga** (Wolof) circumcision ceremony

sai-sai scoundrel

tama talking drum

Tamharit Islamic New Year

tapa stick

tenda port, wharf, riverside

tesito self-reliance, a slogan of Jawara's government, now adopted by development projects

tiko woman's head-tie

Tobaski Muslim festival celebrated by the ritual slaughter of a sheep

toma namesake, a special friend

toubab or **tubab** white person

Vision 2020 APRC political programme

warri traditional board game

wax African-style printed cotton

Wolof ethnic group, dominant in the Kombos

Index

and small print

Map entries are in colour

A

INDEX

A Rough Guide to Rough Guides

In the summer of 1981, Mark Ellingham, a recent graduate from Bristol University, was travelling round Greece and couldn't find a guidebook that really met his needs. On the one hand there were the student guides, insistent on saving every last cent, and on the other the heavyweight cultural tomes whose authors seemed to have spent more time in a research library than lounging away the afternoon at a taverna or on the beach.

In a bid to avoid getting a job, Mark and a small group of writers set about creating their own guidebook. It was a guide to Greece that aimed to combine a journalistic approach to description with a thoroughly practical approach to travellers' needs – a guide that would incorporate culture, history and contemporary insights with a critical edge, together with up-to-date, value-for-money listings. Back in London, Mark and the team finished their Rough Guide, as they called it, and talked Routledge into publishing the book.

That first *Rough Guide to Greece*, published in 1982, was a student scheme that became a publishing phenomenon. The immediate success of the book – with numerous reprints and a Thomas Cook prize shortlisting – spawned a series that rapidly covered dozens of destinations. Rough Guides had a ready market among low-budget backpackers, but soon also acquired a much broader and older readership that relished Rough Guides' wit and inquisitiveness as much as their enthusiastic, critical approach. Everyone wants value for money, but not at any price.

Rough Guides soon began supplementing the "rougher" information about hostels and low-budget listings with the kind of detail on restaurants and quality hotels that independent-minded visitors on any budget might expect, whether on business in New York or trekking in Thailand.

These days the guides – distributed worldwide by the Penguin group – offer recommendations from shoestring to luxury and cover more than 200 destinations around the globe, including almost every country in the Americas and Europe, more than half of Africa and most of Asia and Australasia. Our ever-growing team of authors and photographers is spread all over the world, particularly in Europe, the USA and Australia.

In 1994, we published the *Rough Guide to World Music* and *Rough Guide to Classical Music*, and a year later the *Rough Guide to the Internet*. All three books have become benchmark titles in their fields – which encouraged us to expand into other areas of publishing, mainly around popular culture. Rough Guides now publish:

- Travel guides to more than 200 worldwide destinations
- Dictionary phrasebooks to 22 major languages
- History guides ranging from Ireland to Islam
- Maps printed on rip-proof and waterproof Polyart™ paper
- Music guides running the gamut from Opera to Elvis
- Restaurant guides to London, New York and San Francisco
- Reference books on topics as diverse as the Weather and Shakespeare
- Sports guides from Formula 1 to Man Utd
- Pop culture books from Lord of the Rings to Cult TV
- World Music CDs in association with World Music Network.

Visit **www.roughguides.com** to see our latest publications.

Rough Guide Credits

Text editor: Fran Sandham
Managing Director: Kevin Fitzgerald
Series editor: Mark Ellingham
Editorial: Martin Dunford, Jonathan Buckley, Kate Berens, Ann-Marie Shaw, Helena Smith, Olivia Swift, Ruth Blackmore, Geoff Howard, Claire Saunders, Gavin Thomas, Alexander Mark Rogers, Polly Thomas, Joe Staines, Richard Lim, Duncan Clark, Peter Buckley, Lucy Ratcliffe, Clifton Wilkinson, Alison Murchie, Matthew Teller, Andrew Dickson, Fran Sandham, Sally Schafer, Matthew Milton, Karoline Densley (UK); Andrew Rosenberg, Yuki Takagaki, Richard Koss, Hunter Slaton (US)
Design & Layout: Link Hall, Helen Prior, Julia Bovis, Katie Pringle, Rachel Holmes, Andy Turner, Dan May, Tanya Hall, John McKay, Sophie Hewat (UK); Madhulita Mohapatra,

Umesh Aggarwal, Sunil Sharma (India)
Cartography: Maxine Repath, Ed Wright, Katie Lloyd-Jones (UK); Manish Chandra, Rajesh Chhibber, Jai Prakesh Mishra (India)
Cover art direction: Louise Boulton
Picture research: Sharon Martins, Mark Thomas
Online: Kelly Martinez, Anja Mutic-Blessing, Jennifer Gold, Audra Epstein, Suzanne Welles, Cree Lawson (US); Manik Chauhan, Amarjyoti Dutta, Narender Kumar (India)
Finance: Gary Singh
Marketing & Publicity: Richard Trillo, Niki Smith, David Wearn, Chloë Roberts, Demelza Dallow, Claire Southern (UK); Geoff Colquitt, David Wechsler, Megan Kennedy (US)
Administration: Julie Sanderson
RG India: Punita Singh

Publishing Information

This first edition published October 2003 by
Rough Guides Ltd,
80 Strand, London WC2R 0RL.
345 Hudson St, 4th Floor,
New York, NY 10014, USA.
Distributed by the Penguin Group
Penguin Books Ltd,
80 Strand, London WC2R 0RL
Penguin Putnam, Inc.
375 Hudson Street, NY 10014, USA
Penguin Books Australia Ltd,
487 Maroondah Highway, PO Box 257,
Ringwood, Victoria 3134, Australia
Penguin Books Canada Ltd,
10 Alcorn Avenue, Toronto, Ontario,
Canada M4V 1E4
Penguin Books (NZ) Ltd,
182–190 Wairau Road, Auckland 10,
New Zealand
Typeset in Bembo and Helvetica to an original
design by Henry Iles.

Printed in Italy by LegoPrint S.p.A

328pp includes index
A catalogue record for this book is available from the British Library

ISBN 1-884353083-X

The publishers and authors have done their best to ensure the accuracy and currency of all the information in **The Rough Guide to The Gambia**, however, they can accept no responsibility for any loss, injury, or inconvenience sustained by any traveller as a result of information or advice contained in the guide.

Help us update

We've gone to a lot of effort to ensure that the first edition of **The Rough Guide to The Gambia** is accurate and up to date. However, things change – places get "discovered", opening hours are notoriously fickle, restaurants and rooms raise prices or lower standards. If you feel we've got it wrong or left something out, we'd like to know, and if you can remember the address, the price, the time, the phone number, so much the better. We'll credit all contributions, and send a copy of the next edition (or any other Rough Guide if you prefer) for the best letters.

Everyone who writes to us and isn't already a subscriber will receive a copy of our full-colour thrice-yearly newsletter. Please mark letters: "**Rough Guide Gambia Update**" and send to: Rough Guides, 80 Strand, London WC2R 0RL, or Rough Guides, 4th Floor, 345 Hudson St, New York, NY 10014. Or send an email to **mail@roughguides.com**
Have your questions answered and tell others about your trip at
www.roughguides.atinfopop.com

Acknowledgements

Emma Gregg

Very special thanks to the following people in the UK: Nathan Pope, for his outstanding assistance, patient support and love; Piers Northam, for lasting friendship, and a second home just when I needed it; Max Adam, for his good faith and the opportunity to realise this project; Richard Trillo, whose idea it was; and all the team at Rough Guides, especially Fran Sandham who helped shape the manuscript with assiduous editing and endless good humour. Thanks also to The Gambia Experience for travel arrangements and to Sony UK for handheld computing and digital voice-recording equipment.

In The Gambia, I would like to thank my good friends: Clive Barlow of Birds of The Gambia, for ornithological expertise; Debbie Burns of Cityscape, for help with maps; Ebrima Colley, for excellent language tuition; Francis Glynn, May Rooney, Aimee and everyone at GTS, for ideas and assistance; Malick Jeng and all at Gambia Tourism Authority and the Ministry of Tourism; David Llewellyn-Griffiths, for introductions; Monika Kili-Cole and her team at Gambia River Excursions and Janjang Bureh Camp, for outstanding hospitality; Evamaria Minuth, for times shared during the Roots Festival; Geri Mitchell & Maurice Phillips and everyone at Safari Garden, for guidance, support, understanding and amazing generosity; Suelle Nachif of the African Living Art Centre, for inspiration; Patrick Sothern and his team at West African Tours, for their highly professional assistance and warm good humour; Foday Suso of Basse, Manjai and Brufut, a fantastic friend; Tony Tabbal of the Spy Bar and Green Mamba, for the phone that was a godsend; Mark Thompson and everyone at Bird Safari Camp on Janjanbureh Island; Foday Trawally and Ann Rivington at Madiyana on Jinack Island, for the nights watching shooting stars; Lawrence Williams and James English of Makasutu, for great company and excellent hospitality.

I'd also like to thank the following for their generous assistance: Abi at Geri & Maurice's; Adama Bah at Village Gallery and Gambia Tourism Concern; Ablay Bayo at Tanje Village Museum; Baba Ceesay at NCAC; John Baldwin of Kaira-Du-La Lodge; Farid and Fouzia Bensouda of Coconut Residence; David Clamp at VSO; Famara Drammeh at Abuko; Modou Lamin Faye at Kambeng and Jokor in Brikama; George Foster at Jokor; Modou Gaye at Cityscape; Derek and Jenny Hewitt in Farafenni; Charbel Hobeika of Gambia Tours; Karen Hobbs of the Roots Festival and Naturelle; Ous Jagne at Timbooktoo; Mawdo Jallow at Bao Bolon Wetland Reserve; Khadija Jammeh at Boucarabou; Jette Jarra of African Heritage; Amadou Johnson of Fulladu Camp; Will Knowles of Madox Microlights; Mama of Mama's in Kololi; Alagi Mbye of Maali's Music School; Hu Morris in Kau-Ur; Farma Njie of Discovery Tours; The Professor of Fajara; RM Tours; Lamin Sanyang at Kiang West National Park; Ann Slind at Traditions in Basse; Kawsu Sillah at Kairoh Garden in Tanji; Sulayman Sonko of Tumani Tenda; Helen Stott of Fajara Paradise Villas; and especially Ibrahim, Kalifa, Numo, Alhaji and Ben of West African Tours.

Finally, thanks to the following fellow travellers: Simon and Nicole Angling; Chris and Alexa; Nick Clark; Ludovic Dumont; Patrick Dyke; Harold Goodwin; Sallie Grayson; Marianne Harstad; Dan, Mandy and Manuel Huertas; Baba Ishangi; Joe and Nina; Nigel Killikelly; Sarah McLaughlin and Simon; Angie Silva; Martine Stone; Mark Stratton; Phil and all Geri's yoga class. Warmest thanks go, too, to all the other Gambians and Gambiaphiles I met in The Gambia and in the UK while researching and writing this Rough Guide. Without their inspiration and appreciation the book would never have been possible.

Richard Trillo

Thanks to all those who have worked on and contributed to the Gambia chapter from the Rough Guide to West Africa, especially Adama Bah, Anne Barrett, Lynne Benson, Kabba Camara, Ruth Hunter, Patrick Sothern, Rosemary Long, Paul Hayward, Kebba Nasso and others at the National Environment Agency, Ann Slind, Mr Sidibeh, VSO in London and The Gambia. Thanks also to Melissa Baker and The Map Studio in Romsey, Hampshire, for maps; Tanya Hall for typesetting; Lisa Pusey and Sharon Martins for picture research; and Susannah Wight for proofreading. Many thanks to Fran Sandham for his diligent editing and, most of all, a huge thankyou to Emma for her commitment, enthusiasm and talent.

Photo credits

Cover credits

Main front picture, Dancers, Banjul © Emma Gregg

Small front top picture, Hibiscus flower © Emma Gregg

Back top picture, Monkey © Emma Gregg

Back lower picture, *Pirogue* on river Allahein © Emma Gregg

Colour introduction and things not to miss

Dawn on the River Gambia and Crocodiles, Katchikali © Sue Cunningham

All other images © Emma Gregg

Birds of The Gambia

Little bee-eater, striated heron, intermediate egret, marabou stork, hooded vulture, palm nut vulture, African jacana, whimbrel, Egyptian plover, Senegal thick-knee, Senegal coucal, Verreaux's eagle owl, pied kingfisher, giant kingfisher, little bee-eater, red-throated bee-eater, northern carmine bee-eater, violet turaco, Abyssinian ground hornbill, bearded barbet, yellow-crowned gonolek, purple glossy starling, exclamatory paradise whydah © Nigel Blake

Pink-backed pelican, African pygmy kingfisher, fine-spotted woodpecker, village weaver, northern red bishop © Vogel Documentatie Fonds

Hammerkop, western reef heron, black-headed plover, Abyssinnian roller, grey plantain-eater, rose-ringed parakeet, red-billed hornbill, beautiful sunbird, red-cheeked cordon-bleu © Gerard Mornie

Black and white photos

All images © Emma Gregg

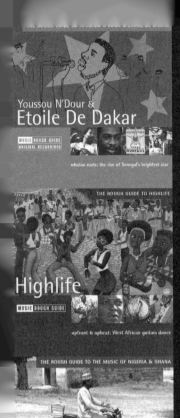

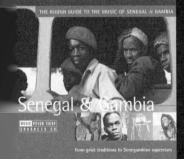

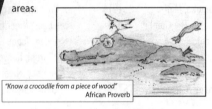